Artificial Intelligence: Advanced Algorithms

Artificial Intelligence: Advanced Algorithms

Edited by
Jeremy Rogerson

| STATES |
ACADEMIC PRESS
www.statesacademicpress.com

Published by States Academic Press,
109 South 5th Street,
Brooklyn, NY 11249, USA

ISBN: 978-1-63989-061-3

Cataloging-in-Publication Data

Artificial intelligence : advanced algorithms / edited by Jeremy Rogerson.
    p. cm.
Includes bibliographical references and index.
ISBN 978-1-63989-061-3
1. Artificial intelligence. 2. Algorithms. 3. Fifth generation computers.
4. Neural computers. I. Rogerson, Jeremy.
Q335 .A78 2022
006.3--dc23

For information on all States Academic Press publications
visit our website at www.statesacademicpress.com

Contents

Preface

The simulation of intelligence in machines is termed as artificial intelligence (AI). The understanding and development of AI is built on the principles of mathematics, computer science, linguistics and information engineering. The current research in artificial intelligence is occurring in the areas of problem solving, reasoning, automated planning and scheduling, knowledge representation, common sense knowledge, etc. Some of the advanced applications of artificial intelligence include understanding human speech, development of self-driving cars, military simulations, and intelligent routing. Algorithms are widely used in artificial intelligence as they are capable of learning from data and improving itself by learning new heuristics. This book presents the complex subject of artificial intelligence in the most comprehensible and easy to understand language. From theories to research to practical applications, case studies related to all contemporary topics of relevance to this field have been included herein. This book will prove to be immensely beneficial to students and researchers in this field.

This book is a comprehensive compilation of works of different researchers from varied parts of the world. It includes valuable experiences of the researchers with the sole objective of providing the readers (learners) with a proper knowledge of the concerned field. This book will be beneficial in evoking inspiration and enhancing the knowledge of the interested readers.

In the end, I would like to extend my heartiest thanks to the authors who worked with great determination on their chapters. I also appreciate the publisher's support in the course of the book. I would also like to deeply acknowledge my family who stood by me as a source of inspiration during the project.

Editor

Yarn tenacity modeling using artificial neural networks and development of a decision support system based on genetic algorithms

M. Dashti[1], V. Derhami[2*], E. Ekhtiyari[1]

1. Textile Engineering Department, Yazd University
2. Electrical and Computer Engineering Department, Yazd University

*Corresponding author: vderhami@yazd.ac.ir (V. Derhami).

Abstract

Yarn tenacity is one of the most important properties in yarn production. This paper focuses on modeling of the yarn tenacity as well as optimally determining the amounts of effective inputs to produce the desired yarn tenacity. The artificial neural network is used as a suitable structure for tenacity modeling of cotton yarn with 30 Number English. The empirical data was initially collected for cotton yarns. Then, the structure of the neural network was determined and its parameters were adjusted by the back propagation method. The efficiency and accuracy of the neural model was measured based on the error value and coefficient determination. The obtained experimental results show that the neural model could predicate the tenacity with less than 3.5% error. Afterwards, utilizing genetic algorithms, a new method is proposed for optimal determination of input values in the yarn production to reach the desired tenacity. We conducted several experiments for different ranges with various production cost functions. The proposed approach could find the best input values to reach the desired tenacity considering the production costs.

Keywords: *Artificial neural network, Genetic algorithm, Yarn tenacity, Modeling, Cotton yarn.*

1. Introduction

The quality and features of yarn determine possibility of using it in production of different fabrics. In this regard, tenacity is of special importance [1]. In fact, the yarn tenacity affects every next step in the processes of using it. This research was performed based on a request from Nakhchin and Nakheaftab factories, which are two distinguished textile production factories located in Yazd, Iran. This research aims at determining the best input values to produce 100% cotton yarn for a desired tenacity.

We are concerned with two constraints: first, although the effective parameters in the yarn tenacity are almost known but it is not clearly determined how these parameters affect the final yarn tenancy. In other words, there is no accurate mathematical model for this purpose. Second, optimal determination of input values to reach a desirable tenacity has not been investigated yet. In fact, nonlinearity and complexity of the relation giving the yarn tenacity in terms of the effective

parameters, have led the textile engineers to determine the values of input materials only by "trial and error" and their former experiences. Investigations show that although there is many research findings focused on modeling of tenacity but only a few of them proposed a practical approach to optimal determination of values for effective inputs. Some usual methods for the yarn tenacity modeling are mechanical models, mathematical models [2], statistical (regression) methods, fuzzy modeling [3], and artificial neural network models [7]. These primary methods (mechanical, mathematical and statistical) require highly experienced personnel as well as numerous of test steps, therefore they could not give accurate models with reasonable computational costs [8].

Artificial Neural Network (ANN) which is inspired from evolution of biological neurons of brain is a powerful method for modeling of complex phenomena. Some of its characteristics such as the ability of learning and generalization, robustness against disturbances, and information parallel processing have made ANN superior to other modeling approaches. Nowadays, ANNs are widely used for solving many engineering problems in modeling, controlling, and patterning recognition [5], [6].

Already in an ANN based yarn tenacity prediction research, the five parameters: spun fibers upper half mean length, package hardness, fineness, proportions of fiber length uniformity, and maturity of fibers content were used as neural network input parameters [7]. The accuracy of this neural model was 12%. In another study, 14 fiber properties have been used as neural network inputs to predict yarn tenacity [8]. These inputs are values of impurity, number of each package impurity (amount of trash), upper half mean length, strength and length increase to the extent on which the fiber is torn (elongation of break), fiber fineness, brightness, yellowness, fiber maturity content, standard fiber fineness (norm), length uniformity, and micronaire. The accuracy of the later neural model was 8%.

Two other papers focused on fiber properties measured by High Volume Instrument (HVI) and included upper half mean length, length uniformity, short fiber content, strength, maturity ratio, fineness, grayness, and yellowness used as neural network input [9],[10].

In this research, we use neural networks in modeling of yarn tenacity of 100% cotton with 30 Ne, where a new approach, which is based on genetic algorithms, is used for optimal determination of values of input materials. The main advantages and innovations on this research are:

> 1- Proposing an accurate neural model for predicting yarn tenacity of 100% cotton yarn. Although there are some research works concerning neural modeling, but our model is a real case study with different inputs and conditions; hence, we use a different structure of ANN.

> 2- Proposing a new idea to find the optimal values of inputs to reach desired yarn tenacity by using genetic algorithms. To the best of our knowledge, this research is the first research of its kind.

The structure of this paper is as follows. In the second section, yarn tenacity and the parameters which affect yarn tenacity are investigated and discussed. The third section deals with introducing neural networks; in the fourth section, modeling of yarn tenacity of 100% cotton with 30 NE (the most popular yarn) using neural network is presented. In the fifth section, a method to find optimal values of inputs to reach a desirable tenacity is proposed. Finally, in the last section, summary and conclusions are provided.

2. Effective parameters on yarn tenacity

The resistance of yarn against tensile forces is called yarn tenacity. It is the minimum force which is needed to tear out that yarn [1]. Several factors are involved in yarn tenancy, and the most important ones are the properties of the fibers used to produce yarn (raw materials) such as: upper half mean length, length uniformity, short fiber content, fibers strength, maturity ratio, yellowness, linear density, and fiber length increase (which is measured by HVI).

Here, the input variables have been chosen with respect to the related research [7,8,10]. The production process was set fixed for the whole time. This means, five adjustable parameters for textile machines such as spin tube, breaker speed, rotor speed, were fixed. Moreover, yarn twist and yarn counts were set constant as well. In this way, in our model, the seven mentioned parameters associated with fiber property were considered as effective parameters on yarn tenacity.

3. Artificial neural networks

Artificial neural network is a structure inspired from the human brain. It is very useful in modeling complex functions. A neural network consists of an interconnected group of artificial neurons where an artificial neuron is a mathematical function representing an abstraction of biological neurons [4].

Figure 1 shows the structure of a neuron. Vector $x = [x_1, ..., x_n]^T$ is input and the scalar y is the output of the neuron.

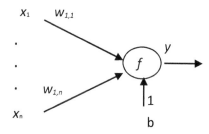

Figure 1. Model of a multi-input neuron

The influence of x_i on y is determined by $w_{1,i}$. Another input is bias parameter that its corresponding weight is 1.

The output of the neuron is computed by:

$$y = f(z) = f(Wx + b) \tag{1}$$

$$z = \sum_{i=1}^{n} x_i w_{1,i} + b = Wx + b \tag{2}$$

$$W = [w_{1,1}, ..., w_{1,n}] \tag{3}$$

The activation function f could be linear or either nonlinear. Here, the designer selects a suitable activation function with respect to the problem features. Table 1 shows some widely used activation functions.

Table 1. Some activation functions

Function	Definition	Range
Linear	$f(z) = z$	$(-\infty, +\infty)$
Logistic	$f(z) = \dfrac{1}{1 + e^{-az}}$, a is slope parameter	$(0, +1)$
Hyperbolic	$f(z) = \dfrac{e^z - e^{-z}}{e^z + e^{-z}}$	$(-1, +1)$
Threshold	$f(z) = \begin{cases} 0 & if \ z < 0 \\ 1 & if \ z \geq 0 \end{cases}$	$\{0, +1\}$

In comparison with single layer networks, multilayer neural networks have more capabilities. Double layers feed forward neural networks (with sigmoid functions in first layer and that of linear in second layer) can estimate any continuous function with arbitrary precision [4].

In this research, we employed a feed forward neural network with two layers, where the first layer is known as the hidden layer. Figure 2 shows the corresponding network structure. This structure is presented as: $n:nh:o$ where n is the number of inputs, nh is the number of hidden layer neurons, and o is the number of output layer neurons. The output of network is computed by:

$$y = f_o(\sum_{i=1}^{nh} o_i w_i^2 + b) \tag{4}$$

$$o_i = f_i(\sum_{j=1}^{n} x_j w_{i,j}^1 + b_i) \quad i = 1, ..., nh \tag{5}$$

where, y is the final output, f_o is the activation function of output neuron, w_i^2 is the weight of link between i-th output neuron in the hidden layer and the final output, b is the bias of output neuron, o_i is the output of i-th neuron in hidden layer, $w_{i,j}^1$ is the weight of link between j-th input and i-th

neuron in hidden layer, b_i is the bias of i-th neuron in hidden layer, and f_i is the activation function in i-th neuron in hidden layer.

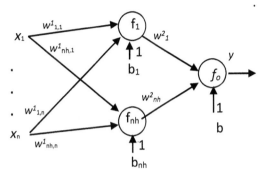

Figure 2. The feed forward neural network.

The weights $(w_{i,j}^1, w_i^2, b_i, b)$ are adjustable parameters that need to be tuned by training. In fact, the objective of network training is adjusting these parameters in such a way that the network generates desired output for different inputs.

4. Modeling

Since neural networks find and learn patterns in the training data, in the first step of modeling, we need some training data. The cotton yarn with 30 NE (Number English) is produced in tenacity range of 13 to 16. Some experiments have already been conducted on cotton fibers and the yarn 30 NE produced from them in order to collect required input data in the mentioned range. As stated in Section 2, seven properties (see Table 2) of cotton fiber are considered as effective parameters on yarn tenacity and they are selected as inputs of our model. The network output would be the yarn tenacity. The activation function for the neurons in the hidden layer is sigmoid and it is linear for the output neuron. Here, we use the obtained data from 33 cotton samples for ring carded spun yarns for input-output data.

The training data must cover the whole input range and need to have a suitable dispersion. Generally, if we use more training data, we would often be more accurate in prediction. In the primary experiments of this research, we used 100 data samples. The obtained result for this data was poor. Therefore, we had to obtain and use more data. Here, we encountered some practical constraints. For example, in measuring yarn tenacity for each sample, first we had to produce the yarn with those input materials. Finally, we totally prepared 990 experimental data for tuning our neural network. During first experiments, we observed that the major problem in training our neural model was over fitting. In fact, we could see an error which was getting smaller and smaller in the course of training (for the training data) but the magnitude of the error for the test data was not acceptable. This phenomenon was due to the fact that during training phase, the network parameters are adjusted to reduce the error for the training data; hence, the network is fitted for the training data and this is why the property of generalization of the neural network degrades considerably. As a result, network's error in the output of the network was too high for any data other than the training data. Providing a solution for the problem, we used some valid data, which are not used for training, but they are only used to stop the training properly to avoid over fitting. After each training epoch, network's error was calculated for valid data and if the training procedure was going in a way that the error was increasing the training would be stopped.

Therefore, we divided our data into three parts: Training data, valid data, and test data. They included 800, 90, and 100 samples, respectively. The test data was used in the final to assess our neural model. The statistical features of the mentioned data shown in Table 2.

4.1. Neural network structure

Previous studies focused on modeling have shown that feed forward networks are suitable for modeling. We used a two layer feed forward neural network for modeling. It consists of seven inputs and one output. The number of neurons in hidden layer is different for these networks. Activation function for neurons in hidden layer is logistic and for the last layer is linear. These networks have been trained using training data regarding the valid data. The training method was the error back propagation algorithm. Results of the experiments on different structures are shown in Table 3.

Table 2. Statistical summary of data for fiber properties

Fibers Characteristics	Fiber Tenacity (CN/Tex)	Fiber Elongation	%50 Average Length	length uniformity	Micronaire	Reflection Degree	Yellowness
Maximum	34	6.9	1.2	83.2	5	80.4	11.4
Minimum	26.5	5.3	0.97	79.2	3.1	73	8
Average	29.05	6.27	1.06	81.57	4.23	77.2	9.34
Standard Deviation	1.41	0.46	0.05	1.05	0.45	2.28	0.72

Table 3. Results of training on different structures of neural networks

Network Structure	7:9:1	7:10:1	7:11:1	7:12:1	7:13:1	7:14:1
Error Percentage for Training Data	3.3%	3.1%	0.8%	3.5%	2%	1.1%
Error Percentage for Test Data	12%	3.5%	10.4%	10.4%	6.4%	11.6%
R2 for Test Data	0.91	0.95	0.90	0.87	0.87	0.83

The first row in the table shows structure of the neural network. The error rate for training data has been given in the second row. The third row shows the error percent for test data, and the determination coefficient [4] has been given in the last row.

As Table 3 shows, the best results have been obtained from the neural network model consisting of 10 neurons in the hidden layer. The training stopped after 106 epochs. The percentage error for this structure in the training phase is 3.1% and 3.5% for the test data. Comparing the similar results from [2, 5] this error is acceptable. Therefore, the ANN with structure of 7:10:1 is selected as a neural model to predict yarn tenacity.

5. Optimal input values for desired tenacity

After finding the suitable neural model, we turn our attention to the determination of input parameters to reach the desired tenacity using Genetic Algorithms (GA). This is, in fact, a multi-goal problem. From one side, the production cost should be minimized and from other side the tenacity of produced yarn should be equal to or higher than the desired tenacity. If the cost reduces but the tenacity is less than the desired value, it would not be acceptable. From the other side, if the tenacity improves but the cost goes too high, it would not be acceptable too. In order to overcome this dilemma, we first convert it into an optimization problem and then propose an approach to solve it by GA. In Section 2, we introduced the seven variables which are effective in yarn tenacity. The cost production function $C(x)$ would be:

$$C(x) = \sum_{i=1}^{7} v_i x_i \qquad (6)$$

Where, v_i is the assigned weight for the i-th variable x_i. Weights show how effective each parameter is in the cost function. In other words, more expensive variables are expressed by higher weights.

The evaluation criterion in GA is the fitness function. Here, the algorithm looks for the responses in such a way that the fitness function decreases to a minimum value. The space of the problem is defined by all combinations of the values of variables x_i where they fall in the ranges mentioned in Table 2. Our objective is to reach the desired tenacity while the cost function (Eq. 6) is minimized. The most important challenge in using GA is defining the suitable fitness function. Here, the fitness function is defined as:

$$Fit.F = K * f(e) + C(x) \qquad (7)$$

$$e = T_{desired} - T_{actual}(x)$$

$$T_{actual}(x) \approx Output\ of\ NeuralModel\ of\ Tenacity$$

$$(8)$$

$$f(e) = \begin{cases} e & e > 0 \\ 0 & Otherwise. \end{cases} \qquad (9)$$

In the above fitness formula, the first term is the error function. The error is equal to the difference between the desired tenacity and the actual tenacity ($T_{actual}(x)$). The actual tenacity is the tenacity of produced yarn with x_i's (the amounts of input materials). We use the neural model obtained in Section 4, to predict the actual tenacity for each x and finally to compute $f(e)$ in Eq. (9). In the first relation, K serves as a weight parameter.

Each intermediate solution for a problem in GA is called a chromosome. A chromosome consists of genes, corresponding to a series of values given to the problem variables (in our case x_i's). The number of genes is equal to the number of variables; therefore in our case, each chromosome will have seven genes. Using values of genes in chromosome as the neural model input, we can get the tenacity of the yarn as well as the production cost using Eq.6. In this way, the fitness function can be computed for each chromosome.

If the predicted tenacity (output of neural model) is less than the desired tenacity, then the first term in fitness function would be positive and its amount is error proportion. In a situation where the predicated tenacity is equal or greater than desired tenacity, the first term in fitness function would be zero. The second term stands for the production cost function. As the cost increases, the fitness function will increase, too.

Regarding the amount of K in Eq. 7, since the main objective is to reach the desired tenacity, K has to be determined in such a way that GA finds answers having first term equal to zero. Since the maximum of cost function is 1000, we set K to 1000 as well. This value for K lets one thousandth of error from the desired tenacity be equal to one unit in the second term (cost function). This will guide our GA model to find the solutions with values in first term equal to zero.

In general, a GA is inspired from evaluation theory. It looks for a chromosome that minimizes the fitness function. The algorithm begins with a random population (some chromosomes), then it uses present population to generate new population based on the following steps in each iteration [11]:

1. The value of fitness function is computed for each chromosome in the current population.
2. The algorithm selects some chromosomes based on their fitness values. These chromosomes are called parents and used to generate next generation. Some well known approaches for selection of parents are: Roulette-wheel selection, rank selection, and elitist selection.
3. The algorithm generates children with applying crossover operation on selected parents.
4. Mutation on a child is changing one or more of its properties randomly. Mutational children are produced in this step.
5. The obtained children are added to the population.

The algorithm continues until it finds a child who fits the desired criteria.

6. Experimental results

To assess the proposed approach, we performed a number of experiments with different desired tenacities and different weights (v_i's) as cost function. The objective was finding the input parameters for yarn production such that the obtained tenacity becomes greater than the desired tenacity and as a result, the production cost is minimized. In the experiments, we used one-point crossover, and mutation rate of 0.1; based on the primary results, the population size was set to 40.

The final experimental results are shown in Table 4. The first column is the desired tenacity, the second column is the obtained tenacity of the produced yarn, the third column is the final value of the fitness function at the termination of the search process in GA, and the last column is the value of V for each experiment.

For efficiency improvement of our algorithm, all input values, x_i, were normalized to be in the range of [0, 1]

Table 4. The results of the experiments

$T_{desired}$	$T_{obtained}$	*Fit.F*	V
14	14.03	660.01	[4 7 3 5 1 2 6]
15	15.01	668.81	[4 7 3 5 1 2 6]
16	16.00	679.67	[4 7 3 5 1 2 6]
14	14.04	718.26	[1 6 3 7 5 2 4]
15	15.00	720.97	[1 6 3 7 5 2 4]
16	16.01	724.81	[1 6 3 7 5 2 4]

Table 4 shows that the proposed approach was capable to find values for the input parameters in a way that the obtained tenacity is satisfactory; the amount of first term of the fitness function is equal to zero and the values of the fitness function are equal to the production cost.

Meanwhile, the obtained values for inputs depend on the amounts of v's. For example, the values in the fourth row, ($T_{desired}$=16, V=[4 7 3 5 1 2 6]), is:

x=[26.754 5.977 0.876 70.510 2.703 64.818 7.216]

and for the last row with the same desired tenacity and V=[1 6 3 7 5 2 4] is:

x=[30.966 4.558 0.855 70.236 2.713 64.890 7.233]

Comparing the two results indicates that the second case, which is the weight of first input variable in the cost function, has been decreased (changed from 4 to 1), the value of this input has been increased. In opposite, the value of forth input variable has been reduced due to its weight increase.

6. Conclusion

In this research, a neural network model of yarn tenacity for 100% yarn cotton 30 NE using empirical data is presented. The output of neural model for test data confirmed the accuracy of the proposed model. Based on the obtained results in modeling section, feed forward neural network with 10 neurons in hidden layers was a suitable structure for modeling of tenacity. We also used GA for optimal determination of values of inputs in yarn manufacturing. The results of the experiment showed that GA with the defined fitness function can find the best values for inputs such that produced yarn with the obtained values of

inputs satisfy the desired tenacity while the production cost becomes minimal. The proposed method can be used to find the best-input values for any kind of yarn production with a desired tenacity. For using the proposed method, a user determines the desired tenacity of yarn and then he/she assigns weights of input materials based on their prices. Afterwards, our proposed method presents the amounts of input materials for yarn production so that the produced yarn has the desired tenacity, and above all, the production cost has been minimized.

References

[1] Taheri, A., (1990). General Technology of Cotton Textile Industry," (in Persian) Aghabik.

[2] Majumdar, P. K., and Majumdar, A., (2004). Predicting the Breaking Elongation of Ring Spun Cotton Yarns Using Mathematical, Statistical, and Artificial Neural Network Models", Textile Research Journal, Vol.74, No.7, pp. 652-655.

[3] Shams Nateri, A. (2005). Using Neuro-Fuzzy For Prediction Ring Spun Yarn Strength From Cotton Fibers Properties", 3rd International Industrial Simulation Conference, June 9-11.

[4] M. Menhaj, (2002). Fundamental of Neural Networks," Amikabir University publication, (in Persian).

[5] Gharehaghaji, A.A., Palhang, M., and Shanbeh, M., (2006). Using Artificial Neural Network Algorithm to Predict Tensile Properties of Cotton-covered Nylon Core Yarns", Esteghlal, Vol. 24, No.2.

[6] Jackowska-Strumillo, L., Ackowski, T., Cyniak, D., Czekalski, J., (2004). Neural Model of the Spinning Process for Predicting Selected Properties of Flax/Cotton Yarn Blends", Abres & Textiles In Eastem Europe, Vol. 12, No. 4, pp. 17-21.

[7] Sette, S., Bouliart, L., Van Langenhove, L. Kiekens, P., (1997). Optimizing the Fiber to Yarn Production Process with a Combined Neural Network/Genetic Algorithm Approach", Textile Research Journal, Vol. 67, No. 2, pp. 84-92.

[8] Cheng, L., Adams, D. L., (1995). Yarn Strength Prediction Using Neural Networks, Part 1: Fiber Properties and Yarn Strength Relationship", Textile Research Journal, Vol. 65, No. 9, pp. 495-500.

[9] Majumdar, A., Majumdar, P. K. , Sarkar, B., (2004). Selecting Cotton Bales By Spinning Consistency Index And Micronaire Using Artificial Neural Networks", AUTEX Research Journal, Vol. 4, No. 1, pp.1-8.

[10] Pynckels, F., Sette, S., Van Langenhove, L., Kiekens, P., and Impe. K. (1995). Use of Neural Nets for Detemining the Spinnability of Fibres"; Journal of the Textile Institute; October Vol. 86, No. 395, pp. 425-437.

[11] Back, T. (1996). Evolutionary Algorithms in Theory and Practice", Oxford University Press, New York.

Noisy images edge detection: Ant colony optimization algorithm

Z. Dorrani[1*] and M. S. Mahmoodi[2]

1. Department of Electrical Engineering, Payame Noor University (PNU), Tehran, Iran.
2. Department of Computer Engineering, Payame Noor University (PNU), Tehran, Iran.

*Corresponding author: dorrani.z@skpnu.ac.ir(Z. Dorrani).

Abstract

The edges of an image define the image boundary. When the image is noisy, it does not become easy to identify the edges. Therefore, a method requests to be developed that can identify edges clearly in a noisy image. Many methods have been proposed earlier using filters, transforms and wavelets with Ant colony optimization (ACO) that detect edges. We here used ACO for edge detection of noisy images with Gaussian noise and salt and pepper noise. As the image edge frequencies are close to the noise frequency band, the edge detection using the conventional edge detection methods is challenging. The movement of ants depends on local discrepancy of image's intensity value. The simulation results compared with existing conventional methods and are provided to support the superior performance of ACO algorithm in noisy images edge detection. Canny, Sobel and Prewitt operator have thick, non continuous edges and with less clear image content. But the applied method gives thin and clear edges.

Keywords: *Ant Colony, Edge Detection, Gaussian Noise, Noisy Image, Salt and Pepper Noise.*

1. Introduction

One of the basic issues in image processing and computer vision is identifying the sudden changes of brightness in an image, or edge detection [1-6]. The edges are defined as the boundary between the objects and the background or the boundary between overlapping objects. If the edges are recognized correctly, the location of all objects in the image can be identified exactly and some basic characteristics, such as the surface and the geometry of the objects will be measured easily [7]. There are many methods for extracting and detecting the edges [6]. Most edge detector programs determine the color or the intensity values of the edge pixels. In images without noise, edges are recognized by the gray level changing at a specific pixel [8]. The higher is the gray level changing, the easier is the detection. However, in some images the gray level changes gradually, and no specific pixel can be identified as the edge pixel. Moreover, noise may cause some grey level changes which are not true. In other words, when affected by noise, two pixels with the same grey levels may find different grey levels in the image [9]. Noise is a random phenomena arising from many sources, such as light intensity, type of camera and lens, mobility, temperature, atmospheric effects, and moisture. The random gray level changes of the pixels appear as some discontinuities in the detected edges. Hence, edge detection in noisy images is a nontrivial problem due to the random damage in the image [8].

To reduce noise effects, Gaussians filtering [10], and some algorithms based on Wavelet Transform [11], mathematical morphology [12], neural networks [13], fuzzy networks [14,15] and an enhanced median filter [16] have been proposed.

The ACO algorithm in [1] and [2] and [17] are proposed for edge detection in without noise images, but in this paper, we used the ACO algorithm for edge detection in image with presence noise. So far this algorithm is not used for edge detection of noisy image. However, a majority of edge detector algorithms, proposed so far, are incapable to remove noise effects precisely. Instead, they optimize their performance in terms of noise effects removal [9]. We show that ACO algorithm can detect edges with presence noise in images.

The remainder of the paper is organized as follows. ACO is introduced briefly in section 2, and ACO implementation for the edge detection problem is explained in section 3. The numerical results are demonstrated in section 4 and the paper is concluded in section 5.

2. Ant colony optimization

ACO algorithms are inspired by the natural behavior of ants which find the shortest paths between their nest and food sources using the deposited pheromone on the ground in an iterative process. Similarly, ACO prepares a set of solution components (paths) and updates it based on a pheromone model (weights of the paths) in each iteration. ACO algorithm constructs the solution with a probabilistic mechanism from the components. The pheromone model is a set of values representing a probability distribution over the search space. The pheromone update is performed to increase the probability of constructing good solutions from the components [17]. ACO algorithm definition Using of the variables used in references [18,19].

To implement ACO algorithm, K artificial moving ants in an area consisting of $M_1 \times M_2$ nodes are considered. The ants construct the components by their probabilistic movement based on the transition probability matrix, P^n. The probability of moving from node i to node j depends on two values associated to the connection of node i to node j: the pheromone value and the heuristic value. The algorithm implementation steps are listed in table 1.

Table 1. ACO algorithm.

step	process
1	Initializing the positions of all K ants and the pheromone matrix τ^0
2	
2-1	Setting the construction-step index n=1:N
2-2	Setting the ant index k=1:K,
3	Moving the kth ant L steps according to an $M_1M_2 \times M_1M_2$ probabilistic transition matrix, P^n
1	Updating the pheromone matrix, τ^n

Accordingly, ACO should perform two main processes iteratively: modifying the probabilistic transition matrix, $p^{(n)}$ and updating pheromone matrix, which are explained in the following. At the n-th step of the algorithm, the k-th ant moves from node i to node j with a probability of:

$$p_{i,j}^{(n)} = \frac{(\tau_{i,j}^{(n-1)})^\alpha (\eta_{i,j})^\beta}{\sum_{j \in \Omega_i} (\tau_{i,j}^{(n-1)})^\alpha (\eta_{i,j})^\beta} \tag{1}$$

where, $\tau_{i,j}^{(n-1)}$ is the pheromone value of node i to node j connection; $\eta_{i,j}$ represents the heuristic information of going from node i to node j and is assumed to be the same for each construction-step; Ω_i is the set of neighbor nodes of the ant a_k that is on node i; α and β are positive constants representing the relation between pheromone information and heuristic information. The pheromone matrix needs to be updated twice during the process. First, the pheromone matrix is updated as:

$$\begin{cases} (1-\rho).\tau_{i,j}^{(n-1)} + \rho.\Delta_{i,j}^{(k)} & if\ (i,j)belongs\ to \\ & the\ best\ tour \\ \tau_{i,j}^{(n-1)} & otherwise \end{cases} \tag{2}$$

where, ρ is the evaporation rate; $\tau_{i,j}^{(n-1)}$ is the pheromone value of node i to node j connection; $\Delta_{i,j}^{(k)}$ is given by the heuristic matrix. Then, the second update is performed after the movement of all K ants within each construction-step as:

$$\tau^{(n)} = (1-\psi).\tau^{(n-1)} + \psi.\tau^{(0)} \tag{3}$$

where, ψ is the pheromone decay coefficient.

3. EDGE detection with ACO

In the edge detection problem, ACO detects the image edges with the ants moving on the image edges and recording the intensity values as estimated pheromone in a matrix which shows the edges information in each situation [1,17].

A number of ants move on a two-dimensional image. Their move with the initial probability on any image pixel is determined with pheromone matrix. This matrix is created according to the definition of edge. In other words, pheromone matrix is created when the difference between two adjacent edges is more than a certain amount. Thus, the ants are led by the changes in the intensity values of edge pixels.

This algorithm performs for the first steps and then in the nth step of construction, one ant being randomly chosen from K total ants and this ant will move over the image for L steps. Ultimately, decision-making Stage is done to determine edges. These steps in order are:

1) Initialization stage

According to the ant system [19], a number of ants are randomly distributed on an image with a size of M1×M2. The primary value of each component of the pheromone matrix, $\tau(0)$, is set to a constant value, τinit.

2) Construction stage

At this stage, a random ant is randomly chosen to perform L movement steps from node (l,m) to a neighboring node (i,j) according to the transition probability [21]

$$p_{(l,m),(i,j)}^{(n)} = \frac{(\tau_{i,j}^{(n-1)})^{\alpha}(\eta_{i,j})^{\beta}}{\sum\limits_{(i,j) \in \Omega_{(i,m)}} (\tau_{i,j}^{(n-1)})^{\alpha}(\eta_{i,j})^{\beta}} \qquad (4)$$

where, $\tau_{i,j}^{(n-1)}$ is the pheromone value of node i to node j connection; $\eta_{i,j}$ represents the heuristic information of going from node i to node j and is assumed to be the same for each construction-step; Ω_i is the set of neighbor nodes of the ant a_k that is on node i; α and β are positive constants representing the relation between pheromone information and heuristic information. The heuristic value, η (i,j), should be determined according to the possible position of pixel (i,j) [22], as:

$$\eta_{i,j} = \frac{1}{z} v_c (I_{i,j}) \qquad (5)$$

where, $z = \sum\limits_{i=1:M_1} \sum\limits_{j=1:M_1} V_c(I_{i,j})$ is a normalized factor,

and $I_{i,j}$ represents the intensity value at position (i,j) in image I; $V_c(I_{i,j})$ is a function of a pixel local group defined by:

$$v_c(I_{i,j}) = f(|I_{i-2,j-1} - I_{i+2,j+1}| + |I_{i-2,j+1} - I_{i+2,j-1}| + |I_{i-1,j-2} - I_{i+1,j+2}| + |I_{i-1,j-1} - I_{i+1,j+1}| + |I_{i-1,j} - I_{i+1,j}| + |I_{i-1,j+1} - I_{i-1,j-1}| + |I_{i-1,j+2} - I_{i-1,j-2}| + |I_{i,j-1} - I_{i,j+1}|). \qquad (6)$$

Function f(0) in (6) is determined using the following four functions [23]:

$$f(x) = \lambda x \qquad \text{for } x \geq 0 \qquad (7)$$

$$f(x) = \lambda x^2 \qquad \text{for } x \geq 0 \qquad (8)$$

$$f(x) = \sin(\frac{\pi x}{2\lambda}) \qquad \text{for } 0 \leq x \leq \lambda \qquad (9)$$

$$f(x) = \frac{\pi x \sin(\frac{\pi x}{\lambda})}{\lambda} \qquad \text{for } 0 \leq x \leq \lambda \qquad (10)$$

where, λ adjusts the shapes of the function (7)-(10). The second issue is to determine the range of the ant's movement. To determine the ant moves range four or eight connection is used.

3) Updating stage

The algorithm performs two updating.
After moving an ant, each component of the pheromone matrix is updated by [20]:

$$\tau_{i,j}^{(n-1)} = \begin{cases} (1-\rho).\tau_{i,j}^{(n-1)} + \rho.\Delta_{i,j}^{(k)}, & \text{If (i,j) is} \\ & \text{visited by} \\ & \text{the current} \\ & \text{k_{th} ant} \\ \\ \tau_{i,j}^{(n-1)} & \text{Other wise} \end{cases} \qquad (11)$$

where, ρ is the evaporation rate; $\Delta_{i,j}^{(k)}$ is given by the heuristic matrix; $\tau_{i,j}^{(n-1)}$ is the pheromone value of node i to node j connection The second update is performed after moving all ants according to (3).

4) Decision stage

A pixel either belongs or does not belong to the edge. Therefore, the decision process is a binary one. A threshold value, T, with an initial value, $T^{(0)}$ which equals the average amount of pheromone matrix, is chosen. The pixels that in two groups can be classified according to the value less than $T^{(0)}$ or greater than $T^{(0)}$. The initial $T^{(0)}$ is computed as follows:

$$T^{(0)} = \frac{\sum\limits_{i=1:M_2} \tau_{i,j}^{(N)} \sum\limits_{j=1:M_2} \tau_{i,j}^{(N)}}{M_1 M_2} \qquad (12)$$

where, the iteration index L=0. Then, Matrix pheromone $\tau^{(N)}$ is divided in two groups using $T^{(L)}$, the first group amounts is less than $T^{(L)}$ and the second group greater than $T^{(L)}$. Mean these two calculate using the following formula that can be [1]:

$$m_L^{(l)} = \frac{\sum\limits_{i=1:M_1} \sum\limits_{j=1:M_2} g_{T^{(l)}}^{L}(\tau_{i,j}^{(N)})}{\sum\limits_{i=1:M_1} \sum\limits_{j=1:M_2} h_{T^{(l)}}^{L}(\tau_{i,j}^{(N)})} \qquad (13)$$

$$m_u^{(l)} = \frac{\sum\limits_{i=1:M_1} \sum\limits_{j=1:M_2} g_{T^{(l)}}^{u}(\tau_{i,j}^{(N)})}{\sum\limits_{i=1:M_1} \sum\limits_{j=1:M_2} h_{T^{(l)}}^{u}(\tau_{i,j}^{(N)})} \qquad (14)$$

where,

$$g_{T^{(l)}}^{L}(x) = \begin{cases} x, & \text{if } x \leq T^{(l)} \\ o & \text{otherwise.} \end{cases} \qquad (15)$$

$$g_{T^{(l)}}^{u}(x) = \begin{cases} x, & \text{if } x \geq T^{(l)} \\ o & \text{otherwise.} \end{cases} \qquad (16)$$

$$h_{T^{(l)}}^{L}(x) = \begin{cases} x, & \text{if } x \geq T^{(l)} \\ o & \text{otherwise.} \end{cases} \qquad (17)$$

$$h_{T^{(l)}}^{u}(x) = \begin{cases} x, & \text{if } x \geq T^{(l)} \\ o & \text{otherwise.} \end{cases} \qquad (18)$$

The new threshold value is the average of the two above values. The iteration index is set to l =l +1.

$$T^{(l)} = \frac{m_L^{(l)} + m_u^{(l)}}{2} \qquad (19)$$

If $\left| T^{(l)}\text{-}T^{(n\text{-}1)} \right| > \varepsilon$, where ε is a very small number, the iteration stages stops then a binary decision to determine edge pixel, is made on each pixel location (i,j), to determine whether it is an edge pixel.

$$E_{i,j} = \begin{cases} 1, & if\ \tau_{i,j}^{(N)}\ \geq T^{(l)} \\ 0 & otherwise \end{cases} \qquad (20)$$

Summary of ACO method in figure 1 is shown.

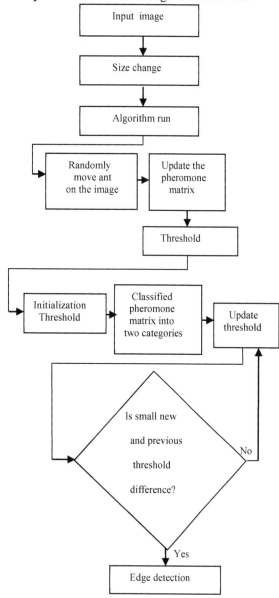

Figure. 1 A review of the performance of ACO algorithm.

4. Simulation results

We evaluate the performance of ACO algorithm in this section. First, a noisy image should be generated. Two types of noise, Gaussian noise, and salt and pepper noise are examined. Algorithm run for image with size $2^n \times 2^n$ and otherwise are resized. The image size is 128×128. The initial values of the pheromone matrix components represent the probability of each pixel to be an edge pixel, which is the same for all pixels at the beginning of the iterations. K ants start moving on the edges, hence the probability of being an edge pixel changes. This process is repeated for L steps, and the pixels probabilities change according to the edge intensity values compared to the ones of the neighboring pixels. At the end, the edge pixels are the ones with the highest number of passing ants. The rest of the algorithm parameters are set in such a way that using initial values of reference [20] trial and error method obtained:

k: total number of ants, which here functions [x] shows high right values that are smaller or equal to x.

τ_{init} = 0.0001 initial value of each component of the pheromone matrix.

α = 3: weighting factor of pheromones information in (4).

β = 0.2: weighting factor of the heuristic information in (4).

Ω: the permissible ant's movement range in (4).

λ=1: the adjusting factor of the functions in (7)-(10).

ρ=0.2: the evaporation rate in (11).

L = 40: total number of ant's movement-steps within each construction-step.

φ = 0.05: the pheromone decay coefficient in (12). To view the algorithm performance two images are examined.

(a)

(b)

figure 2(d), and figure 2(g).Next image is Coins. The above steps are related to this image and results are presented in figures 3(a) to (d).

(a)

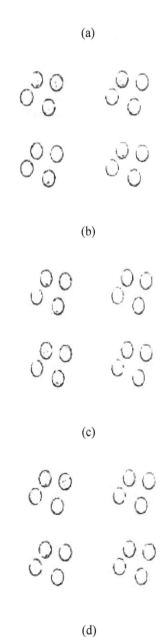

(b)

(c)

(d)

Figure 3. (a) original image (b) edge detection without noise (c) edge detection with salt and pepper noise and intensity=0.02 (d) edge detection with salt and pepper noise and intensity=0.05.

(c)

(d)

(e)

Figure 2. (a) original image (b) edge detection without noise (c) edge detection with salt and pepper noise and intensity= 0.02 (d) edge detection with salt and pepper noise and intensity=0.05 (e) edge detection with Gaussian noise and Intensity=0.05.

Figure 2(a) is the Cameraman image. First, the algorithm is applied to the image without noise. The corresponding results are shown in figure 2(b). Four images obtained according to the four equations in 7-10. Then, figure 2(c) shows the image with salt and pepper noise and intensity=0.02. ACO succeeds in finding the edges. In the next step, noise intensity increases in the image. The computed edges are observed in

Figure 3(a) is original image, figure 3(b) is edge detection without noise, figure (c) is edge detection with salt and pepper noise and figure 3(d) is edge detection with Gaussian noise. ACO succeeds in finding the edges. In the next step, edges of same noisy image detection by, Sobel, figure 4(a), Prewitt figure 4(b), and Canny operators figure 4(c). Comparing the eyes of results can see that Canny, Sobel and Prewitt results depended noise effect, but ACO shows better results.

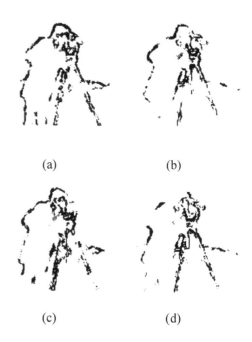

(a)   (b)

(c)   (d)

Figure 5. The results of edge detection with ACO algorithm in reference [1]. (a-d) the proposed ACO based image edge detection algorithm with the incorporation of the function defined in (7-10).

5. Discussion

The purpose of this paper was to find the edges of the image in noisy images. Many methods were applied for this purpose. However, a majority of edge detector algorithms, proposed so far, are incapable to remove noise effects precisely. This paper finds edges in noisy image using ant colony algorithm. Algorithm finds edges in the presence of white Gaussian noise and salt and pepper noise. After the running algorithm gets four different edges of the four types, experiments were conducted to evaluate the performance of the ACO approach in noisy images.

The results of this algorithm were compared with the results of the algorithm used in reference [1] that the results of this reference shown in figure 5.

The algorithm used in this article is performed only by the presence of white Gaussian noise, while the ACO algorithm can be performed by other noises. After running the algorithm gets four different edges of the four types of relationships, that can use in applications according to type and applied fields. Otherwise, edges can combine using operators such as OR. Thus, the used algorithm can be better and be more complete.

6. Conclusion

ACO algorithm has been used for edge detection of noisy images. Edge detection has been performed in the presence of salt and pepper noise and Gaussian noise which are the dominant noise in most images. While the edges frequencies are

(a)

(b)

(c)

Figure 4. edge detection with salt and pepper noise and intensity= 0.1 (a) edge detection with Sobel operator, (b) edge detection with Prewitt operator, (c) edge detection with Canny operator.

close to the noise frequency bands, ACO succeeds in edge detection. We applied ACO algorithm to different images with different noise intensity of the two types of noise. Comparing to a conventional edge detection algorithm performance, referenced in [1], ACO is more effective.

References

[1] Tian, J., et al. (2008). An ant colony optimization algorithm for image edge detection. IEEE Evolutionary Computation, Hong Kong, China, 2008.

[2] He, Q. & Zhang, Z. (2007). A new edge detection algorithm for image corrupted by White-Gaussian noise. International Journal of Electronics and Communications, vol. 6, no. 8, pp. 546-550.

[3] Khashman, A. (2002). Noise-Dependent optimal Scale in Edge Detection. Industrial Electronics, IEEE International Symposium Proceedings, vol. 2, no. 1, pp. 467-471.

[4] Junxi, S., et al. (2003). A multiscale edge detection algorithm based on wavelet domain vector hidden Markov tree model. Elsevier Journal, vol. 37, no.7, pp. 1315-1324.

[5] Kanga, C. & Wanga, W-J. (2007). A novel edge detection method based on the maximizing objective function. The journal of the pattern recognition, vol. 40, no. 2, pp. 609-618.

[6] Bakhshi, H., et al. (2014). A study on Clustering for Clustering Based Image De-Noising. Journal of Information Systems and Telecommunication, vol. 2, no. 4, pp. 196-204.

[7] Hou, Z. J. & Wei, G. W. (2002). A new approach to edge detection, Elsevier Ltd, vol. 35, no.2, pp. 1559-1570.

[8] Xueqin, S., et al. (2010). Edge Detection for Phytoplankton Cellular Based on Multi-wavelets De-noising. Proceedings of the 2nd International Conference on Computer and Automation Engineering (ICCAE), vol. 2, pp. 190-193, 2010.

[9] He, Jianmin, i., et al. (2009). Canny Edge Detection on a Virtual Hexagonal Image Structure. Conferences on Pervasive Computing (JCPC), Tamsui, Taipei, 2009.

[10] Srivastava, G. K. & Verma, R. (2009). A Novel Wavelet Edge Detection Algorithm for Noisy Images. Ultra Modern International Conference Telecommunications & Workshops, St. Petersburg 2009.

[11] Shih, M. (2005). A wavelet-based multiresolution edge detection and tracking Tseng DC. Image Vision Computr, vol. 23, no.1, pp. 441–451.

[12] Lee, J., et al. (2002). Morphologic edge detection. Journal Robotics and Automation, vol. 3, no. 2, pp. 142–156.

[13] Lesions, R. & Woolfson, M. (2004). Application of region based segmentation and neural network edge detection to skin lesions. Comput Med Imag Graphics, vol. 28, no. 1, pp. 61-80.

[14] Akbari, A. S. & Soraghan, J. J. (2003). Fuzzy-based multiscale edge Detection. Electronics Letters, vol. 39, no. 1, pp. 30-32.

[15] Shafiee, M. & Latif, A. (2014). Modified CLPSO-based fuzzy classification system: Color image segmentation. Journal of AI and Data Mining, vol. 2, no. 2, pp. 167-179.

[16] Arastehfar, S., et al. (2013). An enhanced median filter for removing noise from MR images. Journal of AI and Data Mining, vol. 1, no. 1, pp. 13-17.

[17] Prakash Verma, O. & Madasu Hanmandll, M. (2009). A Novel Approach for Edge Detection using Ant Colon Optimization and Fuzzy Derivative Technique. Advance Computing Conference, Patiala, 2009.

[18] Gill J., et al. (2014). Wavelet with Filter Based Method for Edge Detection Using Ant Colony Optimization. International Journal of Advanced Research in Computer Science and Software Engineering, vol. 4, no. 10, pp. 281-285.

[19] Puneet, R. & Maitreyee, D. (2013). Image Edge Detection using Modified Ant Colony Optimization Algorithm based on Weighted Heuristics. International Journal of Computer Applications, vol. 68, no. 15, pp. 5-9.

[20] Rahebi, J., et al. (2011). Biomedical Image Edge Detection using an Ant Colony Optimization Based on Artificial Neural Networks. International Journal of Engineering Science and Technology (IJEST), vol. 3 no. 2, pp. 8211-8218.

[21] Xiaochen, L. & Suping. F. (2015). A convenient and robust edge detection method based on ant colony optimization. Optics Communications, vol. 353, no. 1, pp. 147–157.

[22] Samit, A. & Dipak Kumar, G., (2014). Edge detection using ACO and F ratio. Springer, vol. 8, no. 1, pp. 625–634.

[23] Charu, G. & Sunanda, G., (2013). Edge Detection of an Image based on Ant Colony Optimization Technique, vol. 2 no. 6, pp. 114-120.

3

Modified CLPSO-based fuzzy classification system: Color image segmentation

M. Shafiee[1*] and A. Latif[2]

1. Department of Computer Engineering, Kerman Branch, Islamic Azad University, Kerman, Iran
2. Department of Electrical and Computer Engineering, Yazd University, Yazd, Iran.

*Corresponding author: a.shafiee@iauk.ac.ir (M. Shafiee).

Abstract

Fuzzy segmentation is an effective way of segmenting out objects in images containing varying illumination. In this paper, a modified method based on the Comprehensive Learning Particle Swarm Optimization (CLPSO) is proposed for pixel classification in HSI color space by selecting a fuzzy classification system with minimum number of fuzzy rules and minimum number of incorrectly classified patterns. In the CLPSO-based method, each individual of population is considered to automatically generate a fuzzy classification system. Afterwards, an individual member tries to maximize a fitness criterion which is high classification rate and small number of fuzzy rules. To reduce the multidimensional search space for an M-class classification problem, the centroid of each class is calculated and then fixed in membership function of fuzzy system. The performance of the proposed method is evaluated in terms of future classification within the RoboCup soccer environment with spatially varying illumination intensities on the scene. The results present 85.8% accuracy in terms of classification.

Keywords: *Comprehensive Learning Particle Swarm Optimization, Fuzzy Classification, Image Segmentation, Robotics, RoboCup, LUT Generation, Pattern Recognition.*

1. Introduction

The process of partitioning an image into regions is called image segmentation. The result of the image segmentation is a set of regions that cover the image. All of the pixels in a region are similar with respect to some characteristics, such as color, intensity, or texture. Image segmentation methods divided into five categories: pixel based segmentation [1,2], region based segmentation [3], edge based segmentation [4], edge and region hybrid segmentation [5], and clustering based segmentation [4,6,7]. Color image segmentation using fuzzy classification system is a pixel based segmentation method. A pixel is assigned to a specific color by the fuzzy system, which partitions the color space into segments. Any given pixel is then classified according to the segments it lies in.

Fuzzy rule-based systems applied to solve many classification problems. In many of them, fuzzy classification rules are derived from human experts. Because it is not easy to derive fuzzy rules from human experts, many approaches have been proposed to generate fuzzy rules automatically from the training patterns of the main classification problem [1,2,8,9,10,11].

Solving classification problems with high-dimensional pattern spaces has a significant shortcoming, the more the number of fuzzy rules are, the more the number of dimensions are and the learning time is too high. The Particle Swarm Optimizer (PSO) [12,13] is a computational method that optimizes a problem by iteratively trying to improve a candidate solution with regard to a given measure of quality. Although PSO shares many similarities with evolutionary computation techniques, the standard PSO does not use evolution operators such as crossover and mutation.

PSO emulates the swarm behavior of insects, birds flocking, and fish schooling where these swarms search for food in a collaborative manner. Each member in the swarm adapts its search patterns by learning from its own experience and other members' experiences.

In PSO, a member in the swarm represents a potential solution which is a point in the search space. The global optimum is regarded as the location of food. Each particle has a fitness value and a velocity to adjust its flying direction according to the best experiences of the swarm. The PSO algorithm is easy to implement and has been empirically shown to perform well on many optimization problems [14]. However, it may easily get trapped in a local optimum. In order to improve PSO's performance, we adopt the modified comprehensive learning particle swarm optimizer utilizing a new learning strategy.

In recent years, different methods have been proposed for tuning membership parameters and generating fuzzy rules such as genetic algorithm and PSO. Shamir [15] introduced a human perception based approach to pixel color segmentation using fuzzy systems. Fuzzy sets are defined on the H, S and V components of the HSV color space. The fuzzy rules in this model are defined based on human observations. Tuning fuzzy rules parameters by human expert, significantly affects the classification results and it is a time consuming problem. Marquesan et al. design a color classification system using CLPSO [16]. Image segmentation with the least number of rules and minimum error rate was the main purpose of his work. Enormous search space caused the learning process slow and also his proposed algorithm needed human supervision for defining output color classes. The similar approach using PSO variant algorithm was applied for color image segmentation in [1,2,8,13]. Casillas et al. presented a genetic feature selection process that can be integrated in multistage genetic learning method to obtain fuzzy rule based classification system. It composed a set of comprehensible fuzzy rules with high-classification ability [9]. Yuan et al. designed a fuzzy genetic algorithm to generate classification rules with several techniques such as multi-value logic coding, viability check and composite [10].

Although many color classification methods have been proposed using optimization technique [1,2,8,13,16] and many unsupervised methods for clustering introduced [6,7,17,18,19], no solution have an optimal solution for color image classification to have both high accuracy and time efficiency simultaneously.

In this paper, a modified method based on the Comprehensive Learning Particle Swarm Optimization (CLPSO) is implemented to select an appropriate fuzzy classification system with minimum number of incorrect classified patterns and minimum number of fuzzy rules. In this approach, Centroid of each class is calculated and then fixed in membership function of fuzzy system. As the consequence the search space reduces. Each individual in the population is considered to represent a fuzzy classification system. Then, a fitness function is used to guide the search procedure to select an appropriate fuzzy classification system.

The rest of this paper is organized as follows. Section 2 describes the structure of the fuzzy classification system. Section 3 proposes a modified CLPSO-based method to adjust the fuzzy classification system parameters for pixel classification problem. Section 4 considers classification problems of a humanoid robot vision data to illustrate the learning and the generalization ability of the proposed approach, respectively. Finally, section 5 demonstrates conclusions about the proposed method for solving the classification problem.

2. Fuzzy color classification system

Fuzzy color pixel classification is a supervised learning method for segmentation of color images. In this method, each pixel of an input image assigns to a color class by applying a set of fuzzy rules on it. A set of training pixels, for which the colors class are known, are used to train the fuzzy system.

Figure 1 shows a fuzzy classification system with color pixel on HSI color space as an input. Unlike RGB, HSI separates luminance, from Chroma. This is useful for robustness to lighting changes, or removing shadows.

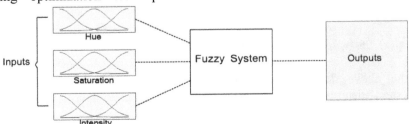

Figure 1. Fuzzy color pixel classification system.

For an M-class classification problem, a rule base of fuzzy classification system considered as follows [12]:

jth Rule:
if x_1 is A_{j1} and x_2 is A_{j2} and ...
and x_m is A_{jm}
then $\underline{x} = (x_1, x_2, ..., x_m)$ belongs to
class H_j with $CF = CF_j$ $j = 1, 2, ..., R$

$$(1)$$

Where R is the number of fuzzy rules and A_{ji} $i = 1, 2, ..., m$, are the premise fuzzy sets of the jth fuzzy rule, $H_j \epsilon \{1, 2, ..., M\}$, is the consequent class output of the jth fuzzy rule, and $CF_j \epsilon [0,1]$ is the grade of certainty of the jth fuzzy rule.

Fuzzy sets are defined on the H, S and I channels with Gaussian membership functions, which are described by (2):

$$\mu_{A_{ji}}\left(m_{(ji,1)}, m_{(ji,2)}, m_{(ji,3)}; x_i\right)$$

$$= \begin{cases} \exp\left(-\left(\dfrac{x_i - m_{(ji,1)}}{m_{(ji,2)}}\right)^2\right), & \text{if } x_i \leq m_{(ji,1)} \\ \exp\left(-\left(\dfrac{x_i - m_{(ji,1)}}{m_{(ji,3)}}\right)^2\right), & \text{if } x_i > m_{(ji,1)} \end{cases}$$

$$(2)$$

Where $m_{(ji,1)}$ determines the center position, $m_{(ji,2)}$ and $m_{(ji,3)}$ are the left and right width values of the membership function, respectively. Hence, the shape of membership function is defined by a parameter vector $\underline{m_{ji}} = [m_{(ji,1)}, m_{(ji,2)}, m_{(ji,3)}]$.

The jth rule is determined by a parameter vector $\underline{r}_j = [m_{j1}, m_{j2}, ..., m_{jM}]$. Also, the set of parameters in the premise part of the rule base is defined as $r = [\underline{r}_1, \underline{r}_2, ..., \underline{r}_R]$.

According to (1), the set of parameters in the consequent part of the rule is defined as $\underline{a} = [H_1, CF_1, H_2, CF_2, ..., H_R, CF_R]$. When the input $x = (x_1, x_2, ..., x_m)$ is given the premise of the jth rule is calculated by the (3).

The class output of the fuzzy classification system with respect to the input x can be determined by (4).

$$q_j(x) = \prod_{i=1}^{M} \mu_{A_{ji}}(x_i) \qquad (3)$$

$$y = \arg \max_{j=1} q_j(x) . CF_j \qquad (4)$$

According to the above description, a fuzzy classification system determines by a set of premise and consequent parameters.

Different parameter sets determine different fuzzy classification systems and so the generated fuzzy classification systems have different performances.

The goal is to find an appropriate fuzzy classification system to have both minimum number of fuzzy rules and maximum number of correct classified pattern.

In the next section, to select an appropriate fuzzy classification system a modified CLPSO is applied.

3. Modified CLPSO-based fuzzy classification system

3.1. Particle swarm optimization

As mentioned before, PSO emulates a swarm behavior and each individual represents some points in the multi-dimensional search space. A particle is a potential solution.

The velocity V_i^d and position X_i^d of the dth dimension of the ith particle are updated as follows:

$$V_i^d \leftarrow V_i^d + c_1 * rand1_i^d * \left(pbest_i^d - X_i^d\right) + c_2 * rand2_i^d * \left(gbest_i^d - X_i^d\right) \qquad (5)$$

$$X_i^d \leftarrow X_i^d + V_i^d \qquad (6)$$

Where $X_i = \left(X_i^1, X_i^2, ..., X_i^D\right)$ is the position of the ith particle, $V_i = (V_i^1, V_i^2, ..., V_i^D)$ represents velocity of ith particle. $pbest_i = (pbest_i^1, pbest_i^2, ..., pbest_i^D)$ is the best previous position yielding the best fitness value for the ith particle; and $gbest = (gbest^1, gbest^2, ..., gbest^D)$ is the best position discovered by the whole population.

c_1 and c_2 are the acceleration constants reflecting the weighting of stochastic acceleration in terms that pull each particle toward pbest and gbest positions, respectively. $rand1_i^d$ and $rand2_i^d$ are two random numbers in the interval of [0, 1].

Although there are numerous variants for the PSO, premature convergence for multimodal problems is the main deficiency of the PSO.

In the original PSO, each particle learns from pbest and gbest simultaneously; restricting the social learning aspect to only to gbest, makes the original PSO converge fast.

Since all particles learn from the gbest even if the current gbest is far from the global optimum, particles may easily be attracted to the gbest region and get trapped in a local optimum.

This matter is critical if the search environment is complex with numerous local solutions.

3.2. Comprehensive learning particle swarm optimization

In the CLPSO, velocity is updated according to (7):

$$V_i^d \leftarrow w * V_i^d + c * rand_i^d \\ * \left(pbest_{fi(d)}^d - X_i^d \right) \qquad (7)$$

Where $f_i = [f_i(1), f_i(2), ..., f_i(D)]$ defines which particles' pbest, the particle i should follow. $pbest_{fi(d)}^d$ can be the corresponding dimension of any particle's pbest including its own pbest, and the decision depends on probability P_{c_i}, referred to as the learning probability, which can take different values for different particles.

For each dimension of particle i, a random number is generated. If this random number is larger than P_{c_i}, the corresponding dimension will learn from its own pbest; otherwise, it will learn from another particles' pbest as follows:

1) First two particles randomly choose out of population.
2) The fitness of these two particles pbest are compared and the better one is selected. In CLPSO, the larger the fitness value is, the better the pbest is defined.

3) The winner's pbest is used as the exemplar to learn from that dimension. The details of choosing f_i are given in Figure 2.

4. Proposed modified CLPSO with fuzzy classification system

Training data contains a mapping from HIS color space **S** to a set of colors **M** which assigns a class label $m_i \in M$ to every point $s_j \in S$ in color space. If each channel is represented by an n-bit value and k = |M| represents the number of defined class labels, then **S → M**, where **S** = {**0, 1, ..., 2ⁿ − 1**}³ and **M** = {**m₀, m₁, ..., m_{k−1}**}. Assuming we have **M** cluster in data set, the centroid of each cluster **C** can be determined by the following equation:

$$C_x = \frac{1}{np} \sum_{j=1}^{n_p} s_{xj} , x \in \{H, S, I\} \qquad (8)$$

Where n_p is the number of points in training set and s_{xj} represents the value of x-channel of the jth point in the training set. Using the cluster

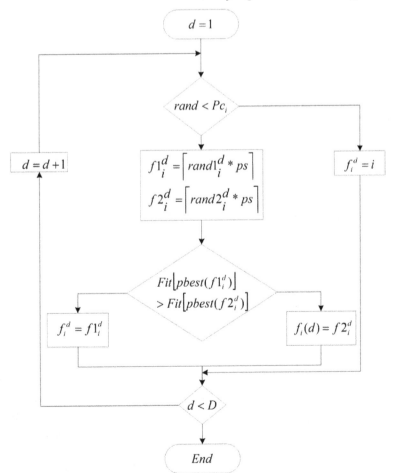

Figure 2. Selection of exemplar dimensions for particle i.

centroids, the center position of the Gaussian membership function of the fuzzy rule system, $m_{(ji,1)}$, can be fixed and therefore, we have a search space reduction. In addition, by having the number of clusters, minimum number of fuzzy rules is calculable and fitness function can be improved.

In the proposed method, each individual is represented to determine a fuzzy classification system. The individual is used to partition the input space so that the rule number and the premise part of the generated fuzzy classification system are determined. Subsequently, the consequent parameters of the corresponding fuzzy system are obtained by the premise fuzzy sets of the generated fuzzy classification system.

A set of L individuals, P which is called population is expressed in the following:

$$\begin{bmatrix} \underline{P_1} \\ \underline{P_2} \\ \underline{P_3} \\ \vdots \\ \underline{P_h} \\ \vdots \\ \underline{P_L} \end{bmatrix} = \begin{bmatrix} \underline{r_1} & \underline{g_1} \\ \underline{r_2} & \underline{g_2} \\ \underline{r_3} & \underline{g_3} \\ \vdots & \\ \underline{r_h} & \underline{g_h} \\ \vdots & \\ \underline{r_L} & \underline{g_L} \end{bmatrix} \qquad (9)$$

In order to evolutionarily determine the parameters of the fuzzy classification system, the individual $\underline{P_h}$ contains two parameter vectors: $\underline{r_h}$ and $\underline{g_h}$. The parameter vector $\underline{r_h} = [\underline{r_1^h} \ \underline{r_2^h} \cdots \underline{r_j^h} \cdots \underline{r_B^h}]$ consists of the premise parameters of the candidate fuzzy rules, where B is a positive integer to decide the maximum number of fuzzy rules in the rule base generated by the individual$\underline{P_h}$. B is all possible combination of clusters centroid for each channel which is $B = C_H \times C_S \times C_I$ where C_H, C_S, C_I is calculated by Eq.8. Likewise, the minimum number of fuzzy rules is equal to the number of main clusters, which is called Q.

Here, $\underline{r_j^h} = [m_{j1}^h \ m_{j2}^h \dots m_{ji}^h \dots m_{jM}^h]$ is the parameter vector to determine the membership functions of the jth fuzzy rule, where $\underline{m_{ij}^h} = [\underline{m}_{(ji,1)} \ \underline{\quad}_{(ji,2)} \ \underline{\quad}_{(ji,P)}^h]$ is the parameter vector to determine the membership function for the ith input variable.

The parameter vector $\underline{g_h} = [g_1^h \ g_2^h \dots g_j^h \dots g_B^h]$ is used to select the fuzzy rules from the candidate rules $\underline{r_h} = [\underline{r_1^h} \ \underline{r_2^h} \cdots \underline{r_j^h} \cdots \underline{r_B^h}]$ so that the fuzzy rule base is generated. $g_j^h \in [0,1]$ decides whether the jth candidate rule $\underline{r_j^h}$ is added to the rule base of the generated fuzzy system or not. If $g_j^h \geq 0.5$,

then the jth candidate rule $\underline{r_j^h}$ is added to the rule base. Consequently, the total number of g_j^h ($j = 1,2,\dots,B$) whose value is greater than or equal to 0.5 is the number of fuzzy rules in the generated rule base.

In order to generate the rule base, the index j of g_j^h ($j = 1,2,\dots,B$) whose value is greater than or equal to 0.5 is defined as $I_r^h \in \{1,2,\dots,B\}$, $r = 1,2,\dots,r_h$ where r_h represents the number of the fuzzy rules in the generated rule base. $\{r_{I_1^h}^h, r_{I_2^h}^h \qquad {}_h\}$ generates the premise part of the fuzzy rule base which is generated by the individual$\underline{P_h} = [\ \underline{r_h} \ \underline{g_h}]$.

For example, assume that $\underline{r_h}$ and $\underline{g_h}$ are denoted as$[\underline{r_1} \ \underline{r_2} \ \underline{r_3} \ \underline{r_4} \ \underline{r_5} \ \underline{r_6}]$ and $[0.12 \ 0.72 \ 0.82 \ 0.35 \ 0.29 \ 0.8]$, respectively. According to $\underline{g_h}$, the generated rule base has three fuzzy rules $\{I_1^h, I_2^h, I_3^h\} = \{2,3,6\}$; therefore, $\{\underline{r_2} \ \underline{r_3} \ \underline{r_6}\}$ determines the premise part of the generated rule base.

The rule base of the generated fuzzy classification system is described as follows:

rth Rule:
if x_1 is $A_{I_r^h 1}^h$ and x_2 is $A_{I_r^h 2}^h$ and ...
and x_m is $A_{I_r^h m}^h$ (10)
then $\underline{x} = (x_1, x_2, \dots, x_m)$ belongs to
class H_r with $CF = CF_r$ $j = 1,2,\dots,r_h$,

Where $A_{I_r^h i}^h$, $i = 1,2,\dots,m$, are the fuzzy sets of the generated rth fuzzy rule. The membership function associated with the fuzzy set is described as follows:

$$\mu_{A_{I_r^h i}^h} \left(m_{(I_r^h i,1)}^h, m_{(I_r^h i,2)}^h, m_{(I_r^h i,3)}^h; x_i \right)$$
$$= \begin{cases} exp\left(-\left(\dfrac{x_i - m_{(I_r^h i,1)}^h}{m_{(I_r^h i,2)}^h} \right)^2 \right), & if \ x_i \leq m_{(I_r^h i,1)}^h \\[4mm] exp\left(-\left(\dfrac{x_i - m_{(I_r^h i,1)}^h}{m_{(I_r^h i,3)}^h} \right)^2 \right), & if \ x_i > m_{(I_r^h i,1)}^h \end{cases} \qquad (11)$$

Assume that N training patterns $(\underline{x_n}, y_n), n = 1,2,\dots,N$, are gathered from the observation of the considered M-class classification problem, where $\underline{x_n} = (x_{n1}, x_{n2}, \dots, x_{nm})$ is the input vector of the nth training pattern and $y_n \in \{1,2,\dots,M\}$, where M is the total number of classes, is the corresponding class output.

In order to determine the consequent parameters H_r and CF_r of the rth fuzzy rule, a procedure is proposed as follows [1]:

Step1. Calculate θ_t, $t = 1, 2, \ldots, M$ for the rth fuzzy rule as follows:

$$\theta_t = \sum_{x_p \in Class\ t} q_r(\underline{x}_p), \qquad t = 1, 2, \ldots, M. \qquad (12)$$

Step2. Determine H_r for the rth fuzzy rule by:

$$H_r = arg\ \max_{t=1}^{M}\ \theta_t. \qquad (13)$$

Step3. Determine the grade of certainty CF_r of the rth fuzzy rule by:

$$CF_r = \frac{\theta_{H_r} - \theta}{\sum_{t=1}^{M} \theta_t} \qquad (14)$$

$$\theta = \sum_{\substack{t=1 \\ t \neq H_r}}^{M} \frac{\theta_t}{M - 1} \qquad (15)$$

In order to construct a fuzzy classification system which has an appropriate number of fuzzy rules and minimize incorrectly classified patterns simultaneously, the fitness function is defined as follows:

$$f_h = fit\left(\underline{p}_h\right) = g_1\left(\underline{p}_h\right) * g_2(\underline{p}_h) \qquad (16)$$

$$g_1\left(\underline{p}_h\right) = NCCP \qquad (17)$$

$$g_2\left(\underline{p}_h\right) = \begin{cases} \left(\dfrac{B - r_h}{B - Q}\right) & B \neq Q \\ \left(\dfrac{r_h}{B}\right) & B = Q \end{cases} \qquad (18)$$

Where NCCP $(\underline{p}_h)$ is the number of correctly classified patterns, r_h is the number of fuzzy rules in the rule base of the generated fuzzy classification system.

The fitness function is designed to maximize the number of correctly classified patterns and minimize the number of fuzzy rules.

In this way, as the fitness function value increases as much as possible, the fuzzy classification system corresponding to the individual will satisfy the desired objective as well as possible.

CLPSO-based method is proposed to find an appropriate individual so that the corresponding fuzzy classification system has the desired performance. The modified proposed procedure is described as follows:

Step1. Initialize the CLPSO-based method.
(a) Set the number of individuals (L), the maximum number of rules (B), the number of generations (K), and the constants for the PSO algorithm (ω_0, ω_1, c).

(b) Generate randomly initial population P. Each individual of the population is expressed as follows:

$$\underline{p}_h = \begin{bmatrix} \underline{r}_h & \underline{g}_h \end{bmatrix}$$

$where$

$$\underline{r}_h = [m^h_{(11,1)}\ m^h_{(11,2)}\ m^h_{(11,3)} \cdots$$
$$m^h_{(1m,1)}\ m^h_{(1m,2)}\ m^h_{(1m,3)} \cdots$$
$$m^h_{(B1,1)}\ m^h_{(B1,2)}\ m^h_{(B1,3)} \cdots \qquad (19)$$
$$m^h_{(Bm,1)}\ m^h_{(Bm,2)}\ m^h_{(Bm,3)}]$$
$$m^h_{(ji,k)}, j \in \{1, 2, \ldots, B\}, i \in \{1, 2, \ldots, M\},$$
$$k \in \{1, 2, 3\}$$
and
$$\underline{g}_h = \begin{bmatrix} g^h_1 & g^h_2 \cdots g^h_j \cdots g^h_B \end{bmatrix}. m^h_{(ji,k)},$$
$$j \in \{1, 2, \ldots, B\}$$
$m^h_{(ji,k)}$ is randomly generated as follow:

$$m^h_{(ji,k)} = m^{min}_{(ji,k)} + \left(m^{max}_{(ji,k)} - m^{min}_{(ji,k)}\right) \times rand \qquad (20)$$

Where the range of the parameter $m^h_{(ji,k)}$ is defined as $[m^{min}_{(ji,k)}, m^{max}_{(ji,k)}]$ and $rand$ is a uniformly distributed random numbers in $[0,1]$, also g^h_j is randomly generated.

(c) Generate randomly initial velocity vectors $\underline{v}_h$, $h = 1, 2, \ldots, L$. Each velocity vector is expressed as follows:

$$\underline{v}_h = \begin{bmatrix} \underline{\alpha}_h & \underline{\beta}_h \end{bmatrix}$$
$where$
$$\underline{\alpha}_h = [\alpha^h_{(11,1)}\ \alpha^h_{(11,2)}\ \alpha^h_{(11,3)} \cdots$$
$$\alpha^h_{(1m,1)}\ \alpha^h_{(1m,2)}\ \alpha^h_{(1m,3)} \cdots$$
$$\alpha^h_{(B1,1)}\ \alpha^h_{(B1,2)}\ \alpha^h_{(B1,3)} \cdots \qquad (21)$$
$$\alpha^h_{(Bm,1)}\ \alpha^h_{(Bm,2)}\ \alpha^h_{(Bm,3)}]$$
$$\alpha^h_{(ji,k)},\ j \in \{1, 2, \ldots, B\},\ i \in \{1, 2, \ldots, M\},$$
$$k \in \{1, 2, 3\}\ and$$
$$\underline{\beta}_h = [\beta^h_1\ \beta^h_2 \cdots \beta^h_B]$$
$\alpha^h_{(ji,k)}$ is randomly generated as follows:

$$\alpha^h_{(ji,k)} = \frac{\left(\alpha^{max}_{(ji,k)} - \alpha^{min}_{(ji,k)}\right)}{20} \times rand \qquad (22)$$

β^h_j is randomly generated as follows:

$$\beta^h_j = \frac{rand}{20} \qquad (23)$$

(d) The fitness value for each particle of the population is calculated and saved. It is being noted that to calculate the fitness value, the fuzzy systems of each particle is tested with training data, individually.

Step2. Generate f_i for each particle as in.

Step3. Update the vector $\underline{g_h} = [g_1^h \ g_2^h \ldots g_j^h \ldots g_B^h]$, as follows:

$$g_{j^*}^h = 1 - g_{j^*}^h, \qquad j^* = rand([1, B]) \qquad (24)$$

Where $rand$ generates an integer random number in interval of $[1, B]$.

Step4. Update velocity and position of each particle according to (6 and 7).

Step5. Mutate the population randomly. At any stage an integer random number, called mutation indicator in range of $[1, L]$, is generated. Particle associated with the selected indicator is selected and its $\underline{g_h}$ vector is replaced by Max-Score vector.

To obtain Max-Score, the total value of all existing rules regardless of $\underline{g_h}$ is achieved using fitness function. Since the fuzzy rules of each cluster is distinctive, the rule with maximum fitness value receives score 1 in Max-Score and the rest of the rules related to the cluster receive score 0. If the particle does not acquire a better fitness value after the mutation, $\underline{g_h}$ will be restored to the previous values before mutation.

Step6. If Max-gen > K then K = K+1 and go to step 2 or it; otherwise stops.

Step7. Based on the individual with the best fitness, the desired fuzzy classification system can be determined.

The flowchart of the modified-CLPSO is given in figure 3.

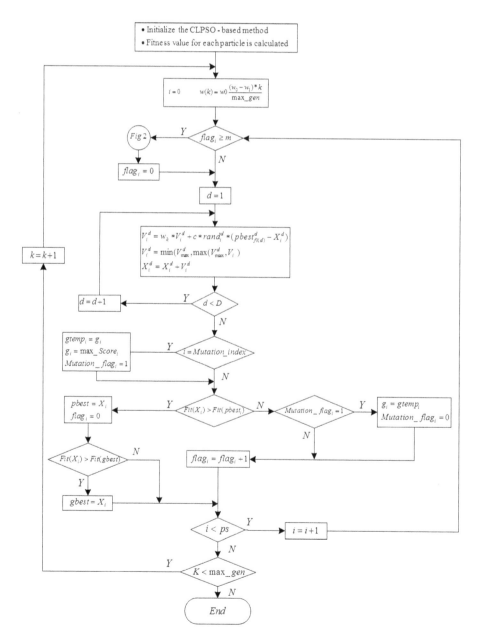

Figure 3. Flowchart of the modified CLPSO.

5. Experimental results

For evaluating the algorithm, one set of images (50 images) was obtained from reference [20] and also we obtain another set (117 images) in varying light condition to measure the robustness of the classifier against the light changes. In providing these images; fluorescent lights and also natural light of ambient without applying any filter were used. A lux-meter with 12 to 12000 lux sensitivity was used and ambient light level for each image was recorded. Light of obtained images was in the range of 100 to 1200 lux.

We implement our scheme on MATLAB R2013 installed on a computer with a Corei7 processor and 8GB RAM. The general parameters of the proposed CLPSO algorithm are listed in Table 1.

Table 1. Proposed method parameters.

Parameters	Symbol	Initialization value
Population size	L	30
Max number of rules	B	$C_{Hn} \times C_{Sn} \times C_{In}$
Min number of rules	Q	Variable
Max number of iterations	K	500
Constants of CLPSO	$(\omega_0, \omega_1, c, m)$	(0.9,0.4,1.49445,4)

For comparison and evaluation of fuzzy classification system, the first set of images was used. After training a fuzzy system with proposed method, its precision was evaluated; table 2 presents the results of this step and Table shows the result of fuzzy pixel classification on 7 samples of data set.

Table 2. Performance of the proposed classification system.

No.	No. of samples	Sensitivity	Specificity	Precision	Accuracy
1	50	0.7312	0.9644	0.6762	0.8582

5.1. Performance of the proposed fuzzy classification system against light changes

To evaluate the robustness of the proposed system against lights changes, set of 117 images in the range of 0 to 1000 lux were used (see Figure 4).

To train the system, a set of pixels in the range of 400 to 700 lux selected and the fuzzy system trained.

Numbers of obtained rules after training were 9 and general precision of classification system was 90%.

Figure 4. Five samples of increasing illumination recorded by lux meter.

To test the system, a set of pixels in the range of 0 to 1000 lux selected and system performance presented in table 4 according to the color and light.

The first column is standard colors defined by RoboCup; the second column is the range of light levels in which the images are taken, the next three columns are the minimum and maximum value of each channel of HSI color space, the result of classification with the proposed fuzzy system is shown in column six, last column shows increase or decrease in classification performance. As shown in the table 4, in the range of 400 to 700 lux, the lowest classification precision related to green, orange and yellow, respectively.

In the range of 0-400 lux, the most decrease in classification precision related to cyan with 37.92

percent, yellow with 20.62 percent and orange with 7.68 percent, respectively.

In this range, it is noticeable that the classification precision for green color increased to 37.09 percent, because of light levels severely reduced in the range of 0-400 lux which places all the data in the correct class.

In the range of 700-1000 lux, classification precision of yellow, green, blue and cyan reduced to 18.33%, 7.5%, 19.58% and 1.2 %, respectively. Therefore, the most robust color to the light changes is pink and the most sensitive color to the light changes is green.

The surveying colors according to robustness against the light changes are pink with 100%, blue with 92.63%, cyan with 86.96%, yellow with 84.92%, orange with 81.37% and green with 77.35%.

Table 3. Result of fuzzy pixel classification tuned by proposed modified CLPSO algorithm.

No.	Input Image	Fuzzy pixel classification output image	Sensitivity	Specificity	Precision	Accuracy
1			0.6099	0.9942	0.9562	0.9799
2			0.6044	0.9791	0.8821	0.8866
3			0.7224	0.9904	0.8997	0.9667
4			0.5949	0.9685	0.7217	0.7827
5			0.7229	0.9824	0.8375	0.8870
6			0.6440	0.9761	0.6629	0.8058
7			0.7747	0.9814	0.6821	0.9276

Table 4. The effect of light changes on system performance.

Color	Lux	Hue		Saturation		Intensity		Classification		Performance
		Min	Max	Min	Max	Min	Max	True	False	
Orange	400-0	3.78	19.27	191.56	232.02	120.00	230.00	75.62	24.37	-7.68
	700-400	7.57	30.47	189.01	234.18	140.00	238.00	83.3	16.6	0
	1000-700	15.14	39.77	76.26	230.44	140.00	243.00	85.20	14.79	+1.9
Yellow	400-0	29.30	42.50	154.06	218.51	116.00	226.00	77.29	22.70	-20.62
	700-400	34.99	43.50	190.85	219.71	153.00	234.00	97.91	2.08	0
	1000-700	36.21	43.86	119.22	219.71	180.00	236.00	79.58	20.41	-18.33
Green	400-0	70.26	108.15	130.00	217.00	84.00	171.00	100	0	+37.09
	700-400	79.90	109.51	107.05	221.45	152.00	212.00	62.91	37.09	0
	1000-700	75.65	111.25	95.21	225.32	163.00	235.00	69.16	30.83	-7.5
Blue	400-0	152.86	170.00	138.70	227.06	80.00	166.00	97.5	2.5	-2.5
	700-400	151.41	158.88	140.03	225.45	120.00	173.00	100	0	0
	1000-700	149.10	157.68	99.41	199.27	144.00	223.00	80.41	19.58	-19.58
Cyan	400-0	115.36	136.45	93.95	221.45	106.00	211.00	62.08	37.92	-37.92
	700-400	118.77	132.19	91.15	218.57	158.00	221.00	100	0	0
	1000-700	115.78	133.84	91.15	219.39	171.00	234.00	98.8	1.2	-1.2
Pink	400-0	229.35	251.7	151.17	221.00	73.00	172.00	100	0	0
	700-400	233.75	246.11	138.68	201.45	94.00	195.00	100	0	0
	1000-700	229.96	79.69	79.69	163.36	127.00	231.00	100	0	0

6. Comparison of the proposed segmentation of the algorithm performance with the existing methods

One of the problems related to optimization techniques is that they are time-consuming. The proposed method has a higher speed compared with the conventional methods.

Figure 5 shows the iteration time table. Firstly, it is observed that all three slopes are approximately equal.

Due to iteration 20, mutations in the particles and the reduction of rules cause the decrease in the calculation complexity and the slope graph.

In figure 6, the overall precision of the existing methods is compared. For this comparison, the results of references [20,21,22] have been used.

In all methods, except for the reference method [20], an optimization algorithm is used to adjust the fuzzy classification system.

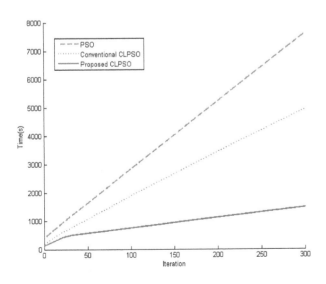

Figure 5. Consumed time graph of PSO, conventional CLPSO and proposed CLPSO methods.

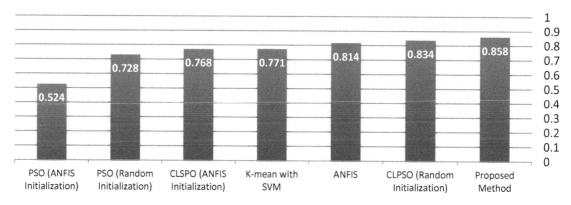

Figure 6. Accuracy of the existing methods.

In all methods, the Gaussian membership function is used, and the goal is to set up a classification system for Robocop competitions.

The main difference of the proposed method with the reference [21] is mainly the modified fitness function and the fixed centroids of the fuzzy membership function.

In [20], the overall precision of classification was not presented and the precision of positive and negative classes were used for expressing the results. For calculating the overall precision of this method, the following equation was used.

$$Balanced\ Accuracy = \frac{Sensitivity + Specificity}{2} \quad (25)$$

The proposed method with 0.858 precision for classifying 8 classes allocated the most precision method among the existing ones.

It is observed that the primary initialization has considerable effects on increasing the accuracy. In addition to the reported accuracy of different methods, the result of classification of each method is shown in figure 7.

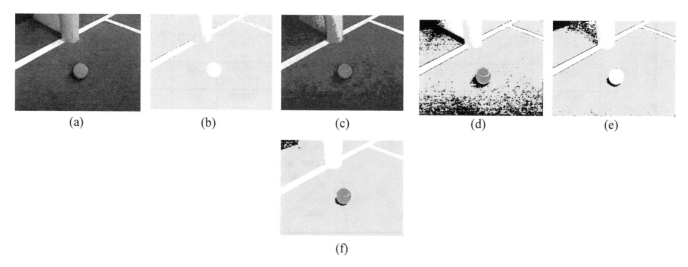

(a)   (b)   (c)   (d)   (e)

(f)

Figure 7. (a) original image, the rest are segmentation result of the test image produced by the following algorithms: (b) PSO random initialization, (c) k-mean with SVM, (d) ANFIS, (e) CLPSO random initialization, (f) proposed method.

One of the important parameters of fuzzy classification system is the number of rules.

As mentioned erliear, the reduction of rules in the fitness function has been taken into consideration and has been one of the main differences between the particle swarm optimization method and ANFIS. In figure 8, the number of obtained rules for various methods has been studied. Due to the

lack of fuzzy methods in reference [20], this method has not been studied in figure 8. Calculations of the number and the cluster centers and using mutation in particles are the main reasons for the dramatic drop off in the number of proposed method rules.

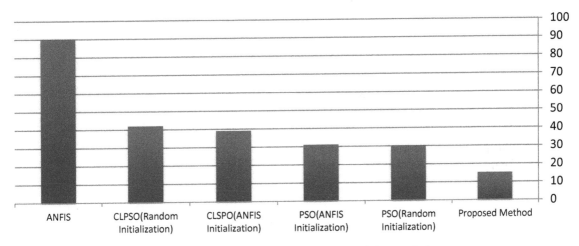

Figure 8. The number of fuzzy rules of the existing methods.

7. Conclusion

In this paper, a comprehensive learning particle swarm optimization (CLPSO) technique with some modifications was proposed to find optimal fuzzy rules and membership functions. Each particle of the swarm codes a set of fuzzy rules. During evolution, a population member tries to maximize a fitness criterion which is here high classification rate and small number of rules. The simulation results show that the selected fuzzy classification system not only has an appropriate number of rules for the considered classification problem but also has a low number of incorrectly classified patterns.

References

[1] Sowmya, B. & Sheela Rani, B. (2011). Colour image segmentation using fuzzy clustering techniques and competitive neural network. Applied Soft Computing, vol. 11, no. 3, pp. 3170-3178.

[2] Reyes, N. H. & Dadios, E. P. (2004). Dynamic Color Object Recognition Using Fuzzy Logic. JACIII, vol. 8, no. 1, pp. 29-38.

[3] Gould, S., Gao, T. & Koller, D. (2009). Region-based segmentation and object detection. Advances in neural information processing systems 22, 2009.

[4] Gupta, A., Ganguly, A. & Bhateja, V. (2013). A Novel Color Edge Detection Technique Using Hilbert Transform. Proceedings of the International Conference on Frontiers of Intelligent Computing: Theory and Applications (FICTA). Springer Berlin Heidelberg, pp. 725-732.

[5] Othmani, A., et al. (2013). Hybrid segmentation of depth images using a watershed and region merging based method for tree species recognition. IVMSP Workshop, 2013 IEEE 11th, pp. 1-4.

[6] Wang, X. Y., Zhang, X. J., Yang, H. Y. & Bu, J. (2012). A pixel-based color image segmentation using support vector machine and fuzzy C-means. Neural Networks, vol. 33, pp. 148-159.

[7] Ji, Z., Xia, Y., Chen, Q., Sun, Q., Xia, D. & Feng, D. D. (2012). Fuzzy c-means clustering with weighted image patch for image segmentation. Applied Soft Computing, vol. 12, no. 6, pp. 1659-1667.

[8] Reyes, N. H. & Messom, C. (2005). Identifying colour objects with fuzzy colour contrast fusion. In 3rd International conference on computational intelligence, robotics and autonomous systems, and FIRA roboworld congress.

[9] Casillas, J., Cordón, O., Del Jesus, M. J. & Herrera, F. (2001). Genetic feature selection in a fuzzy rule-based classification system learning process for high-dimensional problems. Information Sciences, vol. 136, no. 1, pp. 135-157.

[10] Yuan, Y. & Zhuang, H. (1996). A genetic algorithm for generating fuzzy classification rules. Fuzzy sets and systems, vol. 84, no. 1, pp. 1-19.

[11] Borji, A., Hamidi, M. & Moghadam, A. M. E. (2007). CLPSO-based fuzzy color image segmentation. In Proceedings of North American Fuzzy Information Processing Society, pp. 508-513.

[12] Puranik, P., Bajaj, P., Abraham, A., Palsodkar, P. & Deshmukh, A. (2009, December). Human perception-based color image segmentation using comprehensive learning particle swarm optimization. 2nd International Conference on Emerging Trends in Engineering and Technology, pp. 630-635.

[13] Murugesan, K. M. & Palaniswami, S. (2010). Efficient colour image segmentation using exponential particle swarm optimization. In Proceedings of the 12th international conference on Networking, VLSI and signal processing. World Scientific and Engineering Academy and Society (WSEAS), pp. 240-244.

[14] Hu, M., Wu, T. & Weir, J. D. (2012). An intelligent augmentation of particle swarm optimization with multiple adaptive methods. Information Sciences., vol. 213, pp. 68-83.

[15] Shamir, L. (2006, June). Human Perception-based Color Segmentation Using Fuzzy Logic. In IPCV, pp. 496-502.

[16] Maitra, M. & Chatterjee, A. (2008). A hybrid cooperative–comprehensive learning based PSO algorithm for image segmentation using multilevel thresholding. Expert Systems with Applications, vol. 34, no. 2, pp. 1341-1350.

[17] Mishra, S., Satapathy, S. K. & Mishra, D. (2012). CLPSO-Fuzzy Frequent Pattern Mining from Gene Expression Data. Procedia Technology, vol. 4, pp. 807-811.

[18] Yu, Z., Au, O. C., Zou, R., Yu, W. & Tian, J. (2010). An adaptive unsupervised approach toward pixel clustering and color image segmentation. Pattern Recognition, vol. 43, no. 5, pp. 1889-1906.

[19] Wang, X. Y., Wang, Q. Y., Yang, H. Y. & Bu, J. (2011). Color image segmentation using automatic pixel classification with support vector machine. Neurocomputing, vol. 74, no. 18, pp. 3898-3911.

[20] Ishibuchi, H., Nozaki, K., Yamamoto, N. & Tanaka, H. (1995). Selecting fuzzy if-then rules for classification problems using genetic algorithms. IEEE Transactions on Fuzzy Systems, vol. 3, no. 3, pp. 260-270.

[21] Hamidi, M. & Borji, A. (2007). Color image segmentation with CLPSO-based fuzzy. International Journal of Computer Science and Network Security (IJCSNS), vol. 7, no. 6, pp. 215-221.

[22] Budden, D. & Mendes, A. (2014). Unsupervised recognition of salient colour for real-time image processing. RoboCup 2013: Robot Soccer World Cup XVII, vol. 8371, pp. 373-384.

[23] Tan, K. S., Mat Isa, N. A. & Lim, W. H. (2013). Color image segmentation using adaptive unsupervised clustering approach. Applied Soft Computing, vol. 13, no. 4, pp. 2017-2036.

[24] Kashanipour, A., Milani, N. S., Kashanipour, A. R. & Eghrary, H. H. (2008, May). Robust color classification using fuzzy rule-based particle swarm optimization. In Image and Signal Processing, CISP'08, vol. 2, pp. 110-114.

4

FDMG: Fault detection method by using genetic algorithm in clustered wireless sensor networks

A. Ghaffari[*] and S. Nobahary

Department of Computer Engineering, Tabriz branch, Islamic Azad University, Tabriz, Iran.

Corresponding author: a.ghaffari@iaut.ac.ir (A. Ghaffari).

Abstract
Wireless sensor networks (WSNs) consist of a large number of sensor nodes which are capable of sensing different environmental phenomena and sending the collected data to the base station or Sink. Since sensor nodes are made of cheap components and are deployed in remote and uncontrolled environments, they are prone to failure. Thus, maintaining a network with its proper functions even when undesired events occur is necessary and is called fault tolerance. Hence, fault management is essential in these networks. In this paper, a new method has been proposed with particular attention to fault tolerance and fault detection in WSN. The performance of the proposed method was simulated in MATLAB. The proposed method was based on majority vote, which can permanently detect faulty sensor nodes accurately. High accuracy and low false alarm rate helped exclude them from the network. To investigate the efficiency of the new method, the researchers compared it with Chen, Lee, and hybrid algorithms. Simulation results indicated that the proposed method has better performance in parameters such as detection accuracy (DA) and a false alarm rate (FAR) even with a large set of faulty sensor nodes.

Keywords: *Wireless Sensor Networks, Fault Detection, Genetic Algorithm, Fault Diagnosis, Clustering Algorithm.*

1. Introduction

Recent advancements in Micro-Electro-Mechanical Systems (MEMS) technology and wireless communication have promoted the emergence of a new generation technology which is called WSN. It consists of tiny, inexpensive sensors with limited processing and computing resources. These sensor nodes can sense, measure, and gather information from the environment. Hence, they have been used in many applications such as environmental monitoring, object tracking, agricultural lands, office buildings, industrial plants and military systems [1-3].

It is obvious that sensor networks are prone to failure which is mainly due to the fact that many applications require deploying sensors in harsh and contaminated environments such as battlefield. Fault detection and fault tolerance in wireless sensor networks have been investigated in the literature. Moreover, deployed sensor networks may suffer from many faults because of environmental impacts such as lightning, dust and moisture which can reduce the quality of wireless communications and divert sensors from their desirable operations. Moreover, hardware defects of sensors are related to cheap sensors prices which have low quality electronic components; such sensors are used in the construction of sensors which can negatively affect desirable network operations. Also, software bugs have such negative impacts on network operations[4]. These faults can be the cause of data failure and functional failures[5]. Data faults and failures result in inappropriate response of the network manager and faulty nodes bring about inaccurate routing by directing data through intermediate faulty nodes. Accordingly, it is essential to detect and manage faults in WSNs.

As mentioned above, due to the failure of network, there should be a kind of responsibility for avoiding failure so that network fault tolerance is guaranteed. In general, the first step in enhancing fault tolerance in a system is to try to use fault avoidance techniques so as to avoid damaging factors. To achieve this objective, one should use high-technology electronic devices, advanced equipment for designing, constructing and strict compliance of the design roles and testing stages. It should be noted that the first two cases, in particular, will increase the cost of production and is not operational for such networks. On the other hand, the two other cases only ensure reliability of performance accuracy for each sensor node in the construction stage and there is no guarantee for network operation against environmental factors. Consequently, fault avoidance techniques should be used in a network as well as other mechanisms so that network can continue to function properly. These mechanisms are referred to as fault tolerance techniques. The networks having the above-mentioned capability are known as fault-tolerant networks. In general, four types of redundancies, namely, hardware, software, information and time redundancy are used in the development of fault tolerant systems [6]. Using the first two redundancy types significantly increases the cost of production; hence, they are not appropriate for WSNs. In contrast, the other two redundancy types are used in some protocols which are proposed for these networks.

There are several sophisticated techniques and methods for detecting faults in WSNs. For instance, one highly powerful method, i.e. the majority vote method, is appropriate for detecting faults. This method makes use of genetic algorithms (GAs). GA is aimed at using natural evolution and a fitness value for each possible solution to the problem. The best GA choice and candidate is a representation of candidate solutions to the problem in (genotype).The initial population randomly produces a fitness function. It measures and compares each solution in the population; genetic algorithm operates the crossover and mutation functions to produce new Generation. Finally, the algorithm tunes parameters such as population size either finds the best data or finishes the time of execution, etc. Successful application of GAs in sensor network designs [7] has resulted in the development of several other GA-based application-specific approaches in WSN design mostly by the structure of a single fitness function [5,8,9]. Also, it has led to meditation optimality in the evaluation of fitness values[7].However, in the majority of these methods, very limited network characteristics are considered; hence, several requirements of application cases are not taken

into consideration in the performance measure of the algorithm.

However, in this paper, the researchers proposed a new method to solve the problem of majority vote. Moreover, it should be noted that by using GA, the proposed method can detect faulty sensors with high detection accuracy and low false alarm rate. In the proposed method, GA was used in sinking to select the best data and to define the status of each sensor node.

The rest of the paper is organized as follows: Section (2) provides a brief overview of fault detection methods in WSNs and related works; then in section 3, the proposed method was explained and network models are discussed in detail. The results of the simulation are mentioned and evaluated in section 4. Ultimately, section 5 sums up the findings, concludes the study and suggests directions for future works.

2. Related works

In this section, common and related algorithms and methods to fault detection literature are reviewed [10-14]. These methods use majority vote but they can't detect common failure nodes.

Chen et al.[15]have proposed a new distributed fault detection algorithm for wireless sensor networks. In this algorithm, data of sensors were compared twice to achieve a final decision on the status of sensors; moreover, four steps have to be taken and the improved majority voting was used. Two predetermined threshold values, marked up by θ_1 and θ_2, were used. Each sensor node compared its own sensed data with the data of neighbor nodes in the time stamp t; if the difference between them was greater than θ_1, the comparison would be repeated in the time stamp $t+1$; in case the difference was greater than θ_2, too, it was interpreted that data of this node was not similar to data of the neighbor nodes. In the next step, each sensor defined its own status as likely good (LG) if its own sensed data was similar to at least half of the neighbors' data. Otherwise, the sensor status would be defined as likely faulty (LF). In the next step, each sensor can determine its own final status according to the assumption that the sensor status is GOOD (GD) if it determined its status as LG in the previous step and more than half of the neighbors are LG. Then, sensors whose statuses are GD broadcast their status to their neighbors. A sensor node with an undetermined status can determine its status using the status of its neighbors. If a sensor node whose status is defined as LG and receives GD status from its neighbor node whose own sensed data is similar to the data of the sender of this message;

hence, it changes its status to *GD*. If a sensor whose status is defined as *LF* and receives faulty status from its neighbor whose own sensed data is similar to the data of the sender of this message, then it will change its status to faulty. The complexity of this algorithm is low and the probability of fault detection accuracy is very high. This algorithm only detects permanent faults while transient faults are ignored although these types of faults may occur in most of the sensor nodes.

Lee et al. [16] proposed a distributed fault detection algorithm for wireless sensor networks which is simple and highly accurate in detecting faulty nodes. This approach used time redundancy for increasing the tolerance of transient faults. In this method, two predetermined threshold values marked up by θ_1 and q were used. Every node compared its own sensed data with data from its neighbor nodes q times in order to determine whether its data are similar to the data of neighbors or not. In the next step, the sensor status would be defined as fault-free if its sensed data is similar to at least θ_1 of the data of neighbor nodes. Each sensor whose status is determined will broadcast its status to undetermined sensors so that they define their status. Simulation results in that study indicated that fault detection accuracy of this algorithm would decrease rapidly when the number of neighbor nodes was low but fault detection accuracy would increase when the number of neighbor nodes was high. The disadvantage of this algorithm is that it is not able to detect common mode failures.

As mentioned above, most fault detection algorithms [6, 16-20] in WSNs compare their own sensed data with the data of neighbor nodes. If their data is similar to at least half of the data sensed by neighbors, the cited sensor will be considered as fault-free. Comparison-based fault detection methods suffer from several deficiencies. They are unable to detect faulty nodes in remote areas where sensors do not have any availability to data of neighbors' nodes in their transceiver boards. The poor performance of algorithms in detecting common mode failures is another problem for these techniques.

With respect to the research gap highlighted above, in this paper, the researchers proposed a distributed method which is able to detect faulty nodes. To increase load balancing and lifetime of WSNs, different clustering algorithms are used. NHEEP[3](anew hybrid energy efficient partitioning approach for WSN clustering) is a clustering approach based on a partitioning technique in which the number of partitions are

determined by the sink. After partitioning, each node can determine which partition is present. For electing a CH (cluster head) inside a partition, different parameters are considered such as position, distance of the nodes and the residual energy of nodes. NHEEP takes two important parameters into account for selecting cluster head node as follows:

Energy: Due to the lack of energy sources needed for regulating the lifetime of WSNs, energy is one of the most important parameters in research on WSNs. The residual energy is very important for the cluster head. Cluster head is negatively affected by high energy consumption of cluster members. Inasmuch as cluster head is responsible not only for gathering data from cluster members but also for processing data aggregation and data transmission to the sink; hence, its energy runs out very quickly. A qualified node for the cluster head is selected to ensure uninterrupted accomplishment of tasks. This node has more residual energy compared with others nodes.

Centrality: Sometimes the density of a node is high but the nodes which are around that node are only in one side of the mentioned node. When the nodes are in the central part of the area, they play an important role in network structure because the central nodes have an important role in transmitting data to the next step. Thus, it is preferable to have cluster heads in central neighborhood to maintain load balance.

In this algorithm, firstly, nodes identify their own clusters and then they try to select the best node in terms of high centrality and high remaining energy in each cluster as cluster head. In this algorithm, the cluster head collects the data of the cluster and sends it to the other cluster heads to send to the sink through multi-hop approach.

In the next section, the proposed fault detection algorithm is described. In this method, the network is clustered by using NHEEP [3] algorithm.

Then, in the stability phase, before the transmitting data to the cluster head, faulty sensors will be detected according to the fault detection algorithm. This fault detection phase is repeated in proportion to the existing noise in the operational area. In the time slot, fault detection process takes place, and data sensing and transmission will stop. After the mentioned time slot, the network continues its operation again.

3. Proposed method
In this section, fault model, variables and assumptions used in the proposed method are described.

Fault model:
In detecting WSN faults, nodes with faulty state and permanent communication faults are spotted. Since selfish sensor nodes with malfunctioning behavior are still capable of routing information, they could participate in the network operation. However, the sensor nodes with a permanent communication fault (including lack of power) are eliminated from the network [23-24].

Definitions:
The notations used in proposed fault detection algorithm are listed as follows:
- n: total number of sensor nodes distributed throughout the environment;
- M: number of clusters in the network;
- $L=[N/M]$: length of chromosomes;
- x_i: data of i-nodes;
- $|x_i - x_j|$: fitness function;

- θ_1: predetermined threshold value;
- R_r: the best selected gen among all gens

The proposed fault detection algorithm includes three phases: (a) setup and clustering process, (b) fault detection phase, and (c) Data transmission and updating phase. The above-mentioned three phases are described below.

3.1. Set up and clustering processes
In this phase, the deployed sensor nodes identify their neighbor nodes, create neighbor table and create clustering process. For creating the neighbor table, each sensor node sends a hello message at the beginning to identify its neighbors. Hello message includes the identification number of sensor nodes, node coordination and residual energy level of nodes. Figure 1 shows the structure of the hello packets as follows:

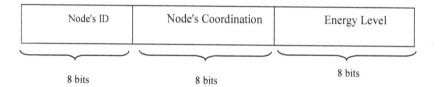

Figure 1. Structure of HELLO message.

The neighbor nodes receiving the hello message respond to the sender node by sending echo message. This echo message includes the node's ID (Identifications), its distance to sink, and

energy level (residual energy) of neighbor nodes. Figure 2 represents the format and number of bits of response package message (echo packet) as follows:

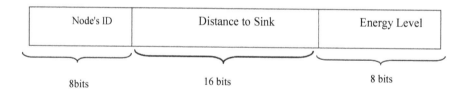

Figure 2. Structure of response (echo) message.

All nodes receive the parameters of their neighbor nodes and store them in the neighborhood table. At this stage, nodes automatically try to select a cluster and their cluster heads. Clustering operation in the proposed method was carried out with the partitioning algorithm which was described in the previous section. For selecting cluster heads, the proposed scheme took the following parameters into account: centrality and residual energy. After choosing cluster heads, cluster member nodes introduce themselves to the cluster head and practically justify their membership in the cluster. In the next step, the cluster members gather the information from the occurred events and send the data packets to the

sink node after data aggregation processing. Figure 3 depicts clustered WSN model with faulty sensor nodes, faulty cluster head, fault-free sensor nodes and fault-free cluster head nodes.

3.2. Fault detection phase
During the normal operation of network, nodes send their data to the cluster head. However, in the fault diagnosis and fault detection phase, each member node of the cluster sends data to nodes of each cluster head. Thus, cluster heads will select the best data of the clusters by applying genetic algorithm and sending them to the sink. Also, sink applies GA whose properties are determined in the following section. The best data is selected between cluster head data previously sent to sink

and the status of each cluster head is determined   by the sink.

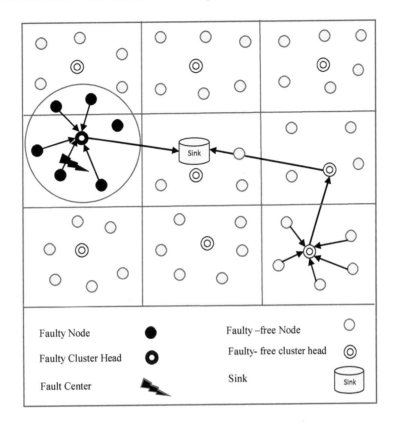

Figure 3. Wireless sensor network with fault-free and faulty nodes and cluster head.

The selected data of sink is broadcast as a message to all the cluster heads. Fault-free cluster heads can determine the status of the cluster nodes but faulty cluster heads should be changed and given to a healthy cluster head. Figure 4 depicts the structure and number of bits of a broadcast message. Cluster head with a faulty plate is

detected by broadcasting messages to all members of the cluster to choose their cluster head node again. It is obvious that the choice of a new cluster head node is healthy. If 30% or less nodes on the cluster nodes as well-known nodes are allowed to join, the cluster nearby nodes is proportional to their distance.

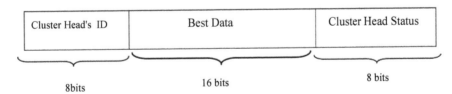

Figure 4. Structure of broadcast message.

Cluster head with a faulty plate is detected by broadcasting messages to all members of the cluster to choose their cluster head node again. It is obvious that the choice of a new cluster head node is healthy. If 30% or less nodes on the cluster nodes as well-known nodes are allowed to join, the cluster nearby nodes is proportional to their distance.

Before determining θ_1 parameter of member nodes, a definite threshold fitting data network is determined. If the dispute is declared as the best

dispute in a particular node, it is greater than θ_1. Nodes will be regarded as faulty nodes; otherwise, the node is known to be healthy. The proposed method reveals that the decision about nodes' status and cluster heads are determined in the sink. Indeed, the method introduced in this paper is a combined approach for selecting the best data based on genetic algorithms.

In the first generation, a chromosome whose genes are real numbers and whose chromosome length is equal to the number of nodes in each cluster. Number of nodes in each cluster is denoted by the symbol L. Values of each gene is equal to the amounts of data sensed by each node. In the proposed algorithm, the number of generations is one thing and the fitness function is used between each gene and other genes of chromosome according to (1). Hence, the last gene will continue using the same gene L and each of the obtained data is gathered and placed in the W and generalizes the corresponding gene in an array according to (2).

Finally, the fitness of a gene (least amount of conflict with other genes) is the most as the genes in the chromosome (R_r) is selected.

$$F = |x_i - x_j| \qquad (1)$$
$$W_1 = |x_1 - x_1| + |x_1 - x_2| + \ldots + |x_1 - x_{L-1}| + |x_1 - x_L|$$
$$W_2 = |x_2 - x_1| + |x_2 - x_2| + \ldots + |x_2 - x_{L-1}| + |x_2 - x_L|$$

$$\vdots$$

$$W_L = |x_L - x_1| + |x_L - x_2| + \ldots + |x_L - x_{L-1}| + |x_L - x_L| \qquad (2)$$

Figure 5 shows the chromosome of the best gene.

W_1	W_2	...	W_L

Figure 5. The chromosome of the best gene.

For ensuring the accuracy of selecting correct data in each cluster, the algorithm repeats it 10 times to set chromosomes $R_0, R_1, \ldots, R_9$.

Then, the highest fitness chromosome is selected. Repeating the fitness function diminishes the probability of transient fault occurrence in the network.

3.3. Data transmission and updating phase

Data transmission phase corresponds to network application based on event occurrence; alternatively, the sensed data collected to the cluster head node and it forwards the aggregated data to the sink.

Since faulty node detection consumes considerable energy, it is not used in all the stages of data collection. In each cluster, sensor nodes send data to the cluster head.

Cluster node controls, aggregates and sends data to the sink.

In the proposed algorithm, new cluster head will be selected if cluster head node is faulty or its battery is low. In this case, cluster members select a new cluster head. Figure 6 illustrates the pseudo code of the first and third stages.

Algorithm phase 1(layer 1)
1:    Step 1: Each node S_i sets its status to H, send hello message to each node, and each node is neighbor sends reply message.
2:      Establish clusters and definite cluster head.
3:      Step 2: Fault detection done for first time (and in each R_r round)
4:      Each node S_i sends its data to CH_i (for example $r=10$)
5:        for $k=1$ to rs_i sends data to CH_i
6:         for $j=1$ to L do
7:          $W_k = |s_i^k - s_j^k|$
8:          Best(i)=Min(W_i)
9:      Send Best(i) for each cluster to sink
10: for $j=1$ to i do
11:    $W_i = |Best_i - Best_j|$
12:    Total Best=Min(W)
13: Each CH_i determines its status
14:      if $|X_{CH_i} - TotalBest| \leq \theta_1$ then $T_{CHi} = H$
15:        else $T_{CHi} = F$
16:      if $T_{CHi} = F$ then   elect another CH_i
17: Each S_i determines its status
18:      if $|X_{S_i} - TotalBest| \leq \theta_1$ then $T_{Si} = H$
19:        else $T_{Si} = F$
20: Step 3: Send data to sink and update network status

Figure 6. Pseudo code of the first to third stages.

4. Simulation results
4.1. Network model

The proposed method was simulated in MATLAB software. n sensors were randomly deployed in $A*A(\mathrm{m}^2)$ square area which was aimed at collecting data during each round. It was assumed that the sink was in the middle of the area with the coordinate of ($A/2$, $A/2$). The simulation was repeated in 1000 cycles and the simulation parameters were indicated in Table 1. The following two metrics, detection accuracy (DA) and false alarm rate (FAR) are used to evaluate the performance, where DA is defined as the ratio of the number of faulty sensor nodes detected to the total number of faulty nodes and FAR is the ratio of the number of fault-free sensor nodes diagnosed as faulty to the total number of fault-free nodes [23]. In this simulation and performance evaluation, nodes with some transient faults are treated as fault-free nodes [23]. A simple model for radio hardware energy dissipation was used where the transmitter dissipates energy to run radio electronics, and power amplifier and the receiver dissipates energy to run the radio electronics.

Based on the model, the network had the following features:

- All nodes were uniformly distributed within a square area.
- Each node has a unique *ID*.
- Each node has a fixed location.

- All nodes can perform data aggregation.
- Transmission energy consumption was proportional to the distance of the nodes.

Both free space and multi-path fading channel models were used for the experiments of this study based on the distance between the transmitter and receiver. Thus, energy consumption for transmitting a packet was calculated for l bits over distance d by (3) as follows [21]:

$$E_{tx}(l,d) = E_{tx-elec}(l) + E_{tx-amp}(l)$$

$$= \begin{cases} E_{tx}(l,d) = l.E_{elec} + l.\varepsilon_{fs}d^2 & d < d_0 \\ l.E_{elec} + l.\varepsilon_{amp}.d^4 & d > d_0d_0 \end{cases} \quad (3)$$

According to the above-mentioned energy consumption model, if the distance between sensor node and base station (BS) is less than a threshold d_0, as calculated by (4), the free space (f_s) model will be used; otherwise, the multi-path (mp) model will be used [21]. The d_0 parameter can be calculated as follows [21]:

$$d_0 = \sqrt{\frac{\varepsilon_{fs}}{\varepsilon_{amp}}} \quad (4)$$

Table 1 shows the values of ε_{fs} and ε_{amp}. Energy consumption for receiving a packet of l bits is calculated according to (5) [21] as follows:

$$E_{RX}(l) = E_{RX-elec}(l) = l.E_{elec} \quad (5)$$

The probability of faulty sensor nodes was assumed to be 0.10, 0.2, 0.3, 0.4 and 0.5. The number of included nodes was assumed to be 100 and 150, respectively.

Table 1. Simulation parameters.

Parameter	Value
Number of sensors	100, 150
Area	400×400 (m²)
Sink position	(200, 200)
d_0	87 m
Radio range	70 m
E_{elec}	50nj/bit
ε_{fs} (if destination to BS<=d_0)	10pj/bit/m²
ε_{amp} (if destination to BS >=d_0)	0.0013 pj/bit/m⁴
Initial energy	1j
E_{da} (Data aggregation energy)	10 nj/bit/packet
Packet size	4000 bits
Simulation repeate	1000 cycles

4.2. Simulation results and performance evaluation

The efficiency of the proposed method was evaluated and compared with Lee [16] and Chen [15] algorithms in terms of detection accuracy and false alarm rate parameters. Whereas DA was defined as the ratio of the number of detected faulty nodes to the total number of faulty nodes, FAR was defined as the ratio of the number of fault-free nodes that are detected as faulty node to the total number of fault-free nodes [22]. Table 2 compares the fault detection accuracy in the proposed scheme, Chen [15], Lee [16] and Hybrid [6] algorithms.

Table 2. Fault detection accuracy in the proposed method, Chen [15], Lee [16] and hybrid [6] algorithms.

				Algorithms				
Chen [15]	Lee [16]	Hybrid [6]	Proposed	Chen [15]	Lee [16]	Hybrid [6]	Proposed	P
0.984	0.986	0.988	1	0.984	0.986	0.988	1	0.1
0.982	0.984	0.985	1	0.982	0.984	0.985	1	0.2
0.96	0.97	0.977	1	0.96	0.97	0.977	1	0.3
0.97	0.50	0.6	1	0.95	0.5	0.6	1	0.4
0	0	0	0.42	0	0	0.1	0.34	0.5
		n=150				*n*=100		

Figures 7 and 8 show the comparison of the proposed algorithm with the algorithms of Chen [15], Lee [16], and hybrid [6] respectively, in terms of detection accuracy and false alarm rate with 100 nodes in network.

When the probability of sensor failure was 0.1, the detection accuracies of Chen [15], Lee [16], and hybrid [6] algorithms were 0.986, 0.984, 0.988 and 0.986 respectively. However, the detection accuracy of the proposed algorithm was equal to

1.When the probability of the sensor failure was 0.25, the detection accuracies of Chen [15], Lee [16], and hybrid [6] algorithms were 0.975, 0.97, and 0.977, respectively. However, it should be noted that the detection accuracy of the proposed algorithm was equal to 0.981. When the probability of sensor failure was 0.25, the false alarm rate in Lee [16] and Chen [15] algorithms

was 0.0018 and 0.0021, respectively. In contrast, the false alarm rate of the proposed algorithm was equal to 0.0013.

Figures 9 and 10 compare the proposed algorithm with that of Chen [15] and Lee [16] in terms of detection accuracy and false alarm rate when there were 150 nodes in the network.

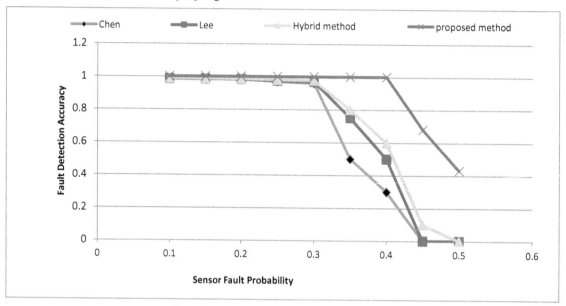

Figure 7. Fault detection accuracy when $N=100$.

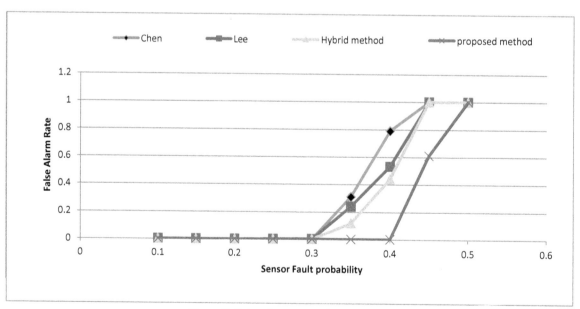

Figure 8. False alarm rate when $N=100$.

When the probability of sensor failure was 0.1, the detection accuracy in both Lee [16] and Chen [15] algorithms was 0.999. However, the detection accuracy of the proposed algorithm was equal to 1.

When the probability of the sensor failure was 0.25, the detection accuracy of Lee [16], Chen [15], and hybrid [6] algorithms were 0.993, 0.991,

0.991 and 0.994, respectively. Nevertheless, the detection accuracy of the proposed algorithm was equal to 0.994.

Similarly, when the probability of sensor failure was 0.15, then, the false alarm rate of Chen [15] algorithm was 0.0001. In contrast, the false alarm rate of Lee [16], hybrid [6] and the proposed algorithm was equal to zero.

When the probability of sensor failure was 0.25, the false alarm rate of Lee [16], Chen [15], and hybrid [6] algorithms were 0.0012, 0.0014, 0.0007and 0.0004, respectively but that of the proposed algorithm was equal to 0.0006. In other words, as the probability of sensor failure increases, the false alarm rate of the proposed algorithm was less than those of Lee [16] and Chen [15] algorithms. Based on figures 7 and 8,

the researchers can draw the conclusion that the detection accuracy increases as the number of neighbors' increases but false alarm rate decreases. Furthermore, as the probability of sensor failure increases, detection accuracy of the proposed algorithm will be higher than those of Lee [16] and Chen [15] algorithms.

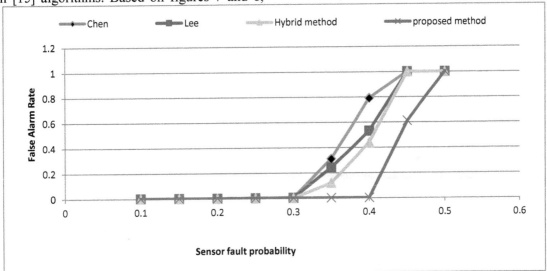

Figure 9. Fault alarm rate when N=150.

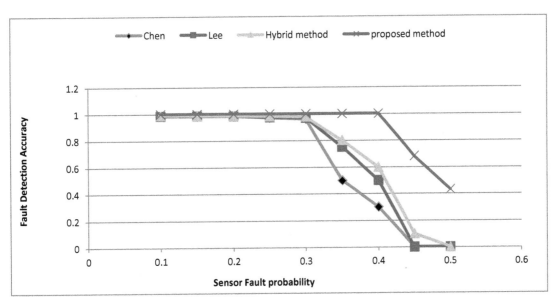

Figure 10. Fault detection accuracy when N=150.

5. Conclusion and directions for further research

Inasmuch as the failure rate of WSNs is remarkable, fault tolerance should be regarded as a significant attribute in these networks; this feature can be utilized to detect faulty nodes and emit them from the network. This paper presents a distributed fault detection algorithm for wireless

sensor networks. In this paper, based on GAs, researchers proposed a new method for detecting faulty node. The proposed method was also intended to detect permanent faults in sensor nodes with an extremely high detection accuracy and low fault alarm rate in the network. The proposed algorithm is simple and detects faults in WSN with high accuracy. Faulty sensor nodes are identified based on comparisons between neighboring nodes and dissemination of the decision made at each node and each cluster. Simulation results revealed that the proposed method demonstrates better performance across parameters such as *DA* and *FAR* even when the number of faulty sensor nodes is high.

A direction for further research can use a combination of the method proposed in this paper with a learning automata technique for fault detection and network fault tolerance enhancement.

References

[1] Ian, F. A., Weilian, S., Sankarasubramaniam, Y. & Cayirci, E. (2002). Wireless sensor networks: a survey. Computer networks, vol. 38, pp. 393-422.

[2] Yick, J., Mukherjee, B. & Ghosal, D. (2008). Wireless sensor network survey. Computer networks, vol. 52, pp. 2292-2330, 2008.

[3] Babaei, S., B., Zekrizadeh N. & Nobahari, S. (2012). NHEEP: A New Hybrid Energy Efficient Partitioning Approach for Wireless Sensor Network Clustering. International Journal of Information and Electronics Engineering, vol. 2, pp. 323-327.

[4] Chenglin, Z., Xuebin, S., Songlin, S. & Ting, J. (2011). Fault diagnosis of sensor by chaos particle swarm optimization algorithm and support vector machine. Expert Systems with Applications, vol. 38, pp. 9908-9912.

[5] Warriach, E., Nguyen, T., Aiello, M. & Tei, K. (2012). Fault detection in wireless sensor networks: a hybrid approach. ACM/IEEE 11th International Conference onInformation Processing in Sensor Networks (IPSN), pp. 87-88.

[6] Warriach, E., Nguyen, T., Aiello, M. & Tei, K. (2012). A hybrid fault detection approach for context-aware wireless sensor networks. 2012 IEEE 9th International Conference onMobile Adhoc and Sensor Systems (MASS), pp. 281-289.

[7] Jourdan, D. & Weck, O. (2004). Layout optimization for a wireless sensor network using a multi-objective genetic algorithm. 2004-Spring. 2004 IEEE 59th Vehicular technology conference (VTC), pp. 2466-2470.

[8] Aldosari S., & Moura, J. (2004). Fusion in sensor networks with communication constraints. In Proceedings of the 3rd international symposium on Information processing in sensor networks, pp. 108-115, 2004.

[9] Mitchell, R. & Chen, R. (2014). survey of intrusion detection in wireless network applications. Computer Communications, vol. 42, pp. 1-23, 2014.

[10] Bari, A., Jaekel, A., Jiang, J. & Xu, Y. (2012). Design of fault tolerant wireless sensor networks satisfying survivability and lifetime requirements. Computer Communications, vol. 35, pp. 320-333.

[11] Ding, M., Chen, D., Xing, K. & Cheng, X. (2005). Localized fault-tolerant event boundary detection in sensor networks. 24th Annual Joint Conference of the IEEE Computer and Communications Societies. Proceedings IEEE in INFOCOM, 2005, pp. 902-913, 2005.

[12] Geeta, D., Nalini, N. & Biradar, R. C. (2013). Fault tolerance in wireless sensor network using hand-off and dynamic power adjustment approach. Journal of Network and Computer Applications, vol. 36, pp. 1174-1185.

[13] Jiang, P. (2009). A new method for node fault detection in wireless sensor networks. Sensors, vol. 9, pp. 1282-1294.

[14] Kaushik, B., Kaur, N. & Kohli, A. K. (2013). Achieving maximum reliability in fault tolerant network design for variable networks. Applied Soft Computing, vol. 13, pp. 3211-3224.

[15] Chen, J., Kher, S. & Somani, A. (2006). Distributed fault detection of wireless sensor networks. in Proceedings of the 2006 workshop on dependability issues in wireless ad hoc networks and sensor networks, pp. 65-72.

[16] Lee, S., Choe, H., Park, B., Song, Y. & Kim, C. (2011). LUCA: An energy-efficient unequal clustering algorithm using location information for wireless sensor networks. Wireless Personal Communications, vol. 56, pp. 715-731.

[17] Banerjee, I., Chanak, P., Rahaman, H. & Samanta, T. (2014). Effective fault detection and routing scheme for wireless sensor networks. Computers & Electrical Engineering, vol. 40, pp. 291-306.

[18] Cho, K., Jo, M., Kwon, T., Chen, H. & Lee, D. (2013). Classification and experimental analysis for clone detection approaches in wireless sensor networks. IEEE journal of Systems, vol. 7, pp. 26-35.

[19] Mahapatro, A. & Khilar, P. (2013). Fault diagnosis in wireless sensor networks: A survey. IEEECommunications Surveys & Tutorials, vol. 15, pp. 2000-2026.

[20] Xie, M. Hu, J., Han, S. & Chen, H. (2013). Scalable hypergrid k-NN-Based online anomaly detection in wireless sensor networks. IEEE Transactions onParallel and Distributed Systems, vol. 24, pp. 1661-1670.

[21] Heinzelman, W. B., Chandrakasan, A. P. & Balakrishnan, H. (2002). An application-specific protocol architecture for wireless microsensor networks. IEEE Transactions on Wireless Communications, vol. 1, pp. 660-670.

[22] Guo, S., Zhong, Z. & He, T. (2009). Find: faulty node detection for wireless sensor networks. In Proceedings of the 7th ACM conference on embedded networked sensor systems, pp. 253-266.

[23] Lee, M. & Choi, Y. (2008). Fault detection of wireless sensor networks. Computer Communication, vol. 31, no. 14, pp. 3469–3475.

[24] Ghaffari, A. (2015). Congestion control mechanisms in wireless sensor networks. Journal of network and computer applications, vol.52 , pp. 101-115.

5

Predicting air pollution in Tehran: Genetic algorithm and back propagation neural network

M. Asghari Esfandani and H. Nematzadeh*

Department of Computer Engineering, Sari Branch, Islamic Azad University, Sari, Iran.

Corresponding author: nematzadeh@iausari.ac.ir (H. Nematzadeh).

Abstract

Suspended particles have deleterious effects on human health and one of the reasons why Tehran is effected is its geographically location of air pollution. One of the most important ways to reduce air pollution is to predict the concentration of pollutants. This paper proposed a hybrid method to predict the air pollution in Tehran based on particulate matter less than 10 microns (PM_{10}), and the information and data of Aghdasiyeh Weather Quality Control Station and Mehrabad Weather Station from 2007 to 2013. Generally, 11 inputs have been inserted to the model, to predict the daily concentration of PM_{10}. For this purpose, Artificial Neural Network with Back Propagation (BP) with a middle layer and sigmoid activation function and its hybrid with Genetic Algorithm (BP-GA) were used and ultimately the performance of the proposed method was compared with basic Artificial Neural Networks along with (BP) Based on the criteria of - R^2-, RMSE and MAE. The finding shows that BP-GA $R^2 = 0.54889$ has higher accuracy and performance. In addition, it was also found that the results are more accurate for shorter time periods and this is because the large fluctuation of data in long-term returns negative effect on network performance. Also, unregistered data have negative effect on predictions. Microsoft Excel and Matlab 2013 conducted the simulations.

Keywords: *Artificial Neural Networks, Genetic Algorithm, Air Pollution, PM_{10}.*

1. Introduction

Air pollution IS one of the biggest environmental problems in Tehran. Several factors are involved in Tehran pollution and their geographical factors are more important. Daily large amounts of toxic gases, Types of pollutants, Suspended hazardous materials vehicles, Factories, industrial sites, power plants and refineries, and numerous residential units are added to the air of the city [12]. Air pollution is a serious risk to the environment and causes serious respiratory and skin diseases, especially for the elderly and children. The environmental and health problems caused by air pollution in large cities have become a major challenge.[10] Air pollution is one of the world's problems with the development of industrialization and with increasing the number of cities, the amount and intensity day by day. [6] Tehran's main air pollutants include: CO, SO2, HC, O3, NOX and PM that 80% of car fuel and the remainder are created by factories and homes heating equipment. Particulate matter affects on

human health, such as the impact of the lungs, respiratory system, asthma and deaths. It was reported that the detrimental effects of particulate matter on human health, is mostly due to being exposed to concentrations of particles. One of the most effective actions to control and reduce air pollution is to estimate the pollutants density and to describe the state of air quality in comparison with the standard conditions [7]. This paper tries to estimate and predict the air pollution of Tehran with two approaches. First, basic ANN was used with randomly generated weights. Second, GA was applied to generate the initial weights of ANN. The results finally showed that the hybrid method of GA and ANN have better performance. The structure of the paper is as follows: Section two introduces algorithms and techniques in the literature related to the study. Section 3 describes the main methodology of the research. Section 4 discusses the research model and its estimation method and research databases and also the results are presented. Finally, section 5 provides conclusions and future works.

2. Literature review

Neural networks or more specifically artificial neural networks rooted in many fields of science. Neurology, Mathematics, statistics, physics, computer science and engineering are examples of mentioned sciences [5,6,7]. Most recently Multi Layer Perceptron (MLP) has been widely used to predict pollutants so that in most large cities around the world for MLP has been used to predict air pollutant. The results of these methods that have been applied for different pollutants are good. The results of several studies that have been done in this context also show that the performance of neural networks is better in comparison with traditional statistical methods such as multivariate regression and auto regression models [1]. Taisa and Barrozo (2007) developed a method to predict Uberlandia Brazil air pollutions using neural networks [1]. The research direction in the field tends develop tools for modeling the distribution of air pollution in near future. Gryvas and Chaloulakou (2006) tried to predict PM10 hourly concentration using neural networks in four major stations in Athens [3]. Cecchetti et al (2004) have done the same research in Milan Italy using Artificial Neural Network [4] Bruelli et al (2007) proposed a two-day ahead prediction with concentration on five particles in Palermo Italy [2]. In Belgium country Data between 1997 and 2000 have used to predict the average concentration of particulate matter for the next day and there were some efforts to predict the air pollution index in Shanghai and Santiago using neural network as well. Nejadkoorki and Baroutian (2012) presented a model based on neural network which was able to predict daily average concentration of PM_{10} in a densely populated area of Tehran [8]. The method had a warning system in order to reduce their unnecessary trips in polluted areas in Tehran. Davar et al (2013), proposed an Artificial Neural Network Model to predict the annual PM_{10} greenhouse gas emissions. In that research artificial neural networks, were trained by using following variables: Gross domestic product, Gross domestic energy consumption, Burning wood, the motorized, manufacture of paper and paperboard, production of sawn timber, production of copper, production of aluminum, production of pig iron and crude steel production. The results show a very good performance of the ANN model in contrast to the Multivariate regression model. [9] Information about the three

stations Fatemi and Aghdasie and bazar is intended to predict PM_{10}. During the years 1779-1781, the neural network is used MLP. The answers are compared with the values obtained from multivariate regression model and the results represent MLP method is superior [11].

3. Proposed methods

In this section, the techniques of artificial neural network, and genetic algorithm used in research are briefly presented and introduced.

3.1. Back-propagation neural network

The neural network model is built to estimate air pollution, from forward multilayer network with back-propagation learning algorithm, which is a supervised learning method. The network structure consists of an input layer, with 22 neurons (11*2=22), in which we have 11 variables and 2 is the number of days of study (Our goal is to use the data from yesterday and today to predict PM_{10}). The output layer represents the concentration of PM_{10}. The number of neurons of the intermediate layer is calculated by trial and error, The number of neurons in hidden layer will vary from 2 to 10 (Trying=3) and Each test is done 3 times. Finally, we compare these with the best, and each one was better, the number of hidden layer neurons is. When the sixth consecutive epoch had this error are increased, train stops. Also an output layer represents the concentration of PM_{10}. Figure 1 shows the proposed back-propagation neural network model. And table 1 shows the characteristics of neural networks. After training (training ends after 25 epochs), ANN would be tested with unused data in the training phase and consequently the results and network performance would be assessed.

3.2. Genetic algorithm

Since the back propagation error algorithm is very slow for real problems, genetic algorithm is used to select the initial weight. Genetic algorithm is a heuristic optimization method, which acts on the basis of evaluation in nature and searches for the final solution among a population of potential solutions [13].

In other words, using neural network and combining it with genetic algorithm the performance (speed of achieving better solutions) and precise results would be increased. Indeed, as we have our own neural network, this time Genetic Algorithm calculates its initial weight. In this research, in both training and testing phase of genetic algorithm was used to optimize the basic ANN behavior. The objective function is Z=fit_nn (w), in which the input are the initial weights that should be calculated and the output is the summation of errors that should be minimized. The specifications of the GA used in the hybrid approach of BP-GA is presented in table 2. Figure 2 shows the development of genetic algorithm during 300 generations, the black dots are the best of the 20 chromosomes the blue dots are the average of 20 chromosomes in each generation. Genetic algorithm calculates the initial weights for using in Artificial Neural Network. After training (Training test ends after 20 epochs), Network with data that is not used in the training would be assessed and its performance would be checked using statistical index. The general structure and the methodology of the research are presented in figure 3.

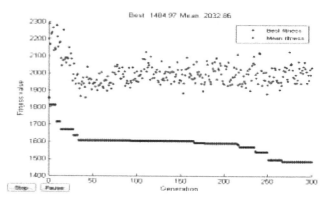

Figure 2. The development of genetic algorithms.

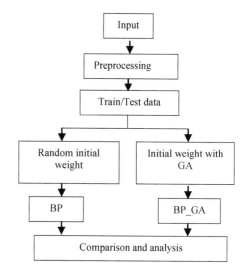

Figure 3. Research methodology.

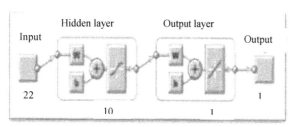

Figure 1. Model of back-propagation neural network (BP).

Table 1. Specification of (BP).

Value	Concept
Trial and error (2-10)	The number of neurons in middle layer
3	Trying
Sigmoid	Activation function of the hidden layer
Linear	Activation function of output layer
levenberg marquardt function	Training the network
max_fail=6	Stop condition

Table 2. Specification of (BP - GA).

Value	Concept
Array of real numbers	View (encoded) chromosome
20	The initial population
300	Number of generations
0.8	Probability of crossover
0.03	Probability of mutation
Z=fit_nn(w)	The objective function
Roulette wheel	Selection function
number of generations=300	Stop condition

4. Simulation and evaluation

Not all air quality monitoring stations have recorded a continuous concentration of pollutants; therefore, in this study, those stations have been ignored. Aghdasiyeh station period only was chosen because it has a more complete course of data in hours (2000-2014). The meteorological station and the airport having a period of more perfect location closer to the air pollution monitoring stations, were studied (2007-2013) The data were recorded on a daily basis. When two air pollution stations and air quality data with our accession will join and make our final data from 2007 to 2013. Unique factors rainfall, relative humidity, wind speed, temperature play a decisive role on the spread of pollutants, especially particulate matter. For example, humidity has a negative impact on air particulates. Input variables to network included variable time (Day , month , year , weekdays and holidays) and meteorological variables (Minimum temperature , average temperature , maximum temperature , humidity , wind speed and PM_{10}).The difference between these two sets of data is that, time variables do not need prediction when working with models and they can basically inserted to the model as inputs. However, meteorological data should be inserted to the model as predicted data. The information in Aghdasiyeh Weather Quality Control Station and Mehrabad Weather Station in Tehran from 2007 to 2013 was collected as a real case study in this paper. Aghdasiyeh station was selected because it had more complete course of records in its database. Table 3 shows the location of the stations under study. The information of 2400 days (from 2007 to 2013) was used. Eleven parameters have been selected as input parameters to our models. These parameters were year, month, day, minimum temperature, mean temperature, maximum temperature, humidity, velocity, week day, holidays from Mehrabad station and PM10 from Aghdasiyeh station To clean existing data and review the situation and quality control the following preprocessing issues were considered:

- Controlling suspicious data and their comparison with the same data in previous and following days.
- On some days, air pollution data led to a gap were not registered. This can happen due to a mistake in the data recording device. These data were excluded from the study. Thus the information of 2400 days decreased to 1362 days means that 1038 days air pollution data were not recorded.
- Normalizing data through conversion was to a range of [0, 1]. Normalization of data prevents to have larger weights. To do so, (1) is used:

$$X = \frac{x - x_{min}}{x_{max} - x_{min}} \tag{1}$$

where, x_{min} is minimum and x_{max} the maximum input vector x, and X is its normalization. The input data after preprocessing were divided to train and test data. 80% percent of the input data were selected as training set (almost 1090 individuals) and 20% have been selected as a testing set (almost 272 individuals). The next step

is to assess and evaluate the accuracy of the models. The evaluation is done based on four famous criteria: Mean Square Error, Root Mean Square Error, Mean Absolute Error, and assessment coefficient (R2) shown in (2),(3), and (4).

$$RMSE = \sqrt{\sum_{i=1}^{n} \frac{(c_i - m_i)^2}{n}}, \ MSE = (RMSE)^2 \tag{2}$$

In which Ci is optimal value that has been estimated by the model, mi the amount which has been calculated and n the number of data pairs which have been observed. RMSE value is usually positive and the ideal value equals to zero. The algebraic sign of the MAE; indicates the error value is positive or negative. In (3), assuming MAE is positive (negative) shows that the estimated value is higher (lower) than the measured value. The ideal value equals to zero. In (4), R^2 shows the dependence between two data groups. The ideal value for R^2 equals to one. The closer R^2 to one, more dependent the data groups are.

$$MAE = \sum_{i=1}^{n} \frac{(c_i - m_i)}{n} \tag{3}$$

$$R^2 = \left[1 - \frac{\sum_{i=1}^{n} |(c_i - m_i)|^2}{\sum_{i=1}^{n} (m_i)^2} \right] * 100 \tag{4}$$

For simulation and implementation purpose, Microsoft Excel 2013 was used for pre-processing and data preparation (eliminate suspicious cases, data normalization, etc.) as well as Matlab 2013 for implementing ANN with Back Propagation (BP), ANN with Back Propagation (BP) and its hybrid with GA (BP-GA). The evaluation of two methods was shown in tables 4 and 5. According to tables 4 and 5 BP-GA is the better model among in comparison with BP since it has the smallest amount of MSE, RMSE, and MAE in the testing set. It also has the greatest R^2. Figures 4 and 5 show the distribution of test data in three models in which black dots are real answers and red dots are predictions.

5. Conclusions and suggestions

As discussed in previous studies [11] to forecast air pollution in Tehran on ANN and linear regression were used, and artificial neural networks and genetic algorithms to predict the composition of PM_{10} in Tehran have not been used. The results of this paper can be compared with the results of previous studies. This is because both types of input data as well as the methods are similar but, the comparison algorithms vary. In this regard, the paper on Tehran air quality prediction using a combination of neural networks and genetic algorithms better than the results obtained in [11].

They say the results of the 2006 $R^2 = 0.57$ for 2005 and 2006 are separated $R^2 = 0.54$ and for 2004 to 2006 apart seized $R^2 = 0.5$ and concluded that the results for one year is better than two years and three years, as two years are better than three years.

Table 3. Aghdasiyeh and Mehrabad stations.

Station	Station location	Latitude	Longitude
Aghdasiyeh	Nobonyad Plaza, Shahid Langari Road	43.75°40′ 35′′	15.12°20′ 51′′
Mehrabad	In the vicinity of northern Tehran, Shahid langari Roadside	35° 47′ 57′′	5° 29′ 7′′

Table 4. Evaluation of BP, BP-GA (Train phase).

Method	TRAIN			
	R^2	MSE	RMSE	MAE
BP_GA	0.74823	714.7516	26.7348	17.9929
BP	0.69793	832.0611	28.8455	18.7362

Table 5. Evaluation of BP, BP-GA (Test phase).

Method	TEST			
	R^2	MSE	RMSE	MAE
BP_GA	0.54889	1756.7358	41.9134	25.7154
BP	0.53932	1778.8447	42.1764	25.5921

However, we examined data for seven years (2007-2013) and found that R^2 =0.54889. It is clear that with neural network $R^2 = 0.53$ and the combination of neural networks and genetic algorithms $R = 0.54889$ and because we got better results data for seven years rather than. One, two, and three years. The results are shown in table 6.

In this paper, two models have been proposed to predict Tehran air pollution based on information from Aghdasiyeh Weather Quality Control Station and Mehrabad Weather Station. The accuracy and performance of the two models are decreased respectively: BP-GA and BP. In other words, the error rate increases. The lack of input data does not affect the predictive ability of the models considerably. It should be mentioned that having more input data and solving the problem of data fluctuation could lead to have better predictions. One of the main limitations of the research is that the prediction models have more accurate results for shorter period of time rather than longer period of time. Two future works are identified for this research. First, more input data can be fed to the

network in order to have more accurate result. This research mostly focused on PM_{10}. Second, other heuristic algorithms like swarm intelligence algorithms can be used to increase the performance and accuracy.

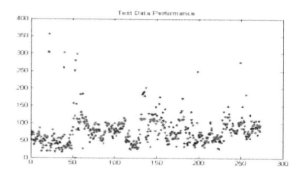

Figure 4. Distribution of test data in the BP-GA.

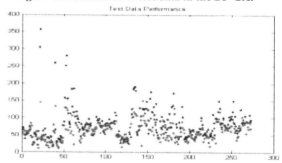

Figure 5. Distribution of test data in the BP.

Table 6. Comparison of previous studies and proposed methods.

Location	RMSE	R^2	Method	Year
Proposed method	41.9134	0.54889	BP_GA	2007-2013
	42.1764	0.53932	BP	2007-2013
	46.2596	0.575	BP	2006
	54.3565	0.546	BP	2006 − 2005
[11]	54.7014	0.5	BP	2007 − 2005

References

[1] Lira, T. S., Barrozo, A. S. & Assis A. J. (2007). Air quality prediction in Uberlandia, Brazil, using linear models and neural networks, 17th European Symposium on Computer Aided Process-Eng, vol. 24, pp. 51-56.

[2] Bruelli, U., Piazza, V., Pignato, L., Sorbello, F. & Vitabile, S. (2007). Two days ahead prediction of daily maximum concentration of SO2, O3, PM10, NO2, CO in the urban area of Palermo, Italy, Atom. Env, Vol. 41, no. 14, pp. 2967-2995.

[3] Grivas, A. & Chaloulakou. A. (2006). Artificial neural network model for prediction of PM10 hourly concentration, In Great Area of Athens, Greece, Atomospheric Environ, vol. 40, pp. 1216-1229.

[4] Cecchetti, M., Corani,G. & Guariso, G. (2004). Artificial neural network prediction of PM10 in the

Milan area, Inte. IEMSS International Congress Osnabrack.

[5] Haykin, S. (1999). Neural network, a comprehensive foundation, Prentice Hall International Inc, Second Edition.

[6] Dimitriou, K., Paschalidou, A. & Kassomenos, P. (2013). Assessing air quality with regards to its effect on human health in the European Union through air quality indices, EcologicalIndicators, vol. 27, pp. 108-115.

[7] Nayak, P., Sudheer, K. P., Rangan, D. M. & Ramasastri, K. S. (2005). Short-term flood forecasting with a neuro fuzzy model, Water Reso Res, pp. 2517-253.

[8] Nejadkoorki, F. & Baroutian, S. (2012). Forecasting Extreme PM10 concentrations Using Artificial Neural Networks", Pages: 277-284.

[9] Davor, Z.A., Viktor, V.P., Dragan, S.P., Mirjana, Đ. R. & Aleksandra, A. P. (2013). PM10 emission forecasting using artificial neural networks and genetic algorithm input variable optimization", Science of the Total Environment, Pages: 511-519.

[10] Tavakoli, M, & Esmaili,A. (2013). Artificial neural networks to predict the concentration of particulate matter air of Tehran, The second national conference on environmental protection and coarser, Hamedan.

[11] Soltaniye, M, Moslehi,P. & Yari, M. (2012). The concentration of suspended particles in the air in Tehran predicted by neural network models and compare multiple regression model, Sanati Sharif University, Tehran.

[12] Rahimi, N, (2012). The effect of geographic factors on air pollution in Tehran, Air Pollution Management Conference, Sharif University.

[13] Majidnezhad, V. (2014). A novel hybrid method for vocal fold pathology diagnosis based on Russian language, Journal of AI and Data Mining, Shahroud university , vol. 2, no. 2, pp. 141-147.

6

On improving APIT algorithm for better localization in WSN

S. M. Hosseinirad [1*], M. Niazi [2], J. Pourdeilami [2], S. K. Basu [1], and A. A. Pouyan [2]

1. Department of Computer Science, Banaras Hindu University, India.
2. Department of Computer Engineering, Shahrood University of Technology, Shahrood, Iran.

*Corresponding author: hosseinirad@gmail.com (S. M. Hosseinirad).

Abstract
In Wireless Sensor Networks (WSNs), localization algorithms could be range-based or range-free. The Approximate Point in Triangle (APIT) is a range-free approach. We propose modification of the APIT algorithm and refer as modified-APIT. We select suitable triangles with appropriate distance between anchors to reduce PIT test errors (edge effect and non-uniform placement of neighbours) in APIT algorithm. To reduce the computational load and avoid useless anchors selection, we propose to segment the application area to four non-overlapping and four overlapping sub-regions. Our results show that the modified-APIT has better estimation's performance of localization for different sizes of network for both grid and random deployments in terms of average error and time requirement. For increasing the accuracy of localization and reduction of computation time, every sub-region should contain minimum 5 anchors. Variations of the size of a network and radio communication radius of anchors affect the value of average error and time requirement. To have more accurate location estimation, 5 to 10 anchors per sub-region are effective in modified-APIT.

Keywords: *WSN, Localization, APIT, Anchor, Coverage.*

1. Introduction

WSNs contain tiny and smart sensors nodes which are battery-operated (limited life-time) [1]. They have limited storage, processing, communication capacity to sense various physical phenomena in the environment. WSNs greatly extend our ability to track, monitor and control a physical phenomenon [2]. Applications include industrial process monitoring and control, military and civilian applications, healthcare, environment and habitat monitoring, home automation, traffic control, etc. [3]. The typical tasks of networked sensor nodes are to collaborate and aggregate huge amount of sensed data from the physical environment. Sensors are deployed either inside a phenomenon being monitored or very close to it. WSNs are highly distributed self-organized systems [4].

WSNs have attracted a lot of research attention in the recent years. It offers a rich area of research, in which a variety of multi-disciplinary tools and concepts are employed [5]. WSN protocols and algorithms must possess self-organizing capabilities. This allows random deployment in inaccessible terrains or hostile terrains.

Localization issue in WSN has attracted a lot of research effort in the recent years [6]. Estimation of the physical positions of the nodes is one of the fundamental and critical issues in Geographical Positional System (GPS) [7]. Accurate estimation of location is useful in sensor network services such as information processing, sensing coverage [8], location directory service [9], management and operation of the network [10], location-based routing protocols [11], etc.

The positional information is essential to many location-aware sensor network communication protocols, such as packet routing and sensing coverage [12]. When an abnormal event occurs, the sensor node detecting the event needs the positional information to locate the abnormal event and report to the special node called the Base Station (BS) or sink(s). BS has higher capability compared to an ordinary sensor node.

Many different protocols and algorithms were proposed for localization in WSN. It is a challenging task to design practical algorithms for node localization, given the constraints that are usually imposed on the sensors [13].

Sensors may be deployed in an application area manually or randomly. Manual sensor deployment is applicable when the size of network is not large. Generally, in the case of harsh or hostile environment large number of sensors is randomly deployed. Positions of sensors are unknown because of random distribution, while applications in this type of networks need to know the source of the received information.

The Approximate Point in Triangle (APIT) is a range-free approach [14]. The main idea of APIT is to consider overlapping triangles. Localization with APIT algorithm leads to PIT test problem and the issue of time. In this paper, to reduce the computational load and avoid useless anchors selection, and increase the location estimation accuracy in APIT algorithm, we propose modification of the APIT algorithm and refer as modified-APIT. The paper is organized as: section 2 deals with localization algorithms, section 3 deals with APIT algorithm, section 4 deals with results and discussion, and section 5 concludes the paper.

2. Localization algorithms

The proposed localization protocols may be divided into two categories: range-based and range-free [15]. The range information can be acquired by using different protocols. These protocols use absolute point-to-point distance estimates (range) or angle estimates for calculating location [16]. The simplest possible localization solution is to attach a GPS. Time of Arrival (TOA) technique is used to estimate distance based on measurement of signal propagation time between two communicating nodes. It uses GPS as the basic localization system [17]. The Time Difference of Arrival (TDOA) measurement uses ultrasound signals to make the distance information estimation possible for nodes [18]. Measurements that are based on signal propagation time can be affected by multipath fading and noise interference; therefore, TOA and TDOA are impractical solutions for WSN localization. To augment and complement TDOA and TOA technologies, an Arrival of Angle (AOA) technique has been proposed that allows nodes to estimate and map relative angles between neighbours. It needs additional expensive hardware like a directional antenna or a digital compass [19]. So, AOA is not a good choice for

resource limited networks. Received Signal Strength Indicator (RSSI) technology has been proposed for hardware-constrained systems. It is another method based on signal strength and distance relation [20]. All range-based localization algorithms are relatively precise, but present a costly solution (expensive and energy consuming) for localization in large scale WSN [21].

Considering the hardware limitations of WSN devices, solutions using range-free localization are being pursued as a cost-effective alternative to the more expensive range-based approaches [22]. Generally, the positions of sensor nodes are not to be engineered or predetermined. The range-free protocols make no assumption about the availability or validity of such information as are required in the range-based estimates.

The centroid algorithm is simple and economic. It requires a lot of anchor nodes broadcasting their positions (via GPS) to compute position as the center of the connected anchor nodes. All the sensor nodes should be connected to the anchor node for good localization results [23]. However, it results in large errors in the case of low anchor ratio or distribution of them is not even, since the nodes are not uniformly distributed and the relationship between hop counts and geographic distances is very weak [24]; therefore, estimated locations tend to be inaccurate.

Distance Vector-Hop (DV-Hop) algorithm has been proposed based on distance vector routing concept [25]. It assumes a heterogeneous network consisting of sensing nodes and anchors. Instead of single-hop broadcasts, anchors flood and broadcast their location information throughout the network maintaining a running hop-count at each node along the way [26]. Consequently, other anchors can obtain minimum hop count to other anchors.

3. APIT algorithm and its modification

The APIT algorithm requires a small percentage of anchors and employs a novel area-based approach to perform location estimation by segmentation of the field. Moreover, these nodes can be equipped with high-powered radio transmitter.

The main idea of APIT for localization of nodes is to consider overlapping triangles. The vertices of these triangles are anchors. Bounding triangles are obtained using any group of three reference nodes, rather than the coverage area of a single node. In the APIT algorithm, the sensor nodes receive location information from the nearby anchors initially.

Second, the Point in Triangulation (PIT) test checks whether a sensor node is in a virtual triangle that is formed by connecting the three anchors from which signals are received. After the PIT test is done, the APIT algorithm aggregates the results through a grid SCAN algorithm [27]. The APIT algorithm calculates the Centre of Gravity (COG) of the intersections of all the overlapped triangles in which the node resides to determine its location.

Localization with APIT algorithm leads to two major issues: (i) PIT test problem, and (ii) anchor selection problem leading to increased time requirement. To solve these issues, we modify the APIT algorithm and call it the modified-APIT algorithm. By selecting suitable triangles with appropriate distance (discussed later) between anchors, we reduce PIT test errors (edge effect and non-uniform placement of neighbours) in APIT algorithm. To reduce the computational load and avoid selection of useless anchors, we propose to segment the application area to four non-overlapping and four overlapping sub-regions.

3.1. PIT test

The purpose of PIT test is to check whether a node is inside a triangle that is formed by three anchors. Every time, the node selects three possible anchors and apply the PIT test. When a node M is inside $\triangle ABC$, if M is shifted in any direction, the new position must be nearer to (or further from) at least one of the anchors A, B or C. Also, when a node M is outside of $\triangle ABC$ and M is shifted, there must exist a direction in which the position of M is closer to (or further from) all the three anchors A, B and C. When there is a direction such that a point adjacent to node M is closer to (or further from) anchors A, B and C simultaneously, then M is outside of $\triangle ABC$. Otherwise, M is inside $\triangle ABC$. This is named Perfect PIT test (PPIT). It can correctly determine whether node M is inside $\triangle ABC$ or not.

To perform PIT algorithm in WSN without the need of node movement, approximate PIT test method has been proposed that takes advantage of high node density in WSNs. To emulate the movement of a node in the PPIT, node uses neighbor information, exchanged via beaconing. If no neighbor of node M is closer to (or further from) all the three anchors A, B and C simultaneously, it is assumed that M is inside $\triangle ABC$. Otherwise, M is outside this triangle. APIT can only check a few directions (neighbors).

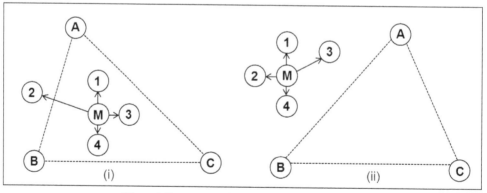

Figure1. In-to-out and out-to-in error situations.

It may be incorrect in the selection of its decisions (Figure 1) to determine the node's position. Although, node M is inside the triangle but APIT decides that it is outside.

The node is near to the edges and some of its neighbors are outside the triangle and further from all anchors in relation to node M. Consequently, node M mistakenly considers it is outside the triangle due to edge effect (In-to-out error, Figure 1 (node A). Although, node M is outside the triangle but since none of its neighbors are closer to (or further from) all anchors simultaneously, node M assumes it is inside the triangle (Out-to-in error, Figure 1 (node B).

3.2. Removing anomalies in PIT test

Selecting suitable triangles of anchors in PIT test is an important issue. In-to-out and out-to-in errors in PIT test is caused by edge effect and non-uniform placement of neighbors. When the triangles formed do not have appropriate sides and areas, these errors mostly occur (Figure 2).

The triangles of anchors should satisfy two conditions. These are: (i) sides of triangles should be comparable within a range. Narrow triangles should be eliminated from the considered set of triangles, because few number of nodes reside inside a very narrow triangle (one of its sides is short and the other two are very long)

Most of the neighbors of a node are located outside the triangle. Sides (x, y, z) of a triangle are to satisfy (1), where α and β are scalars.

$$(\alpha \times z \leq x + y \leq \beta \times z \text{ and } \alpha \times y \leq x + z \leq \beta \times y)$$

where $\alpha = 0.7$ and $\beta = 1.4$.　　(1)

(ii) Because of random deployment of anchors in the environment, short distances among anchors are possible. In such a situation, they may form triangles with very small areas where a few nodes only can reside inside these triangles. They do not

have utility in node localization process. Consequently, triangles with area less than a threshold are eliminated from the considered set of triangles. The area size should satisfy (2), where λ and γ are scalars.

$$\lambda \times A_{\text{Application}} \leq A_{\text{Triangle}} \leq \gamma \times A_{\text{Application}}$$

where $\lambda = \frac{1}{16}$ and $\gamma = \frac{1}{4}$　　(2)

$A_{\text{Application}}$ is the area of the field of interest and A_{Triangle} is the area of the selected triangle.

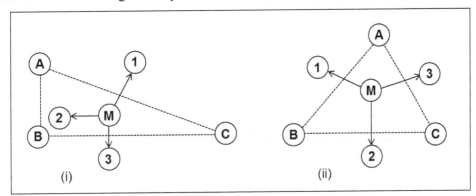

Figure 2. Two instances of inappropriate triangles.

3.3. Appropriate anchor selection problem

Extension of covering area can lead to discontinuity of coverage, computational overload, and increase in localization errors. In APIT algorithm, anchors advertise their locations by using maximum power of radio communication. In addition to consumption of energy, it wastes the sensor nodes resources as well. Possibility of useless anchors selection is one of the major problems that may occur while using APIT algorithm in large area increasing the system cost. Receiving of signal by a sensor node

from an anchor is not adequate for selection in localization. To reduce computational load and useless anchors selection, we propose that a new device named Super Anchors (SA) should be used in the environment. SAs are high-powered equipment with wide radio communication range and it broadcasts signal in the whole environment. They help other sensors to conserve energy and prevent wastage of resources. Segmenting the application area to four sub-regions, four SAs are located in the four corners.

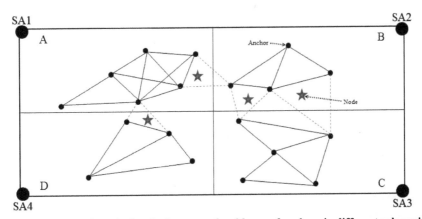

Figure 3. Non-formation of triangles because of residence of anchors in different sub-regions.

By comparing received signal strength of SAs, every node can determine its location in the sub-regions. Sensor nodes select only close by anchors co-located in the sub-region to estimate their

location. With wide radio communications range, an anchor broadcasts its location information over a long distance.

Sometimes, more than one triangle may be formed in APIT algorithm for the specified nodes which are located near the external borders, but the nodes maybe outside of all of these triangles.

Whole of the covering area except the formed triangle could be determined as a possible node location and COG (Centre of Gravity) is calculated for a large but wrong region. After the environment is equipped with SAs, the effect of location miscalculation error is decreased. The maximum error may be equal to the distance of the sub-region corners from its center (Figure 3). After addition of the SAs, same miscalculation error may happen for the nodes located near to the internal sub-region borders and it has negative effect on localization algorithm. The maximum error may be equal to the distance of the sub-region corner and its center. Triangles with dashed lines (Figure 3) can be used to localize the specified node.

To solve miscalculation of the nodes located near the internal sub-region borders, we propose to segment the environment to four non-overlapping and four overlapping regions. Each overlapping region covers about 30% of regions. Based on the received signals from the SAs, every node is able to determine its location in a sub-region through comparison of the received signal strengths. A node is co-located with a SA from which it has received signal of highest strength. After determination of the nearest SA, every node can estimate its sub-region (including overlapping and non-overlapping sub-region) location in the application area through comparison of the strengths of received signals. If the received signal strength from SA 'A' is greater than 70%

of the signal strength received from SA 'B' and if the signal strength of SA 'B' be greater than 70% of the signal strength of SA 'A' then the node is located in the overlapping region. Otherwise, it is located in the sub-region corresponding to the greater signal strength of the SAs. Through the same rule, a node determines the left or the right half of the environment. Based on the proposed method, every node may be located in a sub-region or an overlapping region. The anchors which are least common in one region are selected for triangle formation. Figure 4 shows non-localized nodes (□ and □) in the domain with four sub- regions, because they are located near the internal borders of the sub-regions (no triangles are formed). The nodes □ and □ have been successfully localized after segmenting the environment to four overlapping sub-regions in addition to considering four sub-regions (Figure 4).

The anchors #1, #2 and #3 have been used to localize the node □. Figure 4 shows that the anchor #1 is located in regions 4 and 8, and anchor #2 is located in regions 4, 7 and 8, and anchor #3 is located in regions 1, 5 and 8. These anchors are common in region 8, so they can be used to form triangles. Anchors #4, #5 and #6 have participated in node ★ localization. Anchor #4 is placed in regions 3, 6 and 7, and anchors #5 is placed in regions 3 and 7, and anchor #6 is placed in regions 2, 5 and 6. The common region of these anchors in region 6, they can be used to localize the node ★.

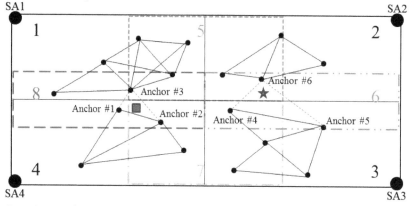

Figure 4. Localization of nodes ★ and ■ after segmentation of field to four non-overlapping and four overlapping sub-regions.

4. Results and discussion

In our study we applied APIT and modified-APIT algorithms on three different network sizes (100, 225, and 400) in a square shaped application area. Figures 5(a) and (b) show the localized sensors with APIT and modified-APIT respectively for a WSN with 100 sensors (the blue sensors determine locations of localized anchors sensors

and black sensors determine locations of localized ordinary sensors).

The algorithms are coded in MATLAB version 7 on Intel(R) core $i5$ CPU 650 3.2 GHz running Windows 7 professional. In APIT algorithm every sensor node is able to receive all anchors' signals to estimate its location. We assume limited percentage of sensor nodes (almost 10%) is equipped with GPS (anchors) to find and advertise its location. When the size of network is low, modified-APIT algorithm is not useful. For example, in a network with 100 sensor nodes, 10 sensors are used as anchors (10%). Therefore, in

every sub-region 2.5 anchors probably are deployed but to form a triangle three anchors are required. Also, for estimation accuracy we need more than one triangle for every sensor node.

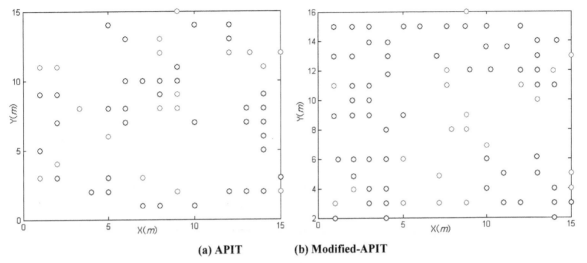

(a) APIT   (b) Modified-APIT

Figure 5. Localized sensors with APIT and modified-APIT.

We define a threshold for the number of anchors in every sub-region and we use minimum 5 anchors in every sub-region. Based on this, we assume that in a network of size 100, 20% of the sensor nodes are anchors. In addition to estimation accuracy, to conserve the energy, we find the threshold value for anchors' radio communication radius based on the number of localized sensors. We compare the APIT and modified-APIT algorithms based on average error and computational time. Average error is calculated by (3).

$$\text{Average error} = \frac{\sum_{i=1}^{n} |\text{Exact Location}_i - \text{Estimated Location}_i|}{n} \quad (3)$$

In the first part of this study, we apply APIT algorithm for three different sizes of network (100, 225, and 400) with grid and random deployments. Table 1 shows that the APIT algorithm has better performance for all sizes of network with random deployment in terms of average error and time requirement.

Table 1. Result of APIT algorithm.

WSN Size	Grid Deployment			Random Deployment		
	Time (s)	Avg. Error	No. of Sen.	Time (s)	Avg. Error	No. of Sen.
100	62.96	3.12	80	52.07	2.97	80
225	1245.48	3.83	202	1246.36	4.67	202
400	110039.1	6.82	360	109949.36	6.11	360

By increasing the size of the network, average error increases linearly and the time requirement increases non-linearly. In a large size network, sensors localization needs lots of time to calculate their location through the APIT algorithm. In the second part of this study we apply the modified-APIT algorithm on three different sizes of network (100, 225, and 400) with grid and random deployments (Table 2).
APIT consumes more time for sensors localization with more average error compared

with modified-APIT algorithm. Also, anchors have to consume more energy for location advertisement. In modified-APIT algorithm, by varying radio communication radius of anchors between 6m and 9m, all sensor nodes are localized. In the modified-APIT algorithm, the average value of this radius is 8m for grid and random deployments. Variation of the size of a network and the value of radio communication radius of anchors affect value of average error and localization time. Increasing the size of the network, the average error increased linearly but the amount of time required increased non-linearly. When the size of a network is increased, the number of anchor nodes in every sub-region is also increased. For example in a network with 225 sensors, every sub-region has 5 anchors and every sensor node can use 10 triangles for location estimation. When the size of the network is 400, every sub-region contains 10 anchors and sensors can use at least 120 triangles for localization. The results illustrate that with increment of anchors in every sub-region, the average error and time requirement are also increased. Therefore, for having more location estimation accuracy, we propose that 5 to 10 anchors per sub-region be used.

Table 2. Result of modified-APIT algorithm.

WSN Size	Grid Deployment				Random Deployment			
	R(*m*)	Time (*s*)	Avg. Error	No. of Sen.	R(*m*)	Time (*s*)	Avg. Error	No. of Sen.
	5	1.18	1.81	78	6	2.43	1.75	66
100	**6**	**2.05**	**1.83**	**80**	**7**	**3.57**	**1.83**	**80**
	7	2.51	1.87	80	8	3.67	1.85	80
	7.5	19.63	2.8	201.4	7.5	25.33	2.84	195
225	**8.5**	**24.05**	**2.83**	**202**	**8.5**	**27.73**	**2.93**	**202**
	9.5	34.42	2.96	202	9.5	30.64	2.72	202
	8	66.83	3.53	358	7	70.19	2.74	348
400	**9**	**92.46**	**3.63**	**360**	**8**	**105.41**	**3.12**	**360**
	10	103.27	3.73	360	9	18622	3.83	360

5. Conclusion

We proposed modification of the APIT algorithm and studied efficacy of the modified algorithm in terms of average error and computational time and compare with those of APIT with segmentation of the application area to four non-overlapping and four overlapping sub-regions. Our results show that the modified-APIT algorithm has better performance in terms of average error and time requirement for all sizes of network with random and grid deployments. To increasing accuracy of localization and prevention of localization complexity, every sub-region should contain minimum 5 anchors. Variations in the size of a network and radio communication radius of anchors affect average error and time requirement. Localization in a large size network using APIT algorithm needs lots of time compared to modified-APIT algorithm. APIT algorithm localizes sensor nodes with more average error compared with the modified-APIT algorithm. Also, in APIT algorithm, anchors consume more energy to advertise their locations. It reduces anchors' lifetime. For more accurate location estimation, 5 to 10 anchors per sub-region are effective in modified-APIT. Sensors localization based on the modified-APIT algorithm through clustering approach is our future plan of study.

References

[1] Akyildiz, I. F., Su, W., Sankarasubramaniam, Y. & Cayirci, E. (2002). Wireless sensor networks: a survey. Journal of Computer Networks, vol. 38, pp. 393-422, DOI: 10.1016/S1389-1286(01)00302-4.

[2] Anastasi, G., Conti, M., Di Francesco, M. & Passarella, A. (2009). Energy conservation in wireless sensor networks: A survey. Journal of Ad Hoc Networks, vol. 7, no. 3, pp. 537–568, DOI: 10.1016/j.adhoc.2008.06.003.

[3] Arampatzis, T., Lygeros, J. & Manesis, S. (2005). A Survey of Applications of Wireless Sensors and Wireless Sensor Networks. In: the Proceeding of 13th Mediterranean Conference on Control and Automation Limassol, pp. 27-29, DOI:10.1109/.2005.1467103.

[4] Akyildiz, I. F. & Kasimoglu, I. H. (2004). Wireless Sensor and actor Networks: Research Challenges. Journal of Ad Hoc Networks, vol. 2, no. 4, pp. 351-367, DOI: 10.1016/j.adhoc.2004.04.003.

[5] Zheng J. & Jamalipour, A. (2009). Wireless Sensor Networks, a networking perspective. Wiley, New York.

[6] Pal, A. (2010). Localization Algorithms in Wireless Sensor Networks: Current Approaches and Future Challenges. Journal of Network Protocols and Algorithms (Macrothink Institute), vol. 2, no. 1, DOI: 10.5296/npa.v2i1.279.

[7] Hofmann-Wellenhof, B., Lichtenegger, H. & Collins, J. (1993). Global Positioning System: Theory and Practice. Springer, New York.

[8] Yan, T., He, T. & Stankovic, J. A. (2003). Differentiated Surveillance Service for Sensor Networks. Proceedings of the 1st international

conference on Embedded networked sensor systems, USA, pp. 51-62.

[9] Li, J., Jannotti, J., De Couto, D. S. J., Karger, D. R. & Morris, R. A. (2000). Scalable location service for geographic ad-hoc routing. In: the Proceeding of International Conference on Mobile Computing and Networking (MOBICOM), pp. 120-130, DOI: 10.1145/345910.345931.

[10] Gengzhong, Z. & Qiumei, L. (2010). A Survey on Topology Control in Wireless Sensor Networks. In: the Proceeding of Second International Conference on Future Networks (ICFN 2010), pp. 376-380, DOI: 10.1109/ICFN.2010.31.

[11] Ko, Y. B. & Vaidya, N. H. (1998). Location-Aided Routing (LAR) in Mobile Ad Hoc Networks. In: the Proceeding of International Conference on Mobile Computing and Networking (MOBICOM) (1998), DOI: 10.1145/288235.288252.

[12] Xu, Y., Heidemann, J. & Estrin, D. (2001). Geography-informed Energy Conservation for Ad Hoc Routing. In: the Proceeding of International Conference on Mobile Computing and Networking (MOBICOM), vol. 1, DOI: 10.1145/381677.381685.

[13] Yu, K., Hedley, M., Sharp, I. & Guo, Y. J. (2006). Node Positioning in Ad Hoc Wireless Sensor Networks. Journal of IEEE International Conference on Industrial Informatics (2006), pp. 641-646, DOI: 10.1109/INDIN.2006.275636.

[14] He, T., Huang, C., Blum, B. M., Stankovic, J. A. & Abdelzaher, T. (2005). Range-Free Localization and Its Impact on Large Scale Sensor Networks. ACM Transactions on Embedded Computing Systems, vol. 4, no. 4, pp. 877-906, DOI: 10.1145/1113830.1113837.

[15] Datta, S., Klinowski, C., Rudafshani, M. & Khaleque S. (2006). Distributed localization in static and mobile sensor networks. In: the Proceeding of IEEE International Conference on Wireless and Mobile Computing, Networking and Communications, (WiMob'2006), pp. 69-76, DOI: 10.1109/WIMOB.2006.1696397.

[16] Garcia-Morchon, O. & Baldus, H. (2009). The ANGEL WSN Security Architecture. In: the Proceeding of third International Conference on Sensor Technologies and Applications (SENSORCOMM), pp. 430-435, DOI: 10.1109/SENSORCOMM.2009.71.

[17] Patwari, N., Hero, A., Perkins, M., Correal, N. & Dea, R. (2003). Relative location estimation in Wireless Sensor Networks. Journal of IEEE Transactions on Signal Processing (2003), pp. 2137-2148, DOI: 10.1109/TSP.2003.814469.

[18] Doherty, L., Pister, K. S. J. & El Ghaoui, L. (2001). Convex Position Estimation in Wireless Sensor Networks. In: the Proceeding of twentieth Annual Joint Conference of the IEEE Computer and Communications Societies (INFOCOM), vol. 3, pp. 1655-1663, DOI: 10.1109/INFCOM.2001.916662.

[19] Niculescu, D. & Nath, B. (2003). Ad Hoc Positioning System (APS) using AoA. In: Twenty-Second Annual Joint Conference of the IEEE Computer and Communications. IEEE Societies (INFOCOM), vol. 3, pp. 1734-1743, DOI: 10.1109/INFCOM.2003.1209196.

[20] Kumar, P., Reddy, L. & Varma, S. (2009). Distance measurement and error estimation scheme for RSSI based localization in Wireless Sensor Networks. In: the Proceeding of Fifth International Conference on Wireless Communication and Sensor Networks (WCSN), pp. 1-4, DOI: 10.1109/WCSN.2009.5434802.

[21] Liu, C., Wu, K. & He, T. (2004). Sensor Localization with Ring Overlapping Based on Comparison of Received Signal Strength Indicator. In: the Proceeding of IEEE International Conference on Mobile Ad-hoc and Sensor Systems (IEEE Cat. No.04EX975 2004), pp. 516-518, DOI: 10.1109/MAHSS.2004.1392193.

[22] Le, V. D., Dang, V. H., Lee, S. & Lee, S. H. (2008). Distributed localization in wireless sensor networks based on force-vectors. In: the Proceeding of International Conference on Intelligent Sensors, Sensor Networks and Information Processing (2008), pp. 31-36, DOI: 10.1109/ISSNIP.2008.4761958.

[23] Meguerdichian, S., Koushanfar, F., Potkonjak, M. & Srivastava, M. B. (2001). Coverage problems in wireless ad-hoc sensor networks. In: the Proceeding of twentieth Annual Joint Conference of the IEEE Computer and Communications Societies (INFOCOM), vol. 3, pp. 1380-1387, DOI: 10.1109/INFCOM.2001.916633.

[24] Sheu, J. P., Li, J. M. & Hsu, C. S. (2006). A distributed location estimating algorithm for wireless sensor networks. In: the Proceeding of IEEE International Conference on Sensor Networks, Ubiquitous, and Trustworthy Computing (SUTC). vol. 1, DOI: 10.1109/SUTC.2006.1636179.

[25] Rudafshani, M. & Datta, S. (2007). Localization in Wireless Sensor Networks. In: the Proceedings of the 6th international conference on Information processing in sensor networks (IPSN'07), pp. 51-60, DOI: 10.1145/1236360.1236368.

[26] Tian, S., Zhang, X., Liu, P., Sun, P. & Wang, X. (2007). A RSSI-based DV-hop Algorithm for Wireless Sensor Networks. In: the Proceeding of International Conference on Digital Object Identifier (WICOM 2007), pp. 2555-2558, DOI: 10.1109/WICOM.2007.636.

7

Optimization of fuzzy membership functions via PSO and GA with application to quad rotor

B. Safaee and S. Kamaleddin Mousavi Mashhadi*

School of Electrical Engineering, Iran University of Science and Technology, Tehran, Iran.

Corresponding author: sk_mousavi @iust.ac.ir (S. K Mousavi).

Abstract

Quad rotor is a renowned under-actuated unmanned aerial vehicle (UAV) with widespread military and civilian applications. Despite its simple structure, the vehicle suffers from inherent instability. Therefore, control designers always face a formidable challenge in their stabilization and control goal. In this paper, the fuzzy membership functions of the quad rotor fuzzy controllers are optimized using nature-inspired algorithms such as particle swarm optimization (PSO) and genetic algorithm (GA). Finally, the results of the proposed methods are compared, and a trajectory is defined to verify the effectiveness of the designed fuzzy controllers based on the algorithm with better results.

Keywords: *Fuzzy Controller, GA, Membership Functions, PSO, Quad Rotor.*

1. Introduction

Quad rotor is a kind of unmanned aerial vehicle (UAV) with 4 rotors in a cross-configuration that has been widely employed in civil and military applications including traffic surveillance, inspections, monitoring, aerial photography, search, and rescue in hazardous environments that are inaccessible for human involvement. Compared to other UAVs, they have a simple structure, low cost, easy maintenance, vertical take-off and landing capability, and rapid maneuvering. Quad rotors are under-actuated systems. They possess some advantages over single-blade helicopters in that they can be controlled by changing the rotor speed and have a simpler design and an easier control due to their fixed pitch blades. Quad rotors are inherently unstable based on several reasons elaborated as follow. First, their dynamic model features include non-linearity, high coupling, being under-actuated and static instability. Secondly, quad rotors are affected by body gravity, air resistance, propeller driving force, gyro impacts, and so on. Therefore, basically there is uncertainty in the dynamic model, which accentuates the need for a proper controller. Several controlling methods have been proposed including intelligent PID algorithm [1], LQR [2], loop forming H_∞ method,

sliding mode variable structure control algorithm [3], adaptive controller [4], feed-back linearization algorithm, back-stepping algorithm [5], hybrid control algorithm and so on [6]. In the following literature, some recent methods have concisely been presented. In [7], a passivity-based adaptive back stepping controller has been proposed to control a type of quad rotor. Reference [8] adopts a robust control for automatic tracking, taking-off, and landing. In [9], a feedback linearization method has been introduced based on the piecewise bilinear model. In [10], the performance of the quad rotor in the presence of wind disturbances has been assessed when back-stepping and feedback linearization controllers are applied on the quad rotor. Literature [11] has introduced the design of a neural adaptive controller using an extreme learning machine (ELM) to control the Euler angles of a quad rotor. A PD fuzzy control has been proposed in [12] to control the attitude. In [13], the controlling goal is to design an intelligent fuzzy controller in an effort to optimize the controller input. An adaptive fuzzy control strategy has been proposed in [14] to solve the problem of trajectory tracking for quad rotors in the presence of model parameter uncertainties and external disturbances. In order to reach the desired attitude and height, a linear active disturbance rejection control (LADRC) approach is utilized for the quad rotor control. LADRC has the capacity to estimate and compensate for the generalized disturbance, and reduce the system to a unit gain double integrator, which can be easily implemented and is robust to environmental disturbances [15]. In [16], a new non-linear controller has been proposed using a back-stepping-like feedback linearization method to control and stabilize the quad rotor. A novel asymptotic tracking controller has been proposed in [17] for a quad rotor using the robust integral of the signum of the error (RISE) method and the immersion and invariance (I & I)-based adaptive control methodology. In [18], the designers have endeavored to gain the stability and tracking control problem of a quad rotor in the presence of modeling error and disturbance uncertainties associated with aerodynamic and gyroscopic effects, payload mass, and other external forces/torques induced from an uncertain flying environment. A PD sliding surface in the sliding mode control has been considered in [19] for a vertical take-off and landing aircraft. A control scheme based on back-stepping control and its combination with fuzzy system has been introduced in [20] to decrease the chattering phenomenon. A control algorithm for a finite-time tracking of a quad rotor has been introduced in [21]; it is based upon the use of feed-back linearization method and finite-time output control. The proposed multi-Lyapunov function-based switching control algorithm in [22] is employed to achieve tracking of Cartesian space motion and the heading angle of a quad rotor.

In this paper, a fuzzy controller due to its capability to handle non-linear systems and model uncertainties is proposed to control both the transitional and angular movements of a quad rotor. Choosing a proper fuzzy membership functions is a time-consuming task, especially when there are a number of fuzzy controllers in the system simultaneously. The main contribution of this paper is to overcome this problem by means of parametrically defining fuzzy membership functions and tuning them based on the minimization of a specific objection function. GA and PSO are selected as the optimizing methods owing to their capability in locating global minima. This paper is organized as follows. Section 1 deals with a brief discussion of the quad rotor configuration and dynamic model. Next, the quad rotor fuzzy controller design is discussed in

section 2. Section 3 concerns a concise introduction of PSO and GA. Finally, the simulation results derived from the proposed algorithms are compared and a trajectory is defined to illustrate the superiority of the best designed fuzzy controller over the not optimized fuzzy controller in section 5.

1.1. Quad rotor configuration

According to figure 1, the front and rear rotors rotate clockwise, while the right and left rotors rotate counter-clockwise. Increasing (decreasing) the speed of all rotors with the same amount generates the vertical motion or thrust. A roll motion can be obtained by increasing (decreasing) the left rotor speed, while decreasing (increasing) the speed of the right rotor. Similarly, a pitch motion is controlled by an increase (a decrease) in the speed of the rear rotor while decreasing (increasing) the front rotor speed. The yaw angle is achieved by increasing the clockwise pair speeds and decreasing the counter-clockwise pair speeds, simultaneously.

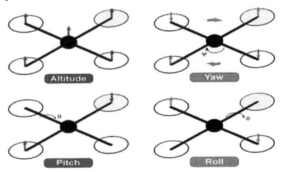

Figure 1. Quad rotor dynamics [23].

2. Model dynamics of quad rotor vehicle
2.1. Reference frames

In order to obtain the quad rotor model, we need to introduce three frames, as follow:

The inertial frame, $F_i = (\vec{x}_i, \vec{y}_i, \vec{z}_i)$, is an earth-fixed coordinate system with the origin located on the ground, for example, at the base station. By convention, the x-axis points towards the north, the y-axis points towards the east, and the z-axis points towards the center of the earth.

The body frame, $F_b = (\vec{x}_b, \vec{y}_b, \vec{z}_b)$, with its origin located at the center of gravity (COG) of the quad rotor, and its axes aligned with the quad rotor structure such that the x-axis $\vec{x}_b$ is along the arm with front motor, the y-axis $\vec{y}_b$ is along the arm with right motor, and the z-axis $\vec{z}_b = \vec{x}_b \times \vec{y}_b$, where '$\times$' denotes the cross-product.

The vehicle frame, $F_v = (\vec{x}_v, \vec{y}_v, \vec{z}_v)$, is the inertial frame with the origin located at the COG of the quad rotor. The vehicle frame has two variations, F_ϕ and F_θ. F_ϕ is the vehicle frame, F_v, rotated about its z-axis $\vec{z}_v$ by an angle ψ so that $\vec{x}_v$ and $\vec{y}_v$ are aligned with $\vec{x}_b$ and $\vec{y}_b$, respectively. F_θ is the frame F_ϕ rotated about its y-axis, $\vec{y}_\phi$, by a pitching angle, θ, such that $\vec{x}_\phi$ and $\vec{z}_\phi$ are aligned with $\vec{x}_b$ and $\vec{z}_b$, respectively. Figure 2 shows these main frames [23].

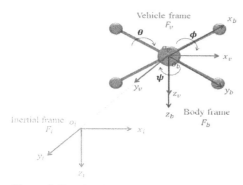

Figure 2. Inertial, body and vehicle frames [23].

2.2. Quad rotor kinematics

If we define $P_F^T = \left[p_x, p_y, -p_z \right]$ as quad rotor position and $\Omega_F^T = [\phi, \theta, \psi]$ as the orientation within a given frame, then the correlation between the quad rotor speeds in the three pre-defined frames can be stated as [23]:

$$\begin{bmatrix} \dot{p}_x \\ \dot{p}_y \\ -\dot{p}_z \end{bmatrix}_{F_i} = \begin{bmatrix} \dot{p}_x \\ \dot{p}_y \\ \dot{p}_z \end{bmatrix}_{F_v} = \left[R_{F_v}^{F_b} \right]^T \begin{bmatrix} \dot{p}_x \\ \dot{p}_y \\ \dot{p}_z \end{bmatrix}_{F_b} \quad (1)$$

where, $\left[R_{F_v}^{F_b} \right]^T$ is the rotational matrix mapping the F_b frame to the F_v frame and is defined as:

$$\left[R_{F_v}^{F_b} \right]^T =$$

$$\begin{bmatrix} C\theta C\psi & S\varphi S\theta C\psi - C\phi S\psi & C\varphi S\theta C\psi + S\phi S\psi \\ C\theta S\psi & S\varphi S\theta S\psi + C\phi C\psi & C\varphi S\theta S\psi - S\phi C\psi \\ -S\theta & S\phi C\theta & C\phi C\theta \end{bmatrix} \quad (2)$$

where, 'S' stands for 'Sin' and 'C' stands for 'Cos', for simplicity. The relation between the angular speeds in the body and the vehicle frames can be obtained using the rotational matrixes, as follows:

$$\begin{bmatrix} \dot{\phi} \\ \dot{\theta} \\ \dot{\psi} \end{bmatrix}_{F_b} = R_{F_\phi}^{F_b}(\phi) \begin{bmatrix} \dot{\phi} \\ 0 \\ 0 \end{bmatrix} + R_{F_\phi}^{F_b}(\phi) R_{F_\theta}^{F_\phi}(\theta) \begin{bmatrix} 0 \\ \dot{\theta} \\ 0 \end{bmatrix} +$$

$$R_{F_\phi}^{F_b}(\phi) R_{F_\theta}^{F_\phi}(\theta) R_{F_\psi}^{F_\theta}(\psi) \begin{bmatrix} 0 \\ 0 \\ \dot{\psi} \end{bmatrix} \quad (3)$$

where:

$$R_{F_\theta}^{F_\phi}(\theta) = \begin{bmatrix} 1 & 0 & 0 \\ 0 & cos\phi & sin\phi \\ 0 & -sin\phi & cos\phi \end{bmatrix} \quad (4)$$

$$R_{F_\psi}^{F_\theta}(\psi) = \begin{bmatrix} cos\theta & 0 & -sin\theta \\ 0 & 1 & 0 \\ sin\theta & 0 & cos\theta \end{bmatrix} \quad (5)$$

$$R_{F_\phi}^{F_b}(\phi) = R_{F_\theta}^{F_b}(\theta) = R_{F_\psi}^{F_b}(\psi) = I \quad (6)$$

Therefore,

$$\begin{bmatrix} \dot{\phi} \\ \dot{\theta} \\ \dot{\psi} \end{bmatrix}_{F_b} = \begin{bmatrix} 1 & 0 & -sin\theta \\ 0 & cos\phi & sin\phi cos\theta \\ 0 & -sin\phi & cos\phi cos\theta \end{bmatrix} \begin{bmatrix} \dot{\phi} \\ \dot{\theta} \\ \dot{\psi} \end{bmatrix}_{F_v} \quad (7)$$

It follows that:

$$\begin{bmatrix} \dot{\phi} \\ \dot{\theta} \\ \dot{\psi} \end{bmatrix}_{F_v} = \begin{bmatrix} 1 & sin\phi tan\theta & cos\phi tan\theta \\ 0 & cos\phi & -sin\phi \\ 0 & sin\phi sec\theta & cos\phi sec\theta \end{bmatrix} \begin{bmatrix} \dot{\phi} \\ \dot{\theta} \\ \dot{\psi} \end{bmatrix}_{F_b} \quad (8)$$

The quad rotor equations of motion can be described by (1) and (7).

2.3. Quad rotor dynamics

Before getting into the quad rotor dynamic model based on the Newton- Euler formalism, we need to make some assumptions as:

- Quad rotor is a solid body.
- It has a symmetrical frame.
- Its center of gravity is the center of the rigid body.

The moment of inertia is calculated by supposing the quad rotor as a central sphere of radius r and mass M_o encircled by four point masses representing the motors. Each motor is assumed to have a mass m and joined to the central sphere through an arm of length l. As mentioned earlier, a quad rotor is symmetric about its three axes, and, consequently the inertial matrix is symmetric:

$$J = \begin{bmatrix} j_x & 0 & 0 \\ 0 & j_y & 0 \\ 0 & 0 & j_z \end{bmatrix} \tag{9}$$

Dynamic of the quad rotor in the presence of external forces applied on its center of gravity in the body frame can be derived based on the Newton-Euler formalism, as follows:

$$\begin{bmatrix} MI_{3\times3} & 0 \\ 0 & I_{3\times3} \end{bmatrix} \begin{bmatrix} \ddot{P}_{F_b} \\ \dot{\Omega}_{F_b} \end{bmatrix} + \begin{bmatrix} \dot{\Omega}_{F_b} \times M\dot{P}_{F_b} \\ \dot{\Omega}_{F_b} \times J\dot{\Omega}_{F_b} \end{bmatrix} = \begin{bmatrix} F_{F_b} \\ \tau_{F_b} \end{bmatrix} \tag{10}$$

where, M refers to the total mass of the quad rotor and $F^T = \begin{bmatrix} f_x, f_y, f_z \end{bmatrix}$ and $\tau^T = \begin{bmatrix} \tau_\phi, \tau_\theta, \tau_\psi \end{bmatrix}$ are the applied external force and the torque vectors on the quad rotor center of gravity. Therefore, the transitional and rotational dynamic model would be [23]:

$$\begin{bmatrix} \ddot{p}_x \\ \ddot{p}_y \\ \ddot{p}_z \end{bmatrix}_{F_b} = \begin{bmatrix} \dot{\psi}\dot{p}_y - \dot{\theta}\dot{p}_z \\ \dot{\phi}\dot{p}_z - \dot{\psi}\dot{p}_x \\ \dot{\theta}\dot{p}_x - \dot{\phi}\dot{p}_y \end{bmatrix}_{F_b} + \frac{1}{M}\begin{bmatrix} f_x \\ f_y \\ f_z \end{bmatrix}_{F_b} \tag{11}$$

$$\begin{bmatrix} \ddot{\phi} \\ \ddot{\theta} \\ \ddot{\psi} \end{bmatrix} = J^{-1} \left\{ \begin{bmatrix} 0 & \dot{\psi} & -\dot{\theta} \\ -\dot{\psi} & 0 & \dot{\phi} \\ \dot{\theta} & -\dot{\phi} & 0 \end{bmatrix} J \begin{bmatrix} \dot{\phi} \\ \dot{\theta} \\ \dot{\psi} \end{bmatrix} + \begin{bmatrix} \tau_\phi \\ \tau_\theta \\ \tau_\psi \end{bmatrix} \right\} =$$

$$\begin{bmatrix} \dfrac{j_y - j_z}{j_x}\dot{\theta}\dot{\psi} \\ \dfrac{j_z - j_x}{j_y}\dot{\phi}\dot{\psi} \\ \dfrac{j_x - j_y}{j_z}\dot{\phi}\dot{\theta} \end{bmatrix}_{F_b} + \begin{bmatrix} \dfrac{1}{j_x}\tau_\phi \\ \dfrac{1}{j_y}\tau_\theta \\ \dfrac{1}{j_z}\tau_\psi \end{bmatrix}_{F_b} \tag{12}$$

2.4. Torques and aerodynamic forces

With the kinematic and dynamic model mentioned above, we will be able to define the forces and torques applied on the quad rotor. The forces include the aerodynamic lift generated by each rotor and the gravitational force acting in the opposite direction of the generated total lift. The moments are comprised of the torques generated to obtain the roll, pitch, and yaw movements [23].

Total thrust: the total thrust of the quad rotor is the sum of each propeller thrust:

$$T = T_f + T_r + T_b + T_l \tag{13}$$

Roll torque: this torque can be generated when the thrust of the left rotor increases, while the right thrust decreases:

$$T_\phi = l(T_l - T_r) \tag{14}$$

Pitch torque: this torque is produced by increasing the front rotor thrust and decreasing the rear rotor thrust at the same time:

$$T_\theta = l(T_f - T_b) \tag{15}$$

Yaw torque: this torque, which causes the quad rotor to revolve around its z axis, stems from the clockwise rotation of the front and rear rotors in conjunction with the counter-clockwise of the right and left rotors. In other words, it is the sum of the torques generated by four rotors:

$$\tau_\psi = \tau_f + \tau_b + \tau_r + \tau_l \tag{16}$$

Gravity force or weight: along with other forces, this force is applied on the quad rotor center of gravity. In the vehicle frame, it is represented as:

$$W_{F_v} = \begin{bmatrix} 0 \\ 0 \\ Mg \end{bmatrix} \tag{17}$$

where, g is the gravitational constant. If we map this force from the vehicle frame to the body frame, it can be re-written as follows:

$$W_{F_b} = R_{F_v}^{F_b} \begin{bmatrix} 0 \\ 0 \\ Mg \end{bmatrix} = \begin{bmatrix} -Mg\sin\theta \\ Mg\cos\theta\sin\phi \\ Mg\cos\theta\cos\phi \end{bmatrix} \tag{18}$$

Finally, dynamic equations of the quad rotor considering these forces and torques can be summarized as:

$$\begin{bmatrix} \ddot{p}_x \\ \ddot{p}_y \\ \ddot{p}_z \end{bmatrix}_{F_b} = \begin{bmatrix} \dot{\psi}\dot{p}_y - \dot{\theta}\dot{p}_z \\ \dot{\phi}\dot{p}_z - \dot{\psi}\dot{p}_x \\ \dot{\theta}\dot{p}_x - \dot{\phi}\dot{p}_y \end{bmatrix} + \begin{bmatrix} -g\sin\theta \\ g\cos\theta\sin\phi \\ g\cos\theta\cos\phi \end{bmatrix} + \begin{bmatrix} 0 \\ 0 \\ \dfrac{-f_z}{M} \end{bmatrix} \tag{19}$$

$$\begin{bmatrix} \ddot{\phi} \\ \ddot{\theta} \\ \ddot{\psi} \end{bmatrix}_{F_b} = \begin{bmatrix} \dfrac{j_y - j_z}{j_x} \dot{\theta}\dot{\psi} \\ \dfrac{j_z - j_x}{j_y} \dot{\phi}\dot{\psi} \\ \dfrac{j_x - j_y}{j_z} \dot{\phi}\dot{\theta} \end{bmatrix} + \begin{bmatrix} \dfrac{1}{j_x} \tau_\phi \\ \dfrac{1}{j_y} \tau_\theta \\ \dfrac{1}{j_z} \tau_\psi \end{bmatrix} \tag{20}$$

3. Quad rotor controller design

The proposed controller can control the quad rotor position and attitude, simultaneously. Our aim is to reach the control states $\left(p_x, p_y, p_z\right)$ and Ψ to their desired values ($p_{xd} = 10\,m$, $p_{yd} = 10\,m$, $p_{zd} = 25\,m$, $\Psi_d = \dfrac{\pi}{6}$ rad), and keep the roll and pitch angles close to zero. The control strategy can be seen in figure 3.

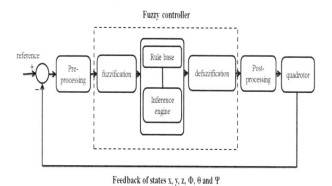

Figure 3. Control strategy [23].

The supposed PWM_{mot} is denoted as the PWM of the front motor (f), back motor (b), left motor (l), and right motor (r). Then the relation between the torques and thrust and PWM_{mot} can be expressed as:

$$T_{mot} = K_T \times PWM_{mot} \tag{21}$$

$$\tau_{mot} = K_\tau \times PWM_{mot} \tag{22}$$

where K_T and K_τ are the dependent parameters of the motors. Hence, we obtain:

$$\begin{bmatrix} PWM_f \\ PWM_r \\ PWM_b \\ PWM_l \end{bmatrix} = G \times \begin{bmatrix} T \\ \tau_\phi \\ \tau_\theta \\ \tau_\psi \end{bmatrix} \tag{23}$$

with:

$$G = \begin{bmatrix} K_T & K_T & K_T & K_T \\ 0 & -l \times K_T & 0 & l \times K_T \\ l \times K_T & 0 & -l \times K_T & 0 \\ -K_\tau & K_\tau & -K_\tau & K_\tau \end{bmatrix}^{-1} \tag{24}$$

In order to aim for the controlling goal, six fuzzy controllers are required. The inference engine implemented in the fuzzy controllers is the Mamdani fuzzy model using the min-max operator for the aggregation and the centroid of area method for defuzzification. All of these controllers have an error, which is the difference between the actual value of a state and its desired value, and the error rate as their inputs. The former is normalized to the interval [-1,1], and the latter is normalized to the interval [-3,3] based on the actuators range. The block diagram of the flight control is depicted in figure 4.

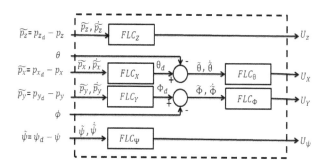

Figure 4. Flight control block diagram.

Each fuzzy controller has three triangular fuzzy membership functions for its each input and one output. Note that the fuzzy membership functions are chosen triangular due to their less sensitivity to the noise and easy implementation [24]. Therefore, nine fuzzy rules can be defined as shown in figure 5. For example, as shown in this figure, the following rule can be defined:

If error (e) is Negative (N) and error rate ($\dot{e}$) is Positive (P), then U is Zero (Z).

$\dot{e}$ \ e	N	Z	P
N	N	N	Z
Z	N	Z	P
P	Z	P	P

Figure 5. Table of fuzzy rules.

The desired angles ϕ_d and θ_d are not explicitly provided but are continuously predicted by FLC_y and FLC_x. As depicted earlier in figure 3, the pre-processing block is responsible for the calculation and normalization of the error and error rate, and the post-processing block employs the output signals of the fuzzy controllers to achieve the PWM value of each motor [23]:

$$PWM_f = Sat(U_z + U_x - U_\psi + Offset)$$

$$PWM_r = Sat(U_z + U_Y + U_\psi + Offset)$$

$$PWM_b = Sat(U_z - U_X - U_\psi + Offset) \qquad (25)$$

$$PWM_l = Sat\left(U_z - U_Y + U_\psi + Offset\right)$$

where, 'offset' is a prior-biased that counteracts the quad rotor weight. The PWM values are confined to a maximum threshold that is highly dependent on the maximum speed of the motors.

4. Membership function optimization
4.1. Genetic algorithm (GA)
GA, as a population-based algorithm, is probably the most popular algorithm due to its widespread applications in complex problems and parallelism. It also has applications in fuzzy systems [25-27]. This algorithm is inspired by the mechanism of natural selection. In a typical GA, every potential solution of a problem is regarded as a chromosome. The chromosome degree of the "goodness" is determined by its fitness value. Each GA initiates with a population of chromosomes. The chromosomes with higher fitness value are more likely to be selected and go through the next parts of the GA cycle, which are crossover and mutation that help the algorithm to culminate in a new generation. A typical GA works as follows [28]:

1. Initiate with a randomly produced population of n chromosomes.
2. Calculate each chromosome fitness.
3. Repeat the following steps until n off-springs have been generated:
    a. Select a pair of chromosomes from the population with less fitness values (for the minimization purpose).
    b. Perform cross-over to the pair to form two new off-springs.
    c. Mutate the two off-springs, and put the resulting chromosome in the new population.

4. Replace the current population with the new one.
5. Go to step 2.

4.2. Particle swarm optimization (PSO)
PSO is inspired by the social behavior of birds. A typical PSO starts with a swarm of particles in a multi-dimensional search space, where each particle represents a potential solution of the problem. Each particle has a position and speed,

which are modified according to (29) and (28), respectively. A particle position is updated according to its best personal position (Bbest) and the best global position of all particles (Gbest), according to (26) and (27):

$$x_i^p(k+1) = \begin{cases} x_i^p(k) & \text{if } f(x_i(k+1)) > f(x_i^p(k)) \\ x_i(k+1) & \text{if } f(x_i(k+1)) \le f(x_i^p(k)) \end{cases} \qquad (26)$$

$$x_g = \min\{x_i^p(k)\} \qquad (27)$$

$$v_i(k+1) = \eta \times v_i(k) + c_1 r_1(k) \times \left(x_g - x_i(k)\right)$$
$$+ c_2 \times r_2(k)\left(x_i^p - x_i(k)\right) \qquad (28)$$

where, η is the inertia factor or each particle momentum, $x_i(k)$ is the current position of particle i, $r_1(k)$ and $r_2(k) \sim U(0,1)$ are random values in the range $[0,1]$, c_1, c_2 are positive weighting constants representing the importance of Gbest and Pbest, respectively, and v_i is restricted to its maximum and minimum value.

The position of particle i is updated as [29]:

$$x_i(k+1) = x_i(k) + v_i(k+1) \qquad (29)$$

The search mechanism of PSO according to what was stated above can be seen in figure 6. PSO application in a fuzzy system can be seen in the literature [30-33].

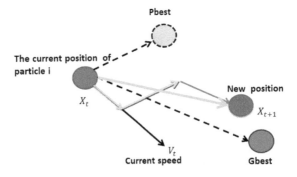

Figure 6. Search mechanism of PSO.

4.3. Problem statement
For the optimization purpose of the fuzzy membership functions, we need to define the parametric fuzzy membership functions. In order to reduce the computational efforts, all of the six fuzzy controllers are assumed identical with the same parametric fuzzy membership functions. Hence, by introducing two parameters like a and b for each membership function of a fuzzy

controller, as illustrated in figure 7, the total number of parameters to be optimized will be six.

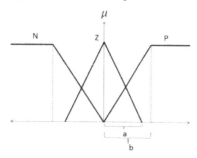

Figure 7. Parameters defined for fuzzy membership functions.

The objective function that should be minimized in order to obtain the fuzzy membership function parameters is chosen as Integral Time Square Error (ITSE):

$$cost = \int_0^t t(ee^T)dt \qquad (30)$$

where, e is the vector including the errors of the states and t denotes the simulation time. This objective function penalizes larger errors more heavily than smaller errors, and can produce the fast settling time.

5. Simulation results

In this section, we present the simulation results derived using the GA and PSO algorithms applied on the fuzzy controllers in the MATLAB software.

The GA and PSO specifications used in the simulation can be seen in tables 1 and 2.

Table 1. Specifications of GA.

Mutation	Cross-over	Selection	Stopping criteria	Population size
Constraint dependent	Scattered	Stochastic uniform	After 200 generations	100

Table 2. Specifications of PSO.

Iterations	c_1, c_2	η	Population size
40	2	1	2^6

The optimized fuzzy membership functions of the fuzzy controllers using GA and PSO can be seen in figure 8.

The blue graph indicates the fuzzy membership functions of the GA algorithm and the red graph shows the fuzzy membership functions of the PSO algorithm.

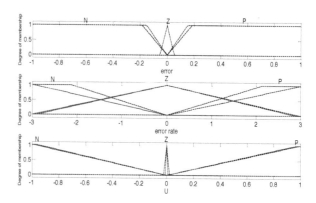

Figure 8. Optimized fuzzy membership functions using GA (blue graph) and PSO (red graph).

Figures 9 and 10 represent the positions and angles of the quad rotor derived from optimized fuzzy controllers with GA and PSO, respectively.

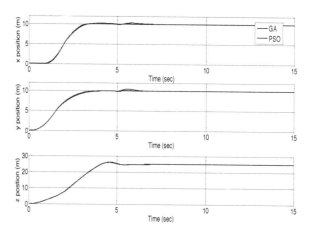

Figure 9. Positions of quad rotor.

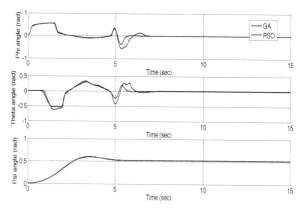

Figure 10. Angles of quad rotor.

We can observe in figures 9 and 10 that all states converged into their desired value ($x_d = 10m$, $y_d = 10m$, $z_d = 25m$, $\psi_d = \frac{\pi}{6}rad$, $\phi_d \approx 0rad$, $\theta_d \approx 0rad$) after a short time. According to figure 9 percent of overshoot is negligible (almost zero). Generally, the position and orientation controls with both GA and PSO depict almost close and satisfactory results.

Table 3 shows the objective function values and total simulation times of the proposed algorithms.

Table 3. Final results of GA and PSO.

Algorithm	Fitness value	Simulation time (s)
GA	8.1102×10^4	3.0045×10^4
PSO	8.054×10^4	2.597×10^4

According to table 3, PSO has both a less fitness value and a less simulation time compared to GA.

Figure 11 illustrates the evolution of fitness vs. total individuals in GA.

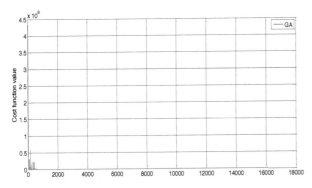

Figure 11. Evolution of fitness value vs. total individuals in GA.

Figure 12 illustrates the evolution of fitness value vs. iterations in PSO algorithm.

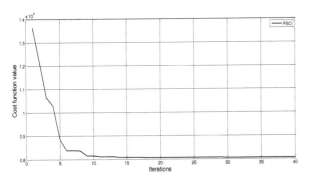

Figure 12. Evolution of fitness value vs. iterations in PSO.

Observing figures 11 and 12 shows that the cost function decreases until it converges a specific value, and this means that those algorithms results will no longer experience improvement.

In order to validate the performance of the fuzzy control approach with optimized membership functions, we define a trajectory comprises x_d and y_d as ramp functions with slope 1 and z_d as a step function. Figure 13 presents the quad rotor trajectory in a 3D space. The optimized fuzzy membership functions are tuned based on PSO.

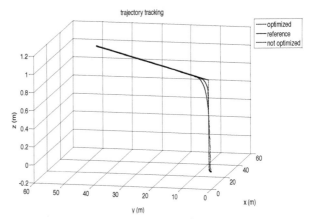

Figure 13. Flight trajectory.

As shown in figure 13, the quad rotor tracking capability has improved with the optimized fuzzy control approach in terms of a faster settling and a rise time.

6. Conclusion

In this paper, the problem of quad rotor flight control was addressed. A fuzzy logic control approach, which does not require the exact mathematical model and has the ability to compensate for the uncertainties and handle non-linearities, was proposed to control the position and orientation of the quad rotor. It comprises six individual fuzzy controllers with Mamdani inference engine. Owing to the high dependence of the fuzzy controllers' performance on their fuzzy membership functions and eliminating the need for the time-consuming trial and error approach, we defined specific parameters for each membership function, and tuned them through minimization of the proposed objective function employing GA and PSO. The investigation of these optimization algorithms applied on the fuzzy controllers was conducted in MATLAB. We compared two proposed methods and observed from the results obtained that both designed fuzzy controllers possess almost close satisfactory performance in the translational and angular quad rotor movement control. To be more specific, considerably small and negligible percent of overshoot and short rise and settling time can be seen in the quad rotor position responses. However when we compared the proposed methods under careful scrutiny, we observed that PSO had a lower fitness value and simulation time. Hence, it can be concluded that the PSO performance outclasses the GA performance in terms of fitness value and simulation time in this case study. Finally, a trajectory was defined to validate the tracking performance of the designed fuzzy controllers whose fuzzy membership functions were optimized by PSO. The simulation result showed that the designed controllers yielded satisfactory performance in term of faster settling and rise time compared to the not optimized fuzzy controllers.

References

[1] Su, J., Fan, P., & Cai, K. (2011). Attitude control of quadrotor aircraft via nonlinear PID. Journal of Beijing University of Aeronautics and Astronautics, vol. 37, no. 9, pp. 1054-1058.

[2] Zhang, Z., & Cong, M. (2011). Controlling quadrotors based on linear quadratic regulator. Applied Science and Technology, vol. 5, pp. 38-42.

[3] Besnard, L., Shtessel, Y. B., & Landrum, B. (2012). Quadrotor vehicle control via sliding mode controller driven by sliding mode disturbance observer. Journal of the Franklin Institute, vol. 349, no. 2, pp. 658-684.

[4] C Diao, C., Xian, B., Yin, Q., Zeng, W., Li, H., & Yang, Y. (2011). A nonlinear adaptive control approach for quadrotor UAVs. In Control Conference (ASCC), 8th Asian Control, Taiwan, pp. 223-228.

[5] Bouabdallah, S., & Siegwart, R. (2005). Backstepping and sliding-mode techniques applied to an indoor micro quadrotor. In Proceedings of the 2005 IEEE international conference on robotics and automation, pp. 2247-2252.

[6] Li, Y., & Song, S. (2012). A survey of control algorithms for quadrotor unmanned helicopter. In Advanced Computational Intelligence (ICACI), 2012 IEEE Fifth International Conference on, pp. 365-369.

[7] Ha, C., Zuo, Z., Choi, F. B., & Lee, D. (2014). Passivity-based adaptive backstepping control of quadrotor-type UAVs. Robotics and Autonomous Systems, vol. 62, no. 9, pp. 1305-1315.

[8] Liu, H., Bai, Y., Lu, G., Shi, Z., & Zhong, Y. (2014). Robust tracking control of a quadrotor helicopter. Journal of Intelligent & Robotic Systems, vol. 75, no. 3-4, pp. 595-608.

[9] Taniguchi, T., Eciolaza, L., & Sugeno, M. (2014). Quadrotor control using dynamic feedback linearization based on piecewise bilinear models. In 2014 IEEE Symposium on Computational Intelligence in Control and Automation (CICA), pp. 1-7.

[10] Araar, O., & Aouf, N. (2014). Quadrotor control for trajectory tracking in presence of wind disturbances. In Control (CONTROL), 2014 UKACC International Conference on, pp. 25-30. IEEE, 2014.

[11] Zhang, Y., Xu, B., & Li, H. (2015). Adaptive neural control of a quadrotor helicopter with extreme learning machine. In Proceedings of ELM-2014 Volume 2. Springer International Publishing, pp. 125-134.

[12] Petruševski, I., & Rakić, A. (2014). Simple fuzzy solution for quadrotor attitude control. In Neural Network Applications in Electrical Engineering (NEUREL), 2014 12th Symposium on. IEEE, pp. 93-98.

[13] Fakurian, F., Menhaj, M. B., & Mohammadi, A. (2014). Design of a fuzzy controller by minimum controlling inputs for a quadrotor. In Robotics and Mechatronics (ICRoM), 2014 Second RSI/ISM International Conference on. IEEE, pp. 619-624.

[14] Yacef, F., Bouhali, O., & Hamerlain, M. (2014). Adaptive fuzzy backstepping control for trajectory tracking of unmanned aerial quadrotor. InUnmanned Aircraft Systems (ICUAS), 2014 International Conference on, Orlando, FL, USA, pp.920-927.

[15] Gao, H., Liu, C., Guo, D., & Liu, J. (2015). Fuzzy adaptive PD control for quadrotor helicopter. In Cyber Technology in Automation, Control, and Intelligent Systems (CYBER), 2015 IEEE International Conference on, pp. 281-286.

[16] Choi, Y. C., & Ahn, H. S. (2015). Nonlinear control of quadrotor for point tracking: Actual implementation and experimental tests. IEEE/ASME transactions on mechatronics, vol. 20, no.3, pp. 1179-1192.

[17] Zhao, B., Xian, B., Zhang, Y., & Zhang, X. (2015). Nonlinear robust adaptive tracking control of a quadrotor UAV via immersion and invariance methodology. IEEE Transactions on Industrial Electronics, vol. 62, no. 5, pp.2891-2902.

[18] Islam, S., Liu, P. X., & El Saddik, A. (2015). Robust control of four-rotor unmanned aerial vehicle with disturbance uncertainty. IEEE Transactions on Industrial Electronics, vol. 62, no. 3, pp. 1563-1571.

[19] Herrera, M., Chamorro, W., Gómez, A. P., & Camacho, O. (2015). Sliding Mode Control: An approach to Control a Quadrotor. In Computer Aided System Engineering (APCASE), 2015 Asia-Pacific Conference on. IEEE, pp. 314-319.

[20] Basri, M. A. M., Husain, A. R., & Danapalasingam, K. A. (2014). Robust chattering free backstepping sliding mode control strategy for autonomous quadrotor helicopter. International Journal of Mechanical & Mechatronics Engineering, vol. 14, no. 3, pp. 36-44.

[21] Margun, A., Bazylev, D., Zimenko, K., & Kremlev, A. (2015). Trajectory-tracking control design and modeling for quadrotor aerial vehicles. In Control and Automation (MED), 2015 23th Mediterranean Conference on. IEEE, pp. 273-277.

[22] Yesildirek, A., & Imran, B. (2014). Nonlinear control of quadrotor using multi Lyapunov functions. In 2014 American Control Conference. IEEE, pp. 3844-3849.

[23] Raza, S. A. (2010). Design and control of a quadrotor unmanned aerial vehicle (Doctoral dissertation, University of Ottawa (Canada)).

[24] Wang, L. X. (1999). A course in fuzzy systems. Prentice-Hall press, USA.

[25] Surmann, H. (1996). Genetic optimization of a fuzzy system for charging batteries. IEEE Transactions on Industrial Electronics, vol. 43, no. 5, pp. 541-548.

[26] Arslan, A., & Kaya, M. (2001). Determination of fuzzy logic membership functions using genetic algorithms. Fuzzy sets and systems, vol. 118, no. 2, pp. 297-306.

[27] Sabzi, H. Z., Humberson, D., Abudu, S., & King, J. P. (2016). Optimization of adaptive fuzzy logic controller using novel combined evolutionary algorithms, and its application in Diez Lagos flood controlling system, Southern New Mexico. Expert Systems with Applications, vol. 43, pp. 154-164.

[28] Martínez-Soto, R., Castillo, O., & Castro, J. R. (2014). Genetic algorithm optimization for type-2 non-singleton fuzzy logic controllers. In Recent Advances on Hybrid Approaches for Designing Intelligent Systems . Springer International Publishing, pp. 3-18.

[29] Maldonado, Y., Castillo, O., & Melin, P. (2013). Particle swarm optimization of interval type-2 fuzzy systems for FPGA applications. Applied Soft Computing, vol. 13, no.1, pp. 496-508.

[30] Shi, Y., & Eberhart, R. C. (2001). Fuzzy adaptive particle swarm optimization. In Evolutionary Computation, 2001. Proceedings of the 2001 Congress on . IEEE., vol. 1, pp. 101 - 106.

[31] Esmin, A. A. A., Aoki, A. R., & Lambert-Torres, G. (2002). Particle swarm optimization for fuzzy membership functions optimization. InSystems, Man and Cybernetics, 2002 IEEE International Conference on, vol. 3, pp. 6-pp.

[32] Safari, S., Ardehali, M. M., & Sirizi, M. J. (2013). Particle swarm optimization based fuzzy logic controller for autonomous green power energy system with hydrogen storage. Energy conversion and management, vol. 65, pp. 41-49.

[33] F. Soleiman Nouri, M. Haddad Zarif and M. M. Fateh (2014). Designing an adaptive fuzzy control for robot manipulators using PSO, Journal of AI and Data Mining (JAIDM), vol. 2, no. 2, pp. 125-133.

8

A topology control algorithm for autonomous underwater robots in three-dimensional space using PSO

Z. Amiri*, A. A. Pouyan and H. Mashayekhi

Department of Computer & IT Engineering, University of Shahrood, Shahrood, Iran.

Corresponding author: z_amiri@shahroodut.ac.ir (Z. Amiri).

Abstract

Data collection from seabed by means of underwater wireless sensor networks (UWSN) has recently attracted considerable attention. Autonomous underwater vehicles (AUVs) are increasingly used as UWSNs in underwater missions. Events and environmental parameters in underwater regions have a stochastic nature. Sensors to observe and report events must cover the target area. A 'topology control algorithm' characterizes how well a sensing field is monitored and how well pairs of sensors are mutually connected in UWSNs. It is prohibitive to use a central controller to guide AUVs' behavior due to ever changing, unknown environmental conditions, limited bandwidth and lossy communication media. In this research, a completely decentralized three-dimensional topology control algorithm for AUVs is proposed. It is aimed at achieving maximal coverage of the target area. The algorithm enables AUVs to autonomously decide on and adjust their speed and direction based on the information collected from their neighbors. Each AUV selects the best movement at each step by independently executing a Particle Swarm Optimization (PSO) algorithm. In the fitness function, the global average neighborhood degree is used as the upper limit of the number of neighbors of each AUV. Experimental results show that limiting number of neighbors for each AUV can lead to more uniform network topologies with larger coverage. It is further shown that the proposed algorithm is more efficient in terms of major network parameters such as target area coverage, deployment time, and average travelled distance by the AUVs.

Keywords: *Underwater Sensor Networks, AUV, PSO Algorithm, Three-dimensional Topology Control, Distributed Artificial Intelligence.*

1. Introduction

Underwater world has an enormous impact on human civilization as it highly affects climate change, food security, minerals and natural resources [1]. However, we still know very little about the underwater environment. Underwater Sensor Networks (UWSNs) provide a promising window of insight and observation that is expected to fill this void. The main mission of an UWSN is to monitor a target field and to detect events. Controlling topology characterizes how well a sensing field is monitored and how well each pair of sensors is mutually connected in WSNs [2]. Controlling topology has a direct impact on the design of wireless sensor networks. Several topology design methods have been proposed in the last decade to control the structures of 2D wireless networks. However, very few studies target design of topologies for 3D wireless sensor networks. The 3D environment introduces new challenges to topology design for UWSNs in terms of coverage, connectivity, and other constraints. The topology control algorithm proposed in this paper, attempts to address several of these constraints, namely distributed control, coverage and connectivity.

Autonomous Underwater Vehicles (AUV) have been used in underwater missions. AUVs can function without tethers, cables, or remote control. They have a multitude of applications in undersea environments. Previous experimental work has shown the feasibility of relatively inexpensive AUV submarines equipped with multiple underwater sensors that can reach any depth in the ocean [3]. This vehicle could independently create an intelligent choice about its next movement location using its neighbors' local information and on-board intelligence without human guidance [4]. The benefits of exploiting a group of AUVs as opposed to single application, become evident when considering performance, costs, fault tolerance and re-configurability [5]. It is prohibitive to use a central controller to guide AUVs' behavior due to ever changing, unknown environmental conditions, limited bandwidth and lossy communication mediums [6].

Zou at el. [4] introduced a three-dimensional topology control mechanism based on the Genetic Algorithm (3D-GA) as a solution for the dispersion of AUVs operating in Underwater Sensor Networks. The goal of their algorithm is to maximize the coverage over a given 3D target field. The proposed algorithm in this paper extends the previous work by the use of Particle Swarm Optimization (PSO) algorithm and considers a global average neighborhood degree as an upper limit on the number of neighbors for each AUV. The proposed algorithm is completely decentralized and utilizes PSO for stepwise decision on AUVs movements. The PSO algorithm is employed to decide on and adjusts the AUV's speed and direction. In the fitness function, the global average neighborhood degree is used as the upper limit of number of neighbors of each AUV. Nodes with higher degrees are more likely to become bottlenecks in the communication graph. Lower node degrees reduce the traffic interference [7]. Therefore, adjusting a node degree can result in better AUV topologies. The algorithm is evaluated in terms of coverage percentage, deployment time and average traveled distance by the AUVs using the Aqua-Sim simulator [8]. Comparing with 3D-GA [4], we show that the algorithm enables AUVs to reach larger coverage with smaller node degrees.

The rest of this paper is organized as follows: Section 2 provides a review on research about AUVs, PSO and other techniques used for topology control in three-dimensional environments, particularly UWSNs. In section 3, the motivation and goal of the research, the UWSNs model and PSO algorithm are introduced. In section 4, the proposed topology control strategy is introduced. In section 5, the results of simulation experiments are presented. Section 6 is devoted to conclusions and future work.

2. Related work

Many WSN applications utilize PSO for various tasks. PSO was introduced by Kennedy and Eberhart [9]. It is a simple and efficient optimization algorithm. It has been applied to address various issues in WSN such as optimal deployment, node localization, clustering and so on. Wang et al. [10] have proposed a virtual force co-evolutionary PSO for dynamic deployment of nodes for the enhanced coverage. Gopakumar et al. [11] have proposed PSO-Loc for localization of n target nodes out of m nodes based on the a priori information of locations of m-n beacons. The approach does not take into account the issues of localization of the nodes that do not have at least three beacons in their neighborhood. Wimalajeewa et al. [12] address the problem of optimal power allocation through constrained PSO. AUVs have been widely used in many commercial and military task s [13] [14], [15] .A behavior fusion method for the navigation of a multi-AUV system in uncertain environments with obstacle avoidance ability is presented [16]. In [17], multi-AUV system represents a new state-estimator capable of determining the 3D position of a fish tagged with small, off-the-shelf acoustic transmitters. An algorithm that guides AUVs to protect harbor entrances, underwater surfaces of large maritime vessels and other civilian, and military assets are introduced in [18].

Topology control for WSNs and UWSNs has been studied in different research. Li et al. [2], provided an overview of topology control techniques. It classified existing topology control techniques into two categories: network coverage and network connectivity. Network coverage describes how well the target field is monitored by the sensor network. It is divided into three categories: blanket coverage [19], barrier coverage [20] , and sweep coverage [21]. Once a sensor network is deployed, system operators must know the network condition from time to time. To this end, the plenty of networking services serves as a bridge between the network and system operators, such as flooding, data collection [22], [23], [24] information aggregation [25] and so on. The essence of those operations is to maintain good connectivities of pairs of communicating sensor nodes temporally and spatially. Thus, in the network connectivity, two types of mechanisms have been utilized to maintain an efficient sensor connectivity topology: power management mechanisms (i.e., the temporal control) [26], [27] and power control mechanisms (i.e., the temporal control) [28].

Urrea et al. [29] implemented dynamical system model for force-based genetic algorithm which could be used as a topology control algorithm to achieve a uniform deployment of autonomous mobile nodes over an unknown two-dimensional area. In the work of Kusyk et al. [30], a topology control algorithm that makes use of game theory and genetic algorithms for faster deployment of mobile nodes compared with FGA in a two dimensional environment is presented. Three-dimensional topology control, compared to two-dimensional approaches, has a wider range of applications especially for many commercial and military missions in underwater environments. Zou et al. introduced a three-dimensional genetic algorithm-based topology control mechanism (3D-GA) as a solution for the dispersion of AUVs operating in Underwater Sensor Networks [4].

The average neighborhood degree or mean node degree is considered in different papers [31], [32], [33]. Urrea et al. [32] introduced different GA applications for knowledge sharing bio-inspired mobile agents to obtain a uniform distribution of the nodes over an area. The main objectives are to obtain a uniform distribution over the given area, to provide the agents with a balanced number of neighbors, and to improve NAC. This article proposed an analytical model to calculate the mean node degree to be used in the fitness evaluations.

3. Prerequisites

In this section, we describe the major challenges in UWSN and the motivation and goals for our approach, and also briefly describe the PSO algorithm.

3.1. Challenges in UWSN

Some major challenges for the topology control in UWSNs are as follows [4]:

- The communication among AUVs should be kept at minimum because of the limited available communication bandwidth.
- The movements of AUVs are arbitrary. Thus, the network topology can have unpredictable changes.
- Bit error rate when communicating among AUVs in underwater environments is much higher than comparable terrestrial distance communications. AUVs may experience down-time or limited communication ranges due to malfunctions or destruction from harsh underwater environments.

3.2. Motivation and goals

To monitor an underwater target area, AUVs should be uniformly distributed such that the maximum coverage is achieved. Each AUV can monitor a limited surrounding area by means of its

sensor devices. In this paper, a sphere with radius R is considered as both the sensing and communication areas. The degree of an AUV is defined as the number of its neighbors, i.e. the AUVs are within its communication range. Figure 1 shows an example where AUVs protect a specific area. They can detect an unknown object in their sensing area (e.g., a sea mine) and will send the obtained information to a data collection point. Here, an AUV self-positioning approach is introduced to achieve the uniform distribution in the target area. There are three main objectives for the proposed algorithm.

- The first objective is achieving maximal coverage of the target area.
- The second objective is to keep the network connectivity among the AUVs by preventing the isolated AUV(s) in the network.
- The third objective is limiting the upper bound of node degree to achieve larger coverage of the target area. In addition, nodes with a high degree have a high likelihood of becoming bottlenecks in the communication graph and lower node degrees reduce the traffic interference [7].

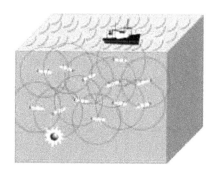

Figure 1. Several AUVs protecting an area.

3.3 PSO Algorithm

Particle swarm optimization [9] is a heuristic global optimization method. It is inspired by natural life, like bird flocking, fish schooling and random search methods of evolutionary algorithms. It can be observed from the nature that animals, especially birds, fish, etc. always travel in a group without colliding. This is because each member follows the group by adjusting its position and velocity using the group information. Thus, it reduces individual's effort for searching of food, shelter, etc. [34].

PSO consists of a population (called a swarm) of candidate solutions (called particles). System is initialized with a population of random solutions. All the particles have a fitness value, which can be calculated using a fitness function. The fitness function in a PSO evaluates the relative goodness of the particles in each iteration. All the particles preserve their individual best performance (pBest). They also know the best performance of their group. They adjust their velocity considering their best performance and also considering the best performance of the best particle (gBest). The velocity and position of the particle are calculated according to (1) and (2). These equations are borrowed from [35]. The various steps of a PSO are depicted in the flowchart shown in Figure 2.

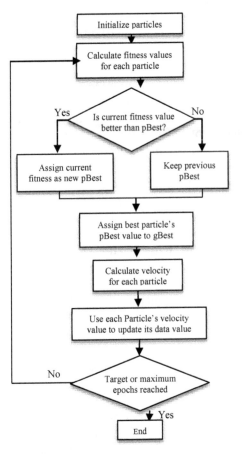

Figure 2. Flowchart of PSO algorithm.

$$v_i^{k+1} = \omega v_i^k + c_1 r_1^k \left(pBest_i^k - x_i^k\right) \\ + c_2 r_2^k (gBest^k - x_i^k)$$ (1)

In (1), v_i^k and x_i^k stand for the velocity vector and position of the particle i at time k respectively. $pBest_i^k$ is the solution with the best fitness that particle i has obtained up to time k. $gBest^k$ is the solution with the best fitness among all particles up to time k. c_1 and c_2 are acceleration coefficients that represent the likelihood of the particle choosing its own solution or following the behavior of the swarm. Usually, c_1 is equal to c_2 and they are equal to 2. r_1 and r_2 are uniformly distributed random numbers in the range of [0,1] and these values are regenerated for each velocity update. ω is the inertia weight. The influence that the last speed has on the current speed can be

controlled by inertia weights. According to experiments, ω is confined from 0.9 to 0.4 according to the linear decrease [35]. The position of the particle within the search space is iteratively updated by adding a velocity vector to the current position using (2).

$$x_i^{k+1} = x_i^k + v_i^{k+1}$$ (2)

4. Proposed method
In this section, a statistical analysis for approximating average neighborhood degree and the proposed topology control algorithm are introduced.

4.1. Statistical analysis for average neighborhood degree
A statistical analysis is described to obtain the average neighborhood degree of AUVs in a uniform distribution on the 3D target area. The objective is to approximate the optimum number of neighbors depending on the network density, communication range and environment size. The topology control algorithm uses this value as the upper limited number of neighbors of each AUV. In the experiments, it is shown that limiting number of neighbors for each AUV can lead to more uniform network topologies with larger coverage of the target area.

Consider two nodes located randomly in a 3D environment with volume V. The probability of one node being in the communication range of the other is defined as follows:

$$P_c = \frac{\frac{4}{3}\pi R^3}{V}$$ (3)

The probability of a node having k neighbors in a region with volume V will then follow the binomial distribution shown in (4).

$$P_c^{(k)} = \binom{N-1}{k}(P_c)^k(1-(P_c))^{N-1-k}$$ (4)

In (4), N is the number of nodes, k is number of neighbor and P_c is obtained from (3). Hence, the average number of neighbor nodes can be calculated as follows:

$$d_{ave} = \sum_{k=0}^{N-1} kP_c^{(k)} =$$

$$\sum_{k=0}^{N-1} k\binom{N-1}{k}(P_c)^k(1-(P_c))^{N-1-k}$$ (5)

To illustrate the concept, the average neighbor degree for 10-50 nodes with communication range [10m-20m] located in a 50*50*50 space, is plotted in Figure 3. This figure shows when the number of AUVs or communication range increase, the average neighbors degree also increase.

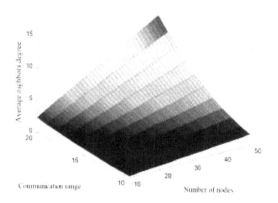

Figure 3. Average neighbors degree in r=[10,20], N=[10,50] and S=50*50*50.

4.2. Topology control algorithm

In this section, we present the proposed topology control algorithm to achieve maximum and uniform distribution, while maintaining the network connectivity. The topology control algorithm proceeds in rounds. In each round, each AUV transmits its location and the number of neighbors to the nodes in its neighborhood. Based on this local information from the neighbors, each AUV executes one iteration of its local PSO (each AUV executes a version of the PSO independently). PSO generates the next movement locations that are more optimally situated. If it can not find a position to improve uniformity, the AUV remains in its current location.

PSO is a swarm of particles. Each particle represents a potential solution composed of the next movement direction and speed of the vehicle. The fitness of each particle is computed. The AUV then selects the best solution in the current generation and performs the movement if fitness is improved; otherwise, the vehicle remains in its current position. This algorithm allows AUVs to adapt their movements while basing their decisions only on local information extracted from their surroundings. Thus, they do not use a centralized infrastructure.

4.2.1. Particles in PSO

As mentioned, each AUV can move freely in the three-dimensional space. Each particle has a velocity vector $v = (V_x, V_y, V_z)$. V_x, V_y and V_z represent velocity in the x, y and z dimensions respectively. Therefore, a particle includes the next movement direction and speed of the AUV in a 3D Cartesian space. Initially, PSO randomly generates n candidate particles within the maximum travelled distance in one step (D_{max}).

Without loss of generality, we selected D_{max} to be equal to R in our implementation. The position of the particle within the target area is iteratively updated by adding the velocity vector to its position through using (1) and (2) in section 3.2. In each generation if fitness is improved, the AUV selects the best particle in the current generation and performs movement to new position according to velocity vector of best particle. In this paper, c_1 and c_2 are both equal to 2 and the inertia weight is set to higher values at the beginning of search process, and reduced gradually in each iteration (0.9-0.4).

4.2.2 Fitness function

The PSO algorithm running on an AUV generates several candidate solutions in each iteration. Fitness function is used to evaluate the relative goodness of each solution. Here, the fitness function is based on the distance between an AUV and its neighbors, degree of neighbors and the average neighborhood degree. For each particle (solution), the new position of the AUV after one time unit adhering to the movement suggested by the best particle, can be calculated from (2).

Assuming this new position for AUV and re-computing distances to its current neighbors, the partial fitness of the AUV relative to neighbor j (F_j) can be computed by (6). This is borrowed from [4].

$$F_j = \begin{cases} F_{max} & \text{if } \delta_j > R \text{ and } d_j = 1 \\ \dfrac{R_{int}}{\delta_j} - 1 & \text{if } 0 < \delta_j < R_{int} \\ 0 & \text{if } R_{int} \le \delta_j \le R \end{cases} \quad (6)$$

In (6), R is the communication range of the AUV, R_{int} is an internal margin close to R, δ_j is the AUV's Euclidean distance to the jth neighbor, d_j is the degree of the jth neighbor and F_{max} is the maximum penalty fitness.

In order to maximize the coverage of a limited number of AUVs, it is desirable to locate the AUVs as far as possible from each other. However, as the connectivity of the AUVs should be maintained and isolating AUVs is prohibited. Therefore, in the partial fitness function, neighbors positioned very close to the AUV will receive larger (worse) values compared with those located farther away (but still within communication range). The best partial fitness belongs to neighbors with distance between R_{int} and R illustrated in Figure 4.

Total fitness F for each candidate solution in an AUV with degree d, is calculated as the sum of all the partial fitness values (7). If degree of the AUV is larger than a threshold, the solution is less appropriate. This penalty is considered to force uniform distribution of AUVs. d^{th}, calculated in (8), is set to be one unit larger than the average neighborhood degree (d_{ave}) discussed in section 4.1.

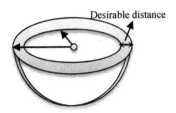

Figure 4. Desirable distance of AUVs from each other.

$$F = \begin{cases} \sum_{j=1}^{d} F_j & \text{if } 1 \leq d \leq d_{th} \\ (d_{th})^4 + \sum_{j=1}^{d} F_j & \text{if } d > d_{th} \\ F_{max} & \text{otherwise} \end{cases} \quad (7)$$

$$d_{th} = round(d_{ave} + 1) \quad (8)$$

5. Evaluation
5.1. Performance metrics
The performance metrics used for evaluation in this research are described below.

- Deployment time

Total deployment (DT) time is defined as the duration from the initial placement of AUVs within an unknown space until convergence of the algorithm [4]. Total deployment time is an important performance metric for the evaluation of node self-positioning approaches in time-critical situations in civilian and military applications.

- Normalized Volumetric Coverage

Normalized Volumetric Coverage (NVC) defines the amount of space covered by vehicles with respect to the size of the total deployment space [6] . We define that a point p (xp, y_p, z_p) is covered by the ith AUV located at (x_i, y_i, z_i) if their mutual distance is less than the communication range R *as* declared in (9).

$$\sqrt{(x_i - x_p)^2 + (y_i - y_p)^2 + (z_i - z_p)^2} < R \quad (9)$$

NVC is the ratio between the volume of the region covered by AUVs and the total target space. The

percentage of the space covered by all the AUVs is given in (10). V_i is a region covered by i^{th} AUV and V is the volume of the target space.

$$NVC = \frac{(\cup_{i=1}^{N} V_i)}{V} \quad (10)$$

NVC is a positive real number with maximum value of 1. When NVC is 1, the space is completely covered by the AUVs.

- Average Travelled Distance

The average travelled distance by each node is related to the required energy for its movement [36]. Thus, one important metric assessing performance of node self-spreading algorithms is ATD. Since movement is a highly power-consuming operation, reducing the traveling distance for each node is an important task. This task can significantly extend the lifespan of a network [37]. Let $D(A_i^0, A_i^t)$ denote the total distance traveled by the ith AUV up to time t. We define ATD (t) as the average distance traveled by nodes until time t as (11).

$$ATD(t) = \frac{1}{N} \sum_{i=1}^{N} D(A_i^0, A_i^t) \quad (11)$$

5.2. Experimental results
We evaluate performance of our algorithm by implementing the simulations in the Aqua-Sim simulator. This simulator is developed on the basis of NS-2 for UWSNs. In what follows, we consider several settings in which a team of AUVs enters an unknown geographical space. For all settings, AUVs are initially deployed randomly in the environment.

The approximation value of coverage with respect to the number of AUVs is examined. In the next part, the performance of the algorithm with and without the degree bound is examined. When degree is not bounded, the first two conditions of (7) are combined in the first condition and d_{th} is ignored. Then, the impact of reducing mobility of AUVs in each step is examined. In the last part, performance of the algorithm is compared with 3D-GA [4]. The parameters of the experiments are shown in
Table 1.

5.2.1. Coverage
In this experiment, the goal is to find the approximate coverage in space with respect to number of AUVs. Number of AUVs is varied from 14 to 30. Each experiment is repeated ten times and the average NVC is reported in Figure 5. When the number of nodes is increased, NVC grows and with at least 28 AUVs, 99 percent of

the space is covered. In the next experiments, we will use 28 AUVs in the environment.

Table 1. Parameters in all experiments.

Parameter	Description	Values (Default)
N	Number of AUVs	14-30(28)
R	Communication range	10
S	Dimension of the target space	30*30*30
R_{int}	The internal communication margin	9

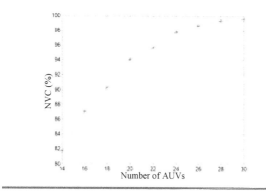

Figure 5. NVC versus number of AUVs.

5.2.2. The effect of bounding the node degrees

In this experiment, 28 AUVs are considered with two approaches of bounded and unbounded node degrees. Figure 6 and 7 present the results of the two approaches, respectively.

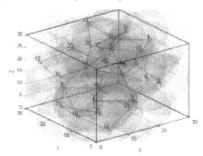

Figure 6. Final distribution of AUVs (bounded node degree).

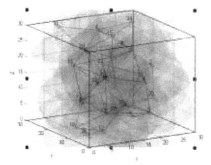

Figure 7. Final distribution of AUVs (unbounded degree).

In Figure 8, the percentage of NVC respect to time step is shown. With the limited node degree, the percentage of NVC is 99.67% and with unlimited degree, value is 96.10%. Thus, by penalizing the fitness based on the node degree we

can improve NVC in space. Figure 9 represents ATD with respect to time steps. Deployment time can also be achieved from this diagram. When limiting node degree the value of ATD is 54m and deployment time is 38s. Without limiting node degree ATD is 40.24m and the deployment time is 33s. The Result shows when limiting node degree ATD and DT will increase. Therefore, a tradeoff exists between shorter travel with faster deployment and maximal coverage.

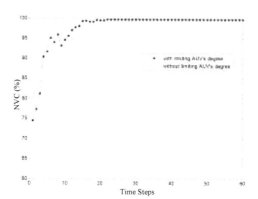

Figure 8. NVC vs. time step with and without limiting AUV's degree.

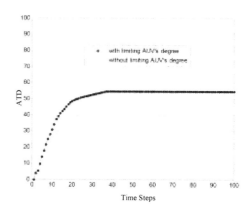

Figure 9. ATD vs. time step with and without limiting AUV's degree.

5.2.3. Impact of reducing AUV's movement

Results from previous experiment show that with limiting node degrees, ATD increases. Since movement is a highly power-consuming operation, reducing the traveling distance for each node is an important task. Here, we propose a method for reducing ATD, in which running PSO and changing location in each step is performed with probability p in each AUV.

Three scenarios are considered to compare with the impact of reducing AUV's movement. In the first scenario, node degrees are not bounded (scenario 1), in the second experiment they are bounded (scenario 2), and in last scenario degree of AUVs is bounded and in each step AUVs move with p=0.7 (scenario 3). This value is obtained empirically.

For each scenario, we repeated the experiment ten times, and the results are shown in Table 3-4. For each scenario, the average of NVC, ATD and DT are displayed in Table 5. Scenario one has least travelled distance and deployment time, but the final coverage is less. Comparing scenarios two and three, results show that when reducing AUV's

movement, the average travelled distance decreases considerably, though NVC slightly decreases. However, the deployment time also increases to some extent. Thus, in situations where energy is more important than time, the strategy of scenario 3 can be used. As previously noted, a tradeoff exists between shorter travelled distanced with faster deployment and maximal coverage.

Table 2. Results of ten experiments with scenario 1 (unbounded node degree).

Test Number	1	2	3	4	5	6	7	8	9	10
ATD(DT)	57.29	34.11	42.28	30.88	29.52	40.28	40	41.49	30.46	44.05
NVC(DT)	94.29	97.07	96.9	95.65	96.51	96.15	94	96.35	95.67	96.73
DT	48	38	39	28	32	31	33	32	37	31

Table 3. Results of ten experiments with scenario 2 (bounded node degree).

Test Number	1	2	3	4	5	6	7	8	9	10
ATD(DT)	48.41	63	68.61	55.66	39.81	45.9	67.49	37.41	65.08	60.1
NVC(DT)	99.89	99	99.04	99.1	99.48	99.4	99.02	99.01	99.44	99.39
DT	30	41	49	35	26	39	50	32	42	36

Table 4. Results of ten experiments with scenario 3 (bounded node degree and p=0.7).

Test Number	1	2	3	4	5	6	7	8	9	10
ATD(DT)	50.87	38	48.82	39.31	27.37	31.1	41.27	57.63	45.83	51.89
NVC(DT)	98.76	99	99.02	98.28	99.42	98.33	98.87	99.06	98.68	99.98
DT	42	52	56	32	30	35	41	45	39	49

Table 5. Average of NVC, ATD and DT for 3 scenario.

	Unbounded node degree (scenario 1)	Bounded node degree (Scenario 2)	Bounded node degree and p=0.7 (scenario 3)
NVC	95.94	99.29	98.97
ATD	39.01	55.11	43.189
DT	34.9	38	42.1

5.2.4. Comparison with 3D-GA

In this experiment, we compare our algorithm using the three scenarios described before, with 3D-GA [4]. We implemented 3D-GA in Aqua-Sim. 3D-GA is repeated (with parameters of Table 1) ten times and the average NVC, ATD and DT are presented in Table 6. Results show 3D-GA has smaller NVC and DT after convergence and DT with respect to all the three scenarios of our algorithm (Table 5) but AUVs travel longer to converge with respect to scenarios 1 and 3 and they travel shorter with respect to scenario 2.

At last we consider 4 experiments with scenarios 1-3 and 3D-GA. The diagram of NVC and ATD for these experiments is shown in Figure 10 and Figure 11, respectively. (In 3D-GA all AUVs are initially deployed along the x-axis, so initial value of NVC for 3D-GA is smaller than our methods.)

Table 6. Average of NVC, ATD and DT for 3D-GA.

NVC	ATD	DT
92.31	48.6	25

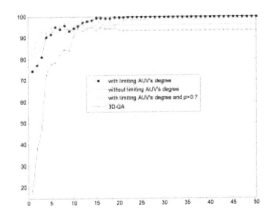

Figure 10. NVS vs. time step for scenarios 1-3 and 3D-GA.

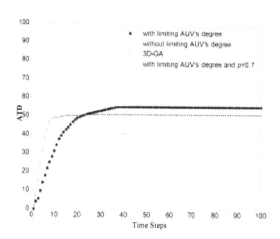

Figure 11. NVS vs. time step for scenarios 1-3 and 3D-GA.

6. Conclusion and directions for future research

In this paper, we proposed a three-dimensional PSO algorithm to operate as a decentralized topology control mechanism for AUVs. The proposed algorithm does not require a central control unit. It runs autonomously at each AUV to adjust its speed and direction. AUVs actively collect information from their neighbors to decide on their location. We also introduced a fitness function, which tends to bind the degree of nodes based on average neighborhood degree. This enhanced capacity is used to provide a near-optimum number of neighbors depending on the network density.

The method is quite capable of establishing an efficient topology. It has been revealed by a performance analysis in terms of metrics such as average coverage, travelled distance and deployment time. The experimental results based on simulation shows that by limiting AUV's degree, spatial coverage is increased. This consequently reduces the traffic interferences. It is achieved at the price of increased travelled distance and coverage time. Therefore, a tradeoff exists between shorter travel distances with faster deployment, and maximal coverage. By applying the proposed method travelled distance decreases, coverage time has significantly been increased. Hence, this strategy establishes a significant tradeoff between energy consumption and coverage time. Enhancing the PSO fitness function through introducing the impact of energy consumption in fitness remains as a direction for future research. Another research direction should be focused on assessing the impact of removal of AUVs due to hostile activities or malfunction of some AUVs.

References

[1] Abbas, W. b., Ahmed, N., Usama, C. & Syed, A. A. (2014). Design and evaluation of a low-cost, DIY-inspired, underwater platform to promote experimental research in UWSN. Ad Hoc Networks, Elsevier, In Press, 2014.

[2] Li, M., Li, Z. & Vasilakos, A. (2013). A Survey on Topology Control in Wireless Sensor Networks: Taxonomy, Comparative Study, and Open Issues. Proceedings of the IEEE , vol. 101, no. 12, pp. 2538 – 2557.

[3] Akyildi, I. F., Pompili, D. & Melodia, T. (2005). Underwater acoustic sensor networks research challenges. Ad Hoc Networks, vol. 3, pp. 257-279.

[4] Zou, J., Gundry, S., Kusyk, J. & Uyar, M. (2013). 3D genetic algorithms for underwater sensor networks. Ad Hoc and Ubiquitous Computing, vol. 13, pp. 10-22.

[5] Sorbi, L., De Capua, G. P., Fontaine, J.-G. & Toni, L. (2012). A Behavior-Based Mission Planner for Cooperative Autonomous Underwater Vehicles. Marine Technology Society Journal, vol. 46, no.2, pp. 32-44, 2012.

[6] Zou, J., Gundry, S., Kusyk, J., Sahin, C. & Uyar, U. (2012). Particle Swarm Optimization based Topology Control Mechanism for Holonomic Unmanned Vehicles Operating in Three-dimensional Space. in Sarnoff Symposium (SARNOFF), Newark, NJ, (2012).

[7] Chiwewe, T. & Hancke, G. (2011). A Distributed Topology Control Technique for Low Interference and Energy Efficiency in Wireless Sensor Networks. Industrial Informatics, IEEE Transactions on , vol. 8, no. 1, pp. 11-19, 2011.

[8] Xie, P., Zhou, Z., Peng, Z. & Yan, H. (2009). Aqua-Sim: An NS-2 based simulator for underwater sensor networks. OCEANS 2009, MTS/IEEE Biloxi - Marine Technology for Our Future: Global and Local Challenges, Biloxi, MS 2009.

[9] Kennedy, J. & Eberhart, R. (1995). Particle swarm optimization. in Proceedings of the IEEE International Conference on Neural Networks, vol. 4, pp. 1942–1948., 1995.

[10] Wang, X., Wang, S. & Ma, J. J. (2007). An improved co evolutionary particle swarm optimization for wireless sensor networks with dynamic deployment. Sensors, vol. 7, pp. 354–370.

[11] Gopakumar, A. & Jacob, L. (2008). Localization in wireless sensor networks using particle swarm optimization. in in Proceedings of the IET International Conference on Wireless, Mobile and Multimedia Networks 2008. pp. 227–230.

[12] Wimalajeewa, T. & Jayaweera, S. K. (2008). Optimal power scheduling for correlated data fusion in wireless sensor networks via constrained PSO," IEEE Trans. Wireless Commun., vol. 7, no 9, pp. 3608–3618.

[13] Hagen, P., Fossum, T. & Hansen, R. (2008). Applications of AUVs with SAS. in Proceedings of OCEANS 2008, Quebec City, QC, 2008.

[14] Sariel, S., Balch, T. & Stack, J. (2006). Distributed multi-AUV coordination in naval mine countermeasure Missions. Georgia Institute of Technology, 2006.

[15] Pentzer, J., Crosbie, B., Bean, T., Canning, J., Frenzel, J., Anderson, M. & Edwards, D. (2010). Measurement of magnetic field using collaborative AUVs. in Proceedings of OCEANS, Sydney, 2010.

[16] Kang, X. D., Xu, H. L. & Feng, X. S. (2009). Fuzzy logic based behavior fusion for multi-AUV formation keeping in uncertain ocean environment. in in Proc. OCEANS, MTS/IEEE Biloxi—Marine Technol. Future, Global Local Challenges, pp. 1–7., 2009.

[17] Yukun, L., Kastein, H., Peterson, T. & White, C. (2014). A multi-AUV state estimator for determining the 3D position of tagged fish. in Intelligent Robots and Systems (IROS 2014), Chicago, IL, 2014.

[18] Jianmin, Z., Gundry, S., Kusyk, J. & Sahin, C. (2013). Bio-inspired topology control mechanism for autonomous underwater vehicles used in maritime surveillance. in EEE International Conference Technologies for Homeland Security (HST), 2013.

[19] Wang J. & Zhong, N. (2006). Efficient point coverage in wireless sensor networks. J. Combinat. Optim, pp. 291-304.

[20] Saipulla, A., Westphal, C., Liu, B. & Wang, J. (2013). Barrier coverage with line-based deployed mobile sensors. Ad hoc Networks, vol. 11, no. 4, pp. 1381–1391, 2013.

[21] Min, X., Kui, W., Yong, Q. & Jizhong, Z. (2009). Run to Potential: Sweep Coverage in Wireless Sensor Networks in IEEE Int. Conf. Parallel Process, Vienna, 2009.

[22] Yao, Y., Qing, C. & Vasilakos, A. (2013). EDAL: An Energy-Efficient, Delay-Aware, and Lifetime-Balancing Data Collection Protocol for Wireless Sensor Networks. Mobile Ad-Hoc and Sensor Systems (MASS), 2013 IEEE 10th International Conference on, pp.182-190, 14-16 Oct. 2013.

[23] Yao, Y., Cao, Q. & Vasilakos, A. (2014). An Energy-Efficient, Delay-Aware, and Lifetime-Balancing Data Collection Protocol for Heterogeneous Wireless Sensor Networks. Networking, IEEE/ACM Transactions on (Volume:PP , Issue: 99), vol. 23, no. 3, pp. 810-823, 2014.

[24] Liu, X.-Y., Zhu, Y., Kong, L., Liu, C., Gu, Y., Vasilakos, A. & Wu, M.-Y. (2014). CDC: Compressive Data Collection for Wireless Sensor Networks. IEEE Transactions on Parallel & Distributed Systems, vol. 26, no. 8, pp. 2188-2197.

[25] Liu, X., Jun, L. & Vasilakos, A. (2011) Compressed data aggregation for energy efficient wireless sensor networks. in Sensor, Mesh and Ad Hoc Communications and Networks (SECON), Salt Lake City, UT, 2011.

[26] Sengupta, S., Das, S., Nasir, M., Vasilakos, A. V. & Pedrycz, W. (2012). An Evolutionary Multiobjective Sleep-Scheduling Scheme for Differentiated Coverage in Wireless Sensor Networks. IEEE Transactions on Systems, Man, and Cybernetics, Part C, vol. 42, no. 6, pp. 1093-1102.

[27] Han, K., Luo, J., Liu, Y. & Vasilakos, A. V. (2013). Algorithm Design for Data Communications in Duty-Cycled Wireless Sensor Networks: A Survey. Communications Magazine, IEEE, vol. 51, no.7, pp. 107-113.

[28] Rodoplu, V. & Meng, T. (1999). Minimum energy mobile wireless networks. IEEE J. Sel. Areas Commun., vols. 17, no. 8, pp. 1333–1344.

[29] Urrea, E., Sahin, C. S., Uyar, M. U., Conner, M., Bertoli, G. & Pizzo, C. (2010). Estimating behavior of a GA-based topology control for self-spreading nodes in manets. Proceedings of International Conference on Military Communications (MILCOM), 2010.

[30] Kusyk, J., Urrea, E., Şahin, C. Ş. & Uyar, M. Ü. (2011). Game theory and genetic algorithm based approach for self-positioning of autonomous nodes. Ad Hoc & Sensor Wireless Networks, vol. 6, pp. 119-138.

[31] Hökelek, İ., Uyar, M. & Fecko, M. (2005). Random-Walk based Analysis of Virtual Backbone in Manets. Communications and Computer Networks , Marina del Rey, CA, USA, 2005.

[32] Urrea, E., Şahin, C. Ş., Hökelek, İ., Uyar, M. Ü., Connera, M., Bertolic, G. & Pizzo, C. (2009). Bio-inspired topology control for knowledge sharing mobile agents. Ad Hoc Networks, vol. 7, no. 4, pp. 677–689.

[33] Bettstetter, C. (2002). On the Minimum Node Degree and Connectivity of a Wireless Multihop Network. MobiHoc Proceedings of the 3rd ACM International Symposium on Mobile ad Hoc Networking & Computing; , New York, NY, USA., 2002.

[34] Kuila, P. & Jana, P. K. (2014). Energy efficient clustering and routing algorithms for wireless sensor networks: Particle swarm optimization approach. Engineering Applications of Artificial Intelligence, vol. 33, pp. 127–140.

[35] Bai, Q. (2010). Analysis of Particle Swarm Optimization Algorithm. Computer and Information Science, Vols. 3, No 1, pp. 180-184.

[36] Heo, N. & Varshney, P. (2003). A Distributed Self Spreading Algorithm algorithm for mobile wireless sensor networks. in Wireless Communications and Networking, 2003. WCNC 2003. 2003 IEEE (Volume:3), New Orleans, LA, USA, 2003.

[37] Gundry, S., Kusyk, J., Zou, J. & Sahin, C. (2012). Performance evaluation of differential evolution based topology control method for autonomous MANET nodes. in Computers and Communications (ISCC), 2012 IEEE Symposium on, Cappadocia, 2012.

9

Sub-transmission sub-station expansion planning based on bacterial foraging optimization algorithm

H. Kiani Rad and Z. Moravej*

Faculty of Electrical & Computer Engineering, Semnan University, Semnan, Iran.

Corresponding author: zmoravej@semnan.ac.ir (Z. Moravej).

Abstract

In the recent years, significant research efforts have been devoted to the optimal planning of power systems. sub-station expansion panning (SEP), as a sub-system of power system planning, consists of finding the most economical solution with the optimal location and size of future sub-stations and/or feeders to meet the future load demand. The large number of design variables and combination of discrete and continuous variables make the sub-station expansion planning a very challenging problem. So far, various methods have been presented to solve such a complicated problem. Since the bacterial foraging optimization algorithm (BFOA) yield to proper results in power system studies, and it has not been applied to SEP in sub-transmission voltage level problems yet, this paper develops a new BFO-based method to solve the sub-transmission sub-station expansion planning (STSEP) problem. The technique discussed in this paper uses BFOA to simultaneously optimize the sizes and locations of both the existing and new installed sub-stations and feeders by considering reliability constraints. To clarify the capabilities of the proposed method, two test systems (a typical network and a real one) are considered, and the results of applying GA and BFOA to these networks are compared. The simulation results demonstrate that BFOA has the potential to find more optimal results than the other algorithms under the same conditions. Also the fast convergence and consideration of the real-world network limitations, as the problem constraints, and the simplicity in applying it to real networks are the main features of the proposed method.

Keywords: *Bacterial Foraging Optimization Algorithm, Genetic Algorithm, Sub-station Expansion Planning.*

1. Introduction

Along with the electric power consumption growth, new power system equipment are needed to overcome the possible lack of adequacy problems, so that with the least costs, various operational constraints are met. In the so-called sub-station expansion planning (SEP), the problem is to determine the required expansion capacities of the existing sub-stations as well as the locations and sizes of new sub-stations together with the required availability times, so that the loads can be adequately supplied [1].

Usually, according to the geographic distribution of actual consumers, the service areas of an electric power distribution system are divided into many small irregular areas, which are called "electrical domains". Each domain has a load-point showing the power consumption of customers in this domain. Moreover, there are some candidate places for installing new sub-stations as well as the possibility of expanding some of the existing ones.

Various constraints should also be observed during the optimization process such as the maximum permissible voltage drop, maximum allowable capacity of feeders, maximum permitted capacity of sub-station equipment, accessibility to upward and downward networks, and considering enough space for possible future developments [2].

The expansion cost components include new sub-station installation cost, no-load and loading loss cost in sub-stations' transformers, and also, the installation and loss cost of feeders. The solution that leads to the minimum total expansion and operational costs and satisfies the constraints is considered as the optimal solution to the SEP problem. So far, different algorithms have been developed by researchers for this purpose. Most of the existing methods can be categorized into two groups, numerical methods and heuristic ones. Mixed integer linear programming (MILP) [3,4], non-linear programming (NLP) [5], dynamic programming (DP) [6], ordinal optimization (OO) [7], and direct solution [8] are from numerical methods.

The other group consists of heuristic methods which are listed as follow.

Genetic algorithm (GA): GA is applied for the solution of the SEP problem [9-12]. SEP is solved by GA in combination with quasi-Newton [13], optimal power flow (OPF) [14], and branch exchange [15].

Tabu search (TS): The SEP problem, considering DG and uncertainties, is solved by TS with an embedded Monte Carlo simulation-based probabilistic power flow model [16]. Multi-objective TS solves a dynamic SEP [17]. TS and simulated annealing (SA) have been applied to solve SEP, and it has been concluded that TS is more efficient than SA [18].

Particle swarm optimization (PSO): The medium-voltage (MV) and low-voltage (LV) networks are simultaneously designed by a discrete PSO (DPSO) [19]. A modified DPSO solves SEP considering DG and cross-connections [20]. SEP, considering DGs and storage units, is solved by a modified PSO with local search [21]. An evolutionary PSO solves the SEP under uncertainty considering the DG units [22].

Ant colony system (ACS): A dynamic ACS algorithm solves SEP, considering the installation of DG together with the reinforcement of feeders and sub-stations [23].

Simulated annealing (SA): SEP has been solved by SA in conjunction with MILP in [24].

Artificial bee colony (ABC): ABC algorithm computes the network reinforcements and the commitment schedule for the installed generating units [25].

Shuffled frog leaping algorithm (SFLA): SFLA considers placement and sizing of DGs optimally with respect to the reliability indices improvement [26].

Practical heuristic algorithms: A minimum spanning tree method solves the feeder routing problem in distribution networks including DG [27]. A heuristic method solves SEP in order to increase the penetration of DG units [28]. SEP is solved by a branch-exchange technique in combination with minimum spanning tree [29] and DP [30]. A heuristic method for dynamic SEP has been proposed based on back-propagation of the planning procedure starting from the final year [31].

Bacterial foraging optimization (BFO): A BFO technique solves the optimal feeder routing problem [32]. The multi-stage radial distribution system expansion planning problem in the presence of the distributed generator in a multi-objective optimization framework has been addressed in [33]. The complex multi-objective optimization problem has been solved using BFO. Reference [34] analyzes the impacts of the characteristics of electricity generation and consumption of micro-grid on the distribution network losses and the reliability of electric power supply to consumers. Considering these impacts, a distribution network flexible planning model containing micro-grid has been established and solved by the bacteria colony chemotaxis (BCC). Also [35] applies the BCC algorithm to distribution network planning, and makes some improvements about the algorithm.

In [36], a new mathematical model for unified sub-station planning of two voltage levels has been presented that makes the total cost of two voltage levels as the objective function and the geographical information as the restrictive condition, while the BCC algorithm optimizes the problem.

In most of the methods proposed for SEP, the effect of uncertainty on the input parameters is ignored. However, the study of the provided papers presents such items that include uncertainty studies. Information gap decision theory, robust optimization, stochastic modeling, and fuzzy logic theory are the main methods used for applying uncertainty to input parameters [37-42].

By reviewing the previous studies, it can be concluded that the heuristic methods have many applications that can be used to solve the SEP problem. GA and PSO are the most popular heuristic algorithms, and usually, they lead to more optimal results.

According to references [33-35], it is evident that bacterial foraging optimization algorithm (BFOA) has been applied mainly to the distribution networks, and has not been applied to the sub-transmission voltage level networks. The only paper that has applied BFOA to the planning studies for high-voltage levels is Ref. [36]. The presented study is in the transmission voltage level, and it has some drawbacks like ignoring network configuration for low-voltage level and ignoring the downstream network expansion.

Since BFOA obtains proper results for power system studies [32-36, 43-46], and it has not been applied to the STSEP problem yet, this paper develops a new BFO-based method to solve the STSEP problem. The results of applying the presented method to the SEP problem are compared with those of GA and PSO as the most famous heuristic methods.

Solution of STSEP is obtained by investigating the pre-determined candidates. In this method, the candidates are obtained by dividing the area under study into certain squares, and then considering the center of each square as the candidate for a new sub-station installation. Clearly, by using smaller squares, the results become more accurate. However, this leads to more computational effort and solution time. After finding the candidates, BFOA is applied to find the best solution among the available solutions. Some important features of the proposed approach are its applicability to transmission and sub-transmission networks, its fast convergence, and having the capability of applying to large-scale networks.

This paper is organized as follows. Section 2 provides the sub-station expansion planning problem. Section 3 introduces the BFO algorithm. The results of applying the proposed method to a typical and a real network are presented in section 4. Finally, section 5 concludes the paper.

2. Sub-station expansion planning

The power system planning studies consist of studies for the next 1–10 years or higher. This planning aims to decide on installation of new equipment as well as upgrading the existing ones to adequately meet the load growth in a foreseen future [1].

This equipment may include the followings:
• Generation facilities
• Sub-stations
• Transmission lines and/or cables
• Capacitors/Reactors

This paper focuses on the case of sub-stations. The aim of sub-station expansion planning is to determine a set of decision variables including sub-stations' locations, sizes, and associated service areas with minimum expansion cost respecting technical constraints [47].

Mathematically, the problem can be defined as (1)-(6):

$$Fitness = \sum_{i=1}^{n_s} C_i^S + \sum_{i=1}^{n_s} \sum_{j=1}^{n_l} C_{ij}^F . d_{ij} . \beta_{ij}$$
$$+ \sum_{h=1}^{n_y} PW^h . \sum_{i=1}^{n_s} \sum_{j=1}^{n_l} \alpha . \gamma . \beta_{ij} . C^l . P_{ij}^{loss}$$
$$+ \sum_{h=1}^{n_y} PW^h . \sum_{i=1}^{n_s} \alpha . C^l . P_i^{iron}$$
$$+ \sum_{h=1}^{n_y} PW^h . \sum_{i=1}^{n_s} \alpha . \gamma . C^l . P_i^{cu} . \left(\frac{S_i^s}{CS_i} \right)^2 \tag{1}$$

$$PW = \frac{1 + \inf\_r}{1 + \text{int}\_r} \tag{2}$$

$$P_{ij}^{loss} = \frac{\left(S_j^l\right)^2 . d_{ij} . r_{ij}}{|V_n|^2}, \quad \forall i \in \Omega^s, \quad \forall j \in \Omega^l \tag{3}$$

$$S_i^s = \sum_{j=1}^{n_l} \beta_{ij} . \left(S_j^l + P_{ij}^{loss}\right), \quad \forall i \in \Omega^s \tag{4}$$

$$\psi^{\min} . CS_i \leq S_i^s \leq \psi^{\max} . CS_i, \quad \forall i \in \Omega^s \tag{5}$$

$$\left| \frac{S_j^l . \sum_{k=1}^{n_s} \left[\beta_{kj} . d_{kj} . z_{kj}\right]}{V_n} \right| \leq \Delta V_{\max}, \quad \forall j \in \Omega^l \tag{6}$$

where n_s is total number of selected sub-stations, n_l is number of load points, n_y is the number of years at the planning period, d_{ij} is the distance between nodes i-j (km), β_{ij} is the binary decision variable that is equal to 1 if sub-station i supplies load point j and is 0 otherwise, α is the number of hours in a year (8760), γ is the loss factor, C_i^s is the total expansion and maintenance cost of sub-station i within the planning period (\$), C_{ij}^F is the construction cost of feeder located between nodes i-j (\$/km), C^l is the per unit cost of energy loss (\$/kWh), PW is the present worth factor, P_{ij}^{loss} is the copper losses of feeder located between nodes i-j (kW), P_i^{iron} is the iron loss in sub-station i (kW), P_i^{cu} is the copper loss in sub-station i at the rated loading (kW), S_i^s is the total power provided by sub-station i (MVA), CS_i is the specified capacity of sub-station i (MVA), $\inf-r$ is the inflation rate, $\text{int}-r$ is the interest rate, S_j^l is the expected load demand at node i (MVA), r_{ij} is the resistance per length of feeder constructed between nodes i-j (Ω/km), V_n is the nominal voltage magnitude (V), Ω^s is the set of selected sub-stations (existing and proposed), Ω^l is the set of load points (electrical domains), $\psi^{\min}$ is the minimum permissible loading percentage of sub-stations, $\psi^{\max}$ is the maximum permissible loading percentage of sub-stations, Z_{ij} is the impedance per length of feeder constructed between nodes i-j (Ω/km), and $\Delta V_{\max}$ is the maximum allowed voltage drop.

The objective function of the SEP problem is presented in (1), where the terms show expansion costs of the selected sub-stations, total required cost for expanding the medium voltage feeders, total cost associated with the medium voltage feeder losses, sub-stations' no-load loss cost, and sub-stations' loading loss cost, respectively.

Equations (5) and (6) exhibit the SEP constraints. Each feeder, regarding its conductor type, is able to transfer a certain amount of power. Also due to the reliability considerations, the sub-stations should have less loading than the nominal capacity. These requirements are guaranteed by (5). Finally, constraint (6) ensures the proper supply of electric consumers with permissible voltage drop at the load points [47].

BFOA, as a powerful tool for solving the above complicated optimization problem, will be discussed in the following section.

3. Bacterial foraging optimization algorithm

BFO method was first invented by Passino [48]. This algorithm is inspired from the natural selection that tends to eliminate the animals with poor foraging strategies, and favor those having successful foraging strategies. The foraging strategy is governed basically by four processes namely chemotaxis, swarming, reproduction, elimination and dispersal [49]. According to [50], the four processes of the algorithm are as follows:

3.1. Chemotaxis

The chemotaxis process includes the characteristics of movement of bacteria in search for food, and it consists of two processes namely swimming and tumbling. A bacterium is said to be "swimming" if it moves in a pre-defined direction and "tumbling" if it moves in an altogether different direction. Let j be the index of the chemotactic step, k be the reproduction step, and l be the elimination dispersal event. Let $\theta^i(j,k,1)$ be the position of the ith bacteria at the jth chemotactic step, kth reproduction step and lth elimination dispersal event, C be the size of the step taken in the random direction specified by the tumble, and ϕ be the angle of the direction that is randomly generated in the range of $(0, 2\pi)$. The position of the bacteria in the next chemotactic step after a tumble is given by (7):

$$\theta^i(j+1,k,l) = \theta^i(j,k,l) + C \times \angle\phi \qquad (7)$$

If the health of the bacteria improves after the tumble, they will continue to swim to the same direction for the specified steps or until the health degrades.

3.2. Swarming

Bacteria exhibit a swarm behavior, i.e. a healthy bacterium tries to attract another one, so that together they reach the desired location (solution point) more rapidly. The effect of swarming is to make the bacteria congregate into groups and move as concentric patterns with a high bacterial density. In mathematical terms, the swarming behavior can be modeled as (8):

$$J_{cc}\left(\theta^i(j,k,l), \theta(j,k,l)\right) = \sum_{i=1}^{s} J_{cc}^t\left(\theta^i, \theta\theta\right)$$

$$= \sum_{t=1}^{s}\left[-d_{attract}\exp\left(-\omega_{attract}\sum_{m=1}^{p}\left(\theta^i_m - \theta^t_m\right)^2\right)\right] \qquad (8)$$

$$+ \sum_{t=1}^{s}\left[-d_{repellant}\exp\left(-\omega_{repellant}\sum_{m=1}^{p}\left(\theta^i_m - \theta^t_m\right)^2\right)\right]$$

where, $J_{cc}\left(\theta^i, \theta\right)$ is the cost function value to be added to the actual cost function to be minimized to present a time-varying cost function, s is the total number of bacteria, p is the number of parameters to be optimized, and $d_{attract}$, $\omega_{attract}$, $d_{repellant}$, and $\omega_{repellant}$ are different coefficients that must be chosen properly.

3.3. Reproduction

In this step, the population members having sufficient nutrients will reproduce, and the least healthy bacteria will die. The healthier half of the population is substituted with the other half of bacteria being eliminated, owing to their poorer foraging abilities. This keeps the population of bacteria constant in the evolution process.

3.4. Elimination-Dispersal

In the evolution process, a sudden unforeseen event may drastically alter the evolution, and may cause the elimination and/or dispersion to a new environment. Elimination and dispersal help in reducing the behavior of stagnation, i.e. being trapped in a premature solution point or local optima.

4. Numerical results

4.1. Results of applying BFOA to a typical network

In this section, a typical network is assumed, and the results of sub-station expansion planning using BFOA are obtained. In the horizon year (2020), the typical network consists of 31 load centers and 5 existing sub-stations [51]. The network parameters, feeder parameters, investment cost of the existing sub-stations, and new sub-station installation cost are presented in [51].

In this paper, the candidates are acquired by dividing the area under study into a number of small squares, and the center of each square is considered as the candidate point.

In order to compare the performance of the proposed algorithm with other methods, at first, the SEP results for the proposed network are obtained by GA and PSO as the well-known methods in SEP.

In order to make sure that GA, PSO, and BFOA have really found the best solution, the simulations are executed many times, and the best results are considered as the optimum solution.

Figure 1 depicts the results of applying GA on a typical network. After running the program, all the loads are fed by sub-stations in the horizon year. As it can be seen, six new sub-stations have been installed, and two of the existing sub-stations have been expanded. Table 1 provides more details.

After running the program, the genetic algorithm is converged after about 560 iterations in 327 seconds.

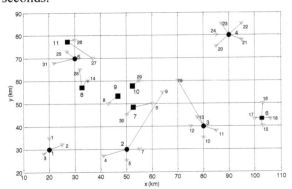

Figure 1. Results of applying GA to solve SEP problem on a typical network.

▼: Load Centers, ●: Existing Sub-stations, ■: New Sub-stations

Table 1. Detailed results of applying GA to solve SEP problem on a typical network.

Number of new installed sub-stations	6
Sum of loads	152 (MW)
Sum of the new sub-stations capacity	105 (MVA)
Installation cost of the new sub-stations	10,500,000($)
Expanded sub-stations	2,4
Sum of the old sub-stations expansion capacity	30 (MVA)
Expansion cost of the old sub-stations	860,000($)
Low-voltage expansion cost	1,125,000 ($)
Total cost of expansion	12,485,000($)

Figure 2 depicts the results of applying PSO to a typical network. After running the program, all of

the loads are fed by sub-stations in the horizon year. Six new sub-stations have been installed in the positions shown and one sub-station has been expanded. Table 2 provides more details.

After running the program, PSO is converged after about 530 iterations in 312 seconds.

In the following, the results of applying BFOA to a typical network are presented.

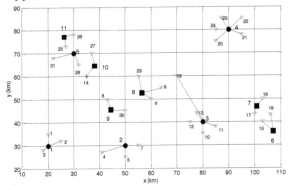

Figure 2. Results of applying PSO to solve SEP problem on a typical network.

▼: Load Centers, ●: Existing Sub-stations, ■: New Sub-stations

Table 2. Detailed results of applying PSO to solve SEP problem on a typical network.

Number of new installed sub-stations	6
Sum of loads	152 (MW)
Sum of new sub-stations capacity	120 (MVA)
Installation cost of new sub-stations	12,000,000($)
Expanded sub-stations	4
Sum of old sub-stations expansion capacity	15 (MVA)
Expansion cost of old sub-stations	430,000($)
Low-voltage expansion cost	502,000 ($)
Total expansion cost	12,932,000($)

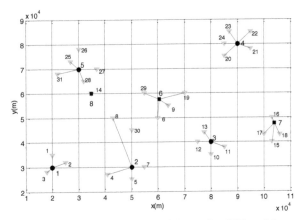

Figure 3. Results of applying BFOA to solve SEP problem on a typical network.

▼: Load Centers, ●: Existing Sub-stations, ■: New Sub-stations

figure 3 and table 3 show the results. It is clear that by installing three new sub-stations in the positions shown and by expanding two existing sub-stations, the loads will be adequately supplied in the horizon year. For more details, see table 3. After running the program, the BFO algorithm is converged after about 480 iterations in 263 seconds.

Table 3. Detailed results of applying BFOA to solve SEP problem on a typical network.

No. of new installed sub-stations	3
Sum of loads	152 (MW)
Sum of capacity of new sub-stations	90 (MVA)
Installation cost of new sub-stations	9,000,000($)
Expanded sub-stations	2,4
Sum of expansion capacity of the old sub-stations	30 (MVA)
Expansion cost of old sub-stations	860,000($)
Low-voltage expansion cost	1,575,000($)
Total expansion cost	11,435,000($)

By comparing tables 1, 2, and 3, it is clear that the expansion cost of the network by BFOA is lower. Thus, the solution presented by BFOA is preferable.

By considering the results of GA, PSO, and BFOA, it is clear that GA and PSO fall in local minima and are not as able as BFOA at solving the SEP problem. In other words, BFOA is more able than GA and PSO to find an optimal solution to SEP. Also by considering the results of GA and PSO in tables 1 and 2, it is clear that GA is better than PSO in finding an optimal solution to SEP. Therefore, in section 4.2, the BFOA results are compared with the GA results in applying to a real presented network.

4.2. Results of applying BFOA to a real network

In order to illustrate the capabilities of the proposed method, the algorithm is carried out on a real network, and the results obtained are compared with those for GA. The considered network is a part of Iran's electric grid, and consists of 92 load centers in the horizon year (2020), while the existing sub-stations are 19 [51].

Table 4. Results of applying GA to a Real network.

No. of new installed sub-stations	7
Sum of loads	328 (MW)
Sum of capacity of new sub-stations	120 (MVA)
Installation cost of new sub-stations	12 (M$)
Expanded sub-stations	6, 10
Sum of expansion capacity of old sub-stations	30 (MVA)
Expansion cost of old sub-stations	860,000($)
Low-voltage expansion cost	7,020,000($)
Low-Voltage Loss	8.8 MW
Sum expansion cost	19,880,000($)

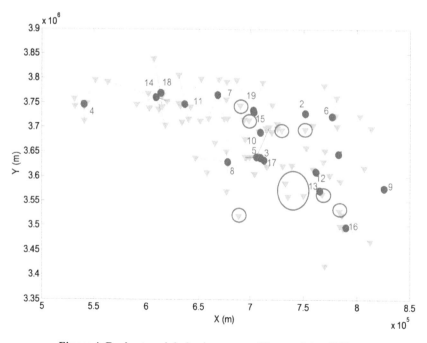

Figure 4. Real network in horizon year without solving SEP.

▼: Load Centers, ●: Existing Sub-stations, ■: New Sub-stations

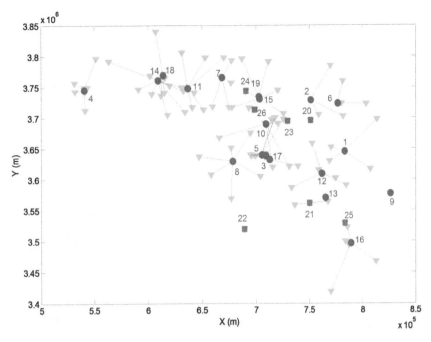

Figure 5. Results of applying GA to solve SEP problem on a real network.

▼: Load Centers, ●: Existing Sub-stations, ■: New Sub-stations

As the loads are increased in the horizon year, some of the loads are not supplied without expanding the existing network (those shown in figure 4 with a circle around them). Thus there is a need to expand the network by installing new sub-station(s) and/or by expanding some existing sub-stations.

To find the best solution to the SEP problem on the real presented network, GA and BFOA are executed on the network, and the results are illustrated in figures 5 and 6, and tables 4 and 5.

As shown in figure 5, GA solves the SEP problem by installing seven new sub-stations and by expanding two existing sub-stations. Also the total cost of the network expansion is 19,880,000 dollars. On the other hand, figure 6 shows that BFOA finds the SEP solution by installing six

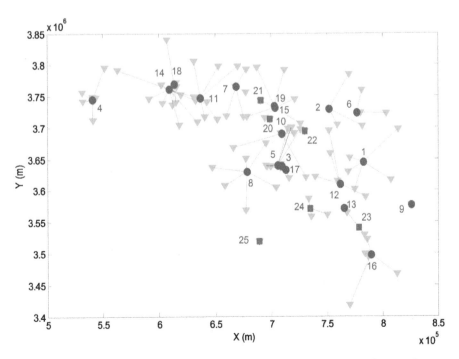

Figure 6. Results of applying BFOA to solve SEP problem on a real network.

▼: Load Centers, ●: Existing Sub-stations, ■: New Sub-stations

new sub-stations and by expanding one existing sub-station. Table 5 declares that the total cost of the network expansion by this method is 18,321,820 dollars.

Table 5. Results of applying BFOA to a real network.

No. of new installed sub-stations	6
Sum of loads	328 (MW)
Sum of capacity of new sub-stations	105 (MVA)
Installation cost of new sub-stations	10,500,000($)
Expanded sub-stations	1
Sum of expansion capacity of old sub-stations	15 (MVA)
Expansion cost of old sub-stations	430,000($)
Low-voltage expansion cost	7,391,820($)
Low-Voltage Loss	9.3 MW
Sum cost of expansion	18,321,820($)

With deeper looks at figures 5 and 6, it is obvious that sub-station No. 22 in figure 5 and sub-station No. 25 in figure 6 feed a load that the voltage droop constraint does not permit other sub-stations to feed it. Thus a new sub-station has been installed just to supply this load. Also in the horizon year, due to exhaustion, the lifetime of sub-station no. 13 is over, and no load is allocated to the sub-station. Thus, to feed the nearby loads, sub-station No. 13 has been replaced by sub-station No. 21 in figure 5, and by sub-station No. 23 in figure 6.

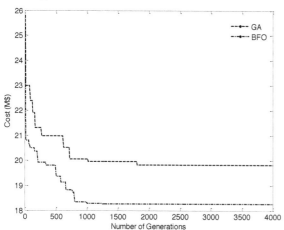

Figure 7. Convergence curve for BFOA and GA.

By comparing the results of GA and BFOA, it is clear that both methods have the ability to find proper solutions to SEP but BFOA is more able than GA to find an optimal solution to SEP. Also BFOA is faster than GA in finding the SEP results. This fact is obvious from figure 7.

According to this figure, GA is converged after about 1800 iterations and 1257 seconds, whereas BFOA is converged after about 1000 iterations and 543 seconds.

5. Conclusion

Sub-station expansion planning is one of the important parts of the power system expansion planning studies. The diversity of decision variables in the SEP problem has made the solution process more difficult. This paper introduced a new method for solving SEP as an optimization problem. The optimization method was based on BFOA. To demonstrate the capabilities of BFOA, GA and PSO were used as the benchmark methods for assessing validity. A typical and real network was assumed, and the results of SEP by the use of GA, PSO, and BFOA were obtained. The results obtained showed that GA was more capable than PSO, and BFOA was more efficient than GA in finding the solutions. The results of applying BFOA to a real network showed the functional capabilities of the presented method. Other features of this method are the capability to be applied to the sub-transmission and transmission networks, high speed of convergence, high quality of solutions, consideration of real-world network limitations as SEP constraints, and its simplicity in applying to real networks.

References

[1] Seifi, H. & Sepasian, M. S. (2011). Electric Power System Planning. Springer.

[2] Georgilakis, P. S. & Hatziargyriou, N. D. (2015). A Review of Power Distribution Planning in the Modern Power Systems Era: Models, Methods And Future Research. Electric Power Systems Research, vol. 121, pp. 89-100.

[3] Alizadeh, B. & Jadid, S. (2014). Accelerating the Composite Power System Planning by Benders Decomposition. Journal of Operation and Automation in Power Engineering, vol. 2, no. 1, pp. 1-9.

[4] Shu, J., et al. (2012). A New Method for Spatial Power Network Planning in Complicated Environments. IEEE Transactions on Power Systems, vol. 27, no. 1, pp. 381–389.

[5] Wong, S., Bhattacharya, K. & Fuller J. D. (2009). Electric Power Distribution System Design and Planning in a Deregulated Environment. IET Generation, Transmission & Distribution, vol. 3, no. 12, pp. 1061–1078.

[6] Ganguly, S., Sahoo, N. C. & Das, D. (2013). Multi-Objective Planning Of Electrical Distribution Systems Using Dynamic Programming. International Journal of

Electrical Power & Energy Systems, vol. 46, pp. 65–78.

[7] Lin, X., et al. (2014). Distribution Network Planning Integrating Charging Stations of Electric Vehicle With V2G. International Journal of Electrical Power & Energy Systems, vol. 63, pp. 507–512.

[8] Samui, A., Samantaray, S. R. & Panda, G. (2012). Distribution System Planning Considering Reliable Feeder Routing. IET Generation, Transmission & Distribution, vol. 6, no. 6, pp. 503–514.

[9] Nazar, M. S., Haghifam, M. R. & Naˇzar, M. (2012). A Scenario Driven Multi-Objective Primary–Secondary Distribution System Expansion Planning Algorithm in The Presence of Wholesale–Retail Market. International Journal of Electrical Power & Energy Systems, vol. 40, no. 1, pp. 29–45.

[10] Mendoza, J. E., López, M. E., Pena, H. E. & Labra, D. A. (2012). Low Voltage Distribution Optimization: Site, Quantity and Size of Distribution Transformers. Electric Power Systems Research, vol. 91, pp. 52–60.

[11] Chen, T. H., Lin, E. H., Yang, N. C. & Hsieh, T. Y. (2013). Multi-Objective Optimization for Upgrading Primary Feeders With Distributed Generators From Normally Closed Loop to Mesh Arrangement. International Journal of Electrical Power & Energy Systems, vol. 45, no. 1, pp. 413–419.

[12] Mendoza, J. E., López, M. E., Fingerhuth, S. C., Pena, H. E. & Salinas, C. A. (2013). Low Voltage Distribution Planning Considering Micro Distributed Generation. Electric Power Systems Research, vol. 103, pp. 233–240.

[13] Carrano, E. G., Takahashi, E., Cardoso, P., Saldanha, R. R. & Neto, O. M. (2005). Optimal Sub-station Location and Energy Distribution Network Design Using a Hybrid GA-BFGS Algorithm. IEE Proceedings-Generation, Transmission and Distribution, vol. 152, no. 6, pp. 919–926.

[14] Naderi, E., Seifi, H. & Sepasian, M. S. (2012). A Dynamic Approach for Distribution System Planning Considering Distributed Generation. IEEE Transactions on Power Delivery, vol. 27, no. 3, pp. 1313–1322.

[15] Salehi, J. & Haghifam, M. R. (2012). Long Term Distribution Network Planning Considering Urbanity Uncertainties. International Journal of Electrical Power & Energy Systems, vol. 42, no. 1, pp. 321–333.

[16] Koutsoukis, N. C., Georgilakis, P. S. & Hatziargyriou, N. D. (2014). A Tabu Search Method for Distribution Network Planning Considering Distributed Generation and Uncertainties. Proceedings of the IEEE International Conference on Probabilistic Methods Applied to Power Systems, Durham, United States, 2014.

[17] Pereira Junior, B. R., Cossi, A. M., Contreras, J. & Mantovani, J. R. S. (2014). Multi Objective Multistage Distribution System Planning Using Tabu Search. IET Generation, Transmission & Distribution, vol. 8, no. 1, pp. 35–45.

[18] Parada, V., et al. (2010). Heuristic Determination of Distribution Trees. IEEE Transactions on Power Delivery, vol. 25, no. 2, pp. 861–869.

[19] Ziari, I., Ledwich, G. & Ghosh, A. (2011). Optimal Integrated Planning of MV-LV Distribution Systems using DPSO. Electric Power Systems Research, vol. 81, no. 10, pp. 1905–1914.

[20] Ziari, I., Ledwich, G., Ghosh, A. & Platt, G. (2013). Optimal Distribution Network Reinforcement Considering Load Growth, Line Loss, and Reliability. IEEE Transactions on Power Systems, vol. 28, no. 2, pp. 587–597.

[21] Sedghi, M., Golkar, A. & Haghifam, M. R. (2013). Distribution Network Expansion Considering Distributed Generation and Storage Units Using Modified PSO Algorithm. International Journal of Electrical Power & Energy Systems, vol. 52, pp. 221–230.

[22] Samper, M. E. & Vargas, A. (2013). Investment Decisions in Distribution Networks under Uncertainty with Distributed Generation – Part II: Implementation and Results. IEEE Transactions on Power Systems, vol. 28, no. 3, pp. 2341–2351.

[23] Favuzza, S., Graditi, G., Ippolito, M. G. & Sanseverino, E. R. (2007). Optimal Electrical Distribution Systems Reinforcement Planning Using Gas Micro Turbines by Dynamic Ant Colony Search Algorithm. IEEE Transactions on Power Systems, vol. 22, no. 2, pp. 580–587.

[24] Popoviˊc, Z. N., Kerleta, V. D. & Popoviˊc, D. S. (2014). Hybrid Simulated Annealing and Mixed Integer Linear Programming Algorithm for Optimal Planning of Radial Distribution Networks With Distributed Generation. Electric Power Systems Research, vol. 108, pp. 211–222.

[25] El-Zonkoly, A. M. (2013). Multistage Expansion Planning For Distribution Networks Including Unit Commitment. IET Generation, Transmission & Distribution, vol. 7, no. 7, pp. 766–778.

[26] Heidari, M., Banejad, M. & Hajizadeh, A. (2013). Using The Modified Shuffled Frog Leaping Algorithm for Optimal Sizing and Location of Distributed Generation Resources For Reliability Improvement. Journal of AI and Data Mining, vol. 1, no. 2, pp. 103-110.

[27] Kumar, D., Samantaray, S. R. & Joos, G. (2014). A Reliability Assessment Based Graph Theoretical Approach for Feeder Routing in Power Distribution Networks Including Distributed Generations. International Journal of Electrical Power & Energy Systems, vol. 57, pp. 11–30.

[28] Alvarez-Herault, M. C., et al. (2012). Optimizing Traditional Urban Network Architectures to Increase

Distributed Generation Connection. International Journal of Electrical Power & Energy Systems, vol. 35, no. 1, pp. 148–157.

[29] Domingo, C. M., et al. (2011). A Reference Network Model for Large-Scale Distribution Planning With Automatic Street Map Generation. IEEE Transactions on Power Systems, vol. 26, no. 1, pp. 190–197.

[30] Moreira, J. C., Míguez, E., Vilachá, C. & Otero, A. F. (2012). Large-Scale Network Layout Optimization for Radial Distribution Networks by Parallel Computing: Implementation And Numerical Results. IEEE Transactions on Power Delivery, vol. 27, no. 3, pp. 1468–1476.

[31] Humayd, A. S. B. & Bhattacharya, K. (2013). Comprehensive Multi-Year Distribution System Planning Using Back-Propagation Approach. Generation, Transmission & Distribution, vol. 7, no. 12, pp. 1415–1425.

[32] Singh, S., Ghose, T. & Goswami, S. K. (2012). Optimal Feeder Routing Based On The Bacterial Foraging Technique. IEEE Transactions on Power Delivery, vol. 27, no. 1, pp. 70–78.

[33] Biju, E. R., & Anitha, M. (2015). Reconfiguration Based Expansion Planning and Reliability Evaluation Of Radial Distribution Networks Using BFA. International Journal of Applied Engineering Research, vol. 10, no. 19, pp. 40679-40685.

[34] Fan, P. F., Zhang, L. Z., Xiong, H. Q., Zhang, H., & Wang, D. J. (2012). Distribution Network Planning Containing Micro-Grid Based On Improved Bacterial Colony Chemotaxis Algorithm. Power System Protection and Control, vol. 40, no. 10, pp. 12-18.

[35] Fan, P., Zhang, L., & Wang, Z. (2012). Improved Bacterial Colony Chemotaxis Algorithm for Distribution Network Planning. Advanced Materials Research, vols. 354-355, pp. 1002-1006.

[36] Wenxia, L., Fei, Y., Jianhua, Z., Nian, H., & Lixin, Z., (2008). Study of Multi-Level Sub-Station Planning Approach Based On Bacterial Colony Chemotaxis Algorithm And GIS. 3rd International Conference on Deregulation and Restructuring and Power Technologies, pp. 1014-1019.

[37] Murphy, C., Soroudi, A., & Keane, A. (2015). Information Gap Decision Theory Based Congestion and Voltage Management in The Presence of Uncertain Wind Power. IEEE Transactions on Sustainable Energy, vol. 7, no. 2, pp. 841-849.

[38] Rabiee, A., Soroudi, A., & Keane, A. (2015). Risk-Averse Preventive Voltage Control of AC/DC Power Systems Including Wind Power Generation. IEEE Transactions on Sustainable Energy, vol. 6, no. 4. pp. 1494-1505.

[39] Soroudi, A., Siano, P., & Keane, A. (2015). Optimal DR and ESS Scheduling for Distribution Losses Payments Minimization Under Electricity Price Uncertainty. IEEE Transactions on Smart Grid, vol. 7, no. 1, pp. 261-272.

[40] Rabiee, A., Soroudi, A., & Keane, A. (2014). Information Gap Decision Theory Based OPF with HVDC Connected Wind Farms, IEEE Transaction on Power Systems. vol. 30, no. 6, pp. 3396-3406.

[41] Soroudi, A. (2013). Robust Optimization Based Self Scheduling of Hydro-Thermal Genco in Smart Grids. Energy, vol. 61, no. 1, pp. 262-271.

[42] Soroudi, A. & Amraeeb, T. (2015). Decision Making Under Uncertainty in Energy Systems: State of The Art. Renewable and Sustainable Energy Reviews, vol. 28, pp. 376-384.

[43] Devabalaji, K. R., Ravi K. & Kothari, D. P. (2015). Optimal Location and Sizing of Capacitor Placement in Radial Distribution System Using Bacterial Foraging Optimization Algorithm. International Journal of Electrical Power & Energy Systems, vol. 71, pp. 383–390.

[44] Naveen, S., Sathish Kumar, K. & Rajalakshmi, K. (2015). Distribution System Reconfiguration for Loss Minimization Using Modified Bacterial Foraging Optimization Algorithm. International Journal of Electrical Power & Energy Systems, vol. 69, pp. 90–97.

[45] Mohamed Imran, A. & Kowsalya, M. (2014). Optimal Size and Siting of Multiple Distributed Generators in Distribution System Using Bacterial Foraging Optimization. Swarm and Evolutionary Computation, vol. 15, pp. 58–65.

[46] Devi, S. & Geethanjali, M. (2014). Application of Modified Bacterial Foraging Optimization Algorithm for Optimal Placement and Sizing of Distributed Generation. Expert Systems with Applications, vol. 41, no. 6, pp. 2772–2781.

[47] Mazhari, S. M., Monsef, H. & Falaghi, H. (2012). A Hybrid Heuristic and Learning Automata-Based Algorithm for Distribution Sub-stations Siting, Sizing And Defining The Associated Service Areas. European Transactions on Electrical Power, vol. 24, no. 3, pp. 433-456.

[48] Passino, M. (2002). Biomimicry of Bacterial Foraging for Distributed Optimization and Control. IEEE Control Systems Magazine, vol. 22, pp. 52–67.

[49] Passino, M. (2005). Biomimicry for Optimization, Control, and Automation. Springer Verlag London, pp. 768-816.

[50] Abraham, A., Hassanien, A. E., Siarry, P. & Engelbrecht, A. (2009). Foundations of Computational Intelligence. Springer: studies in computational intelligence, vol. 3, pp. 26-30.

[51] Kord, H. (2010). Substation Expansion Planning Including Load Uncertainties. MS.C. dissertation, Univ. Zanjan, College electrical engineering.

10

Impact of linear dimensionality reduction methods on the performance of anomaly detection algorithms in hyperspectral images

M. Zare-Baghbidi[1*], S. Homayouni[2], K. Jamshidi[1] and A. R. Naghsh-Nilchi[3]

1. Computer Architecture Engineering Department, Faculty of Computer Engineering, University of Isfahan, Isfahan, Iran.
2. Department of Geography, University of Ottawa, Ottawa, Canada.
3. Artificial Intelligent Department, Faculty of Computer Engineering, University of Isfahan, Isfahan, Iran.

*Corresponding author: mohsen.zare@zoho.com (M. Zare-Baghbidi).

Abstract

Anomaly Detection (AD) has recently become an important application of hyperspectral images analysis. The goal of these algorithms is to find the objects in the image scene which are anomalous in comparison with their surrounding background. One way to improve the performance and runtime of these algorithms is to use Dimensionality Reduction (DR) techniques. This paper evaluates the effect of three popular linear dimensionality reduction methods on the performance of three benchmark anomaly detection algorithms. The Principal Component Analysis (PCA), Fast Fourier Transform (FFT) and Discrete Wavelet Transform (DWT) as DR methods, act as pre-processing step for AD algorithms. The assessed AD algorithms are Reed-Xiaoli (RX), Kernel-based versions of the RX (Kernel-RX) and Dual Window-Based Eigen Separation Transform (DWEST). The AD methods have been applied to two hyperspectral datasets acquired by both the Airborne Visible/Infrared Imaging Spectrometer (AVIRIS) and Hyperspectral Mapper (HyMap) sensors. The evaluation of experiments has been done using Receiver Operation Characteristic (ROC) curve, visual investigation and runtime of the algorithms. Experimental results show that the DR methods can significantly improve the detection performance of the RX method. The detection performance of neither the Kernel-RX method nor the DWEST method changes when using the proposed methods. Moreover, these DR methods increase the runtime of the RX and DWEST significantly and make them suitable to be implemented in real time applications.

Keywords: *Hyperspectral Image Processing, Anomaly Detection, Dimensionality Reduction.*

1. Introduction

Hyperspectral imaging is a suitable tool for target detection and recognition in many applications, including search-and-rescue operations, mine detection, and military usages. Hyperspectral sensors are powerful tools for distinguishing between different materials on the basis of each object's unique spectral signatures; these sensors are able to do this because they collect information about surfaces and objects in hundreds of narrow contiguous spectral bands in the visible and infrared regions of the electromagnetic spectrum [1].

Anomaly Detection (AD) is a special kind of target detection (TD) techniques with no priori information about the targets. The main purpose of these algorithms is to find the objects in a given image that are anomalous with respect to their surrounding background [1]. In other words, the point of anomaly detectors is to find the pixels whose spectra significantly differ from the background spectra [2]. The main advantage of these methods is that they don't need priori information about the target signature, nor do they need any form of atmospheric or radiometric corrections on data [3].

The Reed-Xialoi (RX) is the most widely used AD algorithm; it is known as a benchmark anomaly detector for multi/hyperspectral images. This algorithm, which is derived from the generalized likelihood ratio test (GLRT), assumes that the background pixels in a local neighbourhood around the target can be modelled by the multivariate normal (Gaussian) distribution [4,5].

The most reported problem for the RX and many of its modified versions is the "small sample size". This problem concerns the estimation of a local background covariance matrix from a small number of very high dimensional samples. This may result in a badly conditioned and unstable estimate of local background covariance matrix that strongly affects the detection performance of the AD algorithm [6]. The first solution to this problem is enlarging the sample size by expanding the local window size. This solution tries to resolve the non-homogeneity of the local background, which undermines the effectiveness of the covariance matrix estimation. Another solution for this problem is using the Dimension Reduction (DR) [6,7].

The performance of many AD algorithms can be improved by using a pre-processing DR step. The reason is that the hypercube is a relatively large empty space and the most important or interesting information is represented in a few features [8,9]. The DR step, used as a pre-processing step of the AD algorithm, can reduce the inter-band spectral redundancy and ever-present noise. Although the DR is lossy, it increases the separation between anomaly and background signatures. Thus, the detection performance of the anomaly detector is improved.

Another reason for using DR algorithms is that AD algorithms, such as RX, involve the inverse local clutter covariance matrix. This covariance matrix is usually singular, due to the high dimensionality of the hyperspectral data [10]. In addition, in hyperspectral image data, the correlation between the different bands, i.e. information redundancy, is high. As a result, by reducing the number of image bands, the correlation between them is decreased and therefore the problem is solved. Furthermore, since DR brings data from a high order dimension to a low order dimension, it can overcome the "curse of dimensionality" problem [11].

DR techniques are divided into two categories: linear and nonlinear. Although linear techniques do not exploit the nonlinear properties in hyperspectral data, they can be fast enough for real time applications. A popular linear DR method, which is ideally used for small target detection is Principle Component Analysis (PCA) [12]. There are other linear DR methods, such as the Discrete Wavelet Transform (DWT) and Fast Fourier Transform (FFT), which can be used to

improve the performance and runtime of AD algorithms [13,14].

A general framework of an AD scenario is shown in figure 1. For the first step, the spectral dimension of an image cube is reduced through using a DR method. The AD algorithm is then used to analyse new image; the result is a two dimensional matrix named "AD matrix". To specify the locations of anomalies or targets in the image, a post-processing threshold step can be added to the algorithm.

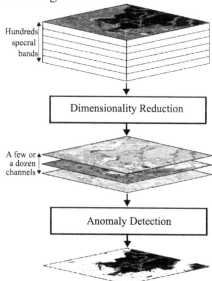

Figure 1. Flowchart of hyperspectral AD using the pre-processing DR method.

In this study, three linear DR methods PCA, DWT and FFT are used as a pre-processing step for three famous AD methods: RX, Kernel-RX and DWEST and the impact of DR step on the performance of the AD methods is evaluated. The Airborne Visible/Infrared Imaging Spectrometer (AVIRIS) and Hyperspectral Mapper (HyMap) datasets are being used to both apply and evaluate the performance of methods on real hyperspectral remotely sensed images using Receiver Operation Characteristic (ROC) curve [15], area under the ROC curve (AUC) [7], visual investigation and runtime of the algorithms.

This paper is organized as follows: Section 2 provides a brief overview of three popular AD methods: RX, Kernel-RX, and DWEST. In section 3, the DR methods (PCA, DWT and FFT) are introduced. The results of the experiments will be discussed in section 4. Lastly, concluding remarks are given in section 5.

2. Anomaly detection methods
2.1. RX detector
The RX algorithm is the most famous AD algorithm, developed by Reed and Yu [16]. RX is

considered to be a benchmark AD algorithm for hyperspectral images; it works as follows: Assume that r is an image pixel vector that has L elements, where L is the number of image's spectral bands. The RX detector is defined by (1).

$$\delta_{rxd}(r) = (r-\mu)^T C_{L \times L}^{-1} (r-\mu) \qquad (1)$$

In this equation, μ is the sample mean and C is the sample data covariance matrix. Finally $\delta_{rxd}(r)$ is the well-known mahalanobis distance that shows the abnormality amount of pixel under test (PUT). The result of AD process is a two-dimensional detection matrix. To determine the exact location of targets (anomalies), a threshold should be performed on the detection matrix.

2.2. Kernel-RX detector

The Kernel RX is a nonlinear version of the RX detector, which was introduced by Kown and Nasrabadi [5]. This method is based on the kernel theory. It performs far better than the standard RX detector. The kernelized version of the RX detector is defined by (2). In this equation K_r^T, $K_{\mu_b}^T$ and K_b are defined as follows:

$$\delta_{KRX}(r) = (K_r^T - K_{\mu_b}^T)^T K_b^{-1} (K_r^T - K_{\mu_b}^T) \qquad (2)$$

$$K_r^T = k(X_b, r)^T - \frac{1}{M} \sum_{i=1}^{M} k(x(i), r) \qquad (3)$$

$$K_{\mu_b}^T = \frac{1}{M} \sum_{i=1}^{M} k(x(i), X_b) - \frac{1}{M^2} \sum_{i=1}^{M} \sum_{j=1}^{M} k(x(i), x(j)) \qquad (4)$$

$$K_b = (K_b - 1_M K_b - K_b 1_M + 1_M K_b 1_M) \qquad (5)$$

$k(X_b, r)^T$ represents a vector whose entries are kernels $k(x(i), r)$, $i = 1...M$, and $\frac{1}{M} \sum_{i=1}^{M} k(x(i), r)$ represent the scalar mean of $k(X_b, r)^T$. In addition, K_b is the Gram matrix before centering, and the elements of $M \times M$ matrix $(1_M)_{i,j} = 1/M$.

2.3. DWEST

Dual Window-based Eigen Separation Transform (DWEST) is an adaptive anomaly detector, developed by Kwon *et al.* [17]. This method uses two windows, called "inner windows" and "outer windows", both of which are designed to maximize the separation between two-classes of data: target class data and background class data. The inner window is used to capture targets in the window; the outer window is used to model the local background. This algorithm extracts targets by projecting the differential mean between two windows onto the eigenvectors, which are associated with the first few largest Eigen-Values

of the difference covariance matrix. If the covariance matrix of the inner and outer windows is named C_{in} and C_{out}, the difference covariance matrix which represents the differential second-order statistics between the two classes, is defined in the following way:

$$C_{diff} = C_{inner} - C_{outer} \qquad (6)$$

The eigenvalues of C_{diff} are divided into two groups, negative values and positive values. The eigenvectors associated with a small number of large positive eigenvalues of C_{diff} can successfully extract the materials in the inner window that are spectrally distinctive. If the mean of inner and outer windows represented by m_{in} and m_{out}, and the eigenvectors represented by the positive eigenvalues in this set are donated by $\{v_i\}$, the DWEST detector projects the differential mean of two windows (which is defined by (7)) onto $\{v_i\}$ by (8) [18,19].

$$m_{diff} = m_{inner} - m_{outer} \qquad (7)$$

$$\delta^{DWEST}(r) = \left| \sum_{v_i} v_i^T m_{diff}(r) \right| \qquad (8)$$

3. Dimensionality reduction methods
3.1. PCA

PCA is the best known technique for data reduction. The main purpose of PCA is to reduce a dataset that consists of a large number of interrelated variables, while retaining the variation of the dataset as much as possible. This purpose is achieved by transforming the data into a new set of variables, the principal components (PCs), which are both uncorrelated and ordered so that the first few PCs retain most of the variation present in all of the original variables [20]. An important problem in PCA-RX is the number of PCs that determine the amount of band reduction for a hyperspectral image.

3.2. DWT

As a different DR method, one can use the DWT to reduce the dimension of a hyperspectral image; it was first investigated for AD methods by Zare-Baghbidi et al. [13]. A pixel within the hyperspectral image, like a signal, has low frequency components for its major part, and high frequency components for its minor part. Thus, the main behaviour of a signal can be found in approximation coefficients of the DWT, which are related to low frequencies of the main signal [21]. As an example, Figure 2 presents the spectral signature of a given pixel a from a hyperspectral image with 64 bands (part [a]). The four-level DWT coefficients of this signal, obtained using the Daubechies4 wavelet transform [22], are presented in part (b) of figure 2. As can be seen, only four samples, which are related to low frequencies in the original signal, carry relevant information about the signal. However, the rest of samples do not contain any relatively important information. Therefore, these samples can be discarded without losing significant information. As a result, the first four samples are the approximation coefficients of the main signal and are used to detect the anomalies.

The DWT DR method first calculates the DWT coefficients of every pixel in a hyperspectral data cube using the Daubechies8 wavelet. This wavelet transformation decomposes the main signal until eight samples are left. The eight samples provided in a matrix are called the "approximation matrix". The approximation matrix is an image that has eight bands; this matrix is an abstract of the original image and can represent the main behaviour image data. Therefore, the anomaly detectors can be performed on this matrix.

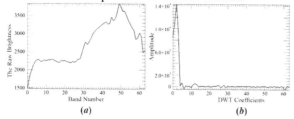

Figure 2. (a) A spectrum pixel of a hyperspectral image, (b) 4-level DWT of the main signal.

3.3. FFT

For the purpose of AD, the DFT can be used in a three-step framework (see Figure 3) [14]. In the first step, the Discrete Fourier transform (DFT) of every image pixel is calculated using the Fast Fourier Transform (FFT) [23]. The "DFT amplitude" of the "DFT values" is then calculated. The results are stored in a matrix named "amplitude" (Figure 3.b). The last step uses a few bands of the amplitude matrix, which are related to low frequencies (and high values) of the main image. A new matrix is formed by this process. This new matrix is actually the abstract of the FFT amplitude matrix (Figure 3.c). The size of this abstract matrix is related to the amount of band reduction, and can be selected during the experiment.

$$
\begin{bmatrix} x & \cdots & x \\ \vdots & \ddots & \vdots \\ x & \cdots & x \end{bmatrix} \quad \begin{bmatrix} |X| & \cdots & |X| \\ \vdots & \ddots & \vdots \\ |X| & \cdots & |X| \end{bmatrix} \quad \begin{bmatrix} |X| & \cdots & |X| \\ \vdots & \ddots & \vdots \\ |X| & \cdots & |X| \end{bmatrix}
$$
$$
\qquad (a) \qquad\qquad (b) \qquad\qquad (c)
$$

Figure 3. (a) Hyperspectral image matrix, (b) FFT Amplitude of hyperspectral matrix, (c) Abstract of FFT Amplitude matrix [14].

4. Experimental results
4.1. HyMap data

This hyperspectral data is an image of the Cooke City in Montana, collected by HyMap (Hyperspectral Mapper) sensor. This image, which released for Target Detection Blind Test project, has 126 spectral bands with wavelengths from 453 to 2496 nanometers (nm) and an approximate ground sampling distance (GSD) of 3 meters [24]. During the image acquisition campaign, 12 real targets were located in an open grass region. Targets of this image are divided into two parts: self-test and blind-test. Because only the real location of the self-test targets is available, this part of the image cannot be used to evaluate the performance of the AD algorithms. Due to this limitation, some self-test targets (red cotton, blue cotton, yellow nylon, and red nylon) were selected and implanted in another part of the image. To implant the targets in this sub-image (named "Img-I") a target implanted method [25] has been used. For this method, a synthetic sub-pixel anomaly, z, is a combination of both the target and background, as shown in (9). In this equation, t and b shows (i.e., denotes) the target and background respectively. Therefore, sub-pixel (z) consists of the target's spectrum with fraction f, and the background's spectrum with fraction ($1-f$) [25].

$$z = f.t + (1-f).b \qquad (9)$$

This implantation method does not include the adjacency effects of the target spectrum on the local background pixels. To have a more realistic condition, the background pixels, which are neighbours of the targets, can be affected by a target pixel. This effect can be achieved by using a Gaussian function with a width of w, as shown in (10), where p_i is the spatial distance between background pixel (z_i) and the target pixel (t) [4].

$$z_i = \exp\left(-\frac{\rho_i^2}{w^2}\right).f.t + \left(1 - \exp\left(-\frac{\rho_i^2}{w^2}\right).f\right).b_i \qquad (10)$$

To construct the desired image, according to figure 4, a part of the main image is selected; the targets are then implanted in the selected sub-image (Figure 4(a)). To apply the effect of the background on targets and make sub-pixels, outlines of targets have been selected and combined with their adjacent background according to (9) with the coefficient $f=0.6$. To apply the effect of anomalies on the background pixels (10) is used. The final image with implanted targets includes sub-pixel and full-pixel (or multi-pixel) targets. As a result, this image seems to be a perfect data for testing AD and TD algorithms.

The truth location of the targets that are either sub-pixel or full-pixel is shown in figure 4(b).

Figure 4. A natural color composite of the HyMap data cube, (a) selected sub-image with implanted targets (Img-I), (b) truth location of targets [26].

4.2. AVIRIS data

Two other sub-images have been extracted from a hyperspectral image of a naval air station in San Diego, California, collected by the AVIRIS sensor [27, 28]. This data cube has 189 useful spectral bands with wavelengths from 400 to 2500 nm and a GSD of 3.5 meters (see Figure 5).

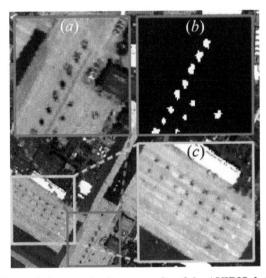

Figure 5. A natural color composite of the AVIRIS data cube, (a) sub-image with real targets (Img-II), (b) truth locations of targets in Img-II and (c) sub-image with real targets (Img-III) [14].

The first sub-image, named Img-II, is an 80×80 pixel data cube that contains some military targets as anomalies and is used to evaluate the exact detection performance of algorithms using Receiver Operation Characteristic (ROC) curve (Figure 5(a)). The truth location of targets in this sub-image is shown in figure 5(b). The second sub-image, named Img-III, is an image window with 100×100 pixels. This sub-image contains 38 anomalous targets, which may be either helicopters or helipads, as shown in figure 5(c).

This sub-image is used in some TD works [29]; it is also used to evaluate the runtime of anomaly detectors.

4.3. Implementation

To evaluate the performance of the AD and DR methods, three AD algorithms, namely, the RX, Kernel-RX, and DWEST, have been implemented in the standard mode (without a pre-processing DR step) and with the three mentioned DR methods. Algorithms have been addressed according to table 1.

Table 1. Addressing AD algorithms.

Main Algorithms	Algorithms using PCA DR method	Algorithms using DWT DR method	Algorithms using FFT DR method
RX	PCA-RX	DWT-RX	FFT-RX
Kernel-RX(KRX)	PCA-KRX	DWT-KRX	FFT-KRX
DWEST	PCA-DWEST	DWT-DWEST	FFT-DWEST

One of the most important decisions for AD algorithms is the detection window size [4]. Although there is no specific method for choosing these windows [4], the size of the inner window should be almost as large as the biggest target in the scene. In addition, the size of the outer window should be large enough to provide a sufficient number of background samples for simulating the local background [30]. According to the both above-mentioned rules and the results of the experiment, the inner and outer window size for Img-I are selected 3×3 and 11×11 pixels, respectively. The inner and outer windows for Img-II are selected 5×5 and 13×13 pixels and these values for Img-III are selected 5×5 and 11×11 pixels, respectively.

An important decision for the DR methods is the amount of reduction that determines the number of image/feature bands after the DR step. This parameter should be selected according to two metrics: performance and runtime. In this study, according to the experiments the band number of output images is assumed to be 8. Therefore, at the pre-processing step, the spectral bands of the main image are reduced to 8 useful bands.

4.4. Detection performance evaluation

The ROC curve is the best way to evaluate the detection performance of AD algorithms. The ROC is a curve that shows the true detection rate (TDR) versus the false alarm rate (FAR) in a particular scenario. The TDR and FAR can be computed by varying the detection threshold and counting both the number of true detection targets and the corresponding number of false alarms in every threshold value [1]. To evaluate the detection of algorithms more accurately, the AUC is used. This value is an exact criterion; it is widely used to evaluate the detection performance of target detection algorithms [7]. Another way to evaluate the performance of algorithms is the visual investigation. This evaluation can be a good criterion using the post-processing threshold step. In this study, the evaluation of algorithms for Img-I and Img-II datasets is done using the ROC curve and the AUC value; in addition, the Img-III data is used to evaluate algorithms visually.

4.4.1. AD results of Img-I

Figure 6 shows the ROC curves of the RX detector family for Img-I. The ROC curves of the Kernel-RX and DWEST families shown in figures 7 and 8, respectively. The AUC values of all algorithms are presented in table 2. According to these criteria, the following results can be inferred.

The detection performance of the RX method in the standard mode is very weak in general; however, the use of the per-processing DR methods increases its performance significantly. According to the AUC values, although the DWT-RX and FFT-RX methods exhibit the best performance among the RX family, the performance of all the methods that use DR as a pre-processing step are almost superior.

The performance of Kernel-RX method does not change using PCA or FFT DR methods as a pre-processing step and DWT does not noticeably reduce its performance. For the DWEST family, DWT-DWEST performs best and the performance of other methods is almost same. Of all the methods that are applied to Img-I, the DWT-DWEST performs best and the RX method performs worst. The performance of other

methods is acceptable for detection of anomalies.

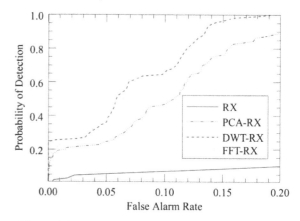

Figure 6. ROC curves of the RX AD family for Img-I.

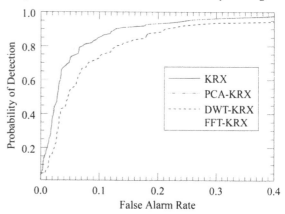

Figure 7. ROC curves of the Kernel-RX AD family for Img-I.

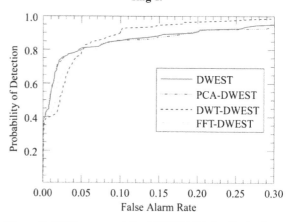

Figure 8. ROC curves of the DWEST AD family for Img-I.

Table 2. AUC values of the AD methods applied to Img-I.

AD Algorithm	Without DR	PCA DR	DWT DR	FFT DR
AUC (RX)	0.427	0.895	0.934	0.933
AUC (KRX)	0.940	0.940	0.904	0.942
AUC (DWEST)	0.949	0.944	**0.962**	0.950

4.4.2. AD results of Img-II

The ROC curves of the RX, Kernel-RX and DWEST families, applied to Img-II, are shown in figures 9, 10, and 11, respectively; the AUC values of these methods are shown in table 3. According to these criteria, the following results can be inferred.

The performance of RX method used without DR step is very weak; using DR pre-processing step increases its performance significantly. The performances of RX family using the DR step are almost the same. In the Kernel-RX family the Kernel-RX and PCA-KRX have the best performance and the performance of DWT-KRX and FFT-KRX are same. According to the results, the performance of all methods of this family is almost the same. The performance of DWEST family in all cases is almost the same and this mean DR step does not change the performance of it. Among all AD algorithms applied to Img-II, the DWT-DWEST and FFT-DWEST methods exhibit the best performance; the RX method performs worst. The performance of the other methods is good. These results are almost the same as the results inferred from the evaluation of the algorithms on Img-I.

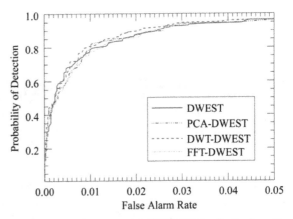

Figure 11. ROC curves of DWEST AD family for Img-II.

Table 3. AUC values of the AD methods applied to Img-II.

AD Algorithm	Without DR	PCA DR	DWT DR	FFT DR
AUC (RX)	0.511	0.967	0.968	0.976
AUC (KRX)	0.972	0.972	0.967	0.966
AUC (DWEST)	0.990	0.989	**0.991**	**0.991**

4.4.3. AD results of Img-III

Img-III is used to evaluate the performance of anomaly detectors in a real scene. Because the truth location of the targets in this image is not available, the detection performance of AD algorithms is investigated visually. To achieve a better visual investigation, a threshold step is added at the end of the AD procedure. To execute this post-processing step, a cut-off threshold is needed; this value can be calculated adaptively using (11) [31]:

$$\tau_\alpha = \mu_d + Z_\alpha \times \sigma_d \qquad (11)$$

Where τ_α is the cut-off threshold that declares whether a pixel is a target or not, μ_d and σ_d are the mean and standard deviation of the output of the AD algorithm, respectively, and Z_α is the z statistic at the significant level of α, which controls the number of pixels declared to be anomalies. Figure 12 shows the output of the threshold step using the adaptive cut-off threshold of (11).

According to these results, the performance of RX is very weak. In addition, DR step increases its performance significantly. The performance of Kernel RX family is almost the same. This family suffers from False Alarm Rate (FAR) that reduces their performance. The performance of the DWEST family algorithms is almost the same.

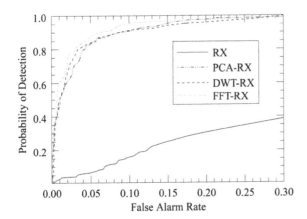

Figure 9. ROC curves of the RX AD family for Img-II.

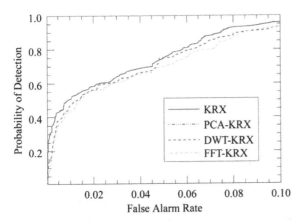

Figure 10. ROC curves of the Kernel-RX AD family for Img-II.

4.5. Runtime evaluation

To evaluate the speed of the AD methods, a computer system with an "Intel Core i5-2410M,

2.3GHz" processor and four GB of Random Access Memory (RAM) is used to measure the runtime of algorithms on Img-III, in equal conditions.

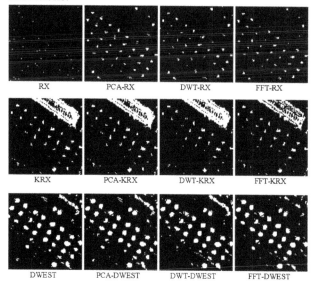

Figure 12. Detection results of algorithms applied to Img-III.

The runtime of the DR methods is shown in table 4 and the runtime of the AD methods, which includes the runtime of related DR pre-processing methods, is shown in table 5. In addition, figure 13 compares the runtime of the methods using a column chart.

Table 4. Runtime of DR methods applied to Img-III.

DR method	PCA	DWT	FFT
Runtime (s)	0.4530	5.062	**0.125**

Table 5. Runtime of AD methods applied to Img-III.

AD Algorithm	Without DR	PCA DR	DWT DR	FFT DR
Runtime (RX)	102.52	2.78	7.44	**2.44**
Runtime (KRX)	303.36	187.05	192.02	187.13
Runtime (DWEST)	295.20	3.44	8.02	3.14

According to these results, with using the dimension reduction techniques, the FFT DR method has the best runtime. Among the AD families, the RX family has best runtime; nevertheless the Kernel RX family has the worst runtime.

The runtime of the RX and DWEST families that use the DR step is acceptable; these methods can be used in real-time applications by using parallel processing or hardware implementation of algorithms using field programmable gate array (FPGA) [32,33]. Of all the methods, the FFT-RX has the best runtime: its runtime is about 124 times better than the slowest method, the Kernel-RX.

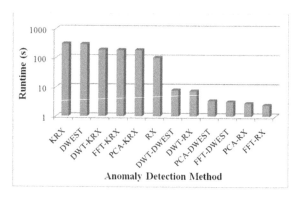

Figure 13. Runtime comparison of various anomaly detectors applied to Img-III.

5. Conclusion

This paper evaluated the impact of linear dimensionality reduction methods on the performance of anomaly detection algorithms. By reducing the dimensions of the hyperspectral image as a pre-processing step, the detection performance and runtime of AD algorithms are improved. PCA, DWT and FFT as the main DR methods have been used to evaluate the performance of RX, Kernel-RX and DWEST AD algorithms. The results of the experiment on the AVIRIS and HyMap datasets were assessed using the ROC curve, the AUC values, and a visual investigation. According to these results, these DR methods increase the detection performance of RX method significantly and do not diminish the performance of Kernel-RX and DWEST methods. In addition, DR methods improve the runtime of RX and DWEST detectors significantly but this improvement about Kernel-RX is not much. FFT has the best runtime among DR methods and FFT-RX has the best runtime among AD methods. Based on these results, the DR methods, as a pre-processing step, can improve the performance of some AD algorithms and runtime of all algorithms. This runtime improvement makes the algorithms suitable for real-time application of TD in hyperspectral remotely sensed data.

Acknowledgments

The authors would like to thank the Digital Imaging and Remote Sensing group, Center for Imaging Science, Rochester Institute of Technology, Rochester, NY, for providing the HyMap dataset, and the EXELIS VIS Company for making the AVIRIS dataset accessible.

References

[1] Matteoli, S., Diani M. & Corsini, G. (2010). A tutorial overview of anomaly detection in hyperspectral images. IEEE Aerospace and Electronic Systems Magazine, vol. 25, no. 7, pp. 5-28.

[2] Borghys, D., Truyen, E., Shimoni, M. & Perneel, C. (2009). Anomaly detection in hyperspectral images of complex scenes. in Proceedings of 29th Earsel Symposium, MAI, Chania.

[3] Acito, N., Corsini, M. & Cini. A. (2004). Experimental performance analysis of hyperspectral anomaly detectors. in Image and Signal Processing for Remote Sensing X, Bellingham, WA, pp. 41-51.

[4] Khazai, S., Homayouni, S., Safari, A. & Mojaradi, B. (2011). Anomaly Detection in Hyperspectral Images Based on an Adaptive Support Vector Method. IEEE Geoscience and Remote Sensing Letters, vol. 8, no. 4, pp. 646-650.

[5] Kwon, H. & Nasrabadi, N. M. (2005). Kernel RX-algorithm: a nonlinear anomaly detector for hyperspectral imagery. IEEE Transactions on Geoscience and Remote Sensing, vol. 43, no. 2, pp. 388–397.

[6] Matteoli, S., Diani, M. & Corsini, G. (2009). Different approaches for improved covariance matrix estimation in hyperspectral anomaly detection. Proceedings of Riunione Annuale GTTI, pp. 1–8.

[7] Khazai, S., Safari, A., Homayouni, S. & Mojaradi. B. (2011). A Performance Comparison Between Recent Anomaly Detectors on Hyperspectral Images. in International Conference on Sensors and Models in Photogrammetry and Remote Sensing, Tehran, Iran.

[8] Bruce, L. M., Koger, C. H. & Li, J. (2002). Dimensionality reduction of hyperspectral data using discrete wavelet transform feature extraction. IEEE Transactions on Geoscience and Remote Sensing, vol. 40, no. 10, pp. 2331–2338.

[9] Landgrebe, D. (2002). Hyperspectral image data analysis. IEEE Signal Processing Magazine, vol. 19, no.1, pp. 17 – 28.

[10] Nasrabadi, N. M. (2008). Regularization for spectral matched filter and RX anomaly detector. Proceedings of SPIE, vol. 6966, pp. 696604-696604-12.

[11] Scott, D. W. (1992). The curse of dimensionality and dimension reduction, in Multivariate Density Estimation: Theory, Practice, and Visualization. New York: Wiley, ch. 7, pp. 195–217.

[12] Ma, L., Crawford, M. M. & Tian, J. (2010). Anomaly Detection for Hyperspectral Images Based on Robust Locally Linear Embedding. Journal of Infrared Millimeter and Terahertz Waves, Springer, pp. 753-762.

[13] Zare-Baghbidi, M., Jamshidi, K., Naghsh-Nilchi, A.-R. & Homayouni, S. (2011). Improvement of Anomaly Detection Algorithms in Hypespectral Images using Discrete Wavelet Transform. Signal and Image Processing : An International Journal, vol. 2, no. 4, pp. 13–25.

[14] Zare-Baghbidi, M., Homayouni, S. & Jamshidi, K. (2015). Improving the RX Anomaly Detection Algorithm for Hyperspectral Images using FFT. MSEEE, Journal of modeling and Simulation in Electrical & and Electronic Engineering (MSEEE), vol. 1, no. 2, pp. 89-95.

[15] Kerekes, J. (2008). Receiver operating characteristic curve confidence intervals and regions. IEEE Letters on Geoscience and remote sensing, vol. 5, no. 2, pp. 251–255.

[16] Reed, I. S. & Yu, X. (1990). Adaptive multiple-band CFAR detection of an optical pattern with unknown spectral distribution. IEEE Transactions on Acoustics, Speech and Signal Processing, vol. 38, no. 10, pp. 1760–1770.

[17] Kwon, H., Der, S. Z. & Nasrabadi, N. M. (2003). Projection-based adaptive anomaly detection for hyperspectral imagery. in Proceedings 2003 International Conference on Image Processing, Barcelona, Spain, vol. 1, pp. I-1001-4.

[18] Chang, C.-I. & Hsueh, M. (2006). Characterization of anomaly detection in hyperspectral imagery. Sensor Review, vol. 26, no. 2, pp. 137-146.

[19] El-Rewainy, A., Farouk, E. & Fouda, A. (2009). A Comparison Study of Dual Window-Based Anomaly Detection Algorithms for Hyperspectral Imagery. in 13th International Conference on Aerospace Science & Aviation Technology, Cairo, Egypt, pp. 1-10.

[20] Jolliffe, I. (2002). Principal component analysis. 2nd edition. New York: Springer, p. 1.

[21] Polikar, R. (2011). The Wavelet Tutorial, Part IV, Multiresolution Analysis: The Discrete Wavelet Transform, [Online]. Available: http://users.rowan.edu/~polikar/WAVELETS/WTpart4.html [Accessed: 20-Sep-2011].

[22] Daubechies, I. (1988). Orthonormal bases of compactly supported wavelets. Communications on Pure and Applied Mathematics, vol. 41, no. 7, pp. 909-996, Oct.

[23] Cochran, W. T. et al. (1967). What is the fast Fourier transform?. Proceedings of the IEEE, vol. 55, no. 10, pp. 1664-1674.

[24] Snyder, D., Kerekes, J. & Fairweather, I. (2008). Development of a web-based application to evaluate target finding algorithms. IGARSS 2008, pp. 915–918. Stefanou, M. & Kerekes, J. P. (2009). A method for assessing spectral image utility. IEEE Transactions on Geoscience and Remote Sensing, vol. 47, no. 6, pp. 1698-1706.

[25] Zare-Baghbidi. M. & Homayouni, S. (2013). Fast Hyperspectral Anomaly Detection for Environmental Applications. Journal of Applied Remote Sensing, Vol. 7, 073489, doi:10.1117/1.JRS.7.073489.

[26] Porter, W.M. & Enmark, H.T. (1987). A system overview of the airborne visible/infrared imaging spectrometer (AVIRIS). SPIE, Imaging Spectroscopy II, vol. 834, pp. 22–31.

[27] ITT Visual Information Solution. (2011). ENVI Tutorials. [Online]. Available: http://www.ittvis.com/portals/0/tutorials/envi/18_SAM _BandMax.zip [Accessed: 26-Sep-2011].

[28] He, Y., Liu, D. & Yi, S. (2011). Recursive spectral similarity measure-based band selection for anomaly detection in hyperspectral imagery. Journal of Optics, vol. 13, no.1, pp. 1–7.

[29] Goldberg, H. R. (2007). A performance characterization of kernel-based algorithms for anomaly detection in hyperspectral imagery. M.S. thesis, University of Maryland, College Park.

[30] Rosario, D. S. (2008). Algorithm Development for Hyperspectral Anomaly Detection. Ph.D. dissertation, University of Maryland, College Park.

[31] Molero, J. et al. (2011). Fast Anomaly Detection in Hyperspectral Images with RX Method on Heterogeneous Clusters. Journal of Supercomputing, vol. 58, no. 3.

[32] González, C. et al. (2012). FPGA Implementation of the N-FINDR Algorithm for Remotely Sensed Hyperspectral Image Analysis. IEEE Transactions on Geoscience and Remote Sensing, vol. 50, no. 2, pp. 374–388.

11

Wireless sensor network design through genetic algorithm

S.M. Hosseinirad*, S.K. Basu

Department of Computer Science, Banaras Hindu University, India

Corresponding author: hosseinirad@gmail.com (S.M. Hosseinirad)

Abstract

In this paper, we used WSN design, as a *multi-objective optimization problem* through Genetic Algorithm (GA) technique. We examined the effects of GA parameters including population size, mutation probability, and selection and crossover methods on the design. Choosing suitable parameters is a trade-off between different network criteria and characteristics. Type of deployment, effect of network size, radio communication radius, deployment density of sensors in an application area and location of base station are the WSN's characteristics, which were investigated in this paper. The simulation results of this study indicate that the value of radio communication radius has direct effect on radio interference, cluster-overlapping, sensor node distribution uniformity and communication energy consumption. The optimal value of radio communication radius depends on network deployment density rather than network size and deployment type. Location of the base station affects radio communication energy, cluster-overlapping and average number of communication per cluster head. BS located outside the application domain is preferred over that located inside. In all the network situations, random deployment has better performance compared to grid deployment.

Keywords: *Wireless sensor network, cluster head, genetic algorithm, active sensor, base station.*

1. Introduction

Wireless sensor networks (WSNs) have become an essential part of many applications over the past decades [1]. Compared to computer networks, WSNs are small, cheap but have lower power, limited processing, storage, and radio communication capabilities [2]. Depending on the application, one or more sensors are deployed to perform monitoring, tracking, or surveillance [3]. WSNs are used to monitor complex processes in different areas. They are densely scattered either inside or very close to a phenomenon being monitored [4]. Sensors are usually intended to last for a long period of time, such as months or even years [5]. The network operates when power is available [6].

WSNs have attracted a lot of research attention in the recent years [7]. It offers a rich area of research, in which a variety of multi-disciplinary tools and concepts are employed [8]. Due to economic and technological reasons, most available wireless sensor devices are highly constrained in terms of computational, memory, power, and communication capabilities. It has been the focus of considerable research efforts in the areas of communications (protocols, routing, coding, and error correction), electronics (energy efficiency, miniaturization), and control (networked control systems, theory and applications) [9].

Size of network, radio communication radius, type of deployment, location of base station (BS), and density of deployment are some of the fundamental design issues of WSNs [10]. These issues, such as whether sensor nodes are to be deployed randomly or manually? Whether the location of BS is inside or outside the application area? are to be settled before topology initialization. Some of the most important parameters in WSN design are energy consumption, coverage, connectivity, data redundancy, and radio interference [11].

WSNs have dynamic topology. It varies over time. Design and construction of an efficient topology for WSNs is a multi-objective optimization problem [12]. Optimizing one or more parameters regardless of others may cause negative effects on the performance and lifetime of WSNs. For example, optimizing communication energy consumption directly affects coverage, connectivity and radio interference.

To solve and optimize a complex problem in the real world, different methods such as genetic algorithm [13], ant colony optimization [14], and imperialist competition algorithm [15-16] have been proposed. GA is a very simple and powerful simulation technique to optimize problems based on searching in multi-modal landscape. The main goal in GA is to generate and evolve solutions very close to the optimal solution. It is applied in many different domains such as engineering, computational science, and mathematics. GA is based on natural evolution. It includes different steps such as *initialization, fitness calculation*, and application of different operators such as *selection, crossover,* and *mutation* [17].

We study WSN design in terms of network size, communication and operation energies, cluster distribution uniformity, radio interference, and data redundancy. In the first part of this paper, we try to tune GA parameters under the framework of our WSN model. In the second part of this paper, we study WSN parameters in terms of network size, communication and operation energies, cluster distribution uniformity, radio interference, and data redundancy and find near optimal values of these parameters based on fine-tuned parameters of GA. The paper is organized as follows: section 2 deals with WSN design issues, section 3 deals with our WSN model, section 4 deals with GA, section 5 deals with results and discussion, and section 6 concludes the paper.

2. WSN design issues

Energy optimization is one of the most important issues in WSN design [18]. Unlike the wired network, WSN energy resources are much bounded. Sensor nodes are battery powered which have limited capacity and lifetime [19]. Recharge or replacement of sensors' batteries is very difficult or impossible in some cases. When batteries are drained out, sensors are not able to stay alive and function. When some nodes of a WSN fail, the WSN has to reorganize and reroute the messages. Using optimized network topologies and suitable network protocols, WSN's lifetime can be increased from months to years. Increasing the lifespan of WSN is an important design consideration.

By reducing the *radio communication range* and minimizing data processing load in sensors, energy can be conserved in a WSN. More than 20% of sensors' energy is consumed in radio communications [20]. Short radio communication range and limited bandwidth are important goals of WSN design.

Type of deployment is also an important consideration in WSN design [21]. Deployment could be deterministic (where sensors are placed manually) or random (sensors are deployed randomly) [22]. The deterministic method is used for small size networks. Random method is used for larger networks with higher density of node deployment. If any sensor node fails, another close by sensor node compensates for the failure by taking additional work load. The network in such a situation functions with reduced performance.

Network topology determines the way different devices on the network are arranged, and how they communicate with each other [23]. The main motivation behind topology design is to build a network that saves energy and preserves important characteristics such as connectivity, and coverage. WSN topology is dynamic and changes with time according to the network's conditions. Large scale WSNs are, in general, homogenous and all the sensors have equal capabilities. Selection of suitable topology and implementation of efficient network protocols are other important design challenges. Reducing the transmission power of the nodes needs packet delivery through multiple hops. As the direct communication (single-hop) to the base station (BS) drains battery very quickly, all the sensors use multi-hop communication (hierarchical architecture) with short radio distances [24]. It reduces communication energy consumption and network traffic [25].

In the *hierarchical topology*, the application domain area is divided into some sub-domains which are named clusters. Usually, the sensors with more energy and better geographical positions are eligible to be selected and act as cluster heads (CHs). Total number of CHs is generally in the range 5% to 15% of the number of sensors in the network [26]. The members of a cluster communicate with the BS via CHs, and CHs act as relay nodes to carry on data to the BS via single-hop communication paths.

After data are gathered from the cluster members, preprocessing of data is done in the corresponding CH. The CHs forward preprocessed data to the BS. In large scale WSNs, preprocessing of data in CHs reduce energy consumption and data redundancy. Also, clustering of nodes balances the network traffic load dynamically. Selecting suitable CHs and the way of organizing these clusters are still two basic problems in WSN design.

Lack of connectivity and coverage are two undesirable effects of non-uniform cluster deployment. Generally, it is assumed that all clusters are in circular shape with a cluster radius (R_{CH}). How to find an optimal value of R_{CH} is an important issue, as it determines the number of clusters in a deployment. To determine cluster uniformity, cluster-overlapping is a parameter to measure in a WSN domain.

Radio interference is another issue in wireless communication leading to data inaccuracy and wastage of energy resources [27]. To simulate wireless communication and radio interference of wireless sensors, some radio models are proposed [28]. In the first radio model, it is assumed that the radio channel is symmetric so that the energy required to transmit a message from node A to node B is the same as the energy required to transmit a message from node B to node A. As all the sensors are homogeneous, every sensor node has equal radio capability with the same communication radius (R_{rx}). Optimizing the value of R_{rx} is essential, because it determines the extent of radio interference, accuracy of data communication and network connectivity.

Data redundancy is another important consideration in WSN design [29]. Data redundancy wastes memory space, energy and other network resources [30]. In random deployment, sensors are deployed with high density. The sensing radius (R_{sen}) indicates the maximum sensing coverage area which is monitored by a sensor node. To reduce data redundancy, every CH performs data fusion of the received data from active sensors.

WSNs are designed for *specific applications* and usages. In addition to the important issues such as energy consumption, coverage, and connectivity, some parameters of the specific application should also be taken into account in considering a design.

3. WSN Model

This section describes the WSN model studied and used in the rest of the paper. In our proposed model, we assume that all the sensor nodes are stationary and identical in capabilities. A sensor node can function in two modes: (i) a cluster head (CH), (ii) an active sensor (ACS), depending on the role assigned to a sensor node dynamically. The model deals with radio communication, data sensing, energy consumption, sensor placement, and topology aspects of WSN. Sensor nodes can be deployed manually or randomly in the application area. We use a cluster-based topology with single-hop transmission. It is assumed that remote BS can always communicate with all the sensors directly. CHs are required to communicate over relatively

longer distances; therefore, their batteries drain more quickly than those of other sensor nodes. CHs have to gather data from the members of the corresponding clusters, preprocess the data, and forward it to the BS after data fusion.

The main issues in a WSN design are *reducing energy consumption*, optimizing deployment of sensors, reducing radio interference, enhancing network coverage and network connectivity. Radio communication and sensing coverage areas of the sensor nodes are in a circular shape. Every sensor node has a sensing coverage radius (R_{sen}) and radio communication radius (R_{rx}) associated with it. The overlapping of sensing areas, intersection of clusters and overlapping of radio coverage of two sensor nodes can be obtained by Eq. (1).

$$A = 2R^2 \cos^{-1}(\frac{d}{2R}) - \frac{1}{2}d\sqrt{4R^2 - d^2} \qquad (1)$$

where R represents the clusters, sensing or radio communication radii and d is the Euclidean distance between two sensor nodes. Sensor nodes consume energy for sensing, processing, and radio transmission. A major part of energy is used for radio communication. In the first radio model, ACS communicates over short radio distances [26]. Data transmission energy consists of transmitting (E_{Tx}) and receiving (E_{Rx}) energies [30]. Thus, to transmit a *k*-bit message over a distance of *d* using the first radio model may be given by Eq. (2).

$$E_{Tx}(k,d) = E_{Tx-elec}(k) + E_{Tx-amp}(k,d) \qquad (2)$$

$$= \begin{cases} k \times E_{elec} + k \times \varepsilon_{fs} \times d^2 & d < d_0 \\ k \times E_{elec} + k \times \varepsilon_{mp} \times d^4 & d \geq d_0 \end{cases}$$

where d_0 is the threshold distance defined as $d_0 = \sqrt{\frac{\varepsilon_{fs}}{\varepsilon_{mp}}}$, ε_{fs} is the energy loss to send 1-*bit* message by transmitter amplifying circuit in elemental area in free space model, and ε_{mp} is the energy to send 1-*bit* message by transmitter amplifying circuit in multi-path fading model, $E_{Tx-elec}$ is the energy spent by the transmit circuit, E_{Tx-amp} is the energy-cost of the transmission amplifying circuit, $E_{Rx-elec}$ signifies the energy-cost of the receiving circuit, and E_{elec} is the energy expense to transmit or receive 1-*bit* message by the transmitting or the receiving circuit. The energy spent in receiving data can be given by Eq. (3).

$$E_{Rx}(k,d) = (E_{Rx} + E_{BF}) \times k \qquad (3)$$

where E_{BF} is the beam forming energy. Not only do distances transmit, but the number of transmit and receive operations for each message also has to be minimized. The energy consumption for data fusion ($E_{\text{da-fus}}$) is represented by Eq. (4).

$$E_{da-fus}\left(k,d\right) = k \times E_{da} \qquad (4)$$

Total energy which a sensor node consumes for communication ($E_{\text{CE-Sen}}$) may be represented by Eq. (5).

$$E_{CE-Sen}\left(k,d\right) = E_{Tx}\left(k,d\right) + E_{Rx}\left(k,d\right) + E_{da-fus}\left(k,d\right) \qquad (5)$$

WSN's total energy consumption for communication can be represented by Eq. (6).

$$CE = \sum_{i=1}^{n} E_{CE-Sen_i}\left(k, d_i\right) \qquad (6)$$

Operation energy (OE) is different for different nodes. In the present model, OE of a node in CH mode is assumed to be ten units of operation energy and an active sensor consumes two units of operation energy. The exact value of OE is related to electro-mechanical characteristics of a sensor node. The OE of sensors is calculated by Eq. (7) in this study.

$$OE = 10 \times N_{CH} + 2 \times N_{ACS} \qquad (7)$$

where N_{CH} is the total number of CH nodes and N_{ACS} is the total number of ACS.

Network connectivity has to cover all sensor nodes. If an ACS cannot access its CH within its radio coverage, it is disconnected from the network. This sensor node becomes out of range and is represent by ACS$_{\text{out}}$. Total number of out of range sensors (N_{ACSout}) is obtained by counting how many ACS$_{\text{out}}$ are there.

Every CH should have some nodes belonging to the cluster; otherwise, it becomes a useless cluster head (CH$_{\text{useless}}$). In our study, we try to minimize number of useless clusters. The total number of useless cluster heads represented by $N_{\text{CHuseless}}$ is obtained by counting how many CH$_{\text{useless}}$ are there.

For every CH, a predefined number of nodes are allocated depending on the hardware and communication capabilities of the nodes. If a CH provides services for more than the maximum number of ACSs, it is called an overloaded cluster head (CH$_{\text{overload}}$). We also assume in our model that every CH can provide services to ten ACSs at most. Total number of overloaded cluster heads ($N_{\text{CHoverload}}$) is obtained by counting how many CH$_{\text{overload}}$ are there.

4. Genetic Algorithm

Genetic algorithm is a search heuristic which was proposed by John Holland and his students in Michigan University in 1975 [13]. GA does searching through a population of points. A large number of points increase the number of calculations and decrease speed. GA works with coded parameters not with parameters itself. Genes are used to represent the coded parameters. Representing and encoding of parameters in GA can be done in different ways such as binary, decimal or any other base. A predefined collection of genes is named chromosome. GA deals with a population of individuals, where each individual is a potential solution represented as a chromosome. Each population evolves through a number of generations. A fitness function is applied to each member (chromosomes) of the population. Chromosomes are selected for recombination based on fitness. Better chromosomes have higher chances of being carried to the next generation (elitist). In the crossover step, two different chromosomes (parents) are selected for recombination from which two children are created. To prevent premature convergence to local optima, mutation operator is used. In this set up, WSN design reduces to multi-objectives optimization. This multi-objective optimization is defined by Eq. (8).

$$f = \min\left\{\sum_{i=1}^{9} J_i W_i\right\} \qquad (8)$$

J_1 through J_9 represents the objective parameters and W_1 through W_9 represents the weight of each parameter in the objective function (Table 1).

To represent WSN parameters in a chromosome, we use binary encoding scheme: 1 for cluster head and 0 for active sensor. For example, a chromosome '101000…101' means "CH, ACS, CH, ACS, ACS, ACS, …, CH, ACS, CH". The length of every chromosome is determined by the number of WSN's sensors alive. For example, a WSN with 100 sensor nodes alive, the length of every chromosome is 100. We use elitist GA, that is, a chromosome with the highest fitness value is retained in the next generation. The fitness function is defined by Eq. (9).

$$f = \frac{1}{N_{ACS} \times W_1 + N_{CH} \times W_2 + CH_{overlap} \times W_3 + CH_{overload} \times W_4 \cdots} \\ \frac{1}{+R_{radio} \times W_5 + OE \times W_6 + CE \times W_7 + CH_{useless} \times W_8 + ACS_{out} \times W_9} \qquad (9)$$

Based on normalization, the final values of the weighing coefficients of fitness function are determined as shown in Table 2. The final values of the coefficients are trade-off between energy management, and network connectivity.

5. Results and Discussion

In the first part of this paper, we examined the effects of GA-parameters on simulation and optimization of WSNs under the framework of the proposed model. We first fixed the values of the GA parameters through fine-tuning. To begin the simulation study, we used the values of different GA parameters given in Table 3 and selected a suitable mutation probability based on network size shown in Table 4.

We used five different sizes of the monitoring area: $10m \times 10m$, $15m \times 15m$, $20m \times 20m$, $25m \times 25m$, $30m \times 30m$. We assumed that the initial values for communication energy were as shown in Table 5. We optimized the number of cluster head sensors (N_{CH}), subject to optimal number of active sensors (N_{ACS}) for coverage, minimize cluster-overlapping ($CH_{overlapp}$), cluster head overloading ($CH_{overload}$), radio interference (R_{radio}), operation energy (OE), communication energy (CE), cluster without any member node ($CH_{useless}$), and the number of active sensors out of coverage (ACS_{out}).

Table 1. Correspondence between optimization parameters and objectives.

Objective	Optimization Parameter	GA Symbol
J_1	Total number of active sensors	N_{ACS}
J_2	Total number of cluster heads	N_{CH}
J_3	Total amount of cluster heads overlapping	$CH_{overlapp}$
J_4	Total number of CHs overloaded	$N_{CHoverload}$
J_5	Total value of radio interference	R_{radio}
J_6	Total value of operation energy	OE
J_7	Total value of communication energy	CE
J_8	Total number of CH without any member	$N_{CHuseless}$
J_9	Total number of ACSs out of coverage	N_{ACSout}

Table 2. Weighing coefficients of fitness function.

Weights	Up to 25 Sensors	Up to 100 Sensors	Up to 225 Sensors	Up to 400 Sensors	Up to 625 Sensors	Up to 900 Sensors
W_1	10^{-4}	10^{-2}	10^{-3}	10^{-2}	10^{-3}	10^{-4}
W_2	10^2	10^2	10^2	10^2	10^5	10^7
W_3	10^2	10^2	10^2	10^2	10^8	10^8
W_4	1	1	1	1	1	1
W_5	10^2	10^2	10^3	10^3	10^{-4}	10^{-4}
W_6	10^4	10^5	10^6	10^7	10^{10}	10^{10}
W_7	10^5	10^7	10^7	10^8	10^8	10^8
W_8	1	1	1	1	1	1
W_9	1	1	1	1	1	1

Table 3. Initial values for GA parameters.

Parameters	Description	Values
$P_{selection}$	Selection probability	0.07
$P_{crossover}$	Crossover probability	(0.00035×No. of Generation)+0.4465
N_{GE}	Number of generation	500
$N_{population}$	Number of individuals	50
Sel_{method}	Selection method	rank
Cr_{method}	Crossover method	Two-point crossover method

Table 4. Mutation Probability.

Network Size	Probability of Mutation
Up to 25 Sensors	$0.01 \times e^{\frac{\text{No. of Generation}}{1 \times \sqrt{\text{Size of Network}}}}$
Up to 100 Sensors	$0.01 \times e^{\frac{\text{No. of Generation}}{3 \times \sqrt{\text{Size of Network}}}}$

Up to 225 Sensors	$0.01 \times e^{-\frac{\text{No. of Generation}}{5 \times \sqrt{\text{Size of Network}}}}$
Up to 400 Sensors	$0.01 \times e^{-\frac{\text{No. of Generation}}{5 \times \sqrt{\text{Size of Network}}}}$
Up to 625 Sensors	$0.01 \times e^{-\frac{\text{No. of Generation}}{6 \times \sqrt{\text{Size of Network}}}}$
Up to 900 Sensors	$0.01 \times e^{-\frac{\text{No. of Generation}}{7 \times \sqrt{\text{Size of Network}}}}$

Table 5. Initial values for communication energy.

	Description	Values
R_{sen}	Sensing coverage radius	$5m$
E_{Tx}	Transmission energy	$50nJ/bit$
E_{Rx}	Receiving energy	$50nJ/bit$
E_{BF}	Beam forming energy	$5nJ/bit$
E_{da}	Energy consumption for data fusion	$5pJ/bit$
ε_{amp}	Transmitter amplifier energy	$100pJ/bit$
ε_{fs}	energy to send 1-bit message by transmitter amplifying circuit in elemental in free space model	$10pJ/bit/m^2$
ε_{mp}	energy to send 1-bit message by transmitter amplifying circuit in multi-path fading model	$0.0013pJ/bit/m^2$

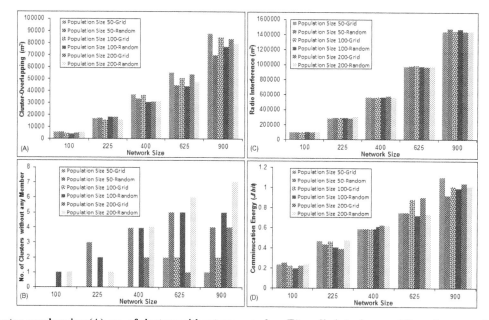

Figure 1. Cluster-overlapping (A), no. of clusters without any member (B), radio interference (C), and communication energy (D) versus network sizes with different population sizes.

To study the effect of population size, we did simulation with three different sizes of population 50, 100, 200 for different network sizes and deployments. Increasing or decreasing the number of chromosomes in the population does not affect cluster-overlapping (Figure 1A), radio interference (Figure 1C) and communication energy (Figure 1D). The number of member-less cluster heads depends on the type of network deployment. Compared to grid deployment, we find more cluster heads without any member in random deployment, which increases with the increasing size of the network (Figure 1B). Deciding an appropriate population size is a trade-off between WSN and GA parameters. Increasing the number of chromosomes in the population increases the CPU time.

To study the effect of selection methods in GA, we used two selection methods: rank and tournament with different type of deployments and WSN sizes. Figure 2(A) illustrates that the tournament selection has lower value of communication energy compared to the rank selection for random and grid deployments when the size of network is small. With larger size networks, the rank selection has lower value of communication energy compared with the tournament selection for random and grid deployments. The rank selection has lower value of cluster-overlapping compared with the rank selection for random and grid deployments in all of the network sizes (Figure 2B). Compared with the rank selection, tournament selection has lower radio interference in all the sizes and types of networks shown in Figure 2(C). By using rank selection, we can minimize operation energy for all the network sizes and deployment types (Figure 2D). We use rank selection for the sake of energy minimization. Energy optimization in a WSN increases the network lifetime and improved the network coverage for small sized networks with tournament selection. When the size of a network is large, rank selection gives better results.

To study the effect of crossover method in WSN design, we used one-point and two-point crossover methods.

We use variable probability of crossover, $P_{crossover}$ = (0.00035×No. of Generation) + 0.4465. Compared with two-point crossover, one-point crossover is more effective in minimizing the value of cluster-overlapping (Figure 3A). Type of crossover does not affect the communication energy; the values of communication energy are very close as shown in Figure 3(B). Network radio interference is minimized with two-point crossover compared with that of one-point crossover shown in Figure 3(C). Figure 3(D) indicates that the type of crossover does not affect $CH_{useless}$, but it depends on the size and type of deployment in the network. Since two-point crossover gives better results than one-point crossover, we use two-point crossover for the rest of the study.

Mutation is an important step in GA. A small change in mutation probability affects the result strongly. To study the effect of mutation probability in WSN design, we use (i) probability of mutation constant ($P_{mutation}$ = 0.001), and (ii) exponential probability of mutation varying with the generation number and the network size.

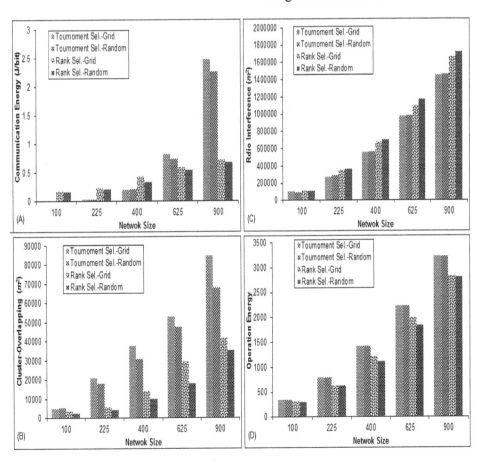

Figure 2. Communication energy (A), cluster-overlapping (B), radio interference (C), and operation energy (D) versus network sizes under different selection methods.

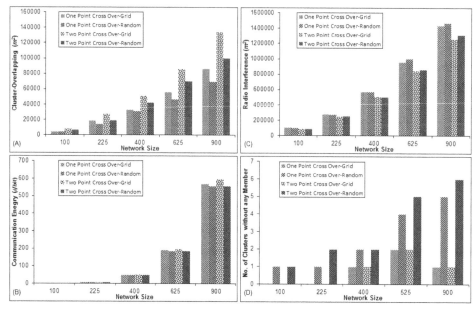

Figure 3. Cluster-overlapping (A), communication energy (B), radio interference (C), and no. of clusters without any member (D) versus network sizes for different crossover methods.

When the mutation probability is changed, the fitness function weights are tuned again. Table 2 shows the fitness function weights for exponential mutation probability and Table 6 shows the different values of the fitness function weights for constant mutation probability.

Figure 4(A) shows that variable probability of mutation is more effective in optimizing cluster-overlapping in both deployment types and sizes of network compared with those with constant probability of mutation. Mutation probability does not affect the average number of communications per cluster (Figure 4B).

Constant probability gives better performance in radio interference compared with variable probability (Figure 4C).

Using variable probability, one can better optimize the communication energy of networks of different types and sizes (Figure 4D). Using exponential mutation probability leads to cluster deployment uniformity, increases in network coverage and lifetime optimization of network communication energy consumption, and decreases in network radio interference.

For finding optimal WSN design parameters and minimizing CPU time, we use *population of size 50*, *rank* selection, *two-point* crossover, *variable probability of crossover*, and *exponential probability of mutation*, which changes with *generation* for *random* and *grid* deployments.

Radio communication radius (R_{rx}) is dependent on the characteristics of WSNs such as *hardware limitation*, *density*, *deployment*. It is optimally fixed with respect to *network connectivity*, and *radio interference*. When the value of R_{rx} is decreased, the network connectivity goes down as well. Increasing the value of R_{rx} leads to more consumption of network energy.

Table 6. Weighing coefficient of fitness function for constant mutation probability.

Weights	Up to 25 Sensors	Up to 100 Sensors	Up to 225 Sensors	Up to 400 Sensors	Up to 625 Sensors	Up to 900 Sensors
W_1	10^{-4}	10^{-2}	10^{-3}	10^{-2}	10^{-3}	10^{-4}
W_2	10^{-2}	10^4	10^6	10^6	10^7	10^8
W_3	10	10^2	10^3	10^4	10^8	10^8
W_4	1	1	1	10^2	1	1
W_5	10^3	10^2	10^2	10^2	10^{-2}	10^{-4}
W_6	10^5	10^5	10^7	10^9	10^{10}	10^{10}
W_7	10^5	10^5	10^5	10^6	10^8	10^9
W_8	1	10^2	10^2	10^2	1	1
W_9	1	1	1	10^2	1	10^2

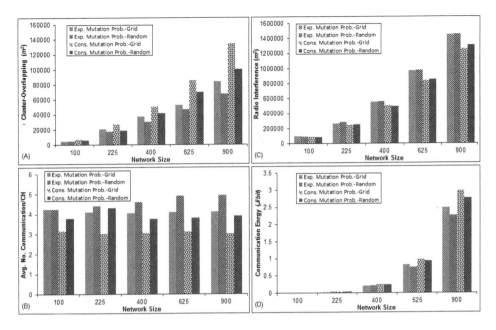

Figure 4. Cluster-overlapping (A), avg. no. of communication/CH (B), radio interference (C), and communication energy (D) versus network sizes for different mutation probabilities.

The simulation results shown in Figure 5 indicate that irrespective of the network size and deployment, the optimal value of R_{rx} is 5 m for the proposed WSN model (Figure 5A), and increasing the value of R_{rx} increases radio interference (Figure 5B), and decreasing its value increases the number of sensors out of range affecting connectivity (Figure 5A).

To study the effect of deployment on WSN design, we studied two types of deployment: *grid* and *random* for five network sizes. *Radio interference* in random deployment is less than that of the grid deployment shown in Figure 6(A). The value of *operation energy* in random deployment is much lower than that of grid deployment when the size of the network is small. When the size of the network is increased, these values are very close shown in Figure 6(B).

Clusters in the network with grid deployment are more *flexible* and have *better cluster distribution uniformity* compared with that of random deployment when the size of the network is small, but by increasing the size of the network, clusters with random deployment become *more flexible* and have *better uniformity* in *cluster distribution* compared with that of grid deployment shown in Figure 6(C).

Grid deployment requires more *communication energy* than random deployment shown in Figure 6(D). Thus, WSN with random deployment *lasts*

longer than a WSN of equal size with a grid deployment.

In WSN design, location of the BS can be *inside* or *outside* of an application area. Figure 7(A) illustrates that outside located BS *reduces* the value of *cluster-overlapping* compared with BS located inside. Therefore, *clusters* in a WSN with outside located BS are *distributed more uniformly*. The average number of communications per cluster for all network sizes and types are *equal* when the BS is located inside. It is less than those in the cases when the BS is located outside. It means that the network can be designed with *less number* of CHs when the BS is *located outside* (Figure 7B). But with inside located BS, the radio interference is lower than outside located BS for all different network types and sizes (Figure 7C). *Outside* located BS affects the value of *communication energy* of the network (Figure 7D).

To study the effect of density, we define *unit* density as *one sensor* per *meter* because the R_{sen} is 1 meter. We experiment with three different densities: 0.5, 1 and 1.5.

If the area size is 100 m^2, we deploy 50 (density is 0.5), 100 (density is 1) and 150 (density is 1.5) sensors in the area. *Radio interference* (Figure 8A), cluster-overlapping (Figure 8B), and the *number of clusters without any member* (Figure 8D) all increase with *increasing* density of deployment, but the number of *active sensors out of range* (Figure 8C) *decreases*.

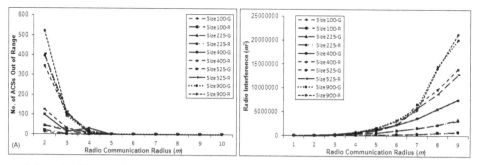

Figure 5. No. of ACSs out of range (A), and radio interference (B) versus radio communication radius.

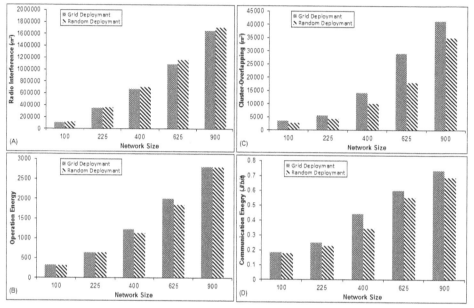

Figure 6. Radio interference (A), operation energy (B), cluster-overlapping(C), and communication energy (D) versus network sizes under grid and random deployments.

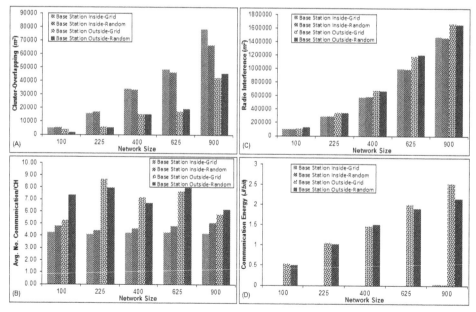

Figure 7. Cluster-overlapping (A), avg. no. of communication/CH (B), radio interference (C), and communication energy (D) versus network sizes for two possible locations of BS.

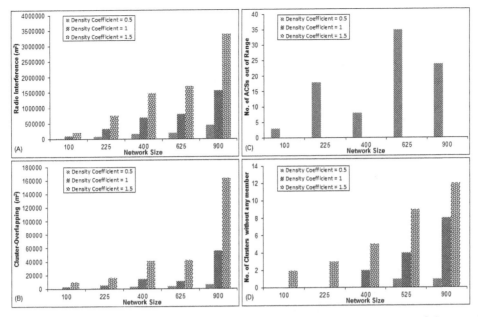

Figure 8. Radio interference (A), cluster-overlapping (B), no. of ACSs out of range (C), and no. of clusters without any member (D) at different densities.

6. Conclusion

We study WSN design through GA by first studying and fixing the GA parameters and then using these values for near optimal WSN design. There are trade-off among different criteria and parameters of WSNs. The algorithm is coded in MATLAB version 7 on Intel® core $i5$ CPU 650 3.2 GHz running Windows 7 professional. With increasing sizes of network, optimization time increases.

The simulation results of this study indicate that deciding an appropriate population size is a trade-off between WSN parameters and GA parameters. In small sized networks, to optimize energy, to increase the network's lifetime and to improve the network's coverage, tournament selection is more efficient. When the size of a network is large, rank selection has better performance. Also, two-point crossover's performance is better than one-point crossover for the proposed model. Exponential mutation probability increases a network's coverage and lifetime, and decreases network communication energy consumption and radio interference.

By increasing the size of a network, optimization time is increased. The simulation results of this study indicate that the value of radio communication radius directly affects radio interference, cluster-overlapping, and uniformity in distribution, communication energy, and number of sensors out of range and CHs without any member. The optimal value of radio communication radius is not dependent on network size and type of deployment, but dependent on the density of network deployment. Outside located BS reduces the value of cluster-overlapping compared with the case when the BS is located inside.

The average number of communications per cluster for all network sizes and types are equal when the BS is located inside. With inside located BS, radio interference value is lower than when the BS is located outside for all deployments and sizes. Outside located BS affects communication energy. Outside located BS is preferred over inside located BS. Sensing radius determines density of a network. Density affects radio communication radius strongly. In all the network situations, random deployment has better performance compared with grid deployment. Future research will focus on WSN design using other optimization methods.

References

[1] Akyildiz I. F., Su W., Sankarasubramaniam Y., Cayirci E. (2002). Wireless sensor networks, a survey Computer Networks, Elsevier, 38, 393-422, doi: 10.1016/S1389-1286(01)00302-4.

[2] G. Anastasi, M. Conti, M. Di Francesco, A. Passarella. (2009). Energy conservation in wireless sensor networks: A survey, Journal of Ad Hoc Networks, Vol. 7, Issue 3, 537-568, doi: 10.1016/j.adhoc.2008.06.003.

[3] Ian F. Akyildiz, Ismail H. Kasimoglu. (2004). Wireless sensor and actor networks, research challenges, Ad Hoc Networks, Elsevier, 2, 351-367, doi: 10.1016/j.adhoc.2004.04.003

[4] Siva Ram Murthy, C. Manoj, B.S. (2004). Ad Hoc Wireless Networks, Prentice Hall PTR, New York.

[5] Arampatzis Th., Lygeros J., Manesis S. (2005). A Survey of Applications of Wireless Sensors and Wireless Sensor Networks, In: Proceedings, of 13th Mediterranean Conference on Control and Automation Limas sol (Cyprus), 719-724, doi: 10.1109/.2005.1467103.

[6] Meer A. Hamza, Sherin M. Youssef, Salma F. Fayed. (2007). A distributed energy efficient query processing in self-organized Wireless Sensor Networks, In: Proceedings, the World Congress on Engineering (WCE), Vol. II, 2-4.

[7] Yanhuai Qu, Jianan Fang, Shuai Zhang. (2010). Modeling the Critical Transmitting Range for Connectivity in Wireless Sensor Networks, In: Proceedings, of International Conference on Multimedia Information Networking and Security.

[8] Akyildiz I. F., W. Su, Y. Sankarasubramaniam, and E. Cayirci. (2002). A survey on sensor networks, IEEE Communications Magazine, Vol. 40, No. 8, Pages 102-114, doi: 10.1109/MCOM.2002.1024422.

[9] Zheng, J., Jamalipour, A. (2009). Wireless Sensor Networks, a networking perspective, Wiley.

[10] Kevin L. Mills. (2007). A brief survey of self-organization in wireless sensor networks, Wireless Communications and Mobiles Computing, 823-834, doi: 10.1002/wcm.v7:7

[11] Moslem Afrashteh Mehr. (2011). Design and Implementation a New Energy Efficient Clustering Algorithm using Genetic Algorithm for Wireless Sensor Networks, World Academy of Science, Engineering and Technology, 430-433.

[12] Konstantinos P. Ferentinos, Theodore A. (2007). Tsiligiridis, Adaptive design optimization of wireless sensor networks using genetic algorithms, Computer Networks, Vol. 51, Issue 4, 1031–1051, doi:10.1016/j.comnet.2006.06.013.

[13] Haupt R. L., Haupt S. E. (2004). Practical Genetic Algorithms, Second Edition, Wiley, New York.

[14] Dorigo M., Blum C. (2005). Ant colony optimization theory, a survey, Theoretical Computer Science, 344, 243-278, doi: 10.1016/j.tcs.2005.05.020.

[15] Atashpaz-Gargari E., C. Lucas. (2007). Imperialist Competitive Algorithm, An algorithm for optimization inspired by imperialistic competition, IEEE Congress on Evolutionary Computation, 4661-4666, doi: 10.1109/CEC.2007.4425083.

[16] S. M. Hosseinirad, S. K. Basu, (2012). Imperialist Approach to Cluster Head Selection in WSN, International Journal of Computer Applications, 1-5.

[17] M. Melanie, (1999). An Introduction to Genetic Algorithms, MIT Press.

[18] Gowrishankar S., Basavaraju T. G., Manjaiah D. H., Subir K. Sarkar. (2008). Issues in Wireless Sensor Networks, In: Proceedings, of the World Congress on Engineering (WCE), Vol. I, 2-4.

[19] D. G. Melese, H. Xiong, Q. Gao, (2010). Consumed energy as a factor for cluster head selection in Wireless Sensor Networks, In: Proceedings, of 6th International Conference on Wireless Communications Networking and Mobile Computing (WiCOM).

[20] Javier Espina, Thomas F., Oliver M. (2006). Body Sensor Networks, Springer publication, New York

[21] Zoran O. Bojkovic, Bojan B. (2008). A Survey on Wireless Sensor Networks Deployment, WSEAS Transaction on Communications, Vol. 7, 1172-1181.

[22] Kenan Xu, Glen Takahara, Glen Takahara. (2006). On the Robustness of Grid-based Deployment in Wireless Sensor Networks, In: Proceedings, of International Wireless Communications and Mobile Computing Conference (IWCMC).

[23] Paolo Santi. (2005). Topology Control in Wireless Ad Hoc and Sensor Networks, ACM Computing Surveys, Vol. 37, No. 2, 164-194.

[24] Garg S., Arya S., Kaler R. S., Gupta U. (2008). Wireless Sensor Network design for Smart Operations, In: Proceedings, of International Conference on Microwave, 850-851, doi: 10.1109/AMTA.2008.4763141.

[25] Stojmenovic Ivan, (2005). Handbook of Sensor Network, Algorithms and Architectures, Wiley, New York.

[26] Heinzelman W. R., Chandrakasan A. (2000). Balakrishnan H., Energy-Efficient Communication Protocol for Wireless Micro-sensor Networks, In: Proceedings, of the Hawaii International Conference on System Sciences, 4-7, doi: 10.1109/HICSS.2000.926982.

[27] Ganesan D., Cerpa A., Wei Ye, Yan Y., Zhao J., Estrin D. (2003). Networking Issues in Wireless Sensor Networks, Elsevier Science, doi: 10.1016/j.jpdc.2004.03.016.

[28] Ferrari G., P. Medagliani, S. Di Piazza, M. Martal`o,. (2007). Wireless Sensor Networks, Performance Analysis in Indoor Scenarios, EURASIP Journal on Wireless Communications and Networking.

[29] Enrique J., Duarte-Melo, Mingyan Liu. (2003). Data-Gathering Wireless Sensor Networks, Organization and Capacity, Elsevier Science, New York.

[30] Ziqing Z., Hai Z., Jian Z., Dazhou Li. (2010). Research on wireless sensors network topology models, Scientific Research Journal in Software Engineering & Applications, 1167-1171.

12

A stack-based chaotic algorithm for encryption of colored images

H. Khodadadi[1*]and O. Mirzaei[2]

1. Department of Computer Engineering, Minab Branch, Islamic Azad University, Minab, Iran.
2. Computer Security Lab, Department of Computer Science and Engineering, Universidad Carlos III de Madrid, Madrid, Spain.

*Corresponding author: habibekhodadadi@gmail.com (H. Khodadadi).

Abstract

In this paper, a new method is presented for encryption of colored images. This method is based upon using stack data structure and chaos, which make the image encryption algorithm more efficient and robust. In the proposed algorithm, a series of data whose range is between 0 and 3 is generated using the chaotic logistic system. Then the original image is divided into four sub-images, which are subsequently pushed into the stack based on the next number in the series. In the next step, the first element in the stack, which includes one of the four sub-images, is popped, and this image is divided into four other parts. Then, based on the next number in the series, four sub-images are pushed into the stack again. This procedure is repeated until the stack is empty. Therefore, during this process, each pixel unit is encrypted using another series of chaotic numbers (generated by the Chen chaotic system). This method is repeated until all pixels of the plain image are encrypted. Finally, several extensive simulations on well-known USC datasets are conducted to show the efficiency of this encryption algorithm. The tests performed show that the proposed method has a really large key space and possesses a high-entropic distribution. Consequently, it outperforms the other competing algorithms in the case of security.

Keywords: *Chaos, Encryption of Colored Images, Chen Chaotic System, Logistic Chaotic System, Stack.*

1. Introduction

The data security is highly considered day after day, given the growth of internet global network and its influence on all aspects of the human life. The internet is used as a platform for transferring our data. Consequently, the protection and security of this data becomes more and more crucial if it is valuable for us. In electronic exchanges, which are increasing day by day, some trustworthy mechanisms are required. These mechanisms should be designed so adequately and accurately that would make the individuals trust the other individual with whom they are communicating. Moreover, it should make the individuals trust the platform that is used for communication. Preserving information security is the foundation of this trust.

Data encryption is one of the best ways to maintain security. Image encryption is one of the main sorts of encryption areas. So far, several algorithms have been developed for this purpose. Among these methods, the application of chaos

for cryptography is highly considered due to its specific features [1]. Chaotic systems are considered as ideal methods for cryptography due to their unique characteristics including sensitivity to initial values, pseudo-randomness, unpredictability, non-periodic, etc. For this reason, the applications of these systems are increasing day by day.

Many encryption algorithms have been proposed based on chaos. In these algorithms, the features of chaotic systems are specially applied in image encryption. In these methods, the pixel values for the image are somehow combined using the numbers generated by the chaotic system. Then the encrypted image is obtained by this combination. Meanwhile, the application of various chaotic functions with different dimensions or the application of a combination of several chaotic functions is very common [2-6]. In [7-9], DNA encoding has been combined with chaotic map for encryption.

In many papers [10-17], the plain-image has first been divided into several sub-images, and then the position of each sub-image is changed pseudo-randomly according to a chaotic map.

A stack-based chaotic algorithm is proposed in this paper for encryption of colored images, different from other research works suggested so far. First of all, a series of data is generated in the range of [0, 3] using the chaotic logistic system. Then the original image is divided into four equal sub-images, and, based on the next number in the produced series, four parts of the image are, respectively, pushed into the stack. In the next step, the first element in the stack, which includes one of the four sub-images, is popped, and this image is divided into four other parts. Then, based on the next number in the series, four sub-images are pushed into the stack again. This procedure is repeated every time until the stack is empty. Thus during this process, every time we reached a pixel unit, we encrypted it with the help of another series of chaotic numbers (generated by the Chen chaotic system). This method was repeated until all pixels of the image were encrypted.

This paper is organized as follows. Section 2 provides a brief description about chaotic systems. Section 3 explains about two fundamental data structures, stack, and queue. It also describes our proposed encryption algorithm in details. Simulation outcomes as well as different security analyses are given in section 4, and finally, section 5 concludes the paper and suggests some future improvements.

2. Chaotic systems

Chaos is a phenomenon that occurs in non-linear definable systems. These systems show a high sensitivity to initial conditions. Moreover, they represent a pseudo-random behavior. Such systems remain stable in the chaotic mode when they meet the Lyapunov exponential equation conditions. The important characteristics of the chaos that make it suitable for encryption purposes are its definable nature along with its pseudo-random behavior. This leads to a condition in which the output of the system seems random from the attackers' viewpoint, while it seems definable from deciphers' viewpoint. As a result, such a system seems very simple and decipherable from deciphers' viewpoint. So many chaotic systems have been introduced so far, which can be classified into two main categories from one viewpoint. The first category includes chaotic systems with specific physical interpretation. These kinds of systems have also been derived using the dynamic equations of real

systems such as the Lorenz chaotic system [18]. The Lorenz chaotic system was the first continuous chaotic system studied. The second category includes the chaotic systems that do not have any physical interpretation. They are only unique mathematical models. In fact, this category of chaotic systems is used as an assessment indicator in the chaos control and synchronization issues. For example, the Chen chaotic system [19] is a good representative of the chaotic system category. It was first presented by Chen and Eta in 1999. The equations governing this system are provided in the following equation:

$$\begin{cases} x & = a(y - x) \\ y & = (c - a)x - xz + cy \\ z & = xy - bz \end{cases} \tag{1}$$

In this equation, a, b, and c are parameters. If a = 35, b = 3, and c = [20, 28.4], then the system is in a chaos state. The chaotic behavior of this system is shown in figure 1.

Logistic system is a simple chaotic system. It is perhaps the simplest example of a dynamic discrete chaotic system that shows a chaotic behavior. The governing equation of this system is as follows:

$$x_{n+1} = \lambda x_n (1 - x_n), x_0 \in (0,1) \tag{2}$$

In this equation, x_0 is the initial value, and λ is the system parameter in the interval [3.57, 4].

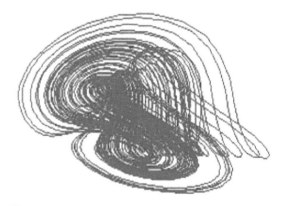

Figure 1. Chaotic behavior of Chen chaotic system.

3. Proposed encryption algorithm
3.1. Stack and queue concepts

Stack and queue are two important and popular data structures in computer science, which are used to solve a variety of data structure problems.

A queue is defined as a list whose elements enter it from one side, named as queue rear, and exit it from the front of the queue. The queue is also known as a FIFO (First in First Out) list because the first element in a queue is the first element that will be served (exited) from the queue [20]. In other words, the order of entry of the elements into the queue is the same as the order of elements leaving the queue. A sample queue is demonstrated in figure 2, and the adding and removing procedures are also illustrated there.

A stack is a list of elements in which each one of the elements can only be added to the list or removed from it from one side (top of the stack). In other words, the elements are removed from the stack in the inverse order they enter the stack [20]. Two basic actions in the stack include PUSH action, in order to add an element to the stack, and POP action, in order to remove an element from the stack. The stack is also known as a LIFO (Last in First Out) list because the last element that enters the stack is the first element that exits it. This data structure and also its basic procedures are demonstrated in figure 3.

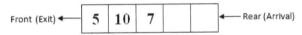

Front (Exit) ← | **5** | **10** | **7** | | | ← Rear (Arrival)

Figure 2. A sample queue as well as removing and adding items.

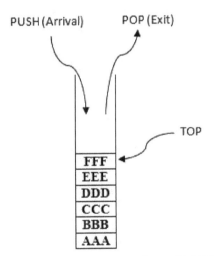

Figure 2. Stack data structure along with PUSH and POP actions.

Referring to figure 3, the six elements AAA, BBB, CCC, DDD, EEE, and FFF are, respectively, pushed in an empty stack. The main procedures of the stack that add and remove the elements can only happen from the top of this data structure. In other words, EEE cannot be removed from the stack before FFF is removed, and DDD cannot be removed from the stack before EEE and FFF are removed, and so forth. As a result, the elements in the list can only be removed or popped in the inverse order they were added or pushed into the stack.

3.2. Stack-based chaotic algorithm for image encryption

The proposed algorithm is a chaotic one, which uses the stack data structure to encrypt the colored images. The algorithm steps are as follow:

Step 1: An empty stack is created with a size exactly the same as the original image. The chaotic logistic system is set to an appropriate initial value. Then a chaotic series of L values is generated after M0 times of execution.

Step 2: X1 series is created from L series using the following equation:

$$x1 = rem(floor((abs(L(i))*(10^{14}))),4) \qquad (3)$$

In this equation, rem(L) returns an integer residual value, floor(L) returns the integer part of the number L, and abs(L) returns the absolute value of L. As a result, X1 series includes the numbers 0, 1, 2, and 3, respectively.

Step 3: The image is divided into 4 equal sub-images, according to figure 4, and the K1 counter is set to M0.

Step 4: First, one part of the image is selected based on the first number in the X1 series. Then the other three parts and this selected part are saved in the stack in a clockwise order. In fact, corresponding rows and columns of the pixels are saved. For example, if the first number of the series was 2, then 3, 0, 1, and 2 are, respectively, saved in the stack. Therefore, the top element of the stack is 2. Finally, one unit is added to the K1 counter.

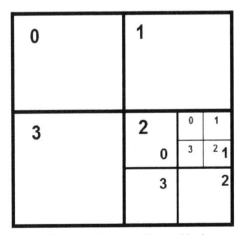

Figure 4. Division of image blocks.

Step 5: The following loop is repeated until the stack is empty:

5.1.   The first (top) element is popped from the stack.

5.2.   If this element only includes one pixel,

the encryption sub-program is called, this pixel is encrypted, and the control is turned back to the beginning of the loop. If this element does not include one pixel, the popped element is divided into 4 equal sub-images according to figure 4. Then, based on the next number in the X1 series (K1th number in the X1 series), the 4 obtained sub-images are pushed into the stack in a clockwise order. At last, one unit is added to the K1 counter. Therefore, the encryption of image pixels becomes more complicated with the help of stack data structure, and, as a result, it is also difficult to find which pixel is encrypted at what step. In order to encrypt each pixel in the original image, the remaining steps are as follow:

Step 6: First, the Chen chaotic system is set to the initial appropriate values. Then three series named x, y, and z are created.

Step 7: X2, X3, and X4 series are created, respectively, according to (4) from x, y, and z series after N0 times of execution. Then the K2 counter is set to N0.

$$x2 = rem(floor[(abs(x(i)) - floor(abs(x(i)))) * 10^{14}], 256) \quad (4)$$

Therefore, all numbers in the X2, X3, and X4 series are in the range of 0-255.

Step 8: Finally, the following steps are done in order to encrypt each pixel in the image (encryption sub-program):

8.1.   The range of pixel values is between 0 and 255 in colored images. The pixel values include the red, green, and blue colors. Therefore, these pixel values and K2th elements of the X2, X3, and X4 series are initially converted to binary forms.

8.2.   XOR operation is applied between the K2th element of the X2 series and the red value of pixel, between the K2th element of the X3 series and the green value of the pixel, and finally, between the K2th element of the X4 series and the blue value of the pixel. These three obtained binary numbers are then converted to decimal numbers. These new numbers are considered as new values of the red, green, and blue pixels.

8.3.   One unit is added to the K2 counter.

In order to decrypt the image, the above-mentioned steps should be performed on an encrypted image. All the steps are shown in figure 5.

4. Simulation results

A good encryption algorithm should produce cipher-images such that they have noticeable differences with their corresponding plain-images from statistical viewpoints. It should also resist all kinds of known attacks. Thus different statistical experiments were conducted to show the efficiency of our proposed encryption algorithm.

The simulations were all implemented using the MATLAB 7.10 software, and the popular USC data base was used as a benchmark for our experiments. The initial value for the logistic system was set to 0.75798, the λ value was set to 3.85, and the Chen system parameters a, b, and c were set to 35, 3, and 26, respectively. Furthermore, the initial values for the x, y, and z series were set to 1, –1.6, and –0.2, respectively. Finally, M0 was set to 2000, while N0 was set to 3000 (the values of series were not used before the M0 and N0 repeats).

In figures 6, 7, 8, and 9, two sample 256 * 256 images are shown along with the histograms of red, green, and blue channels. Moreover, the encrypted image and its histograms of red, green, and blue channels were presented. As it is clear in this picture, the proposed encryption algorithm has encrypted the image appropriately since the image histogram is completely flat.

4.1. Key space analysis

In the proposed algorithm, the Chen and logistic systems were used in the encryption process. The key values were as follow: the initial values for the logistic and Chen systems that needed a 128-bit space and a 32-bit space for storing λ value of logistic system. Furthermore, a, b, and c values in the Chen system needed a 48-bit space, and finally, the N0 and M0 values needed a 64-bit space. Putting all of these values together, the total number of bits needed for storing all the parameters was 272. Therefore, the cryptosystem provided 2^{272} different combinations, and had a large key space.

The key space of the proposed encryption method was compared with some other competitive algorithms, and the results obtained were presented in table 1. Referring to this table, it is clear that the stack based chaotic algorithm has the largest key space in contrast with the others.

4.2. Key sensitivity test

Several key sensitivity tests were performed in this work. Figures 7, 10, and 11 illustrate the sensitivity of our encryption method to the secret keys L, λ, a, b, c, x, y, z, N0, and M0.

Figure 7 is the encrypted image of figure 6 with the actual parameters (cited in section 4). Figure 10 is the encryption result of figure 6 with all the parameters equal to actual ones, except $a = 35.000001$, and, finally, figure 11 is the encryption result of the same image with all the parameters equal to the actual ones except $\lambda = 3.85000001$.

The histograms of the encrypted images with different initial values are also given in figures 10 and 11.

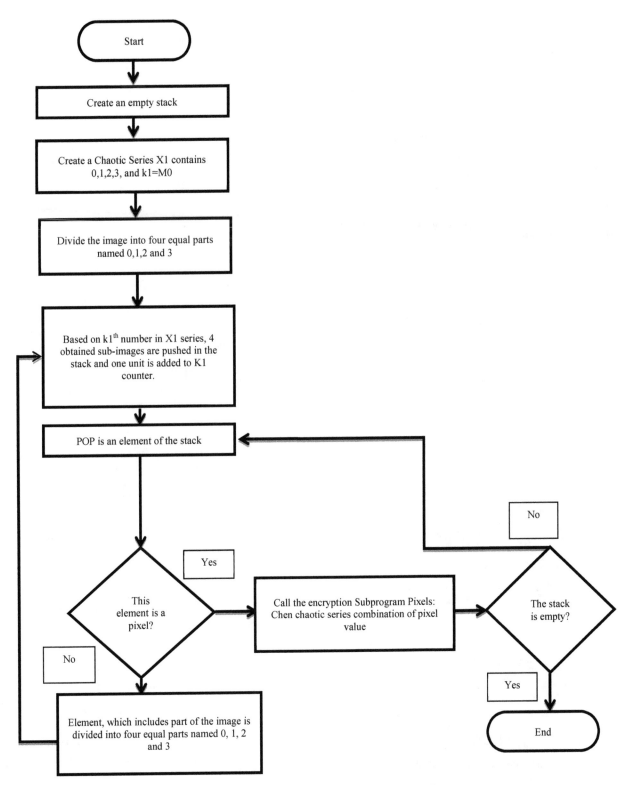

Figure 5 .Proposed encryption algorithms using stack.

Referring to the aforementioned images, it can be concluded that the new chaotic encryption algorithm is sensitive to initial keys such that a small change in their values will generate a completely different decryption result, and, as a result, the plain image cannot be retrieved correctly.

4.3. Similarity of adjacent pixels
Usually, in most parts of an image, the neighbor pixel values are very similar to each other. Therefore, a high level of similarity between neighbor pixels is expected in each image. A good encryption algorithm should decrease this level of similarity in order to minimize the possibility of deciphering the pixel values by comparing the neighbor pixel values [10]. For this reason, 3000 pairs (horizontal, vertical, and diagonal) of the neighbor pixels were selected randomly from both the original ciphered images.

The levels of similarity between these pairs are shown in figure 12 (only red channel was used for our comparisons). As it can be seen, the level of similarity is high in the plain-image, while it decreases in the ciphered one using the proposed encryption algorithm.

Table 1. Comparison of key space between our proposed method and some other references.

Ref.	[7]	[9]	[17]	Our proposed algorithm
Key Space	192	233	240	272

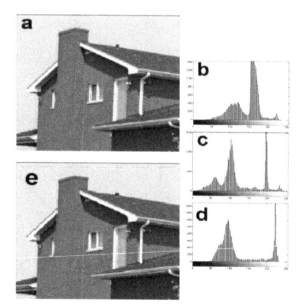

Figure 6. Original image. (b), (c), and (d) are histograms of red, green, and blue channels in original image. (e) Decrypted image.

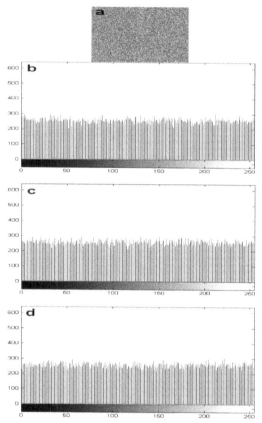

Figure 7. (a) Encrypted image of Fig. 6. (b), (c), and (d) are histograms of red, green, and blue channels.

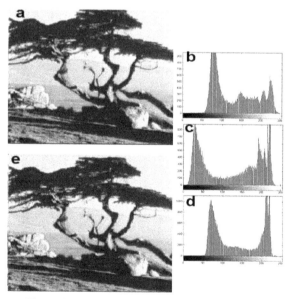

Figure 8. (a) Original image. (b), (c), and (d) are histograms of red, green, and blue channels in original image. (e) Decrypted image.

4.4. Analysis of information entropy
Entropy is one of the most outstanding features that make the images to have a random-like behavior. This parameter was first introduced by Claude E. Shannonin (1949), and can be obtained according to (5).

$$H(S) = \sum_{i=0}^{2^N-1} P(S_i) \log(\frac{1}{P(S_i)}) \qquad (5)$$

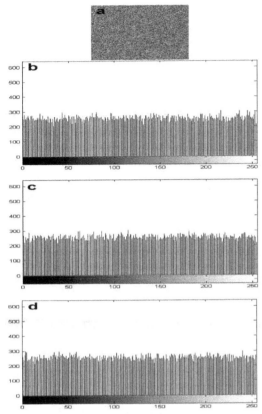

Figure 9. (a) Encrypted image of figure 8. (b), (c), and (d) are histograms of red, green, and blue channels.

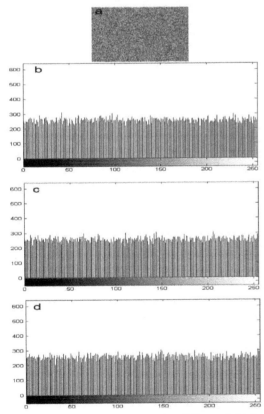

Figure 10. (a) Encrypted image with different initial values (a = 35.000001). (b), (c), and (d) represent histograms of red, green, and blue channels of encrypted image with different initial values.

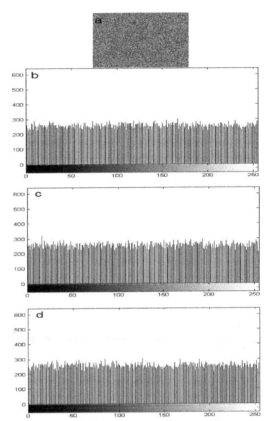

Figure 11. Encrypted image with different initial values (λ = 3.85000001). (b), (c), and (d) represent histograms of red, green, and blue channels of encrypted image with different initial values.

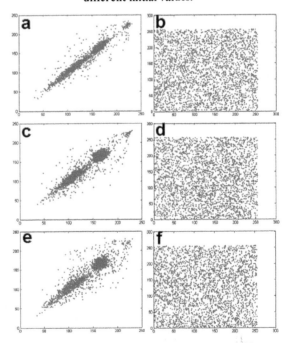

Figure 12. Levels of similarity between two neighbor pixels in red channel of both original and encrypted images from top to bottom in horizontal, vertical, and diagonal.

In this equation, N is the number of grey scale levels in an image (ex: N = 256 for 8-bit image pixels), and P(si) is the occurrence probability of the grey scale "I" in the image. The entropy value is 8 for images that are produced totally randomly. The entropy value for the proposed encryption algorithm were measured for a sample image, and the result obtained was shown in table 2.

Table 2. Entropy of original image and its corresponding encrypted one.

Entropy of plain-image	Entropy of cipher-image
7.0686	7.9989

From table 2, it can be well-understood that the information entropy of the cyphered image is very close to 8. This means that the encrypted images are close to a random source, and that the proposed algorithm is secure against the entropy attack.

Moreover, the information entropy of the proposed encryption method was compared with some other algorithms for the LENA standard image, and the results obtained were all gathered in table 3. As it can be seen, the entropy of our method is higher than the other four competing algorithms. High-entropic distribution implies that an adversary, given the cipher image, is unable or hardly able to compute any predicate on the cipher image with greater probability than an adversary that does not possess it, and, as a result, it is more secure.

Table 3. Comparison of information entropy between our proposed method and some other references.

Ref.	[7]	[16]	[9]	Our proposed algorithm
Information Entropy	7.9890	7.9977	7.9967	7.9991

5. Conclusions and future works

In this paper, a stack-based chaotic algorithm was introduced for the encryption of colored images. In the proposed method, the series generated from the Chen chaotic system were combined with image pixels after initial pre-processing. Then the encrypted image was generated by this combination. The order of pixels encryption was determined by another series of chaotic numbers generated from the logistic system and also the entry/exit mode of either one pixel or part of the image to/from the stack. The experimental results show that the proposed algorithm has a high security, and also a large key space.

Moreover, the following suggestions can be considered as the future extensions of our research work:

1. Some other data structures such as queues and trees can be used, and some other ways can be applied for their composition (e.g. using two or more stacks) to enhance the security of encryption algorithm.

2. Other chaotic systems or a combination of different chaotic systems can be incorporated to our encryption method.

References

[1] Amigo, J. M., Kocarev, L. & Szczepanski, J. (2007). Theory and practice of chaotic cryptography. Physics Letters A, vol. 366, no. 3, pp. 211-216.

[2] Tong, X., Liu, Y., Zhang, M. & Wang, W. (2012). A Novel Image Encryption Scheme Based on Dynamical Multiple Chaos and Baker Map. 11th International Symposium on Distributed Computing and Applications to Business, Engineering & Science, Guilin, China, 2012.

[3] Maksuanpan, S., Veerawadtanapong, T. & San-Um, W. (2014). Robust Digital Image Cryptosystem Based on Nonlinear Dynamics of Compound Sine and Cosine Chaotic Maps for Private Data Protection. ICACT Transactions on Advanced Communications Technology (TACT), vol. 3, no. 2, pp. 418-425.

[4] Gao, H. J., Zhang, Y. S., Liang, S. Y. & Li, D.Q. (2006). A new chaotic algorithm for image encryption. Chaos, Solitons & Fractals, vol. 29, no. 2, pp. 393–399.

[5] Zuo, Y. Z. F., Zhai, Z. & Xiaobin, C. (2008). A New Image Encryption Algorithm Based on Multiple Chaos System. International Symposium on Electronic Commerce and Security, Guangzhou, China, 2008.

[6] Paul, A., Das, N., Prusty, A. K. & Das, C. (2013). RGB Image Encryption by Using Discrete Log with and Lorenz's Chaotic Function. IEEE, 4th International Conference on Computer and Communication Technology (ICCCT), Allahabad, India, 2013.

[7] Liu, L., Zhang, Q. & Wei, X. (2012). A RGB image encryption algorithm based on DNA encoding and chaos map. Computers and Electrical Engineering, Elsevier, vol. 38, pp. 1240-1248.

[8] Som, S., Kotal, A., Chatterjee, A., Dey, S. & Palit, S. (2013). A Colour Image Encryption Based On DNA Coding and Chaotic Sequences. IEEE, 1st International Conference on Emerging Trends and Applications in Computer Science (ICETACS), Shillong, India, 2013.

[9] Wei, X., Guo, L., Zhang, Q., Zhang, J. & Lian, S. (2012). A novel color image encryption algorithm based on DNA sequence operation and hyper-chaotic system. The Journal of Systems and Software, vol. 85, no. 2, pp. 290-299.

[10] Mirzaei, O., Yaghoobi, M. & Irani, H. (2011). A new image encryption method: parallel sub-image encryption with hyper chaos. Nonlinear Dynamics, vol. 67, no. 1, pp. 557-566.

[11] Jiang, H. & Fu, C. (2008). An Image Encryption Scheme Based on Lorenz Chaos System. IEEE, Fourth International Conference on Natural Computation (ICNC), Jinan, China, 2008.

[12] Dongming, C., Zhiliang, Z. & Guangming, Y. (2008). An improved Image Encryption Algorithm

Based on Chaos. IEEE The 9th International Conference for Young Computer Scientists, Hunan, China, 2008.

[13] Wang, Y., Wong, K-W., Liao, X. & Chen, G. (2011). A new chaos-based fast image encryption algorithm. Applied Soft Computing, vol. 11, no. 1, pp. 514–522.

[14] Ye, G. (2010). Image Scrambling encryption algorithm of pixel bit based on Chaos map. pattern recognition letters, vol. 31, pp. 347-354.

[15] Zhu, Z. L., Zhang, W., Wong, K. W. & Yu, H. (2011). A chaos-based symmetric image encryption scheme using a bit-level permutation. Information Sciences, Vol. 181, pp. 1171–1186.

[16] Murillo-Escobar, M. A., Cruz-Hernández, C., Abundiz-Pérez, F., López-Gutiérrez, R. M. & Acosta Del Campo, O.R. (2015). A RGB image encryption algorithm based on total plain image characteristics and chaos. Signal Processing, vol. 109, pp.119-131.

[17] Mazloom, S. & Eftekhari-Moghadam, A. M. (2009). Color image encryption based on Coupled Nonlinear Chaotic Map. Chaos, Solitons & Fractals, vol. 42, no. 3, pp. 1745–1754.

[18] Lorenz, E. N. (1963). Deterministic nonperiodic flow. Journal, J. Atmos. Sci, 1963, vol. 20, no. 2, pp. 130-141.

[19] Chen, G. & Ueta, T. (1999). Yet another chaotic attractor. Journal, Int. J. Bifur. Chaos, vol. 9, no. 7, pp. 1465-1466.

[20] Seymour, L. (1986). Schaum's Outline of Theory and Problems of Data Structures. McGRAW-HILL BOOK Company.

13

Feature selection using genetic algorithm for classification of schizophrenia using fMRI data

H. Shahamat[*] and A. A. Pouyan

Computer Engineering and Information Technology Department, University of Shahrood, Shahrood, Iran.

*Corresponding author: Shahamat@shahroodut.ac.ir (H. Shahamat).

Abstract

In this paper we propose a new method for classification of subjects into schizophrenia and control groups using functional magnetic resonance imaging (fMRI) data. In the preprocessing step, the number of fMRI time points is reduced using principal component analysis (PCA). Then, independent component analysis (ICA) is used for further data analysis. It estimates independent components (ICs) of PCA results. For feature extraction, local binary patterns (LBP) technique is used for the ICs. It transforms the ICs into spatial histograms of LBP values. For feature selection, the genetic algorithm (GA) is used to obtain a set of features with large discrimination power. In the next step of feature selection, linear discriminant analysis (LDA) is used for further extract features that maximize the ratio of between-class and within-class variability. Finally, a test subject is classified into schizophrenia or control group using a Euclidean distance based classifier and a majority vote method. In this paper, a leave-one-out cross validation method is used for performance evaluation. Experimental results prove that the proposed method has an acceptable accuracy.

Keywords: *Schizophrenia, ICA, Feature Extraction, Local Binary Patterns, LDA.*

1. Introduction

Schizophrenia is a common, chronic and debilitating psychiatric disorder. It affects about 1% of the global population, and another 3% has Schizophrenia-type personality disorders [1]. Schizophrenia is the fourth leading cause of disability in the developed counties [2]. In the last years, researchers have tried to propose methods for classification of patients with severe mental illness. It was done to exam differences between patient and controls groups, based on neuroscientific measures [3]. In this regard, researchers have used event-related potentials (ERP) derived from the electroencephalogram (EEG) for finding abnormalities in schizophrenia patients for many years. ERP waveforms obtained through AOD stimuli show good results in separating schizophrenia from normal controls [4, 5]. However, the studies based on ERP have not proven to be sensitive enough to be used in diagnostic purposes.

On the other hand, functional magnetic resonance imaging (FMRI) data have potential to classify different brain disorders including schizophrenia with a higher accuracy than other neuroimaging techniques such as ERPs [6–8]. Since, there exist many challenges in the accurate analysis of fMRI data (such as high dimensionality and noisy nature), many algorithms should be employed for preprocessing, statistical analysis, feature selection, and classification. Many algorithms for dimensionality reduction have been developed. Principal component analysis (PCA) [9] is one of the most popular techniques for dimensionality reduction. PCA constructs a low-dimensional representation of data that describes as much of variance in the data as possible. For FMRI analysis, independent component analysis (ICA) is a useful method, which extracts powerful multivariate features for classification [10,11]. ICA decomposes FMRI data into a product of a set of time courses and independent components (ICs).

These ICs show different activation levels in the normal and schizophrenia groups. Finding an optimal feature selection and extraction method is very important for removing the redundancy and preserving the most discriminative activation patterns from the ICs [3].

Several studies have used FMRI activation levels to discriminate schizophrenia and normal controls. Shinkareva et al. [12] identified groups of voxels showing between-group temporal dissimilarity and worked directly with FMRI time series for classification purposes. In this method, the task-associated stimulus was used to calculate the temporal dissimilarity matrix. However, the rest of data have no such stimulus presented nor are the data task-related. Thus, this method is not applicable for such cases. Ford et al. [13] combined structural and functional MRI data for classification purposes. They used PCA to project the high dimensional data onto a lower dimensional space for the training set. Du et al. [3] proposed a new method to extract classification features from FMRI data collected at rest or during the performance of a task. They proposed a combination of kernel PCA and Fisher's linear discriminant analysis (FLD) for feature identification. Then, a majority vote method was used for classification of subjects into predefined groups.

In this paper, local binary patterns (LBP) [14] is used for feature extraction. Since, after performing this step the data still have a very high dimension, genetic algorithm (GA) is used for feature selection. GA is a search procedure based on the mechanism of natural selection and natural genetics. The first GA was developed by John H. Holland in the 1960s to allow computers to evolve solutions to difficult search and combinatorial problems, such as function optimization and machine learning [15].

GAs offer a particularly attractive approach for problems like feature subset selection since they are generally quite effective for rapid global search of large, non-linear and poorly understood spaces. GAs are based on an imitation of the biological process in which new and better populations among different species are developed during evolution. Thus, unlike most standard heuristics, GA uses information of a population (individuals) of solutions when they search for better solutions.

In this paper, a new approach to discriminate the normal controls and schizophrenia patients is proposed. First, FMRI scans are preprocessed using statistical parametric mapping software version 8 (SPM8) [16], and PCA is used for dimension reduction. Then, independent components of the new data (given by PCA) are estimated using ICA method. For feature extraction, LBP histogram extraction technique is

used for all estimated components. Genetic Algorithm is used for selection of the most significant histogram bins, in next step. Then, linear discriminant analysis (LDA) is performed to further extract features that maximize the ratio of between-class and within-class variability. Finally, a classifier based on Euclidean distance is used for classification. We evaluate the classification performance using a leave-one-out cross-validation method. Figure 1 shows the overall procedure of the proposed method.

The rest of the paper is organized as follows: Section 2 introduces brain FMRI database. In this section the preprocessing steps including preprocessing using SPM8, PCA, and ICA are briefly described. Section 3 explains details of feature extraction using LBP method, and feature selection using GA. Also, in this section, details of GA operators are described. In section 4, we explain the classification process and evaluation of performance of the proposed method. Finally, sections 5 and 6 show experimental results and conclusion.

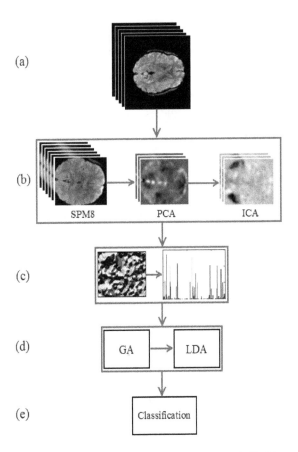

Figure 1. Overall procedure of proposed method: (a) original data, (b) preprocessing using SPM8, PCA, and ICA methods, (c) feature selection using LBP method and its histogram, (d) feature selection using GA and LDA methods, (e) classification using the Euclidean-based classifier.

2. Data and preprocessing
2.1. Database
Multimodal T1 structural MRI, DTI and Resting State FMRI (R-FMRI) datasets of 10 schizophrenia patients (SZ) and 10 (NC) were downloaded from the publicly available NA-MIC dataset [17], but the FMRI scans for case01017 and case01073 do not exist. In this paper, only the fMRI scans are used for further processes. Hence, 18 subjects including 10 NC and 8 SZ are remained for classification. Preprocessing including realignment, normalization, and smoothing, was performed in the statistical parametric mapping software (SPM8) [16]. An example of preprocessing using SPM8 is shown in figure 2.

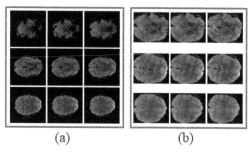

(a)   (b)

Figure 2. Preprocessing using SPM8: (a) original fMRI scan, (b) preprocessed data.

2.2. PCA and ICA
Dimension reduction is one of the key challenges in most FMRI studies. Principle component analysis (PCA) [9] is a mathematical procedure for solving this problem. PCA transforms the original data onto a smaller number of principal components [18]. It is done by finding a linear basis of reduced dimensionality for the data, which the amount of variance in the data is maximal. In this paper, PCA is used for FMRI time point reduction. For FMRI scans, a data matrix $X = [x_1, ..., x_T]$ is constructed. Where, X is a V-by-T matrix, V is the number of voxels, and T is the number of FMRI time points. Finally, PCA is applied to the data matrix X using MATLAB toolbox for dimensionality reduction proposed in [19]. After dimension reduction, ICA method is used for further data analysis. It decomposes data into a set of independent components (ICs), which have very high discrimination power. The ICA analysis of FMRI data is started with X=AS model [3]. Where, $S = [s_1, ..., s_N]^T$ is an N-by-V source matrix, N is the number of sources (the principal components in PCA), V is the number of voxels and s_i is the ith spatial component. The mixing matrix A is an M-by-N matrix where each column a_i represents the time course for the ith source. The goal of the ICA algorithm is to

determine a demixing matrix W such that the sources are estimated using $\hat{S} = WX$ under the assumption of statistical independence of spatial components. Several algorithms for ICA were proposed, and FastICA is one of the most popular of them. FastICA provides a simple way for independent components extraction. It does not depend on any user-defined parameters, and is fast to converge to the most accurate solution allowed by the data [20]. In this paper, ICA is applied to the FMRI scans using FastICA MATLAB toolbox proposed by Hyvarinen [21].

3. Feature extraction and selection
3.1. Local binary patterns
Local binary patterns (LBP) [14] is a simple and efficient image texture operator. Texture analysis based on LBP has excellent discriminative power for many applications in the domain of computer vision. Therefore, it can be used to extract features from medical images [22]. In this paper, LBP technique operates on the ICs, which are estimated by ICA algorithm in the preprocessing step. The LBP operator can be defined as:

$$LBP(x) = \sum_{p=0}^{7} C(v_{x_p}, v_x) 2^p \qquad (1)$$

where, for labeling voxels of ICs using the original LBP, the voxel value v_x at position x is compared to the voxel values v_{x_p} of the eight neighbors of the center position x, as follows:

$$C(v_{x_p}, v_x) = \begin{cases} 1, & v_{x_p} \geq v_x \\ 0, & v_{x_p} < v_x \end{cases} \qquad (2)$$

where, p = 0,1,...,7.

The LBP codes for all voxels in the ICs are calculated, and these coded ICs are transformed into a histogram of LBP values. This paper uses the LBP technique in a 3×3 neighborhood mode (Figure 3). Thus, there will exist $2^8 = 256$ possible texture units (histogram bins) for one IC.

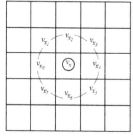

Figure 3. The 3×3 neighborhood in LBP method.

3.2. Feature selection using genetic algorithm
All LBP histograms have 256 bins. Each histogram is considered as a feature vector and

genetic algorithm (GA) is used for feature selection. For 256 bins, there exists 2^{256} subset of bins. Finding a subset of features with sufficiently large discrimination power requires a very large search space. GA is very effective in solving large-scale problems, and can be used to find an optimal or near optimal feature subset [23]. In GA, the individuals are typically represented by n-bit binary vectors. In feature selection problem, each individual would represent a feature subset. It is assumed that the quality of each candidate solution (or fitness of the individual in the population) can be evaluated using a fitness function, with respect to some criteria of interest. GA components are adjusted as follows:

3.2.1. Encoding
Each chromosome in the population represents a candidate solution for feature selection problem. If m is total number of features (here, m = 256), each chromosome is represented by a binary vector of dimension m. If a bit is equal to 0 it means that the corresponding feature is not selected, and if the bit is equal to 1 means the feature is selected [24]. This is the simplest and most straightforward representation scheme.

3.2.2. Initial population
The initial population is generated randomly. A random binary vector creates each chromosome. The number of chromosomes in the initial population is an important issue for GA performance. A large population causes more genetic diversity, but it suffers from slower convergence. A very small population explores only a reduced part of the search space and it may converge to a local extreme.

3.2.3. Fitness function
The fitness function gives the quality of the produced member of the population. In this paper, the quality is measured with the Fisher criterion [3] and GA is used for finding a feature subset (corresponding chromosome), which has maximum or near-maximum amount of Fisher criterion in training data.

3.2.4. Genetic operators
(a) Selection: Roulette wheel selection is used to probabilistically select individuals from a population for later breeding.
(b) Crossover: Single-point crossover operator is used in this paper. The crossover point i is chosen randomly. The new solutions (offspring) will be created using first i bits of one parent and the remaining bits of the other parent.

(c) Mutation: Each individual has a probability P_m to mutate. We randomly choose 10% of the total bits of each selected individual, which should be flipped in the mutation stage.

3.2.5. Genetic algorithm parameters
Finally, GA parameters are adjusted as follows:

1) *Population size*: 100
2) *Number of generation*: 50
3) *Probability of crossover*: 0.7
4) *Probability of mutation*: 0.4
5) *Crossover strategy*: Random single point
6) *The bits of selected chromosomes that will be mutated*: 0.1

3.3. Linear discriminant analysis
Linear Discriminant Analysis (LDA) [25] attempts to maximize the linear separability between data points belonging to different classes. In contrast to most other dimensionality reduction techniques, LDA is a supervised technique. LDA finds a linear mapping M that maximizes the linear class separability in the low-dimensional representation of the data. The criteria that are used to formulate linear class separability in LDA are between-class scatter and within-class scatter. LDA optimizes the ratio between these scatters by finding a linear mapping M that maximizes the Fisher criterion [3]. LDA maps data points onto a d-dimensional space. Where, d < C, and C is the number of classes. In this paper, we deal with a two-class problem. Therefore, d is equal to 1. In general, the projection onto one dimension leads to a considerable loss of information. However, by using LDA, we can achieve a projection that maximizes the class separation and also does not lose within-class compactness. In this paper, MATLAB toolbox for dimensionality reduction [19] is used for applying LDA technique.

4. Classification process and performance evaluation
The classification procedure uses a leave-one-out cross-validation method to evaluate performance of the proposed method. It involves using a single subject for validation data and the remaining subjects as the training set. This is repeated such that each subject is used once as validation data. In this paper, for each left-out test subject, the remaining 17 subjects (including controls and patients) comprise the training set. Our feature extraction method consists of three steps: LBP, GA and LDA. First, histogram of each independent component is extracted using LBP technique, which provides significant features

based on texture information. Second, GA is performed to select the best subset of the LBP histogram. Finally, LDA is used for project-selected features onto one-dimensional space that maximizes the ratio of between- and within-class variability. It should be noted, GA is an optimization method based on stochastic optimization that generates and uses random variables. Thus, to deal with randomization issues, GA will run three times to prove the robustness of the proposed method. For each run, we show the accuracy, sensitivity, and specificity of the obtained classification result. Accuracy is calculated as the ratio between the number of correctly classified subjects and the total number of subjects. Sensitivity and Specificity [3] are defined and calculated as follows:

$$\text{Sensitivity} = \frac{TP}{TP + FN} \quad (3)$$

and,

$$\text{Specificity} = \frac{TN}{FP + TN} \quad (4)$$

where, TP (True positive) is correctly diagnosed patients, FP (False positive) incorrectly identified patients, TN (True negative) correctly diagnosed controls and FN (False negative) incorrectly identified controls. Du et al. [3] proposed a classification algorithm based on Euclidean distance, which shows good results for one-dimensional data. Therefore, we used this algorithm for classification of our data. After obtaining significant features by GA and LDA, the Euclidean distances between the test feature and all training features should be calculated, such that $d_1^{[c]}, ..., d_{n_1}^{[c]}, d_1^{[p]}, ..., d_{n_2}^{[p]}$, where c and p denote the healthy control and the patient group, respectively. By comparing the mean distances between the test data and each training group, the test data will be assigned to closest group. The classification process is used for all slices in all time points for all FMRI scans. Finally, using a majority vote method, the test person is classified to the class receiving the largest number of votes.

5. Experimental results

All FMRI scans contain 200 repetitions of a high resolution EPI scan. In this paper, after preprocessing using PCA method, the number of repetitions is reduced to 10. The PCA method not only reduces the number of repetitions but also maps data onto a new space. After that, in order to further data analysis, an ICA method is used for extraction of independent components (ICs) of the PCA results. Although the dimension of data has been reduced significantly, but data still have a very high dimension. It may causes over-fitting in classification step. Therefore, to obtain a set of features with large discrimination power, LBP operator is used for all ICs, which transform each IC into a spatial histogram of LBP values. In this paper, LBP operator is used in 3×3 mode (see Figure 3), which transforms each brain slice onto a histogram with 256 bins. Then, GA is employed for finding a subset of histogram bins with acceptable discrimination power. In this paper, Fisher criteria are used as a GA fitness function. The GA tries to find a subset of histogram bins from train data, which have most or near most amount of Fisher value. Figure 4 shows examples of increasing fitness value for different generations of GA. Best chromosome in GA is represented by a binary vector with the length of 256. If a bit is equal to 0, it means that the corresponding feature is not selected, and if the bit is equal to 1, it means the feature is selected. After finding an optimal subset of bins, LDA maps these data onto a one-dimensional space. It should be noted, all brain slices in all independent components of the test subjects are classified completely separately. For example, for first slice in first IC of the test subject, the training set includes the only first slices of first ICs of the remaining 17 subjects. When a subject is given for classification, it is preprocessed using mentioned methods, and LBP operator is used for histogram extraction. Then, for each brain slices in each IC, an optimal subset of bins is selected using related best chromosome of GA, and LDA maps these features onto the new space. Finally, comparing the mean distances between a slice of test subject and related slices of each training group will label this slice of test person labeled as a member of nearest group. This process is repeated for all brain slices in all ICs. Then, using a majority vote method, the test subject is assigned to the group, which has maximum votes. As mentioned, GA is a random search, and for performance evaluation of the proposed method, we apply the classification process in three different runs. Table 1 shows classification results in all runs of the proposed method. As can be seen in table 1, all normal subjects in all runs are classified correctly, which causes the sensitivity of 100% in all cases. In the SZ group, "case01018" is classified incorrectly in all runs. In run #1, only 4 SZ subjects were classified correctly. It causes about 78% (14/18) accuracy and 71% specificity. In run #2, in addition to subject "case01018", the subject with number "case01015" is classified incorrectly. Thus, obtained accuracy and specificity are about 89% and 83%, respectively. In run #3, 3 SZ subjects are classified incorrectly, and accuracy 83% and specificity 77% were achieved.

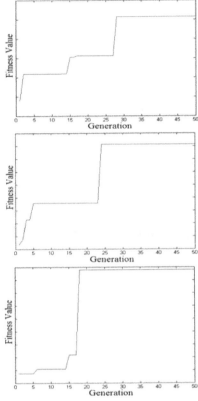

Figure 4. An example of fitness value increasing in order to different generations of GA.

Table 1. Classification results using proposed method for different runs of GA method ($SZ = 1$ & $NC = -1$).

Case number	Diagnosis	Run #1	Run #2	Run #3
case01019	NC	-1	-1	-1
case01020	NC	-1	-1	-1
case01025	NC	-1	-1	-1
case01026	NC	-1	-1	-1
case01029	NC	-1	-1	-1
case01033	NC	-1	-1	-1
case01034	NC	-1	-1	-1
case01035	NC	-1	-1	-1
case01041	NC	-1	-1	-1
case01104	NC	-1	-1	-1
case01011	SZ	-1	1	-1
case01015	SZ	-1	-1	1
case01018	SZ	-1	-1	-1
case01028	SZ	1	1	1
case01039	SZ	1	1	1
case01042	SZ	1	1	1
case01044	SZ	-1	1	-1
case01045	SZ	1	1	1
case01017 case01073	There is not fMRI scans for these subjects			

Table 2 shows the classification performance in different runs of the proposed method. Also, table 2 shows the importance of each step in the

proposed method. When some parts of our method are eliminated, obtained accuracy is lower than complete form of the proposed method. For comparing of the proposed method with state-of-the-art methods, the overall accuracy should be calculated. It is done using an averaging procedure, and the results are shown in table 2. The results prove that our method is comparable with other methods in this area. In order to prove the effectiveness and compatibility of the proposed method, we have compared the proposed method with several state-of-the-art methods including, Ford et al. [26], Pokrajac et al. [27], and Georgopoulos et al. [28] methods, and the results are shown in table 3.

Table 2. Evaluation of classification performance.

GA runs	Sensitivity	Specificity	Accuracy
Run #1	1.00	0.71	0.78
Run #2	1.00	0.83	0.89
Run #3	1.00	0.77	0.83
Average	**1.00**	**0.77**	**0.83**
without PCA	0.67	0.60	0.61
without ICA	0.75	0.64	0.67
without GA	0.20	0.46	0.38
without LDA	0.57	0.64	0.61
without GA & LDA	1.00	0.59	0.60

Table 3. Comparison of obtained accuracy (%) using proposed method with a list of previous research.

Method	Accuracy
Ford	60-80
Pokrajac	68-80
Georgopoulos	77
Proposed method	**83**

6. Conclusion

This paper proposed a GA-based method for classification of schizophrenia using FMRI data. Preprocessing step includes several steps. First, the FMRI scans are realigned, normalized and smoothed using SPM8 software. Then, PCA is used for dimension reduction, and ICA is used for independent components estimation. In feature extraction step, LBP method is used for transforming ICs into spatial histograms of LBP values. For feature selection, GA and LDA are used for spatial histograms for finding the histogram bins with most discrimination power. Finally, a Euclidean-based classifier is used for classification of subjects into predefined groups (SZ or NC). Performance evaluation using the leave-one-out cross validation proved the superiority of the proposed method. The experimental results demonstrate that the proposed method is comparable to other state-of-the-art work.

References

[1] Kandel, E. R. (2000). Disorders of thought and volition: schizophrenia. Principles of neural science, vol. 4, pp. 1188–1208.

[2] Jalili, M. & Knyazeva, M. G. (2011). EEG-based functional networks in schizophrenia. Computers in Biology and Medicine, vol. 41, pp. 1178–1186.

[3] Du, W., Calhoun, V. D., Li, H., Ma, S., Eichele, T., Kiehl, K. A., Pearlson, G. D. & Adali, T. (2012). High classification accuracy for schizophrenia with rest and task fMRI data. Frontiers in human neuroscience 6.

[4] McCarley, R. W., Faux, S. F., Shenton, M. E., Nestor, P. G. & Adams, J. (1991). Event-related potentials in schizophrenia: their biological and clinical correlates and new model of schizophrenic pathophysiology. Schizophrenia research, vol. 4, pp. 209–231.

[5] Ford, J. M. (1999). Schizophrenia: the broken P300 and beyond. Psychophysiology, vol. 36, pp. 667–682.

[6] Levin, J. M., Ross, M. H. & Renshaw, P. F. (1994). Clinical applications of functional MRI in neuropsychiatry. The Journal of neuropsychiatry and clinical neurosciences, vol. 7, pp. 511–522.

[7] Calhoun, V. D., Maciejewski, P. K., Pearlson, G. D. & Kiehl, K. A. (2008). Temporal lobe and "default" hemodynamic brain modes discriminate between schizophrenia and bipolar disorder. Human brain mapping, vol. 29, pp. 1265–1275.

[8] Demirci, O., Clark, V. P., Magnotta, V. A., Andreasen, N. C., Lauriello, J., Kiehl, K. A., Pearlson, G. D. & Calhoun, V. D. (2008). A review of challenges in the use of fMRI for disease classification/characterization and a projection pursuit application from a multi-site fMRI schizophrenia study. Brain imaging and behavior, vol. 2, pp. 207–226.

[9] Hotelling, H. (1933). Analysis of a complex of statistical variables into principal components. Journal of Educational Psychology, vol .24(6), pp. 417-441.

[10] Calhoun, V. D., Kiehl, K. A. & Pearlson, G. D. (2008). Modulation of temporally coherent brain networks estimated using ICA at rest and during cognitive tasks. Human brain mapping, vol. 29, pp. 828–838.

[11] Arribas, J. I., Calhoun, V. D. & Adali, T. (2010). Automatic Bayesian classification of healthy controls, bipolar disorder, and schizophrenia using intrinsic connectivity maps from FMRI data. Biomedical Engineering, IEEE Transactions, vol. 57, pp. 2850–2860.

[12] Shinkareva , S. V., Ombao, H. C., Sutton, B. P., Mohanty, A. & Miller, G. A. (2006). Classification of functional brain images with a spatio-temporal dissimilarity map. NeuroImage, vol. 33, pp. 63–71.

[13] Ford, J., Shen, L., Makedon, F., Flashman, L. A. & Saykin, A. J. (2002). A combined structural-functional classification of schizophrenia using hippocampal volume plus fMRI activation. Engineering in Medicine and Biology, 2002. 24th Annual Conference and the Annual Fall Meeting of the Biomedical Engineering Society EMBS/BMES Conference, 2002. Proceedings of the Second Joint (IEEE), pp. 48–49.

[14] Ojala, T., Pietikäinen, M. & Harwood, D. (1996). A comparative study of texture measures with classification based on featured distributions. Pattern recognition, vol. 29, pp. 51–59.

[15] Holland, J. H. (1975). Adaptation in natural and artificial systems: An introductory analysis with applications to biology, control, and artificial intelligence. (U Michigan Press).

[16] SPM8 - Statistical Parametric Mapping Available: http://www.fil.ion.ucl.ac.uk/spm/software/spm8/ [Accessed June 30, 2013].

[17] MIDAS - Collection NAMIC: Brain Mutlimodality Available: http://insight-journal.org/midas/collection/view/190 [Accessed July 2, 2013].

[18] Sidhu, G. S., Asgarian, N., Greiner, R. & Brown, M. R. G. (2012). Kernel Principal Component Analysis for dimensionality reduction in fMRI-based diagnosis of ADHD. Frontiers in systems neuroscience, vol. 6:74.

[19] Van der Maaten, L. , Postma, E. & van den Herik, H. (2007). Matlab toolbox for dimensionality reduction. Proceedings of the Belgian-Dutch Artificial Intelligence Conference. Vol. 2007, pp 439–440.

[20] Hyvärinen, A. & Oja, E. (1997). A fast fixed-point algorithm for independent component analysis. Neural computation, vol. 9, pp. 1483–1492.

[21] Hyvarinen, A. (1998). The FastICA MATLAB toolbox. Helsinki Univ of Technology.

[22] Unay, D., Ekin, A., Cetin, M., Jasinschi, R. & Ercil, A. (2007). Robustness of local binary patterns in brain MR image analysis. Engineering in Medicine and Biology Society, 2007. EMBS 2007. 29th Annual International Conference of the IEEE (IEEE), pp 2098–2101.

[23] Tan, F., Fu, X., Zhang, Y. & Bourgeois, A. G. (2008). A genetic algorithm-based method for feature subset selection. Soft Computing, vol. 12, pp. 111–120.

[24] Marinakis, Y., Dounias, G. & Jantzen, J. (2009). Pap smear diagnosis using a hybrid intelligent scheme focusing on genetic algorithm based feature selection and nearest neighbor classification. Computers in Biology and Medicine, vol. 39, pp. 69–78.

[25] Fisher, R. A. (1936). The use of multiple measurements in taxonomic problems. Annals of eugenics, vol. 7, pp. 179–188.

[26] Ford, J., Farid, H., Makedon, F., Flashman, L. A, McAllister, T. W., et al. (2003). Patient classification of fMRI activation maps. Medical Image Computing and Computer-Assisted Intervention-MICCAI 2003 (Springer), vol. 2879, pp 58–65.

[27] Pokrajac, D., Megalooikonomou, V., Lazarevic, A., Kontos, D. & Obradovic, Z. (2005). Applying spatial distribution analysis techniques to classification of 3D medical images. Artificial Intelligence in Medicine, vol. 33, pp. 261–280.

[28] Georgopoulos, A. P., Karageorgiou, E., Leuthold, A. C. Lewis,S. M., et al. (2007). Synchronous neural interactions assessed by magnetoencephalography: a functional biomarker for brain disorders. Journal of neural engineering, vol. 4:349.

14

Designing an adaptive fuzzy control for robot manipulators using PSO

F. Soleiman Nouri*, M. Haddad Zarif and M. M. Fateh

Department of Electrical Engineering and Robotics, University of Shahrood, Iran.

Corresponding author: solaimannourifatemeh@yahoo.com (F. Soleiman Nouri).

Abstract

This paper presents a designing an optimal adaptive controller for tracking down the control of robot manipulators based on particle swarm optimization (PSO) algorithm. PSO algorithm has been used to optimize parameters of the controller and hence to minimize the integral square of errors (ISE) as a performance criteria. In this paper, an improved PSO using a logic is proposed to increase the convergence speed. In this case, the performance of PSO algorithms such as an improved PSO (IPSO), an improved PSO using fuzzy logic (F-PSO), a linearly decreasing inertia weight of PSO (LWD-PSO) and a nonlinearly decreasing inertia weight of PSO (NDW-PSO) are with parameter accuracy and convergence speed. As a result, the simulation results show that the F-PSO approach presents a better performance in the tracking down the control of robot manipulators than other algorithms.

Keywords: *Particle Swarm Optimization (PSO), Robot Manipulators, Adaptive Controller, Improved PSO Using Fuzzy Logic (F-PSO), Integral Square of Errors (ISE).*

1. Introduction

Robot manipulators are multi-input/multi-output (MIMO) nonlinear system with couplings that have to face many structured and unstructured uncertainties such as payload parameter, un-modeled dynamics, external disturbance and friction. The design robust controller for robot manipulators and their application is one of the considerable topics in a control field; so many control techniques have been proffered to control robot manipulator such as the PID control method [1], adaptive control [2,3], combined adaptive sliding mode controllers [4], optimal control [5,6] and intelligent approaches [7].

The PSO algorithm comprises a simple structure, and it is easy to be implemented, independent from initial guess and does not need any objective function's gradient. Due to the good characteristics of this algorithm, it has been applied in the diversity of investigation field. For instance, in [9-11], PSO is presented to setting the optimal parameter of PID controller. In [12], proposed to use PSO and its application to train weights of artificial neural network. In [13], the author employed the PSO algorithm to optimize

the parameter of tracking a controller. In [14], PSO is proffered to solve the systems of nonlinear equations. In [15], the proposed algorithm has been used to solve nonlinear optimal control. In [16], the PSO algorithm is used to optimize the parameters of controller to position/force control of constrained robot manipulators.

Fuzzy logic is based on fuzzy set theory. A fuzzy logic controller is composed of its rule base and membership function. Fuzzy logic system was used to approximate any nonlinear function [22,23].

In this paper, the particle swarm optimization utilized to drive the optimal parameters of adaptive controller for robot manipulators. The performance of an improved PSO using fuzzy logic (F-PSO) is compared with PSO with linearly decreasing inertia weight (LDW-PSO), nonlinear inertia weight PSO (NDW-PSO) and improved PSO (IPSO). The simulation results confirmed that the F-PSO has better performance than other algorithm mentioned above. The rest of paper is organized as follows: Section 2 presents the mathematical description of robot manipulator.

Section 3 illustrates the particle swarm optimization. Section 4 shows the design of controller parameters based on PSO. Section 5 illustrates the simulation results on a robot manipulator and comparisons between algorithms. Section 6 concludes the paper.

2. Dynamics of robot manipulators

In the absence of friction or other disturbance, the dynamic equation of a multi-input/multi-output robot manipulator system can be written as [2, 4]:

$$M(q)\ddot{q} + C(q,\dot{q})\dot{q} + G(q) = \tau \tag{1}$$

Where q is a $n \times 1$ vector of generalized coordinate, the position vector of a robot manipulator. $\dot{q}$ is a $n \times 1$ vector of first derivative of generalized coordinate, the velocity of a robot manipulator. $\ddot{q}$ is a $n \times 1$ vector of second derivative of generalized coordinate, the acceleration of a robot manipulator. $M(q)$ is a $n \times n$ symmetric positive definite matrix of manipulator inertia. $C(q,\dot{q})$ is a $n \times 1$ vector of centrifugal and coriolis torque. $G(q)$ is a $n \times 1$ vector of gravitational torque. τ is a $n \times 1$ vector of generalized control input torque or force. The (1) can be stated as follows [2]:

$$M(q)\ddot{q} + C(q,\dot{q})\dot{q} + G(q) = Y(q,\dot{q},\ddot{q})\beta = \tau \tag{2}$$

Where $Y(q,\dot{q},\ddot{q})$ is a $n \times p$ matrix called regressor. β is a $p \times 1$ uncertain vector .

A number of useful properties of robot dynamic is expressed as follows [8]:

Property 1. An appropriate definition of coriolis and centrifugal matrix makes that the

$$N(q,\dot{q}) = \dot{M}(q) - 2C(q,\dot{q}) \quad \text{is} \quad \text{skew}$$

symmetric. This property is very important to stability analysis.

Property 2. The $M(q)$ is a symmetric positive definite matrix, such that:

$$0 < \mu_1 I \le M(q) \le \mu_2 I$$

μ_1, μ_2 are positive constant and I is the identity matrix.

2.1. Adaptive controller design

The control law has been given as follows [2]:

$$\tau = M(q)(\ddot{q}_d - \Lambda(\dot{q} - \dot{q}_d)) + C(q,\dot{q})(\dot{q}_d - \Lambda(q - q_d)) + G(q) + K\sigma \tag{3}$$

Where k is a definite positive matrix, σ is an error of velocity.

$\tilde{q}, \dot{\tilde{q}}, \ddot{q}_r, \dot{q}_r$ are defined as:

$$\tilde{q} = q - q_d, \quad \dot{\tilde{q}} = \dot{q} - \dot{q}_d, \quad \dot{q}_r = \dot{q}_d - \Lambda\tilde{q}, \tag{4}$$

$$\ddot{q}_r = \ddot{q}_d - \Lambda\dot{\tilde{q}}$$

Where $\tilde{q}$ indicates the position tracking error, $\dot{\tilde{q}}$ represents the velocity, $\dot{q}_r$ is called reference Velocity that is utilized to guarantee the convergence of the tracking error, $\ddot{q}_r$ is the reference acceleration, Λ is a positive definite matrix and σ is obtained as:

$$\sigma = \dot{q}_r - \dot{q} = \dot{\tilde{q}} + \Lambda\tilde{q} \tag{5}$$

In the presence of uncertainties, a control law is proposed as:

$$\tau = \hat{M}(q)\ddot{q}_r + \hat{C}(q,\dot{q})\dot{q}_r + \hat{G}(q) + K\sigma$$
$$= Y(q,\dot{q},\dot{q}_r,\ddot{q}_r)\hat{\beta} + K\sigma \tag{6}$$

Where $\hat{M}(q)$ is the estimate of the $M(q)$, $\hat{C}(q,\dot{q})$ is the estimate of the $C(q,\dot{q})$, $\hat{G}(q)$ presented the estimate of the $G(q)$ and also $\hat{\beta}$ denoted the estimate of the β.

Attention to replace the recent control law in the (2), so modeling errors consists of:

$$\tilde{M} = \hat{M} - M \quad \tilde{C} = \hat{C} - C \quad \tilde{G} = \hat{G} - G \tag{7}$$

In order to analysis the stability of the system and obtain convergence tracking error, the Lyapunov function candidate is suggested as follows:

$$v(t) = \frac{1}{2}\left[\sigma^T H\sigma + \tilde{\beta}^T \Gamma^{-1} \tilde{\beta}\right] \tag{8}$$

The adaptation law can be expressed as:

$$\hat{\beta} = -\Gamma Y^{\mathrm{T}} \sigma \qquad (9)$$

Using this upper equation, the derivative of $v(t)$ is given as:

$$\dot{v}(t) = -\sigma^{\mathrm{T}} K_D \sigma \leq 0 \qquad (10)$$

3. Particle swarm optimization

Particle swarm optimization algorithm is a stochastic evolutionary computation approach. It is inspired by the social behavior such as a flock of bird or a school of fish. This algorithm introduced by Eberhart and Kennedy in 1995 [17]. PSO contains a group of solutions that called particles.

These particles are moved in and evaluates the cost function of its position that has been placed in space. Particle adjusted its movement based on corresponding experience of particle and associated experiences of particle that led to the particle moves in the direction of better solution [15]. At each iteration, each particle for updating its velocity and position utilized equations in the following order:

$$V_i^{k+1} = wV_i^k + c_1 rand_1 \times (\mathrm{Pbest}_i^k - X_i^k)$$
$$+ c_2 rand_2 \times (\mathrm{Gbest}^k - X_i^k) \qquad (11)$$

$$X_i^{k+1} = X_i^k + \mathrm{T}_s V_i^{k+1} \qquad (12)$$

Where X_i^k is the current position of ith particle at the kth iteration. T_s is the sampling period. V_i^k is the Current velocity of ith particle at the kth iteration. w is the inertia weight which acquires an important task in the PSO convergence behavior since it is used to balance the global and local search ability. c_1, c_2 are positive constants, correspond to cognitive and social parameter respectively, called learning factors. $rand_1, rand_2$ are random numbers with uniform distribution in the range of 0 to 1. Pbest_i^k is the best position of ith particle at the kth iteration called as personal best. Gbest^k is the global best position among all the particles in the swarm at the kth iteration called global best. The algorithm is repeated several times until the pause condition such as number of iteration or sufficiently good fitness [15].

PSO does exhibit some shortages. It may convergence to a local minimum, therefore researchers try to improve the performance of the PSO with different settings, e.g. w , C_1, C_2 [15].

In this work, we employed the IPSO, NDW-PSO, LDW-PSO and F-PSO, they are approaches that improved the performance of PSO and finally, F-PSO algorithm is compared with the other algorithms.

3.1. Linearly decreasing inertia weight PSO

Linearly decreasing inertia weight PSO was abbreviated to LDW-PSO, the inertia weight decreases linearly from w_{max} to w_{min}, the equation is used for adapting the inertia weight in PSO as follows [19, 20]:

$$w^t = w_{min} + \frac{iter_{max} - t}{iter_{max}} \cdot (\mathrm{w}_{max} - w_{min}) \qquad (13)$$

$iter_{max}$ Denotes to maximum number of iteration and t denotes to current of iteration.

3.2. Nonlinear inertia weight PSO

Nonlinear inertia weight PSO was abbreviated to NDW-PSO. In this mechanism, the inertia weight decreases as same pervious approach but nonlinearity [18].

$$w^t = w_{min} + (\frac{iter_{max} - t}{iter_{max}})^n \cdot (\mathrm{w}_{max} - w_{min}) \qquad (14)$$

3.3. Improved PSO

The values of w , c_1, c_2 is very important to ensure convergent behavior and to optimally trade-off exploration and exploitation. In [21], Author used an improved PSO as follows:

$$w^t = 1/\left(1 + \exp(-\alpha F(gbest^t))^n\right) \qquad (15)$$

$$c_i = 1/\left(1 + \exp(-\alpha F(gbest^t))^n\right) \qquad (16)$$

$$\alpha = 1/\mathrm{F}\left(gbest^t\right) \qquad (17)$$

This adaptation appliance changes in conformity to the rate of the global best fitness improvement.

3.4. Particle swarm optimization with using fuzzy

Fuzzy is used for designing and modeling for system that need to advance mathematics and probabilities. The important part of fuzzy system was a knowledge base that is comprised fuzzy IF-THEN rules. Fuzzy is used to improve the performance of PSO. A fuzzy system will be employed to adjust the learning factors c_1, c_2 with best fitness and iteration. The best fitness measure the performance of the best solution found so far. To design a fuzzy-PSO need to have ranges of best fitness and iteration. Therefore, the best fitness and iteration have to normalize into $[0,1]$ that defined as follows [22, 23]:

$$NCBPE = \frac{CBPE\_CBPE_{min}}{CBPE_{max} - CBPE_{min}} \quad (18)$$

Where $CBPE$ is the current fitness value, $CBPE_{min}$ is the best fitness value and $CBPE_{max}$ is the worst fitness value.

$$Iteration = \frac{iteration}{iteration_{max}} \quad (19)$$

In this mechanism, the best fitness and iteration are inputs and c_1, c_2 are outputs in the fuzzy system. The c_1, c_2 obtained from fuzzy were used to PSO and for adjusting w, we employed the IPSO that mentioned in [15]:

$$w' = 1/\left(1 + \exp(-\alpha F(\text{gbest}^t))^n\right) \quad (20)$$

$$\alpha = 1/F\left(\text{gbest}^t\right) \quad (21)$$

We suggest fuzzy rules:

1. If (iteration is low) and (CPBE is low) then (c1 is low)(c2 is high)
2. If (iteration is low) and (CPBE is medium) then (c1 is medium low)(c2 is medium high)
3. If (iteration is low) and (CPBE is high) then (c1 is medium)(c2 is medium)
4. If (iteration is medium) and (CPBE is low) then (c1 is medium low)(c2 is high)
5. If (iteration is medium) and (CPBE is medium) then (c1 is medium)(c2 is high)
6. If (iteration is medium) and (CPBE is high) then (c1 is medium high)(c2 is low)
7. If (iteration is high) and (CPBE is low) then (c1 is high)(c2 is low)
8. If (iteration is high) and (CPBE is medium) then (c1 is medium high)(c2 is medium low)
9. If (iteration is high) and (CPBE is high) then (c1 is low)(c2 is medium low)

For designing the rules of fuzzy system, it was decided that in early iterations the PSO algorithm must explore and finally exploit.

These approaches usually start with large inertia values, which decrease over time to smaller values. Large values for w facilitate exploration, with increased diversity. A small w promotes local exploitation.

4. PSO controller tuning

The parameters of adaptive control law such as Γ_1, Γ_2, Γ_3, Γ_4, Λ_1 and k_1 is found using PSO.

All the parameters of controller are adjusted to minimize the fitness function based on the integral square of errors that is defined as follows:

$$f = \int_0^T \sum_{i=1}^2 e_i(t)^2 dt \quad (22)$$

Where $e_i(t)$ is the value of tracking error and T is the control system running time.

5. Simulation results

The dynamics of a two links manipulator has been mentioned in section (2), so the element of this equation such as $M(q)$, $C\left(q,\dot{q}\right)$ and $G(q)$ are given as follows [4]:

$$\begin{pmatrix} \tau_1 \\ \tau_2 \end{pmatrix} = \begin{pmatrix} M_{11} & M_{12} \\ M_{21} & M_{22} \end{pmatrix} \begin{pmatrix} \ddot{q}_1 \\ \ddot{q}_2 \end{pmatrix} + \begin{pmatrix} -C\dot{q}_2 & -C\left(\dot{q}_1 + \dot{q}_2\right) \\ C\dot{q}_1 & 0 \end{pmatrix} \begin{pmatrix} \dot{q}_1 \\ \dot{q}_2 \end{pmatrix}, \quad (23)$$

$G(q) = 0$

Where:

$$M_{11} = a_1 + 2a_3 \cos q_2 + 2a_4 \sin q_2 \quad (24)$$
$$M_{12} = M_{21} = a_2 + a_3 \cos q_2 + a_4 \sin q_2 \quad (25)$$
$$M_{22} = a_2 \quad (26)$$
$$C = a_3 \sin q_2 - a_4 \cos q_2 \quad (27)$$
$$a_1 = I_1 + m_1 l_{c1}^2 + I_e + m_e l_{ce}^2 + m_e l_1^2 \quad (28)$$
$$a_2 = I_e + m_e l_{ce}^2 \quad (29)$$
$$a_3 = m_e l_1 l_{ce} \cos \delta_e \quad (30)$$
$$a_4 = m_e l_1 l_{ce} \sin \delta_e \quad (31)$$

In the simulations, the below values have been used in the following order:

$$m_1 = 1 \ , \ l_1 = 1 \ , \ m_e = 2 \ , \ \delta_e = \frac{\pi}{6} \ , \ I_1 = 0.12 \ ,$$

$$l_{c1} = 0.5 \ , \ I_e = 0.25 \ , \ l_{ce} = 0.6$$

The components of matrix of $Y(q, \dot{q}, \dot{q}_r, \ddot{q}_r)$ can be written explicitly:

$$Y_{11} = \ddot{q}_{r1}, \ Y_{12} = \ddot{q}_{r2}, \ Y_{21} = 0, \ Y_{22} = \ddot{q}_{r1} + \ddot{q}_{r2}$$

$$Y_{13} = \left(2\ddot{q}_{r1} + \ddot{q}_{r2}\right)\cos q_2 - \left(\dot{q}_2\dot{q}_{r1} + \dot{q}_1\dot{q}_{r2} + \dot{q}_2\dot{q}_{r2}\right)\sin q_2$$

$$Y_{14} = \left(2q''_{r1} + q''_{r2}\right)\sin q_2 + \left(q'_2 q'_{r1} + q'_1 q'_{r2} + q'_2 q'_{r2}\right)\cos q_2$$ (32)

$$Y_{23} = q''_{r1}\cos q_2 + q'_1 q'_{r1}\sin q_2$$

$$Y_{24} = q''_{r1}\sin q_2 - q'_1 q'_{r1}\cos q_2$$

The desired trajectory is chosen as:

$$q_{d1}(t) = \frac{\pi}{6}\left(1 - \cos(2\pi t)\right)$$

$$q_{d2}(t) = \frac{\pi}{4}\left(1 - \cos(2\pi t)\right)$$ (33)

$\Gamma = diag\begin{bmatrix}3.3 & 0.97 & 1.04 & 0.6\end{bmatrix}, \Lambda = 20I$, $K = 100I$

The controller parameters have been set with PSO, such as :

$\Gamma = diag\begin{bmatrix}\Gamma_1 & \Gamma_2 & \Gamma_3 & \Gamma_4\end{bmatrix}, \Lambda = \Lambda_1 I, K = K_1 I$

The searching ranges are set as follows:

$0 \le \Gamma_1 \le 0.07$, $\quad 0 \le \Gamma_2 \le 0.05$, $\quad 0 \le \Gamma_3 \le 0.15$,

$0 \le \Gamma_4 \le 0.3$, $0 \le \Lambda_1 \le 20$, $0 \le K_1 \le 100$

In all PSO algorithms, $c_1 = c_2 = 2$ [17], w decreases from 0.9 to 0.4, in NWD-PSO n=1.2 [18] and in IPSO n=1.5 [21], population size is set to 10 and maximum number of iteration is set to 50 and each algorithm runs 25 times.

Table 1. Results of comparison between LDW-PSO, NDW-PSO, IPSO, F-PSO.

Control parameters	Real value	LDW-PSO	NDW-PSO	IPSO	F-PSO
Γ_1	0.03	0.0595	0.0591	0.0420	0.0415
Γ_2	0.05	0.0500	0.0499	0.0482	0.0500
Γ_3	0.1	0.1499	0.1499	0.1499	0.1500
Γ_4	0.3	0.3000	0.2999	0.2388	0.2996
Λ_1	20	19.9996	19.9978	19.9986	19.9991
K_1	100.000	99.9987	99.9981	99.9960	99.9869

Table 2. Results of LDW-PSO, NDW-PSO, IPSO and F-PSO algorithm.

Algorithms	Best result	Mean result	Worst result	Std
LDW-PSO	0.0037074	0.0037089	0.0037173	2.5757×10^{-6}
NDW-PSO	0.0037074	0.0037090	0.0037154	2.1170×10^{-6}
IPSO	0.0037083	0.0037322	0.0038063	2.2897×10^{-5}
F-PSO	0.0037076	0.0037111	0.0037155	2.1454×10^{-6}

Table 3. Iteration and time required by LDW-PSO, NDW-PSO, IPSO and F-PSO.

Algorithms	Best result		Average result		Worst result	
	Iterations	Elapse time(s)	Iterations	Elapse time(s)	Iteration	Elapse time(s)
LDW-PSO	35	24228	41	24534	48	24591
NDW-PSO	30	22935	34	23216.7857	35	23456
IPSO	33	24571	45	24673	47	24696
F-PSO	28	27531	32	27561	35	27695

Table 1 exhibits the average of results obtained for adaptive controller parameters and table 2 shows the results ISE for LDW-PSO, NDW-PSO, IPSO and F-PSO, where each algorithm runs 25 times and table 3 shows iteration and necessary time to reach the best, mean and worst results.

Figures 1-6 confirm the success of optimization by F-PSO algorithm compared with the other algorithms for parameters of optimal controller $\Lambda_1, \Gamma_1, \Gamma_2, \Gamma_3, \Gamma_4, K_1$.

These figures are represented from iteration 1 to iteration 50. Figure 7 exhibits the convergence of the optimal ISE. It confirms the superiority of F-PSO algorithm in terms of convergence speed without the premature convergence problem.

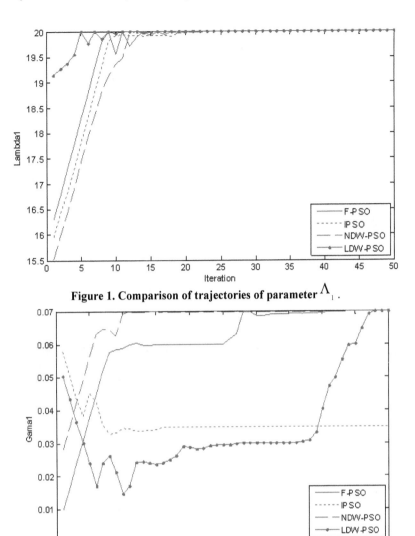

Figure 1. Comparison of trajectories of parameter Λ_1 .

Figure 2. Comparison of trajectories of parameter Γ_1 .

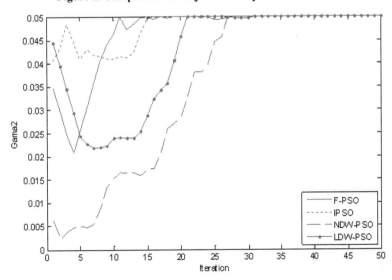

Figure 3. Comparison of trajectories of parameter Γ_2 .

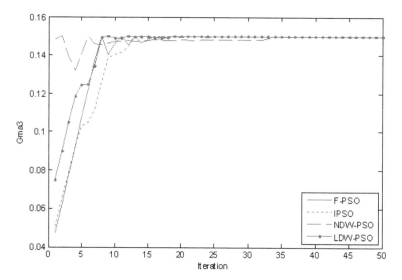

Figure 4. Comparison of trajectories of parameter Γ_3 **.**

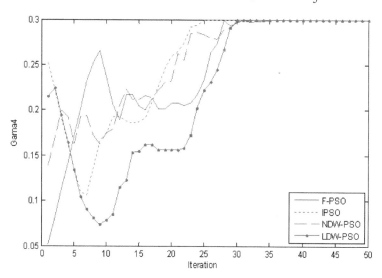

Figure 5. Comparison of trajectories of parameter Γ_4 **.**

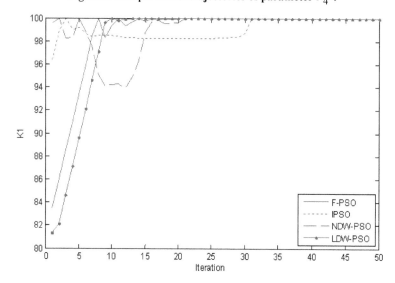

Figure 6. Comparison of trajectories of parameter K_1 **.**

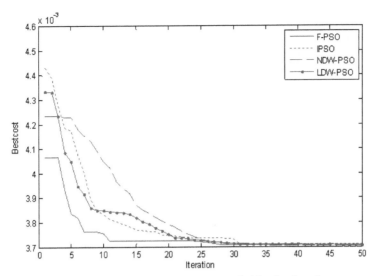

Figure 7. Comparison of convergence of objective function.

6. Conclusion

PSO has been efficient to design the adaptive controller by finding the optimal control parameters. The fuzzy system was proposed for adjusting the parameters for particle swarm optimization. It can improve the quality of result of method in the particle swarm optimization. The simulation results obtained from F-PSO, NDW-PSO, LDW-PSO and IPSO algorithms were compared . The simulation results also show the F–PSO has a better performance for purposes of parameter accuracy and convergence speed than the other algorithms.

References

[1] Alvarez-Ramirez, J., Cervantes, I. & Kelly, R. (2000). PID regulation of robot manipulators. stability and performance. System & Control Letters, vol. 41, pp. 73-83.

[2] Burkan, R. & Uzmay, I. (2005). A model of parameter adaptive law with time varying function for robot control. Applied Mathematical Modelling, vol. 29, pp. 361-371.

[3] Faieghi, M. R., Delavari, H. & Baleanu, D. (2012). A novel adaptive controller for two-degree of reedom polar robot with unknown perturbations. Commun Nonlinear SciNumer Simulate, vol. 17, pp. 1021-1030.

[4] Zeinali, M. & Notash, L. (2010). Adaptive sliding mode control with uncertainty estimator for robot manipulators. Mechanism and Machine Theory, vol. 45, pp. 80-90.

[5] Choi, Y., Chung, W. K. & Youm, Y. (2001). On the Optimal PID Performance Tuning for Robot Manipulators. IEEE/RSJ International Conference On Advanced Intelligent Robots and Systems, Maui, Hawaii, US, 2001.

[6] Wai, R.J., Tu, C. H. & Hsieh, K. Y. (2003). Design of Intelligent Optimal Tracking Control for Robot Manipulator. IEEE/ASME International Conference On Advanced Intelligent Mechatronics, 2003.

[7] Perez P, J., Perez, J. P., Soto, R., Flores, A., Rodriguez, F. & Meza, J. L. (2012). Trajectory Tracking Error Using PID Control Law for Two Link Robot Manipulator via Adaptive Neural Networks. Procedia Technology, vol. 3, pp. 139-146.

[8] Tomei, P. (1991). Adaptive PD controller for robot manipulators. IEEE Trans. Robot. Automat, vol. 7, pp. 565–570.

[9] Girirajkumae, S. M., Jayaraj, D. & Kishan, A. R. (2010). PSO based Tuning of a PID Controller for a High Performance Drilling Machine. International Journal of Computer Applications, vol. 1, pp. 0975-8887.

[10] Cao, S., Tu, J. & Liu, H. (2010). PSO Algorithm-Based Robust design of PID Controller for PMSM. Sixth International Conference on natural Computation, 2010.

[11] Chang, W. D. & Shih, S. P. (2010). PID controller design of nonlinear systems using an improved particle swarm optimization approach. Commun Nonlinear SciNumerSimulat, vol. 15, pp. 3632-3639.

[12] Sun, S., Zhang, J., W, J. & X, L. (2011). The Application of New Adaptive PSO in AGC and AFC Combination Control System. Procedia Engineering, vol. 16, pp. 702-707.

[13] Chen, S. M. & Dong, Y. F. (2011). Satellite Attitude Tracking Controller Optimization based on Particle Swarm Optimization. Procedia Engineering, vol. 15, pp. 526-530.

[14] Jaberipour, M., Khorram, E. & Karimi, B. (2011). Particle swarm algorithm for solving systems of nonlinear equations. Computers and Mathematics with Application, vol. 62, pp. 566-576.

[15] Modares, H. & Naghibi Sistani, M. B. (2011). Solving nonlinear optimal control problems using a hybrid IPSO-SQP algorithm. Engineering Application of Artificial Intelligence, vol. 24, pp. 476-484.

[16] Mehdi, h. & Boubaker, O. (2011). Position/force control optimized by Particle Swarm intelligence for constrained robotic manipulator. 11th International Conference on Intelligent System Design and Applications, 2011.

[17] Kennedy, J. & Eberhart, R. C. (1995). Particle swarm optimization. IEEE International Conference on Neural Networks, vol. 4, pp. 1942-1948 .

[18] Chatterjee, A. & Siarry, P. (2006). Nonlinear inertia weight variation for dynamic adaptation in particle swarm optimization, Computers and Operations research, vol. 33, no. 3, pp. 859-871.

[19] Shi, Y. and Eberhart, R. C. (1998a). Parameter selection in particle swarm optimization. Seventh Annual Conference on Evolutionary Programming, New York, pp. 591-600.

[20] Shi, Y. & Eberhart, R. C. (1998b). A modified particle swam optimizer. Conference on Evolutionary Computation, pp. 69-73.

[21] Modares, H., Alfi, A. & Fateh M. M. (2010). Parameter identification of chaotic dynamic systems through an improved particle swarm optimization, Expert Systems with Applications, vol. 37, pp. 3714-3720.

[22] Shi, Y. (2001). Fuzzy Adaptive Particle Swarm Optimization. Proceeding of the Congress on Evolutionary computation, vol. 1, pp. 101-106.

[23] Melin, P., Olivas, F., Castillo, O., Valdez, F., Soria, J. & Valdez, M. (2013). Optimal design of fuzzy classification system using PSO with dynamic parameter adaptation through fuzzy logic. Expert system with applications, vol. 40, pp. 3196-3206.

15

PSO for multi-objective problems: Criteria for leader selection and uniformity distribution

H. Motameni

Department of Computer Engineering, Sari Branch, Islamic Azad University, Sari, Iran.

*Corresponding author: motameni@iausari.ac.ir (H. Motameni).

Abstract

This paper proposes a method to solve multi-objective problems using improved Particle Swarm Optimization. We propose leader particles which guide other particles inside the problem domain. Two techniques are suggested for selection and deletion of such particles to improve the optimal solutions. The first one is based on the mean of the m optimal particles and the second one is based on appointing a leader particle for any n founded particles. We used an intensity criterion to delete the particles in both techniques. The proposed techniques were evaluated based on three standard tests in multi-objective evolutionary optimization problems. The evaluation criterion in this paper is the number of particles in the optimal-Pareto set, error, and uniformity. The results show that the proposed method searches more number of optimal particles with higher intensity and less error in comparison with basic MOPSO and SIGMA and CMPSO and NSGA-II and microGA and PAES and can be used as proper techniques to solve multi-objective optimization problems.

Keywords: *Multi-objective Optimization, Particle Swarm Optimization, Intensity Distance, Mutation.*

1. Introduction

Optimization means finding one or more solution regarding one or more objectives. One multi-objective problem has more than one objective function which has to be minimized or maximized. The minimization and maximization of functions have a broad usage in scientific research as well as business applications. Multi-objective optimization comes from the real world decision making problems in which one should decide to select a set of solutions rather than a solution. For a set of finite solutions we can have a set of solutions in which two selected solutions have priority over each others. In other words, the solutions of this set are far better than other solutions. This is also called the optimal-Pareto set. In fact, there is one optimal solution in the problem domain but the first set of optimal solutions are selected. Then, user can select the optimal solution among the given best solution [1]. Multi-objective algorithms cannot find the best solutions themselves. Thus, a good technique could be the combination of such algorithms with PSO to find better solutions [2]. PSO is a population based stochastic optimization technique developed by Eberhart and Kennedy, 1995 [3], and inspired by social behavior of bird flocking or fish schooling. The system is initialized with a population of random solutions and searches for optimality by updating generations. In PSO, the potential solutions, called particles, fly through the problem space by following the current optimum particles. Each particle keeps track of its coordinates in the problem space associated with the best solution (fitness) achieved so far. (The fitness value is also stored.) Another "best" value that is tracked by the particle swarm optimizer is the best value, obtained so far by any particle in the neighbors of the particle. When a particle takes all the population as its topological neighbors, the best value is a global best. The particle swarm optimization concept consists of, at each time step, changing the velocity of (accelerating) each particle toward its personal best and local best locations (local version of PSO). Acceleration is weighted by a random term, with separate random numbers being generated for acceleration toward personal best and local best locations [4].

2. Standard PSO algorithm

PSO is initialized with a group of random particles (solutions) and then searches for optima by updating generations. In every iteration, each particle is updated by following two "best" values. The first one is the best solution (fitness) achieved so far. (The fitness value is also stored.) This value is called pbest. Another "best" value that is tracked by the particle swarm optimizer is the best value, obtained so far by any particle in the population. This best value is a global best and called gbest[5,6,32]. When a particle takes part of the population as its topological neighbors, the best value is a local best and is called lbest.

In order to establish a common terminology, in the following we provide some definitions of several technical terms commonly used:

Swarm: Population of the algorithm.

Particle: Member (individual) of the swarm. Each particle represents a potential solution to the problem being solved. The position of a particle is determined by the solution it currently represents.

pbest (personal best): Personal best position of a given particle, so far. That is, the position of the particle that has provided the greatest success (measured in terms of na scalar value analogous to the fitness adopted in evolutionary nalgorithms).

lbest (local best): Position of the best particle member of the neighborhood of a given particle.

gbest (global best): Position of the best particle of the entire swarm.

Leader: Particle that is used to guide another particle towards better regions of the search space. After finding the two best values, the particle updates its velocity and positions with following equations (1) and (2). PSO, includes parallel search algorithms based on population, which with a group of random answers (particles) start, then the optimal solutions of the problem space by date particle location in the search continues. Each particle Multidimensional) depending on the problem (with the two vectors x_{id} and v_{id} represent the location and velocity of the i particle dimension d are to be determined. At each stage of the movement is the, location of each particle of the two values best on the day.

The first value, which is the best experience ever gotten particle by showing p_best the second value is the best experience of all particles obtained by. g_best shown [5,6]. In each iteration, the algorithm after finding two values,

the new particle velocity and position according to (1) and (2) is updated.

$$v_{id}(t+1) = wv_{id}t + c_1.rand(p_{best_{id}(t)} - x_{id}(t)) \quad (1)$$
$$+c_2.rand(g_{best_{id}(t)} - x_{id}(t))$$
$$x_{id} = (t+1)x_{id}(t) + v_{id}(t+1) \quad (2)$$

In (1), W is a linear coefficient of inertia reduced, and is usually in the range [0,1], respectively and from which we in this paper considered equal to 0.2. C1 and C2 are coefficients of learning or acceleration in the interval [0,2] is selected and in most cases for g_best, and the second and third equation (1) will be zero. The particle motion in the previous ones will be moving. This is because, typically W has both the 1.49 level and 2 Use [6,7,8]. We in this paper considered c1 and c2 equal to 1 and 2 [15].

The right side of (1) is composed of three parts:, The first part of a multiple current speed of the particle is, the second part of the third rotation of a particle to the personal experience and basic variety rotate a bit to the experience is the best [2].w, seeking to establish a balance between local and global, for the first time in [9] proposed the specifies motion coefficient global search. In many cases, this leads to premature convergence and the algorithm will be a local optimum. To resolve this problem first in 2002, a new algorithm was presented with the name GCPSO [10] and in this method, a new parameter has been added to the algorithm. The question is if the answer queries about the random particle g_best optimized. The main problem for solving multi-objective optimization using PSO update equation is the speed, because it makes that all particles converge on one point to get a result of each run. To solve this problem, noted in the previous position, the new position stores them. The result of the selection of the initial population is doubled. The method is intended for particle and is selected from among Old and new particles in the initial population as regular and the other one is defeated [2]. To overcome the problem algorithm of premature convergence to a local optimum, in 2002, a new algorithm called GCPSO was presented [10] and in this method, a new parameter was added to the algorithm that would be random searches particle g_best around the optimal solution.

3. Related works

Multi-objective optimization was done in research on transportation planning in which the proposed problem was resource distribution of products [11]. MOPSO was applied to solve the problem.

The problem was divided into sub-solutions and objective functions were described based on variable dependencies. The result showed the robustness and flexibility of the research.

A new technique was proposed in [12] to solve redundancy and reliability in which three functions were used simultaneously; objective function, cost function, and dynamic penalty function. The dynamic function controlled objective and cost function throughout iterations. Deb et al proposed an elitist non dominated sorting genetic algorithm for multi-objective optimization called NSGA-II. NSGA-II used elitism. In different dimensions in contrast with NSGA, NSGA-II worked by composing parent and offspring population and creating Rt. Then, Rt was classified using elitism. If in each class, the population is less than N (population size), all of the class members are chosen for next generation. The rest of the solutions are selected from other elite classes. On the other hand, if the population is greater than N, the better solutions for next generation are chosen based on intensity operator. The intensity is calculated using congestion procedure in objective function space and it can also be calculated in parameter space too. The constraint of the proposed technique was that intensity could offend convergence inside the algorithm in some cases [12]. Both intensity and convergence were targeted in [13] with introducing a new algorithm called MOGA. MOGA can also be used for composite optimization problems. The objective function procedure never guaranteed that a solution with lower rank always has a better scaled fitting F specially when there are solutions with better ranks and higher congestion. This can also offend convergence. However, in NSGA, the mentioned deficiency does not exist since it used queues. Share σ is a parameter that should be initialized at the beginning of algorithm like other GAs.

Deb and his students in an elite category or sorting Non-dominated genetic algorithms) so-called (NSGA_II offered.

NSGA_II of one of the most common methods is EMO multiple Pareto optimal solutions for multi-objective optimization problem acquires [14].

Multi-objective optimization using PSO was used in multi-objective handling system in [15]. The problem had three objectives:

• Minimization of the algorithm's produced pareto in comparison with the main pareto.

• Maximization of the founded solutions' distribution which makes uniform distribution achievable.

• Maximization of solutions in the optimal-Pareto.

Firstly, this algorithm works by initializing the parameters. Then, better solutions are both identified and archived. Next, for each particle a leader is selected from the archive and that particle should move toward its leader. The intensity of particles is small throughout the search space in this algorithm. Likewise in [15] an MOPSO optimizer was introduced for integrated low-carbon distribution system for the demand side of a product distribution supply chain. The proposed MOPSO selected bad solutions for deletion. The optimization occurred based on priority, ranking, and scenario analysis. The optimization of CO2 production and its relevant cost had been targeted in this research.

A new algorithm was proposed in [16] in which particle swarm optimization has been used. Particles produced offsprings in order to apply comparison in optimal-Pareto set. The problem in basic PSO is that the optimal-Pareto set comparison is not originally done in updating the best particle form each particle. To overcome this problem and to increase the sharing level among particles in a group NSPSO composes the entire best particles population (N) with their offsprings (N) and creates a temporary population of size 2N. Then the comparison procedure starts within the entire 2N particles. To do so, the entire population should be sorted in different optimal-Pareto sets as NSGA-II. A special rank is assigned to each particle in accordance with the optimal-Pareto set the particle belongs and receives the particles in the first Pareto the fitness priority of 1 and those in the second Pareto receives the fitness priority of 2 and likewise particles' fitness in each Pareto should have been calculated. In addition to fitness priority, a cumulative distance for each particle must have been calculated as well to guarantee the distribution of optimal particles. Cumulative distance is also used to evaluate the distance of each particle with its neighbours.

In [17] Sigma method as a new way to find the best local guides for each particle of the population has been introduced.

In [18], the CMPSO method has been proposed which was the combination of basic PSO with cumulative distance to solve multi objective problems. Particles are kept in the archive based on the cumulative distance. If a non-optimal solution wants to enter the archive and the archive size is the predefined size, the particle with the smallest cumulative distance in the archive should be selected first and then compared with new particle. The particle with the smaller cumulative distance is selected to be deleted from the archive. Keeping optimal particles in archive causes keeping good solutions and not missing them. Archives keep particles with greater cumulative distance and this leads to have diversity in solutions. Archive members in low density area have greater probability to be converted to optimal situations. This helps the algorithm to find the best optimal-Pareto set.

In [19], a task scheduling using multi-objective genetic algorithm with fuzzy adaptive operators for computational grids and compared with fixed rate of mutation and crossover was proposed. Fuzzy method with a more efficient solution set of values for load balancing, makespan and price.

We have to improve [19] proposed a method and with using experiments, all we show is more efficient and our method provides makespan, price and in some cases load balancing.

In [20], the scheduling job-shop with discrete solution spaces multi-objective problem is solved using an algorithm MOPSO.

In [20,21] flexible job-shop scheduling problem (FJSP), one of the classic problems of planning a multi-objective job-shop is inconsistent and contradictory, and is solved through using algorithm PSO and tabu search (TS).The computational results have proved that the proposed hybrid algorithm in [21] is an efficient and effective approach to solve the multi-objective FJSP, especially for the problems on a large scale. In [22] a method using particle swarm optimization (PSO) is proposed to reduce the communication overhead and reduces the time to complete the process and improves resource utilization of the computational grid. The representations of the position and velocity of the particles in conventional PSO is extended from the real vectors to fuzzy matrices. The proposed approach is to dynamically generate an optimal schedule so as to complete the tasks within a minimum period of time as well as utilizing the resources in an efficient way. In [23], a presented multi-objective particle swarm optimization in systems handling is that multi-objective particle swarm optimization in systems handling is stated these objectives: Minimize the Pareto fronts distance generated by the algorithm and the Pareto front, maximize the development of solutions, so that a smooth and uniform distribution maximize the number of elements found in optimal Pareto. In this algorithm, we first initialize the population and then Non-dominated members are isolated populations. Archives are stored. For each particle of the members of the leadership archive, select

the particles move toward the guide. In this paper, it is proved that the algorithm optimization MOPSO algorithm Optimization NSGAII, PAES, Micro GA Better Performance and better solutions with greater density in more smoothly and with less error is generated. In [24], the integration of low-carbon distribution in EPA using the optimization MOPSO algorithm. Done integration to distribute applicants will be done in the supply chain is presented. MOPSO non-optimal is a set of solutions from the solution desirable and practical search which remove them. Optimization and prioritization, rating and analysis scenario are done. Optimized of greenhouse gases CO_2 and cost optimization are concerned.

Scheduling algorithms plays an important role in grid computing, parallel distributed systems for scheduling tasks and deploys them to appropriate resources. Grid computing system has three objectives makespan, price and balance the load.

In [25] the problem of scheduling independent tasks in heterogeneous distributed systems such as grid using multi-objective optimization algorithm non-dominated density of particles is studied. This paper presents a scheduling algorithm based on multi-objective optimization offers free particles. The work optimized simultaneously two objectives makespan and circulation time.

In [26] takes advantages of genetic algorithm, brings forward a novel heuristic genetic load balancing algorithm and applied to solve grid computing load balancing problem.

In [27], the price and makespan as the main objective, regardless the load balancing by using a GA algorithm for scheduling problem modeling are proposed. In [28], the two types of GA to improve the performance of the scheduling algorithm are presented and minimize the total execution time and meet load balancing.

In [29], the balance is the net charge on the computational grid using genetic algorithms regardless of makespan or fees for network resources represented. In [30], the different load balancing strategy based on a tree representation of a network is studied. This enables conversion of any network architecture to a unique tree with a maximum of four levels. Task scheduling algorithm in [30,31] is considered only load balancing without makespan or price to users consider.

4. Proposed technique

In the proposed technique, each particle is dedicated a random amount. Particles are divided based on optimal or bad solutions archived. For each article a leader is selected and each article should move toward that article. After movement of particles, mutation occurs. Mutation could decrease convergence [14] and this reduction is necessary if the uniform distribution should be achieved. At first, the probability of occurring mutation is high and gradually this probability is decreased. Next, the personal best of each particle should be updated. This continues iteratively and new optimal solutions are archived. Sometimes the replacement of archive elements is necessary specially when we have other candidate optimal solutions and the archive is full. This continues until stop criterion achieves otherwise the leader selection and deletion of extra leaders continue.

4.1. Leader selection

The way how the leaders are selected has great impact on the proposed technique. Thus, a new leader selection is proposed to improve a basic MOPSO algorithm. The selected leaders are the best elements in optimal-Pareto. Two ways are suggested to choose a leader for each particle.

4.1.1. Leader selection (1st approach)

In the first way, a roulette wheel is used to select the M optimal solutions randomly. The places with fewer elements have more probability to be selected because this increases the optimal set domain. The mean of M selected articles is appointed as a leader. This leader selection is shown in figure 1 under the assumption of M=2. As it is shown in figure 1, particle D is the leader of particle A which is the mean of leaders B and C. In the proposed technique, more optimal solutions will be obtained for M = 3. This means that the main leader for each particle is found through calculating the average of three leaders.

Figure 1. Leader selection (1ˢᵗ approach).

4.1.2. Leader selection (2nd approach)

In the second approach, a leader is selected for any of N particles in population. The first approach in leader selection is also applied in which M=3. All the particles should move toward the leader and consequently to the optimal-Pareto. Figure 2 depicted the proposed approach. Particle

D is the selected leader for N particles which is the mean of leaders A and B.

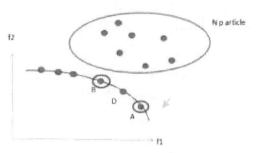

Figure 2. Leader selection (2ⁿᵈ approach).

4.2. Leader deletion

Some of the elements of the archive should be deleted provided that the archive queue becomes full. Through this way new optimal candidate solutions can be inserted to the archive. To delete an element uniformity criterion has been used to keep the set of optimal particles uniform. We want to delete those particles with less intensity distance. The process of leader deletion has been shown in figure 3. Intensity distance is calculated using (6). As it is shown in figure 2, particle A is deleted because of having smaller cumulative distance.

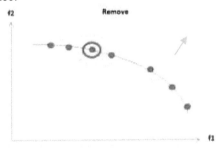

Figure 3. Leader deletion.

$$d_i^2 = \min\{d_{ij}|x^j \in Q, j \neq i\} \tag{3}$$

$$d_i^2 = \min\{d_{ij}|d_{ij}|>d_i^2, x^j \in Q, j \neq i\} \tag{4}$$

$$d_{ij} = \sqrt{\sum_{i=1}^{M}(\mu_k(f_k(x^i)-f_k(x^j)))^2} \tag{5}$$

$$c_{iQ} = (d_i^2+d_j^2)/2 \tag{6}$$

Generally, the proposed technique has been tested using four standard tests in multi-objective optimization. The evaluation criteria in this paper are: the number of elements in optimal-Pareto set, uniformity, and error. The results show that the proposed technique searches more numbers of optimal particles with higher intensity and less error in comparison with basic MOPSO. The proposed technique can be selected as a good replacement in solving multi-objective optimization problem. The proposed algorithm is shown in figure 4.

1	Initialization of the population
2	Separation and archiving optimal particles
3	Tabulating the detected objective search space
4	Leader selection for each particle from archive set and moving toward leader
5	Updating the personal best of each particle
6	ᴐAddition of current optimal particles to the archive
7	Deletion of non-optimal elements in archive
8	Archive elements => dedicated capacity => deletion of extra elements
9	Finish if stopping criterion satisfied otherwise goto step 3

Figure 4. Proposed algorithm.

5. Evaluation

The proposed technique has been evaluated based on three facts:

- The number of elements in optimal-Pareto set: the summation of each particle distance from nearest particle in optimal-Pareto set over the number of detected solutions as in (7). The less GD is, the more elements belonging to the optimal-Pareto set[14].

$$GD = \frac{\sqrt{\sum_{i=1}^{n} d_i^2}}{n} \tag{7}$$

- Uniformity: assuming zero for this parameters means that the element of pareto set has been distributed uniformly as shown in (8)[14].

$$SP = \sqrt{\frac{1}{n-1}\sum_{i=1}^{n}(d-d_i)^2} \tag{8}$$

$$d_i = \min(f_1^i(x) - f_1^j(x) + f_2^i(x) - f_1^j(x))$$

$$d = mean d_i$$

- Error: assuming zero for this parameter means that all produced solutions from the proposed algorithm belong to optimal-Pareto set as (9) [14].

$$ER = \frac{\sum_{i=1}^{n} e_i}{n} \tag{9}$$

5.1. First test function

We use the first test function as in [12] and (10).

$$f_1(x) = x^2 \tag{10}$$

$$f_2(x) = (x - 2^2)$$

For the first test function, the initial population was assumed to be 50, the iteration number was assumed to be 20 and the repository capacity was assumed to be 100.

In tables 1 to 4 the results of the comparison proposed technique by MOPSO and SIGMA and CMPSO is to for first test function. This table has three values of the best, worst and average values of GD, SP, are error.

GD in the SIGMA less than other techniques, and it is for this reason that the number of elements found in less optimal and most repetitive elements is found. However, in the above aspects, the proposed technique is more than GD. As a result of using a less optimal number of elements can be found Sigma.

The sigma error rate in comparison to the proposed high you can conclude that fewer elements have been found to be the optimal set.

In the first part of table 1 shows that the two proposed algorithms have less GD than the basic MOPSO and SIGMA and CMPSO. This means that more detected particles belong to the optimal-Pareto set. In the second part of table 1 shows that the two proposed algorithms have less SP than the basic MOPSO. As a result the distribution is more uniform. Also In the third part of table 1 shows that the error in basic MOPSO is more than the two proposed algorithms. In the Fourth part of table 1 compares the result based on time execution.

Table 1: GD/SP/ERROR/TIME result for first function.

GD/SP/ ERROR	MOPSO	SIGMA	CMOPSO	MOPSO1	MOPSO2
Best	0.2159	0.013288	0.10925	0.1142	0.090054
Worst	0.3274	0.028923	0.62396	0.31341	0.20463
Average	0.25072	0.018854	0.19627	0.18849	0.145853
Best	0.09628	0.11698	0.12946	0.12964	0.090545
Worst	1.2454	0.8231	0.37104	0.87629	0.99389
Average	0.37498	0.364742	0.294364	0.35284	0.433475
Best	0.0826	0.1071	0.0826	0.0741	0.0741
Worst	0.1304	0.1453	0.1304	0.115	0.1071
Average	0.11082	0.12248	0.10834	0.09718	0.09566
TIME		MOPSO1		MOPSO2	
Best		15.1353		4.982	
worst		50.0331		38.7575	
average		31.68764		25.70032	

5.2. Second test function

We use the second test function as in [12] and (11).

$$f_1(x) = \sum_{i=1}^{n-1}(-10\exp(-0.2\sqrt{x_i^2 + x_{i+1}^2})) \tag{11}$$

$$f_2(x) = \sum_{i=1}^{n}(|x_i|^{0.8} + 5\sin x_i^2)$$

For the second test function, the initial population was assumed to be 100, the iteration number was assumed to be 200 and the repository capacity was assumed to be 200.

In tables 5 to 8 the results of the comparison proposed technique by MOPSO and SIGMA and CMPSO is to for second test function. This table has three values of the best, worst and average values of GD, SP, are error. GD in the SIGMA less than other techniques, and it is for this reason that the number of elements found in less optimal and most repetitive elements is found. However, in the above aspects, the proposed technique is more than GD. As a result of using a less optimal number of elements can be found Sigma. The sigma error rate in comparison to the proposed high you can conclude that fewer elements have been found to be the optimal set.

In the first part of table 2 shows that the two proposed algorithms have less GD than the basic MOPSO and SIGMA and CMPSO. This means that more detected particles belong to the optimal-Pareto set. In the second part of table 2 shows that the two proposed algorithms have less SP than the basic MOPSO. As a result the distribution is more uniform. Also In the third part of table 2 shows that the error in basic MOPSO is more than the two proposed algorithms. In the fourth part of table 2 compares the result based on time execution.

Table 2: GD/SP/ERROR/TIME result for second function.

GD/SP/ERROR	MOPSO	SIGMA	CMOPSO	MOPSO1	MOPSO2
Best	2.03851	0.2247	2.5685	1.7619	1.8274
Worst	2.4601	0.4519	2.0385	2.6521	2.3863
Average	2.180802	0.364894	2.26366	2.02984	2.101662
Best	0.0395	0.0494	0.0339	0.0366	0.0303
Worst	0.0769	0.0962	0.1129	0.0926	0.0822
Average	0.06012	0.07812	0.05918	0.05726	0.05332
TIME	MOPSO1			MOPSO2	
Best	40.6679			29.8304	
worst	77.8366			56.6297	
average	55.24176			41.643	

In [14] MOPSO was compared with NSGA-II, microGA, and PAES and the results are shown in table 3. As it is shown in table 3, MOPSO has the smallest GD in comparison with other techniques. Tables 3 are in [14].

Table 3: GD/SP/ERROR result for third function.

GD	MOPSO	NSGA-II	microGA	PAES
Best	0.00745	0.006905	0.006803	0.01467
Worst	0.00960	0.103095	0.010344	0.157191
Average	0.008450	0.029255	0.008456	0.54914
Medium	0.00845	0.017357	0.008489	0.049358
Std. Dev.	0.000051	0.02717	0.000987	0.030744
SP	MOPSO	NSGA-II	microGA	PAES
Best	0.06187	0.018418	0.071686	0.064114
Worst	0.118445	0.065712	0.203127	0.340955
Average	0.09747	0.036136	0.128895	0.197532
Medium	0.10396	0.036085	0.126655	0.186632
Std. Dev.	0.01675	0.010977	0.029932	0.064114
ER	MOPSO	NSGA-II	microGA	PAES
Best	0.18	0.06	0.18	0.10
Worst	0.37	1.01	0.36	0.68
Average	0.2535	0.56	0.27	0.27
Medium	0.255	0.495	0.245	0.245
Std. Dev.	0.04082	0.384516	0.053947	0.10489

5.3. Third test function

We use the third test function as in [12] and (12).

$$f_1(x) = (1 - \exp(-\sum(\frac{x-1}{\sqrt{n}})^2) \tag{12}$$

$$f_2(x) = (1 - \exp(-\sum(\frac{x+1}{\sqrt{n}})^2)$$

For the third test function, the initial population was assumed to be 100, the iteration number was assumed to be 200 and the repository capacity was assumed to be 200.

In table 4 the results of the comparison proposed technique by MOPSO and CMPSO is to for third

test function. This table has three values of the best, worst and average values of GD, SP, are error. GD in the SIGMA less than other techniques, and it is for this reason that the number of elements found in less optimal and most repetitive elements is found.

However, in the above aspects, the proposed technique is more than GD. As a result of using a less optimal number of elements can be found Sigma. The sigma error rate in comparison to the proposed high you can conclude that fewer elements have been found to be the optimal set.

In the first part of table 4 shows that the two proposed algorithms have less GD than the basic MOPSO and SIGMA and CMPSO.

This means that more detected particles belong to the optimal-Pareto set. In the second part of table 4 shows that the two proposed algorithms have less SP than the basic MOPSO and SIGMA and CMPSO. As a result the distribution is more uniform. Also In the third part of table 4 shows that the error in basic MOPSO is more than the two proposed algorithms. In the fourth part of table 4 compares the result based on time execution.

Table 4: GD/SP/ERROR/TIME result for third function.

GD/SP/ERROR	MOPSO	SIGMA	CMPSO	MOPSO1	MOPSO2
Best	0.047057	0.003502	0.046153	0.03973	0.039172
Worst	0.054195	0.016435	0.076365	0.055144	0.044375
Average	0.050508	0.008953	0.055487	0.043991	0.042329
Best	0.096128	0.10691	0.073575	0.082234	0.051319
Worst	0.11224	0.12798	0.11286	0.10116	0.090021
Average	0.104914	0.119148	0.100004	0.092765	0.068794
Best	0.0253	0.0678	0.0238	0.0229	0.0196
Worst	0.0319	0.0833	0.0476	0.0268	0.028
Average	0.02836	0.07502	0.0316	0.02506	0.0245
TIME	MOPSO1			MOPSO2	
Best	65.8227			42.8899	
worst	99.5306			85.4931	
average	756.458			73.79252	

Table 5. GD/SP/ERROR analysis on first test function.

M	GD/SP/ERROR		
	2	5	15
Best	0.1142	0.11619	0.08122
worst	0.31341	0.36649	0.32001
average	0.18849	0.21468	0.179382
Best	0.12964	0.11313	0.16972
worst	0.87629	0.54794	0.3692
average	0.35284	0.23272	0.243934
Best	0.0741	0.0654	0.0741
worst	0.115	0.1228	0.1525
Average	0.09718	0.08546	0.10474

Table 6. GD/SP/ERROR analysis on second test function.

M	GD/SP/ERROR		
	2	5	15
Best	1.7619	1.7713	1.6021
worst	2.6521	2.2464	3.398
Average	2.02984	2.06912	2.42
Best	0.02801	0.03613	0.034087
worst	0.19154	0.058174	0.29466
Average	0.07101	0.046731	0.174293
Best	0.0366	0.0375	0.0328
worst	0.0926	0.0649	0.1111
Average	0.05726	0.04274	0.0686

6. Experimental result
6.1.1. First analysis

This analysis is done to determine the best M, and to calculate the mean of M leaders for the first proposed technique.

Assuming 2, 5, and 15 for M, the results are calculated. Tables 5 to 7 show that the best assumption is M=2 that is few errors, the SP and GD.

Table 7. GD/SP/ERROR analysis on third test function.

GD/SP/ERROR			
M	2	5	15
Best	0.03973	0.034591	0.035432
worst	0.055144	0.050634	0.063236
Average	0.043991	0.039307	0.048697
Best	0.082234	0.053142	0.037104
worst	0.10116	0.086248	0.057453
Average	0.092765	0.067503	0.047034
Best	0.0229	0.017	0.0152
worst	0.0268	0.0244	0.0227
Average	0.02506	0.02092	0.01962

6.1.2. Second analysis

This analysis is done to determine the best N, for the second proposed technique. This analysis also helps to determine how many particles need a certain leader to achieve better optimal-Pareto solutions. Assuming 5, 20, and 50 for N, the results are calculated. Tables 8 to 10 show that the best assumption is N=50 that is few errors, the SP and GD.

Table 8. GD/SP/ERROR analysis on the first test function.

GD/SP/ERROR			
N	5	20	50
Best	0.066882	0.17949	0.090054
worst	0.25464	0.36342	0.20463
Average	0.156502	0.272078	0.145853
Best	0.16708	0.1387	0.20104
worst	1.1823	1.0292	0.99389
Average	0.409728	0.349194	0.596456
Best	0.0654	0.0741	0.0741
worst	0.1379	0.0991	0.1071
Average	0.10332	0.0842	0.09566

Table 9. GD/SP/ERROR analysis on the second test function.

GD/SP/ERROR			
N	5	20	50
Best	1.7194	1.7304	1.8274
worst	2.7931	2.5637	2.3863
Average	2.094	2.05442	2.101662
Best	0.035883	0.038456	0.014392
worst	0.19398	0.20685	0.16151
Average	0.098005	0.12092	0.07814
Best	0.0274	0.0377	0.0303
worst	0.0577	0.0561	0.0822
Average	0.04244	0.04376	0.0533

6.1.3. Third analysis

This analysis is done to determine the dimensions of the problem, for both techniques. The consequences in tables 11 to 13 show that lower dimensions have better results and the proposed techniques is better in comparison with basic MOPSO.

Table 10. GD/SP/ERROR analysis on the third test function.

GD/SP/ERROR			
N	5	20	50
Best	0.042976	0.03617	0.039172
worst	0.064321	0.047743	0.044375
Average	0.051529	0.043034	0.042329
Best	0.052436	0.070877	0.051319
worst	0.081611	0.075822	0.090021
Average	0.065549	0.073381	0.068794
Best	0.0167	0.0182	0.0196
worst	0.0226	0.0261	0.028
Average	0.01964	0.02348	0.0245

Table 11. GD/SP/ERROR analysis on the first proposed technique.

GD/SP/ERROR			
NVAR	3	10	30
Best	1.7619	8.1567	33.367
worst	2.6521	13.6528	45.3985
Average	2.02984	10.9251	37.68592
Best	0.02801	0.020605	0.032489
worst	0.19154	0.83062	0.3059
Average	0.07101	0.231264	0.181066
Best	0.0366	0.027	0.1064
worst	0.0926	0.1892	0.1304
Average	0.05726	0.07266	0.11872

Table 12. GD/SP/ERROR analysis on the second proposed technique.

GD/SP/ERROR			
NVAR	3	10	30
Best	1.8274	9.4872	26.9047
worst	2.3863	11.3522	37.5597
Average	2.101662	10.2596	33.13216
Best	0.014392	0.018486	0.050401
worst	0.16151	0.99951	0.46794
Average	0.07814	0.267326	0.256166
Best	0.0303	0.06	0.0357
worst	0.0822	0.0862	0.1304
Average	0.05332	0.06914	0.0793

As it is shown in table 12, with higher dimensions MOPSO does not work on second test function. It only works for dimensions 3 and 10.

Table 13. GD/SP/ERROR analysis on the second test function.

GD/SP/ERROR		
NVAR	3	10
Best	2.03851	9.4417
worst	2.4601	13.7426
average	2.180802	11.78792
Best	0.045384	0.089812
worst	0.23174	1.5549
average	0.115702	0.611626
Best	0.0395	0.0588
worst	0.0769	0.119
average	0.06012	0.09424

CMPSO is not suitable for higher dimensions with second test function. It only has appropriate results for three and ten dimensions. Based on the comparisons made in table 14 even this result is not optimal.

SIGMA technique is not suitable for higher dimensions with second test function. It only has appropriate results for three and ten dimensions. Based on the comparisons made in table 15 even this result is not optimal.

Table 14: Test results for second test function.

GD/SP/ERROR		
NVAR	3	10
Best	2.5685	12.0271
worst	2.0385	15.5735
average	2.26366	13.45778
Best	0.04189	0.016527
worst	0.13083	1.0559
average	0.073292	0.299453
Best	0.0339	0.0625
worst	0.1129	0.1429
average	0.05918	0.11088

Table 15: Test results for second test function.

GD/SP/ERROR			
NVAR	3	10	30
Best	0.2247	3.6339	16.3493
worst	0.4519	8.3863	42.0749
Average	0.364894	5.32646	32.44846
Best	0.035788	0.11267	1.905
worst	0.15884	2.7703	15.3253
Average	0.083683	1.140006	6.2378
Best	0.0494	0.1875	0.1875
worst	0.0962	0.25	0.5455
Average	0.07812	0.21804	0.38548

7. Discussion

We have changed the leader selection and leader deletion in basic MOPSO to have more uniform distribution in the set of optimal-Pareto particles. The proposed approach also leads to have fewer errors and to detect more optimal particles. In the first leader selection approach, since the mean of M leader is calculated the results solutions will have more uniform optimal-Pareto particles. Likewise the result SP parameter is also smaller than the basic MOPSO and SIGMA and CMPSO. In the second leader selection approach, one leader is considered for N particles. This yields to have more solutions with uniform distribution. Also the time to achieve optimal solutions decreased. For leader deletion the proposed technique helps to increase the optimal-Pareto solutions or in other words, GD will be decreased. Finally, error was also declined.

8. Conclusion

In this paper a technique was proposed to enhance the basic MOPSO. The results prove the enhancement in comparison with the basic MOPSO and SIGMA and CMPSO and NSGA-II and microGA and PAES. In fact the proposed MOPSO has considerable results to detect optimal solutions based on the test functions. Moreover, the proposed MOPSO keeps optimal-Pareto solutions more uniform and with more intensity. As a future work we can make the algorithm and its parameters more accurate to achieve acceptable results for dynamic functions.

References

[1] Deb, K. (2014). Multi-objective optimization. In search methodologies, pp. 403–449. Springer.

[2] Coello Coello, C. A., & Lechuga, M. S. (2002). MOPSO: A proposal for multiple objective particle swarm optimization. Evolutionary Computation, 2002. CEC'02. Proceedings of the 2002 Congress on, vol. 2, pp. 1051–1056. IEEE.

[3] Eberhart, R. C., & Kennedy, J. (1995). A new optimizer using particle swarm theory. Proceeding of the sixth international symposium on micro machine and human science, vol. 1, pp. 39–43. New York, NY.

[4] Sheibani, M. & Meybodi, M. R. (2007). PSO-LA: A new model for Optimization. 12rd Iranian Conference on Computer Engineering. pp:1162-1169, In persian.

[5] Hu, X., Shi, Y. & Eberhart, R. C. (2004). Recent advances in particle swarm. IEEE congress on evolutionary computation, vol. 1, pp. 90–97.

[6] Kennedy, J. & Mendes, R. (2002). Population structure and particle swarm performance.

[7] Cui, X., Potok, T. E. & Palathingal, P. (2005). Document clustering using particle swarm optimization. Swarm Intelligence Symposium, 2005. SIS 2005. Proceedings 2005 IEEE, pp. 185–191. IEEE.

[8] Liu, H. & Abraham, A. (2005). Fuzzy adaptive turbulent particle swarm optimization. Hybrid Intelligent Systems, 2005. HIS '05. Fifth International Conference on. doi:10.1109/ICHIS.2005.49

[9] Shi, Y., & Eberhart, R. (1998). A modified particle swarm optimizer. Evolutionary Computation Proceedings, 1998. IEEE World Congress on Computational Intelligence., The 1998 IEEE International Conference on, pp. 69–73. IEEE.

[10] Van den Bergh, F. & Engelbrecht, A. P. (2002). A new locally convergent particle swarm optimizer. Proceedings of the IEEE international conference on systems, man, and cybernetics, vol. 7, pp. 6–9.

[11] Zheng, Y.-J. & Chen, S.-Y. (2013). Cooperative particle swarm optimization for multiobjective transportation planning. Applied intelligence, vol. 39, no. 1, pp. 202–216.

[12] Khalili-Damghani, K., Abtahi, A.-R. & Tavana, M. (2013). A new multi-objective particle swarm optimization method for solving reliability redundancy allocation problems. Reliability Engineering & System Safety, vol. 111, pp. 58–75.

[13] Kennedy, J. & Eberhart, R. (1995). Particle swarm optimization. Neural Networks, 1995. Proceedings., IEEE International Conference on. http://doi.org/10.1109/ICNN.1995.488968.

[14] DEH, K., Agrawal, S., PRATAP, A. & Meyarivan, T. (2000). A fast elitist non-dominated sorting genetic algorithm for multi-objective optimization: NSGA-II. Lecture notes in computer science, pp. 849–858.

[15] Coello, C. A. C., Pulido, G. T. & Lechuga, M. S. (2004). Handling multiple objectives with particle

swarm optimization. Evolutionary Computation, IEEE Transactions on, vol. 8, no. 3, pp. 256–279.

[16] Liu, Y. (2008). A fast and elitist multi-objective particle swarm algorithm: NSPSO. Granular Computing, 2008. GrC 2008. IEEE International Conference on, pp. 470–475.

[17] IEEE. Mostaghim, S. & Teich, J. (2003, April). Strategies for finding good local guides in multi-objective particle swarm optimization (MOPSO). In Swarm Intelligence Symposium, 2003. SIS'03. Proceedings of the 2003 IEEE, pp. 26-33. IEEE.

[18] Fan, J., Zhao, L., Du, L. & Zheng, Y. (2010). Crowding-distance-based multi-objective particle swarm optimization. Computational Intelligence and Intelligent Systems, pp. 218–225. Springer.

[19] Salimi, R., Motameni, H. & Omranpour, H. (2014). Task scheduling using NSGA II with fuzzy adaptive operators for computational grids. Journal of Parallel and Distributed Computing, vol. 74, no. 5, pp. 2333-2350.

[20] Sha D. Y. & Lin, H. H. (2010). A multi-objective PSO for job-shop scheduling problems. Expert Systems with Applications, vol. 37, no. 2, pp. 1065-1070.

[21] Zhang, G., Shao, X., Li, P. & Gao, L. (2009). An effective hybrid particle swarm optimization algorithm for multi-objective flexible job-shop scheduling problem. Computers & Industrial Engineering, vol. 56, no. 4, pp. 1309-1318.

[22] Liu, H., Abraham, A. & Hassanien, A. E. (2010). Scheduling jobs on computational grids using a fuzzy particle swarm optimization algorithm. Future Generation Computer Systems, vol. 26, no. 8, pp. 1336-1343.

[23] Carlos A, Coello, Coello, Gregorio Toscano Pulido, M, Salazar Lechuga., (2004). Handling multiple objectives with paper swarm optimization, Evolutionary Computation. IEEE Transactions on, pp. 256-279.

[24] Validi, S., Bhattacharya, A., & Byrne, P. J. (2014). Integrated low-carbon distribution system for the demand side of a product distribution supply chain: a DoE-guided MOPSO optimiser-based solution method. International Journal of Production Research, vol. 52, no. 10, pp. 3074-3096.

[25] Subashini, G., Bhuvaneswari, M. C. (2011). Non dominated particle swarm optimization for scheduling independent tasks on heterogeneous distributed environments, vol. 3, no. 1, pp. 1-17.

[26] J. Ma, Lanzhou. (2010). A novel heuristic genetic load balancing algorithm in grid computing, in: Second International Conference on Intelligent Human–Machine Systems and Cybernetics, pp. 166-169

[27] Kardani-Moghaddam, S., Khodadadi, F., Entezari-Maleki, R. & Movaghar, A. (2012). A hybrid genetic algorithm and variable neighborhood search for task

scheduling problem in grid environment. Procedia Engineering, vol. 29, pp. 3808-3814.

[28] Omara, F. A., Arafa, M. M. (2010). Genetic algorithms for task scheduling problem, J. Parallel Distrib. Comput, vol. 70, no. 1, pp. 13–22.

[29] Prakash, S., Vidyarthi, D. P. (2011). Load balancing in computational grid using genetic algorithm, Advances in Computing. vol. 1, no. 1, pp. 8–17. http://dx.doi.org/10.5923/j.ac.02.

[30] Patni, J. C., Aswal, M. S., Pal, O. P. & Gupta, A. (2011). Load balancing strategies for grid computing. In Electronics Computer Technology (ICECT), 3rd International Conference on, vol. 3, pp. 239-243. IEEE.

[31] Peng, H., Li, Q. (2011). One kind of improved load balancing algorithm in grid computing, in: International Conference on Network Computing and Information Security, vol. 1, pp. 347-351. IEEE.

[32] Izakian, Z., Mesgari, M. S. (2015). Fuzzy clustering of time series data: A particle swarm optimization approach. Journal of Artificial Intelligence and Data Mining, vol. 3, no. 1, pp. 39–46. doi:10.5829/idosi.JAIDM.2015.03.01.05.

16

Using a new modified harmony search algorithm to solve multi-objective reactive power dispatch in deterministic and stochastic models

Kh. Valipour[*] and A. Ghasemi

Technical Engineering Department, University of Mohaghegh Ardabili, Ardabil, Iran.

*Corresponding author: kh_valipour@uma.ac.ir (Kh. Valipour.)

Abstract

The optimal reactive power dispatch (ORPD) problem is a very important aspect in power system planning, and it is a highly non-linear, non-convex optimization problem because it consists of both the continuous and discrete control variables. Since a power system has an inherent uncertainty, this paper presents both the deterministic and stochastic models for the ORPD problem in multi-objective and single-objective formulations, respectively. The deterministic model considers three main issues in the ORPD problem including the real power loss, voltage deviation, and voltage stability index. However, in the stochastic model, the uncertainties in the demand and equivalent availability of shunt reactive power compensators have been investigated. To solve them, we proposed a new modified harmony search algorithm (HSA), implemented in single and multi-objective forms. Since, like many other general purpose optimization methods, the original HSA often traps into the local optima, an efficient local search method called chaotic local search (CLS) and a global search operator are proposed in the internal architecture of the original HSA algorithm to improve its ability in finding the best solution because the ORPD problem is very complex, with different types of continuous and discrete constrains, i.e. excitation settings of generators, sizes of fixed capacitors, tap positions of tap changing transformers, and amount of reactive compensation devices. Moreover, the fuzzy decision-making method is employed to select the best solution from the set of Pareto solutions. The proposed model is individually examined and applied on different test systems. The simulation results show that the proposed algorithm is suitable and effective for the reactive power dispatch problem compared to the other available algorithms.

Keywords: *Reactive Power Dispatch, Modified HSA, Multi-objective, System Stability, Stochastic Model.*

1. Introduction

The optimal reactive power dispatch (ORPD) problem can be divided into two parts, known as the real and reactive power dispatch problems. The real power dispatch problem aims to minimize the total cost of real power generation from thermal power plants at various stations [1]. However, reactive power dispatch controls the power system stability and power quality, i.e. voltage stability and power loss. Generally, the objective of ORPD is to minimize the real power loss and increase the voltage stability in the power system, while satisfying various discrete and continues constraints [2].

Recently, many scientific papers have been dedicated to the ORPD problem, which can be classified into two groups, classical and intelligent computing methods. Classical computing methods consist of some well-known mathematical strategies such as linear programming (LP) [3], non-linear programming (NLP) [4], quadratic programming [5], and decomposition technique [6]. This group is computationally fast but they have several limitations like (i) the need for continuous and differentiable objective functions, (ii) easy convergence to local minima. and (iii) difficulty in handling a very large number of variables. Therefore, it is vital to develop some intelligent methods that are capable of overcoming these shortages. In another group, computational intelligence-based techniques have been proposed for the application of reactive power optimization. In [7], a new modified version of honey bee mating optimization called the parallel vector evaluated honey bee mating optimization (PVEHBMO) based on multi-objective formulation has been proposed to solve the RPD problem. In [8], the authors have presented a quasi-oppositional differential evolution to solve the ORPD problem of a power system. In [9], the authors have proposed a multi-objective differential evolution (MODE) to solve the multi-objective optimal reactive power dispatch (MORPD) problem by minimizing the active power transmission loss and voltage deviation, and maximizing the voltage stability, while varying the control variables such as the generator terminal voltages, transformer taps, and reactive power output of shunt compensators. Pareto-efficient 12-h variable double auction bilateral power transactions have been considered in [10]. The effect of that on the economic welfare has been observed, while solving the reactive power dispatch (RPD) by differential evolution using the random localization technique. This has been accomplished by a combination of static and dynamic var compensators. Out of these 12-h variable power transactions, the Pareto-efficient transactions, which are reconciled by planed biding, have provided the maximum global welfare. In [11], the authors have presented a new meta-heuristic method, namely gray wolf optimizer (GWO), which is inspired from gray wolves'leadership and hunting behaviors to solve the optimal reactive power dispatch (ORPD) problem.

The aforementioned papers show that the optimization methods have a good potential to solve the ORPD problem. The ORPD with high optimal variables and constrains requires a more effective method to avoid the local optimal solutions, and it has well-distribution of non-dominated solutions, while satisfying the diversity characteristics. A new meta-heuristic algorithm, mimicking the improvisation process of music players, has been recently developed and named the harmony search algorithm (HSA) [12]. Due to its many positive features, being simple in concept and easy to implement, flexibility, the possibility of using chaotic maps and of developing hybrids from combinations with other techniques, the HSA algorithm has been successfully applied to the optimization of complex mathematical functions with or without constraints [13]. Unfortunately, the standard HSA often converges to local optima. In order to improve the fine-tuning characteristic of HSA, an improved HSA has been proposed, enhancing the fine-tuning characteristic and convergence rate of harmony

search [14-15]. This paper proposes two modifications in the local and global operators. In the local term, a new CLS operator is presented to update each particle in the search space. In the global part, the pitch adjusting rate (PAR) and the distance bandwidth (bw) are rewritten, which are important coefficients in exploration and exploitation. Moreover, HSA is developed as a stochastic optimization algorithm; it can find an optimal solution within a short calculation time. The results obtained from three test systems in the ORPD problem show that the proposed method has a robust convergence and makes an acceptable distribution in the Pareto-optimal solutions.

2. Deterministic formulation of ORPD problem
In this section, the deterministic formulation of the ORPD problem is presented.

2.1. Problem objectives
• *Objective 1: power-loss minimization*
Transmission losses are construed as a loss of revenue by the utility. The transmission loss can be expressed by [7]:

$$J_1 = P_{loss}(x,u) = \sum_{k=1}^{N_l} g_k [V_i^2 + V_j^2 - 2V_i V_j \cos(\theta_i - \theta_j)] \ (1)$$

where, g_k is the conductance of the line i-j, V_i and V_j are the line voltages, and θ_i and θ_j are the line angles at the i and j line ends, respectively, k is the kth network branch that connects bus i to bus j, i = 1, 2, . . . , ND, where ND is the set of numbers of power demand bus, and j = 1, 2, . . . , N_j, where N_j is the set of numbers of buses adjacent to bus j. PG is the active power in lines i and j. x and u are the vector of dependent variables and the vector of control variables, respectively.

• *Objective 2: Minimization of voltage deviation*
The aim of this function is to minimize the absolute voltage deviation of load bus voltages from their desired values:

$$J_2 = VD(x,u) = \sum_{i=1}^{Nd} |V_i - V_i^{sp}| \qquad (2)$$

where, N_d is the number of load buses.
• *Objective 3: Minimization of L-index voltage stability*
It is a static voltage stability measure of power system, which is computed based on the normal load flow solution. *L-index* L_j of the jth bus can be expressed by:

$$\begin{cases} L_j = \left|1 - \sum_{i=1}^{N_{PV}} F_{ji} \dfrac{V_i}{V_j}\right|, j = 1,2,...,N_{PQ} \\ F_{ji} = -[Y_1]^{-1}[Y_2] \end{cases} \qquad (3)$$

where, N_{PV} and N_{PQ} are the number of PV and PQ

buses, respectively. Y_1 and Y_2 refer to the sub-matrices of the YBUS matrix one gets:

$$\begin{bmatrix} I_{PQ} \\ I_{PV} \end{bmatrix} = \begin{bmatrix} Y_1 & Y_2 \\ Y_3 & Y_4 \end{bmatrix} \begin{bmatrix} V_{PQ} \\ V_{PV} \end{bmatrix} \qquad (4)$$

The L-index is calculated for all the PQ buses. L_j shows no load case and voltage collapse conditions of bus j in the range of (0, 1). Thus the objective function is represented by:

$$L = \max(L_j), j = 1, 2, ..., N_{PQ} \qquad (5)$$

In the ORPD problem, an incorrect set of control variables may increase the value of L-index, and leads to a voltage instability. Let the maximum value of L-index be L_{max}. Therefore, to enhance the voltage stability, and to keep the system far from the voltage collapse margin, one gets:

$$J_3 = VL(x, u) = L_{max} \qquad (6)$$

2.2. Objective constraints
• *Constraints 1: Equality Constraints*
In the ORPD problem, the power generation must be equal to the sum of the demand (P_D) and the power loss in the transmission lines:

$$\begin{cases} P_{G_i} - P_{D_i} = V_i \sum_{j=1}^{N_B} V_j [G_{ij} \cos(\theta_i - \theta_j) + B_{ij} \sin(\theta_i - \theta_j)] \\ \\ Q_{G_i} - Q_{D_i} = V_i \sum_{j=1}^{N_B} V_j [G_{ij} \sin(\theta_i - \theta_j) - B_{ij} \cos(\theta_i - \theta_j)] \end{cases} \qquad (7)$$

where, NB is the number of buses; Q_{Gi} is the reactive power generated at the ith bus; and P_{Di} and Q_{Di} are the ith bus load real and reactive power, respectively; G_{ij} and B_{ij} are the transfer conductance and susceptance between bus i and bus j, respectively; V_i and V_j are the voltage magnitudes at bus i and bus j, respectively; and θ_i and θ_j are the voltage angles at bus i and bus j, respectively.
• *Constraints 2: Generation Capacity Constraints*
Generally, the generator outputs and bus voltage constrains by lower and upper limits are as follow:

$$Q_i^{min} \le Q_i \le Q_i^{max}, v_i^{min} \le v_i \le v_i^{max} \qquad (8)$$

Where, P_i^{min} and P_i^{max} are the minimum and maximum values, respectively.
• *Constraints 3: Line-flow constraints*
One of the main constrains in the ORPD problem is the maximum transfer capacity of the transmission line. These constrains can be calculated as follows:

$$|S_{Lf,k}| \le S_{Lf,k}^{max}, k = 1, 2, ..., L \qquad (9)$$

where, $S_{Lf,k}$ is the real power flow of line k; $S_{Lf,k}^{max}$ is the power flow upper limit of line k, and subscript L denotes the number of transmission lines.

• *Constraints 4: Transformer*
The transformer tap setting is restricted by its lower and upper values:

$$T_i^{min} \le T_i \le T_i^{max} \qquad (10)$$

2.3. Problem formulation
As results, the proposed deterministic multi-objective ORPD problem can be formulated as:

$$\min_{x,u} [\underbrace{P_{loss}(x,u)}_{J_1}, \underbrace{VD(x,u)}_{J_2}, \underbrace{VL(x,u)}_{J_3}]$$

$subject \quad to :$

$$g(x, u) = 0 \qquad (11)$$
$$h(x, u) \le 0$$

$where, x^T = [[V_L]^T, [Q_G]^T, [S_L]^T],$

$u^T = [[V_G]^T, [T]^T, [Q_C]^T]$

Where, g and h are the equality and inequality constraints, respectively; $[V_L]$, $[Q_G]$, and $[S_L]$ are the vector of load bus voltages, generator reactive power outputs, and transmission line loadings, respectively; and $[V_G]$, $[T]$, and $[Q_C]$ are the vector of generator bus voltages, transformer taps, and reactive compensation devices, respectively.

3. Stochastic formulation of ORPD problem
In practice, power injections, especially from intermittent renewable sources, and demand are of uncertainties [16-17]. To aim with this cope, in this section, the load uncertainty is developed in the stochastic form in the ORPD problem. Usually the probability distribution of a random variable is represented using a finite set of scenarios. In other words, each scenario (s^{th}) has an associated probability of occurrence (ξ_s). From (1), variable ψ can be defined as:

$$\psi = \sum_{n \in L} pL_n \qquad (12)$$

The expected value for ψ can be given by:

$$E[\psi] = \sum_{s \in S} \xi_s . \psi_s = \sum_{s \in S} \xi_s . \left(\sum_{n \in TL} pL_n \right) = \sum_{s \in S} \sum_{n \in TL} \xi_s . pL_{n,s} \quad (13)$$

Substituting (12) and (13), one gets:

$$\min\{f(x) + E[\psi(y)]\} \qquad (14)$$

Finally, the stochastic formulation of power loss can be calculated as follows:

$$\min_{\substack{v, \delta, tab, q^{SH} \\ P_{slack}, q_G}} f = \sum_{s \in S} \sum_{n \in TL} \xi_s . pL_{n,s}$$

$$P_{p,s}^G + p_{slack,s}^G = P_{l,s}^D + P_{i,s}(v, \delta, tab)$$

$$q_{j,s}^G = Q_{l,s}^D + Q_{i,s}(v, \delta, tab) + q_{k,s}^{SH}$$

$$\underline{Q}_j^G \le q_{j,s}^G \le \overline{Q}_j^G , \underline{Q}_k^{SH} \le q_{k,s}^{SH} \le \overline{Q}_k^{SH} , \underline{V}_i \le v_{i,s} \le \overline{V}_i \quad (15)$$

$$\underline{Tap}_m \le tap_{m,s} \le \overline{Tap}_m , |s_{n,s}| \le \overline{S}_n$$

$$\forall\{i \in B, k \in SH, p \in PV, j \in \{PV \cup slack\},$$

$$l \in PQ, m \in TAP, n \in TL, s \in S\}$$

Constraints Eqs. (7)-(11) in the deterministic model are modified to take into account all the different scenarios of demand $s \in S$, such that modifications are shown in constraints Eq. (15) in the stochastic model.

4. Multi-objective MHSA
4.1. Standard HSA
In this section, the original HSA is briefly introduced; more details can be found in [12].

```
Start
Objective function f(x), x=(x₁,x₂, ...,x_d)^T
Generate initial harmonics (real number arrays)
Define pitch adjusting rate (PAR), pitch limits and bandwidth
Define harmony memory accepting rate (r_accept)
while t<Max number of iterations
    Generate new harmonics by accepting best harmonics
    Adjust pitch to get new solutions
        if (rand>r_accept), choose an existing harmonic randomly
        else if (rand>PAR), adjust the pitch randomly within limits
            else generate new harmonics via randomization
            end if
        Accept the new harmonics (solutions) if better
    end
Find the current best solutions
End
```

Figure 1. Pseudo-code of standard HSA.

This algorithm has three main components, as shown in figure 1. It is clear that the probability of randomization can be given by:

$$P_{random} = 1 - r_{accept} \qquad (16)$$

and the actual probability of adjusting pitches is given by:

$$P_{pitch} = r_{accept} \times PAR \qquad (17)$$

4.2. Modified HSA
This algorithm shows a good performance in an optimization problem, although the main shortage of the HSA algorithm comes from this fact that it may miss the optimum solution or converge to a near optimum solution. However, it has a flexible and well-balanced mechanism to enhance the global and local exploration abilities. Therefore, the following modifications are proposed.

- *Modification of bw and PAR*

Generally, the parameters PAR and *bw* are arbitrarily fixed. It is clear that they can affect the stochastic nature of HSA. Therefore, a time-varying operator is proposed to keep away from this difficulty:

$$PAR_i = PAR_{min} + \frac{i}{H}(PAR_{max} - PAR_{min}) \qquad (18)$$

$$bw_i = bw_{max} \times \exp\left(i \times \frac{\ln\left(\frac{bw_{min}}{bw_{max}}\right)}{H}\right) \qquad (19)$$

where, PAR_{min} and PAR_{max} are the minimum and maximum values for the pitch adjustment rate in the search space, respectively; and H and i are the maximum and current iterations, respectively.

- *Global searching operator*

In order to have an effective global search, combine the genetic operator as follows:

for i=1:N

$$penalty_i = abs(x_i^{best} - x_i^{worst});$$
$$x_i^{New} = x_i^{best} \pm penalty_i;$$
if rand ≤ T $\qquad (20)$
$$x_i^{New} = x_i^{min} + rand \times (x_i^{max} - x_i^{min});$$
end

end

The superscripts *best* and *worst* refer to the global best and worst solutions for variable x, respectively. The parameter *penalty* is the guarantee for the global search ability. In other words, after some evaluations, HSA may reach a local solution and *penalty* goes to zero, and hereby, the algorithm will be stagnated. To avoid this shortage, generate some random harmonies, and replace the worse harmonies. The number of new random harmonies depends on the problem and size of HM. The new random harmonies increase the *penalty* parameter, and lead to new exploration in finding a better solution.

- *Local searching operator (CLS)*

Chaos is a random-like process found in a non-linear, dynamical system, which is non-period, non-converging, and bounded [17]. The proposed CLS-integrated HSA can be formulated as follows:

$$c_{i+1}^j = \begin{cases} 2c_i^j, & if\ 0 < c_i^j \le 0.5 \\ 2(1-c_i^j), & if\ 0.5 < c_i^j \le 1 \end{cases}, j=1,2,...,Ng \qquad (21)$$

where, C_{i+1}^j is the jth chaotic variable of ith iteration. This combination can be summarized as follows:

i) Generate an initial population:

$$X_{cls}^0 = [X_{cls,0}^1, X_{cls,0}^2,...,X_{cls,0}^{Ng}]_{1 \times N_g}$$
$$cx_0 = [cx_0^1, cx_0^2,...,cx_0^{Ng}] \qquad (22)$$
$$cx_0^j = \frac{X_{cls,0}^j - P_{j,min}}{P_{j,max} - P_{j,min}}, j=1,2,...,Ng$$

where, the chaos variable can be obtained by:

$$x_{cls}^i = [x_{cls,i}^1, x_{cls,i}^2,...,x_{cls,i}^{Ng}]_{1 \times N_g}, i=1,2,...,N_{chaos}$$
$$x_{cls,i}^j = cx_{i-1}^j \times (P_{j,max} - P_{j,min}) + P_{j,min}, j=1,2,...,N_g \qquad (23)$$

ii) Measure the chaotic variables:

$$cx_i = [cx_i^1, cx_i^2, ..., cx_i^{Ng}], i = 0,1,2,...,N_{choas}$$

$$cx_{i+1}^j = base\ CLS \quad j = 1,2,...,Ng \qquad (24)$$

$$cx_0^j = rand\,(0)$$

where, N_{chaos} is the number of individuals for CLS; cx_i^{Ng} is the ith chaotic variable; $rand()$ is a random number at the range $(0,1)$; Ng is the number of units; and X_{cls}^i is the current position of the harmony-based chaos theory.

iii): Map the decision variables

iv): Convert the chaotic variables to the decision variables

v): Evaluate the new solution with decision variables.

4.3. Non-dominated sort and crowding distance

In this process, the entire population is sorted with its non-dominated level. Each solution is assigned with a fitness value. Perform the non-dominated sort method on the initial population, and calculate the rank: $rank_1$, $rank_2$, $rank_3$...., etc. After the non-dominated sort is done, the crowding distance is assigned to each solution. The crowding distance is assigned front wise. Compare the crowding distance between two individuals in different fronts [9, 10]. Hereby, the density of the surrounding individuals of i is expressed by i_d, which is the smallest range that contains i but does not contain other points around the individual i . This process can be expressed as follows:

i) For each front F_i, l is the number of individual, i.e. $|F_i| = l$.

ii) For every individual i , set the initial crowding distance $i_d = 0$.

iii) Set $1_d = l_d = \infty$. For each individual i , $P[i].k$ denotes the value for the kth objective function.

iv) Let i cycle be from 2 to $l - 1$, and calculate the following expression to define the crowding distance for each individual

$$i_d = i_d + \sum_{k=1}^{m} \left((P[i+1].f_k - P[i-1].f_k) \middle/ f_k^{max} - f_k^{min} \right) \quad (25)$$

The graphical outlook for non-dominated sort and crowding distance is shown in figure 2.

4.4. Best compromise solution

Fuzzy decision-maker is one of the multi-criteria decision methods that provide the best decision between a set of solutions. It can help the designer to make the best decisions that are consistent with their values, goals, and performances [17]. Hereby, firstly, the solution is assigned with the following triangular membership function:

$$\mu_i = \frac{f_i^{max} - f_i}{f_i^{max} - f_i^{min}} \qquad (26)$$

$$FDM_i = \begin{cases} 0 & \mu_i \le 0 \\ \mu_i & 0 < \mu_i < 1 \\ 1 & \mu_i \ge 1 \end{cases} \qquad (27)$$

where, f_{min} and f_{max} are the maximum and minimum values for the ith function response of the selected k^{th} solution, respectively. The normalized membership function FDM^k can be calculated by:

$$FDM^k = \left[\frac{\sum\limits_{i=1}^{N_{obj}} FDM_i^k}{\sum\limits_{j=1}^{M} \sum\limits_{i=1}^{N_{obj}} FDM_i^j} \right] \qquad (28)$$

where, M is the number of non-dominated solutions, and Nob_j is the number of objective functions. Figure 3 illustrates a typical shape of the employed membership function.

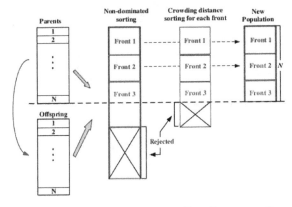

Figure 2. Non-dominated and crowding distance sorting.

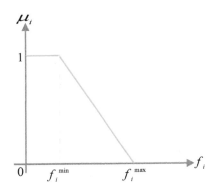

Figure 3. Membership function.

4.5. Pareto-optimal solutions

For a problem with J objectives $(o^1, o^2, ..., o^J)$, a solution $s = (o_s^1, o_s^2, ..., o_s^J)$ dominates another one $s' = (o_{s'}^1, o_{s'}^2, ..., o_{s'}^J)$ if both of the following conditions are satisfied [21]:

- s is no worse than s' in any attributes

- *s* is strictly better than *s'* in at least one attribute.

It can be denoted as s ≻ *s'* or *s'* ≺ s. A solution *s* is defined as covering another one *s'* if s is no worse than *s'* in any attribute. It can be denoted as s ⪰ *s'* or *s'* ⪯ s.

If a solution *s* cannot be dominated by another one *s'*, it can be said that s is non-dominated by *s'*. If a solution *s* is non-dominated by all the other solutions in a solution set *B*, it is called the Pareto-optimal solution in *B*. The set of all the non-dominated solutions of *B* is called the Pareto-set of *B*.

5. Applying MHSA in a multi-objective ORPD problem

The proposed strategy to solve ORPD in the multi-objective framework can be stepped as follows:

Step 1: Generate the initial populations. Firstly, set counter $i = 0$, and generate n random harmony, as follows:

$$D = [D_1, D_2, D_3, ..., D_n] \qquad D_i = (d_i^1, d_i^2, ..., d_i^m) \quad (29)$$

where d_i^j is the jth state variable value of the ith harmony population. For each individual (D_i), the objective function values are calculated.

Step 2: The three conflicted fitness functions, namely J_1, J_2, and J_3 should be minimized simultaneously, while satisfying the system constraints.

Step 3: Update the counter $i = i + 1$.

Step 4: Store the positions of the solutions that represent the non-dominated vectors.

Step 5: Determine the best global solution for the ith harmony from the non-dominated sort. First, these hypercubes consisting of more than one solution are assigned a fitness value equal to the result of dividing any number $x > 1$ by the number of solutions that they contain. Then apply the crowding distance on the fitness values to select the hypercube.

Step 6: Generate a new population of harmonies based on the proposed mutation, local and global operators.

Step 7: Evaluate each solution by the Newton-Raphson power flow analysis method to calculate the power flow and system transmission loss.

Step 8: Update the contents of the repository non-dominated sort together with the geographical representation of the solutions within the hypercube.

Step 9: Update the contents of the repository solutions.

Step 10: If the maximum iteration $iter_{max}$ is satisfied, then the stop optimization process and print final results. Otherwise, go to step 3.

The graphical illustration is shown in figure 4.

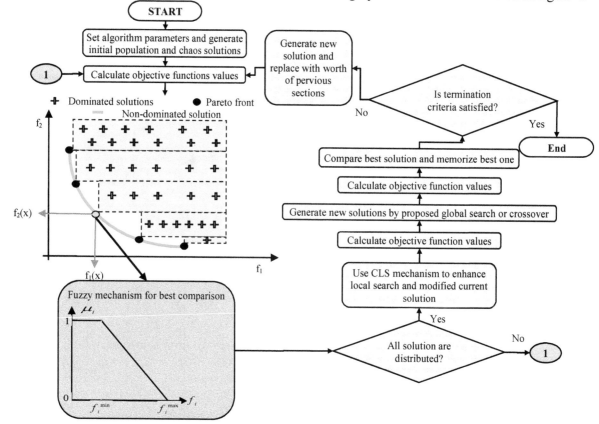

Figure 4. Proposed strategy to solve ORPD problem with modified HAS method.

6. Simulation and discussion

The proposed algorithm was implemented in the MATLAB language 2011a. All simulations were performed on a PC with an Intel Duo Core processor T5800, 2 GHz with a 4GB RAM. In order to access full search ability of the proposed algorithm, test it on the several benchmarks and look at the other articles. As a result, PAR_{min}, PAR_{max}, bw_{min}, and bw_{max} were set with the 0.35, 0.99, 5×10-4, and 0.05 values, respectively. HMCR and HMS were 0.95 and 4, respectively. Also the maximum number of iterations was equal to 500.

6.1. Deterministic model on IEEE 14-bus

At first, the IEEE 14-bus test system was considered with five generator buses (bus 1 was the slack bus, and buses 2, 3, 6, and 8 were PV buses with continuous operating values), 9 load buses and 20 branches, in which 3 branches (4-7, 4-9, and 5-6) were tap changing transformers. Moreover, the candidate buses for shunt compensation were 9 and 14.

Table 1. Results of multi-objective optimization in IEEE 14-bus test system.

Parameters	Case 1		Case 2	
	MHSA	HSA	MHSA	HSA
Vg_2	1.012	1.034	1.132	1.098
Vg_3	1.031	1.065	1.074	1.109
Vg_6	1.029	1.095	1.030	1.165
Vg_8	1.065	1.082	1.072	1.163
T_{4-7}	1.012	1.034	1.028	1.064
T_{4-9}	0.970	0.976	0.907	1.006
T_{5-6}	0.952	0.897	0.989	0.943
Qc_9	0.324	0.302	0.302	0.325
Qc_{14}	0.058	0.047	0.073	0.049
J_1	**1.176**	**1.209**	**1.175**	**1.206**
J_2	**0.205**	**0.243**	0.298	0.652
J_3	0.137	0.135	**0.113**	**0.120**

Parameters	Case 3		Case 4	
	MHSA	HSA	MHSA	HSA
Vg_2	1.093	1.103	1.083	1.053
Vg_3	1.065	1.095	1.094	1.064
Vg_6	1.083	1.163	1.028	1.093
Vg_8	1.001	1.154	1.014	1.172
T_{4-7}	1.039	1.196	1.004	1.106
T_{4-9}	1.042	0.895	1.042	0.953
T_{5-6}	0.987	0.854	0.987	0.803
Qc_9	0.393	0.473	0.386	0.401
Qc_{14}	0.063	0.035	0.057	0.038
J_1	1.195	1.268	**1.177**	**1.210**
J_2	**0.203**	**0.438**	**0.208**	**0.448**
J_3	**0.114**	**0.123**	**0.115**	**0.125**

In order to evaluate the effectiveness of the proposed algorithm in this test system, four different cases were considered as follow:

Case 1: Consider two objective functions; real power loss (J_1) and voltage deviation (J_2).

Case 2: Consider two objective functions; real power loss (J_1) and voltage stability index (J_3).

Case 3: Consider two objective functions; voltage deviation (J_2) and voltage stability index (J_3).

Case 4: Consider all objective functions; J_1, J_2, and J_3.

The numerical results of these case studies with 9 variables were tabulated in table 1, satisfying the system constrains. In all cases, the lower and upper limits of reactive powers were 0-30 MVAr, and these limits for the transformer tap settings and voltage magnitude were considered within the interval 0.9-1.1 p.u, respectively. The simulation results for the algorithms are shown in table 2. It can be seen that the results obtained for MHSA are better than those for the standard HSA algorithm in all cases. The Pareto front of the proposed algorithm for all cases is shown in figure 5.

Moreover, in order to show the robustness of the proposed algorithm to solve the ORPD problem, consider all objective functions, and optimize them by 30 trails that were individually run for 30 times. The simulation results of these trails are given in figure 6.

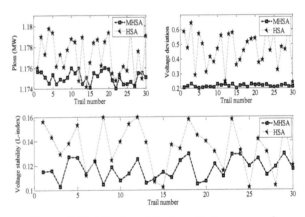

Figure 6. Distribution of final results for proposed algorithm in 30 trials, which simultaneously optimize three objective functions.

It is clear that the variation range of the best total cost during 30 trails simulations is small, which indicates that the MHSA algorithm is stable compared to HSA.

6.2. Deterministic model on IEEE 30-bus

The proposed algorithm was carried out on the IEEE 30-bus test system, which consisted of six thermal plants, 26 buses, and 46 transmission lines. The other useful line data and bus data were taken from [7]. Moreover, it had four transformers, with the off-nominal tap ratio at lines 6–9, 6–10, 4–12, and 28–27. In addition, buses 10, 12, 15, 17, 20, 21, 23, 24, and 29 were selected as shunt VAR compensation buses.

The results of the proposed algorithm were compared with SGA, PSO, GSA, standard HAS, etc, all of which were referred to [7] and [18]. The load of system was $P_{load} = 2.832$ p.u and $Q_{load} =$

1.262 p.u on a 100 MVA base. In this case, the optimization problem had 19 control variables, which were presented in table 2.

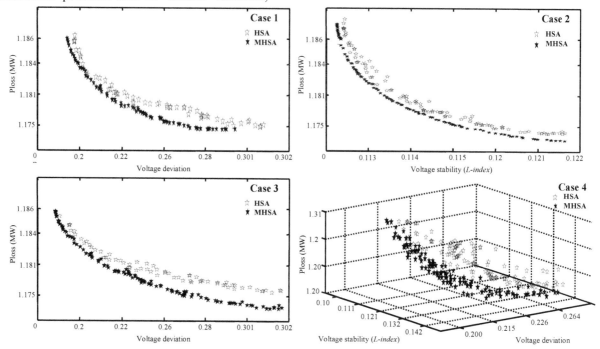

Figure 5. Pareto-optimal front of proposed approach, IEEE 14 bus.

Table 2. Variable limits (p.u.).

	Reactive power generation limits						Voltage and tab setting limits				
Bus	1	2	5	8	11	13	Bus	1	2	5	8	11
Q_G^{max}	0.596	0.48	0.6	0.53	0.15	0.155	V_G^{max}	V_G^{min}	V_{load}^{max}	V_{load}^{min}	T^{max}	T^{min}
Q_G^{min}	-0.298	-0.24	-0.3	-0.265	-0.075	-0.078	1.1	0.9	1.05	0.95	1.05	0.95
				Reactive compensation devices and voltage limits								
				Q_C^{max}	V_G^{max}	V_G^{max}	V_G^{min}					
				0.36	-0.12	1.05	0.95					

Table 3. Comparison of transmission loss for different methods in IEEE 30-bus system.

Algorithm	GAMs	PSO [7]	HSA [7]	DE [7]	SQP [7]	GSA [7]	BBO [7]	BF [18]
Best Ploss (MW)	4.5468	4.9239	4.9059	5.011	5.043	4.51431	4.5511	4.623
Worst Ploss (MW)	4.8932	5.0576	4.9653	---	---	---	---	4.64
Average Ploss (MW)	5.1029	4.9720	4.9240	---	---	---	---	4.68
CPU time, s	11.82	---	---	---	---	94.6938	---	---
Algorithm	CPVEIHBMO [7]	BF [18]	ABC [18]	FF [18]	HBMO [7]	HFA [18]	ALC-PSO [18]	MHSA
Best Ploss (MW)	4.37831	4.623	4.6022	4.5691	4.40867	4.529	4.4793	4.373
Worst Ploss (MW)	4.4901	4.64	4.61	4.578	4.8869	4.5325	4.5036	4.487
Average Ploss (MW)	4.4826	4.68	4.63	4.59	4.6453	4.546	4.4874	4.480
CPU time, s	66.038	---	---	---	67.413	---	---	65.02

The simulation results were tabulated in table 3. As it is evident in this table, the proposed method demonstrates its superiority in the ORPD problem, success rate, and solution quality over the other heuristic methods. Moreover, these results confirm the potential of multi-objective MHSA algorithm to solve real-world highly non-linear constrained multi-objective optimization problems. For the sake of a fair comparison, the results obtained by the MHSA algorithm in term of power loss reduction were compared with the other algorithms [7], in which the constraints and initial settings of the problem were different with the assumed values and constraints (four reactive

compensation devices were installed at buses 6, 17, 18, and 27). Figure 7 shows a comparison between the different algorithms. The results obtained show that the proposed method demonstrates its superiority in computational complexity, success rate, and solution quality over the PSO, GSA, HSA, HBMO, IPM, and DE methods. For the sake of a fair comparison among the developed methods, 10 independent runs were carried out.

6.3. Deterministic model on IEEE 118-bus

For the completeness and comparison purposes, this is the largest practical test system which we can find in the literature with the complete data required for the ORPD problem. In order to test and validate the robustness of the proposed algorithm, the simulations were carried out in the IEEE 118-bus test system. This network consisted of 186 branches, 54 generator buses, and 12 capacitor banks. Nine branches 8-5, 26-25, 30-17, 38-37, 63-59, 64-61, 65-66, 68-69, and 81-80 were tap changing transformers [19].

The capacity of the 12 shunt compensators were within the interval (0, 30) MVAr. All bus voltages were required to be maintained within the range of (0.95, 1.1) p.u. In this regard, consider the following operating condition to compare the performance of the proposed algorithm with the other available methods.

Case 1: To show the effectiveness of the proposed approach, initially, three different objectives namely, transmission loss minimization, voltage profile improvement, and voltage stability index minimization were considered individually. To demonstrate the superiority of the proposed MHSA, the simulation results were compared with the various well-known methods available in the literature, namely, PSO, FIPS, QEA, ACS, DE, SGA, PSO, MAPSO, SOA, TLBO, and QOTLBO. For the convenience of the reader, these methods are collaborated in [20]. The simulation results were tabulated in table 4.

Case 2: In this case study, consider that all the objective functions are simultaneous. The simulation results are given in table 5.

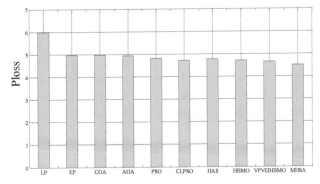

Figure 7. Comparison of proposed method with results exposed in [7].

Table 4. Comparison results for IEEE 118-bus system in case 1.

Index	Loss minimization (MW)									
	MHSA	QOTLBO [19]	TLBO [19]	PSO [19]	ALC-PSO [19]	FIPS [19]	QEA [19]	ACS [19]	GAM	DE [19]
Best	111.092	112.2789	116.4003	118.0	121.53	120.6	122.22	131.90	112.142	128.31
Worst	113.72	115.4516	121.3902	122.3	132.99	120.7	NA	NA	113.731	NA
Mean	112.91	113.7693	118.4427	120.6	123.14	120.6	NA	NA	112.642	NA
Standard deviation	0.012	0.0244	0.0482	NA	0.00	NA	NA	NA	0.014	NA

Index	Voltage deviation minimization (p.u.)				L-index minimization			
	MHSA	QOTLBO [19]	TLBO [19]	GAM	MHSA	GAM	QOTLBO [19]	TLBO [19]
Best	0.1864	0.1910	0.2237	0.1875	0.0603	0.0607	0.0608	0.0613
Worst	0.2201	0.2267	0.2543	0.2412	0.0607	0.0608	0.0631	0.0646
Mean	0.1985	0.2043	0.2306	0.1989	0.0608	0.0611	0.0616	0.0626
Standard deviation	0.0342	0.0356	0.0384	0.0403	0.0402	0.0399	0.0476	0.0488

Table 6. Simulation results obtained by MHSA for case 2 in IEEE 118-bus test system.

Control variables	MHSA	Control variables	MHSA	Control variables	MHSA	Control variables	MHSA
Vg1 (p.u.)	1.0166	Vg49 (p.u.)	1.008	Vg90 (p.u.)	1.0201	QC48 (p.u.)	0.0769
Vg4 (p.u.)	0.999	Vg54 (p.u.)	1.0215	Vg91 (p.u.)	1.009	QC74 (p.u.)	0.0970
Vg6 (p.u.)	1.022	Vg55 (p.u.)	1.0146	Vg92 (p.u.)	1.0048	QC79 (p.u.)	0.1091
Vg8 (p.u.)	1.0244	Vg56 (p.u.)	1.0136	Vg99 (p.u.)	1.0094	QC82 (p.u.)	0.0544
Vg10 (p.u.)	1.0172	Vg59 (p.u.)	1.024	Vg100 (p.u.)	1.0007	QC83 (p.u.)	0.1208
Vg12 (p.u.)	1.0194	Vg61 (p.u.)	1.0061	Vg103 (p.u.)	1.0017	QC105 (p.u.)	0.1087
Vg15 (p.u.)	1.019	Vg62 (p.u.)	1.0194	Vg104 (p.u.)	1.0247	QC107 (p.u.)	0.0861
Vg18 (p.u.)	1.0091	Vg65 (p.u.)	1.0193	Vg105 (p.u.)	1.0251	QC110 (p.u.)	0.0821
Vg19 (p.u.)	1.0166	Vg66 (p.u.)	1.0088	Vg107 (p.u.)	1.0143	T8-5	0.9903
Vg24 (p.u.)	1.0028	Vg69 (p.u.)	1.0141	Vg110 (p.u.)	0.9997	T26-25	1.0141
Vg25 (p.u.)	1.018	Vg70 (p.u.)	1.0001	Vg111 (p.u.)	1.0046	T30-17	0.9896
Vg26 (p.u.)	0.9989	Vg72 (p.u.)	0.9995	Vg112 (p.u.)	1.008	T38-37	0.9907
Vg27 (p.u.)	1.0058	Vg73 (p.u.)	1.013	Vg113 (p.u.)	1.0212	T63-59	1.008
Vg31 (p.u.)	0.9993	Vg74 (p.u.)	1.0201	Vg116 (p.u.)	0.9984	T64-61	0.9917
Vg32 (p.u.)	1.0007	Vg76 (p.u.)	1.0244	QC5 (p.u.)	0.0908	T65-66	1.0193
Vg34 (p.u.)	1.0213	Vg77 (p.u.)	1.0017	QC34 (p.u.)	0.0712	T68-69	1.0193
Vg36 (p.u.)	1.0177	Vg80 (p.u.)	1.0141	QC37 (p.u.)	0.1063	T81-80	1.0157
Vg40 (p.u.)	1.007	Vg85 (p.u.)	1.0113	QC44 (p.u.)	0.0628		
Vg42 (p.u.)	1.0249	Vg87 (p.u.)	0.9983	QC45 (p.u.)	0.1018		
Vg46 (p.u.)	0.999	Vg87 (p.u.)	1.0075	QC46 (p.u.)	0.0624		

It is clear that the proposed method yielded better solutions than QOTLBO, the original TLBO, and the other methods. According to table 5, the minimum system loss obtained by the proposed algorithm is 133.82 MW. In other words, it can be seen that the saving with the proposed method in the system loss is 0.4% better than the best solution for QOTLBO. Moreover, voltage deviation and *L-index* obtained using MHSA is better than QOTLBO and the original TLBO methods. To the reader's convenience, Table 6 summaries the ORPD results obtained by MHSA including the transmission loss, voltage deviation, *L-index*, and optimal settings of control variables.

Table 5. Comparison of test results for multi-objectives of IEEE 118-bus system using different methods.

Index	J_1, J_2, and J_3		
	MHSA	QOTLBO	TLBO
Loss (MW)	133.82	134.4059	137.4324
Voltage deviation (p.u.)	0.2102	0.2410	0.2612
L-index (p.u.)	0.0585	0.0619	0.0627

6.4. Stochastic model on IEEE 30-bus

To validate the proposed stochastic model in a single objective formulation, the numerical results were presented on a six-bus and a modified IEEE 30-bus test system. It consisted of 30 buses, 37 transmission lines, 6 generators, 4 under-load tap changing transformers, and 2 fixed shunt reactive capacitive power banks. For the tests, assume that there are three forecasted levels of demand: 1) low demand, 2) average demand, and 3) peak demand. They are known to happen with 25%, 50%, and 25% probabilities, respectively. Other information is given in section 6.2. Comparison to section 6.2 added a new shunt reactive capacitive compensator at bus 24, whose maximum capacity is 40 MVar. The data for the different levels of demand active and reactive is given in table 7.

Table 7. Demand levels for modified IEEE 30-bus system.

Bus	PD [MW]			QD [MVAr]		
	Low demand	Average demand	Peak demand	Low demand	Average demand	Peak demand
2	16.28	21.70	27.13	9.53	12.70	15.88
3	1.80	2.40	3.00	0.90	1.20	1.50
4	5.70	7.60	9.50	1.20	1.60	2.00
5	70.65	94.20	117.75	14.25	19.00	23.75
7	17.10	22.80	28.50	8.18	10.90	13.63
8	22.50	30.00	37.50	22.50	30.00	37.50
10	4.35	5.80	7.25	1.50	2.00	2.50
12	8.40	11.20	14.00	5.63	7.50	9.38
14	4.65	6.20	7.75	1.20	1.60	2.00
15	6.15	8.20	10.25	1.88	2.50	3.13
16	2.63	3.50	4.38	1.35	1.80	2.25
17	6.75	9.00	11.25	4.35	5.80	7.25
18	2.40	3.20	4.00	0.68	0.90	1.13
19	7.13	9.50	11.88	2.55	3.40	4.25
20	1.65	2.20	2.75	0.53	0.70	0.88
21	13.13	17.50	21.88	8.40	11.20	14.00
23	2.40	3.20	4.00	1.20	1.60	2.00
24	6.53	8.70	10.88	5.03	6.70	8.38
26	2.63	3.50	4.38	1.73	2.30	2.88
29	1.80	2.40	3.00	0.68	0.90	1.13
30	7.95	10.60	13.25	1.43	1.90	2.38

Table 8 shows the reactive power dispatched for reactive sources and the taps settings under load variable transformers by minimizing the active power losses in each demand level. Table 9 shows the voltage magnitude profile.

At load buses, for the three level demands, the voltages are close to their secure lower limit 0.95. However, by the reactive power injection of the fixed or continuous reactive sources installed in some load buses, the voltages are always not as near their secure lower limits.

Table 8. Solution of stochastic model, IEEE 30-bus system.

Bus	Dispatch of Reactive Sources [MVAr]		
	Low demand	Average demand	Peak demand
2	6.48	21.32	59.99
5	21.09	33.75	40.00
8	21.03	36.04	39.98
11	16.32	22.68	24.00
13	7.98	22.56	23.67
24	4.39	9.01	37.26

Bus	Tap Settings of Transformers [pu]		
	Low demand	Average demand	Peak demand
6-9	0.938	0.937	0.951
6-10	1.087	1.094	1.038
4-12	1.028	1.001	1.014
27-28	0.965	0.973	0.949

Table 9. Voltage profile after optimized-30-bus system.

Bus	Low	Ave	Peak	Bus	Low	Ave	Peak
1	0.992	0.978	1.030	16	0.975	1.011	0.997
2	1.008	1.008	1.027	17	1.009	1.011	0.994
3	0.986	1.004	1.032	18	1.007	1.006	1.040
4	0.973	1.020	1.023	19	1.018	0.973	1.034
5	1.012	1.022	1.037	20	1.014	0.976	1.028
6	0.952	1.008	1.020	21	0.971	0.979	1.038
7	0.994	0.980	1.041	22	1.006	1.027	0.992
8	0.964	0.994	1.033	23	0.999	0.990	1.010
9	1.005	0.991	1.024	24	1.017	0.989	1.007
10	0.971	1.001	1.001	25	0.980	1.015	1.019
11	1.001	1.027	0.997	26	0.976	0.976	1.020
12	0.990	1.013	0.997	27	0.997	1.015	1.033
13	1.002	0.972	1.046	28	1.000	0.990	1.030
14	0.998	1.029	1.030	29	0.959	0.985	1.042
15	1.014	0.984	1.014	30	0.980	1.011	1.018

6.7. Statistical analysis and comparison

In this section, the performance of the multi-objective MHSA is compared with NSGA [21] and MOPSO [22] in Spread (SP) index [23]. This indicator is to measure the extent of spread archived among the non-dominated solutions obtained:

$$SP = \frac{d_f + d_l + \sum_{i=1}^{N-1} |d_i - \bar{d}|}{d_f + d_l + (N-1)\bar{d}} \qquad (30)$$

where, N is the number of non-dominated solutions found so far; d_i is the Euclidean distance between neighboring solutions in the obtained non-dominated solutions set, and $\bar{d}$ is the mean of all d_i. The parameters d_f and d_l are the Euclidean distances between the extreme solutions and the boundary solutions of the obtained non-dominated set, respectively. A value of zero for this metric shows that all members of the Pareto optimal set are equidistantly spaced. A smaller value for SP indicates a better distribution and diversity of the non-dominated solutions. Table 10 shows a comparison of the SP metric for different algorithms. It can be seen that the average performance of multi-objective MHSA is much better than the other algorithm results.

Table 10. Comparison of SP-metric for different algorithms.

Index	MHSA	NSGA	MOPSO
Best	0.1683	0.5999	0.2542
Average	0.2789	0.6801	0.3242
Std	0.0089	0.0598	0.0375

7. Conclusion

This paper proposes a modified harmony search algorithm (HSA), which was successfully applied for the ORPD problem solving in deterministic and stochastic models, taking into account the inequality and equality constraints. The ORPD problem was formulated as a multi-objective optimization problem with three conflicted objectives, known as power loss, voltage deviation, and L_{index}. A diversity-preserving mechanism of crowding entropy tactic was investigated to find widely different Pareto optimal solutions. The main contribution of the proposed algorithm can be looked at for the design of local and global search operators and interactive strategy to adjust two significant parameters (i.e. bw and PAR) during the optimization process, which improves its overall performance. The proposed algorithm was evaluated on the three test systems IEEE 14-bus, 30-bus, and 118-bus to demonstrate its effectiveness compared to other available algorithms. It was seen that the ability of the proposed algorithm to jump out of the local optima, the convergence precision, and speed were enhanced remarkably. Furthermore, the results obtained showed the capabilities of the proposed algorithm to generate well-distributed Pareto solutions. Moreover, the uncertainty in generating units in the form of system contingencies was considered in the reactive power optimization procedure by the stochastic model. Hereby, it is expected that the proposed MHSA algorithm is preferred, and it plays a more active role in the reactive power dispatch problem.

References

[1] Ghasemi, A., Golkar, M. J., Golkar, A.& Eslami, M. (2016). Reactive power planning using a new hybrid technique. Soft Comput, vol. 20, pp. 589-605.

[2] Mehdinejad, M., Mohammadi-Ivatloo, B., Dadashzadeh-Bonab, R.& Zare, K. (2016). Solution of optimal reactive power dispatch of power systems using hybrid particle swarm optimization and imperialist competitive algorithms. Int. J. Electr. Power Energy Syst. vol. 83, pp. 104-116.

[3] Kirschen, D. S. & Van Meeteren, H. P. (1988). MW/voltage control in linear programming based optimal power flow. IEEE Trans. Power Syst. vol. 3, pp. 481-489.

[4] Lee, K. Y., Park, Y. M. & Ortiz., J. L. (1985). A united approach to optimal real and reactive power dispatch. IEEE Trans. Power Apparatus Syst. vol. 104, pp. 1147-1153.

[5] Nanda, J., Kothari, D. P. & Srivastava, S. C. (1989). New optimal power dispatch algorithm using Fletcher's quadratic programming method. IEE Electr. Power Gener. Transm. Distrib. vol. 136, pp. 53-161.

[6] Momeh, JA., Guo, SX., Oghuobiri, EC. & Adapa, R. (1994). The quadratic interior point method solving the power system optimization problems. IEEE Trans Power Syst, vol. 9, no. 3, pp. 1327-1336.

[7] Ghasemi, A., Valipour, K. & Tohidi, A. (2014). Multi objective optimal reactive power dispatch using a

new multi objective strategy. Int. J. Electr. Power Energy Syst., vol. 57, pp.318-334.

[8] Basu, M. (2016). Quasi-oppositional differential evolution for optimal reactive power dispatch. Int. J. Electr. Power Energy Syst., vol. 78, pp. 29-40.

[9] Basu, M. (2016). Multi objective optimal reactive power dispatch using multi objective differential evolution. Int. J. Electr. Power Energy Syst., vol. 82, pp. 213-224.

[10] Biswas (Raha), S., Mandal, K. K. & Chakraborty, N. (2016). Pareto-efficient double auction power transactions for economic reactive power dispatch. Applied Energy, vol. 168, pp. 610-627.

[11] Sulaiman, M. H., Mustaffa, Z., Mohamed, M. R. & Aliman, O. (2015). Using the gray wolf optimizer for solving optimal reactive power dispatch problem. Applied Soft Computing, vol. 32, pp. 286-292.

[12] Geem, Z. W., Kim, J. H. & Loganathan, G. V. (2011). A new heuristic optimization algorithm: harmony search. Simulation, vol. 76, no. 2, pp. 60-68.

[13] Kazemi, A., Parizad, A. & Baghaee, H. R. (2009). On the use of harmony search algorithm in optimal placement of facts devices to improve power system security. in: Proceedings of EUROCON, pp. 570-576.

[14] Dash, R. & Dash, P. (2016). Efficient stock price prediction using a Self Evolving Recurrent Neuro-Fuzzy Inference System optimized through a Modified Differential Harmony Search Technique. Expert Systems with Applications, vol. 52, pp. 75-90.

[15] Pandiarajan, K. & Babulal, C. K. (2016). Fuzzy harmony search algorithm based optimal power flow for power system security enhancement. Int. J. Electr. Power Energy Syst., vol. 78, pp. 72-79.

[16] Hu, Z., Wang, X. & Taylor, G. (2010). Stochastic optimal reactive power dispatch: Formulation and solution method. Electr. Power Energy Syst., vol. 32, pp. 615-621.

[17] Ghasemi, A., Gheydi, M., Golkar, M. J. & Eslami, M. (2016). Modeling of Wind/Environment/Economic Dispatch in power system and solving via an online learning meta-heuristic method. Applied Soft Computing, vol. 43, pp. 454-468.

[18] Rajan, A. & Malakar, T. (2015). Optimal reactive power dispatch using hybrid Nelder–Mead simplex based firefly algorithm. Electrical Power and Energy Systems, vol. 66, pp. 9-24.

[19] Power systems test case archive, http://www.ee.washington.edu/research/pstca.

[20] Mandal, B. & Roy, P. K. (2013). Optimal reactive power dispatch using quasi-oppositional teaching learning based optimization. Electrical Power and Energy Systems, vol. 53, pp. 123-134.

[21] Mosavi, A. (2014). Data mining for decision making in engineering optimal design. Journal of AI and Data Mining, vol. 2, no. 1, pp. 7-14.

[22] Shayeghi, H. & Ghasemi, A. (2012). Economic Load Dispatch Solution Using Improved Time Variant MOPSO Algorithm Considering Generator Constraints. International Review of Electrical Engineering, vol. 7, no. 2, pp. 4292-4303.

[23] Deb, K., Pratap, A., Agarwal, S. & Meyarivan, T. (2002). A fast and elitist multiobjective genetic algorithm: NSGA-II. IEEE Trans. Evol. Comput., vol. 6, no. 2, pp. 182-19.

[24] Zitzler, E., Deb, K. & Thiele, L. (2000). Comparison of multiobjective evolutionary algorithms: empirical results. Evol. Comput. J. vol. 8, pp. 125-148.

17

Composite Kernel Optimization in Semi-Supervised Metric

T. Zare[1*], M. T. Sadeghi[1], H. R. Abutalebi[1] and J. Kittler[2]

1. Signal Processing Research Group, Electrical Engineering Department, Yazd University, Yazd, Iran.
2. Centre for Vision, Speech and Signal Processing (CVSSP), Faculty of Engineering and Physical Sciences, University of Surrey, Guildford, Surrey.

*Corresponding author: t.zare@stu.yazd.ac.ir (T. Zare).

Abstract

Machine-learning solutions to classification, clustering, and matching problems critically depend on the adopted metric, which in the past was selected heuristically. In the last decade, it has been demonstrated that an appropriate metric can be learnt from data, resulting in a superior performance as compared with the traditional metrics. This has recently stimulated a considerable interest in the topic of metric learning, especially using the kernel functions, which map the input data to feature spaces with enhanced class separability, and implicitly define a new metric in the original feature space. The formulation of the problem of metric learning depends on the supervisory information available for the task. In this work, we focus on semi-supervised kernel-based distance metric learning, where the training dataset is unlabelled, with the exception of a small subset of pairs of points labelled as belonging to the same class (cluster) or different classes (clusters). The proposed method involves creating a pool of kernel functions. The corresponding kernel matrices are first clustered to remove redundancy in the representation. A composite kernel constructed from the kernel clustering result is then expanded into an orthogonal set of base functions. The mixing parameters of this expansion are then optimised using point similarity and dissimilarity information conveyed by the labels. The proposed method is evaluated on the synthetic and real datasets. The results obtained show the merit of using similarity and dissimilarity information jointly as compared to using just the similarity information, and the superiority of the proposed method over all the recently introduced metric learning approaches.

Keywords: *Distance Metric Learning, Semi-supervised Clustering, Composite Kernels, Pairwise Similarity and Dissimilarity Constraints, Optimization Problem.*

1. Introduction

Distance metrics play a key role in many supervised and unsupervised learning algorithms. The k-nearest neighbour classifier and the k-means clustering algorithm are examples of such supervised and unsupervised algorithms. Selecting an appropriate metric for these algorithms is an important issue. A promising alternative approach is to learn the optimal distance metric from a collection of training data. Distance metric learning has recently received considerable attention [1, 2]. The advocated algorithms in the literature can be divided into three main categories: supervised, unsupervised, and semi-supervised algorithms. A training dataset with explicit class labels or some other supervisory information is required for supervised metric learning [3-7]. Although unsupervised learning such as clustering is known to be highly influenced by the choice of the distance metric, the lack of supervisory information makes the problem of choosing a suitable metric very challenging. In unsupervised distance metric learning, the main idea is to learn a metric that preserves the geometric relationships between most of the observed samples [8]. There is a deep connection between unsupervised distance metric learning methods and unsupervised dimensionality reduction approaches. The main advantage of these algorithms is that they do not require laborious labelling of the training data to provide supervisory information, although their performance is usually lower. These issues have recently motivated the development of a compound solution known as semi-supervised learning. In semi-supervised approaches, a large quantity of unlabelled data and a limited amount of labelled data or some other supervisory knowledge are used to learn a distance metric. One kind of supervisory information for metric learning is expressed in the form of pairwise similarity and/or dissimilarity relationships [9]. The use of these constraints for distance metric learning, and especially semi-supervised distance metric learning, has lately become very popular [10-12]. Compared to the explicitly labelled data, pairwise constraints are weaker but more natural than the clustering concepts. Xing et al. [13] have proposed an iterative approach to learn a Mahalanobis metric using pairwise constraints for the clustering task. Bar-Hillel et al. [14] have proposed a non-iterative algorithm using only pairwise similarity constraints called relevant component analysis (RCA). The RCA algorithm has been extended to a generalized form that makes use of both the pairwise similarity and the dissimilarity constraints in [15]. In the above-mentioned methods, the distance metric learning procedure can be summarized as a process of mapping the associated data to a new feature space using a linear learned transformation and then applying the Euclidean distance in the resultant feature space. However, a linear transformation may not necessarily be a desirable transformation for a given problem or a complicated structure of the training data. In these cases, the kernelized version of the metric learning algorithms can be seen as offering a more general alternative [16, 18].

A kernel function can be considered as a function that implicitly transfers two data points to a new feature space using a non-linear mapping function. It measures their associated similarity by computing the inner product of the projected samples. An important issue in kernel-based approaches is how to find an appropriate kernel and/or how to set the kernel parameter(s). The type of kernel function and the value(s) of kernel parameter(s) play a key role in these algorithms. A typical solution to this problem is to apply cross-validation in order to select the best kernel function among a set of candidates. However, this procedure is time-consuming. Moreover, there is no guarantee that the best possible solution will be found. The other solution to this problem is to use an appropriate combination of different kernel functions. Within this framework, several different algorithms have been proposed for computing composite kernels [19, 20]. It has been shown that the performance of some pattern recognition algorithms such as Support Vector Machine (SVM) classifier and kernel-based feature extraction approaches can be improved by applying composite kernel techniques.

Kernelized versions of metric learning algorithms have already been proposed in [16-18]. However, the methods are not sufficiently flexible because they are based on a fixed kernel function without any generalisation property. In other works, a distance metric learning framework is used for determining the elements of the kernel matrix [21, 22]. However, a common problem of these methods is that a large number of variables are required to be learned. In fact, as the size of a kernel matrix is proportional to the number of training samples, the number of unknowns is usually very large. Soleymani et al. have proposed an iterative kernel-based metric learning algorithm that reduces the number of variables to the number of the related constraints [23].

To date, the problem of metric learning using composite kernel functions has not been studied very extensively. In [24] and [25], the idea of weighted summation of different kernels has been considered within the framework of supervised distance metric learning. In [24], the authors have propose a method that learns a set of Mahalanobis metrics, one for each feature space induced by the respective kernels. The kernel weights and the Mahalanobis metrics are learned using an iterative optimization procedure that is computationally complex. In [25], assuming a linear combination of a set of kernels, several distance metric learning objectives have been defined in order to learn the kernel weights. In our previous work [26], we used composite kernels in semi-supervised metric learning, given a set of pairwise similarity constraints and a limited number of kernels.

As a main contribution, in this paper, we show how to construct a composite kernel matrix for a set of similarity and dissimilarity constraints. For this purpose, first an initial composite kernel matrix is produced by combining a set of kernel matrices. The eigen-decomposition of the matrix is then performed. The resulting eigen-vectors are linearly combined with weights obtained using a semi-supervised distance metric learning objective. Effectively, we rescale the axes of the new feature space (eigen-vectors) induced by the composite kernel so that the pairwise similarity and dissimilarity constraints are satisfied. We finally use the learned kernel matrix in a kernel-based k-means clustering algorithm.

The rest of the paper is organized as what follows In Section 2, the related works are briefly reviewed. In Section 3, our proposed method of composite kernel-based metric learning, which uses both pairwise similarity and dissimilarity constraints, is presented. In the method, a composite kernel is used as the base kernel, and a set of mixing variables are determined. These variables are computed by analytically solving an optimization problem. Our experimental studies are reported in Section 4, where the performance of the method is compared to some other states of the art approaches. Finally, Section 5 offers the concluding remarks.

2. Related works and proposed method

Recently, kernel-based semi-supervised metric learning has attracted the attention of many researchers [16, 18, 21, 22]. In [21], Chang and Yeung have proposed two kernel-based metric learning methods, which are called the kernel-$\mathbf{A}$ and kernel-β methods. They use a set of similarity constraints to guide the learning process. These methods use a pre-specified kernel such as a specific RBF kernel to form the kernel matrix $\mathbf{K}_{N \times N}$. In the kernel-$\mathbf{A}$ method, the target kernel matrix is defined as $\tilde{\mathbf{K}} = \mathbf{A}\mathbf{K}\mathbf{A}^T$, where $\mathbf{A}$ is an $N \times N$ adaptation matrix. The elements of $\mathbf{A}$ are determined using a criterion expressed in terms of pairwise similarity information penalized by a regularization term. They are calculated by applying an iterative algorithm. In the kernel-β method, the kernel matrix $\mathbf{K}$ is first decomposed into a set of base kernels by applying the eigen-decomposition operation. The weighted sum of the base kernels is then used as the final kernel matrix, where the weights are determined analytically using a constraint imposed by identically labelled pairs. For handling large datasets, they extend the kernel-β method to a scalable method by applying low-rank approximation to the kernel matrix [18]. The main limitation of the kernel-β method and its extension is that the target kernel is computed using a linear combination of eigen-matrices, derived from an RBF kernel with a specific width. Thus the diversity of the basic kernel matrix is limited. Therefore, the performance of the method heavily depends on the adopted kernel function (i.e. RBF kernel) and its parameter. Moreover, only pairwise similarity constraints are considered in the learning process.

In the kernel-$\mathbf{A}$ method and in [22], the learning process exploits similarity and/or dissimilarity measures. In these methods, an optimization procedure is used to determine the elements of the base kernel. The authors show that here the choice of the base kernel is not as critical as in the case of the kernel-β method. However, the number of the variables that have to be adjusted is very large.

The kernel-based metric learning method introduced in [23] reduces the adjustable variables to the number of constraints. However, the iterative algorithm used to determine the unknown parameters is time-consuming.

As mentioned in our previous work [26], we used composite kernels in semi-supervised metric learning, given a set of pairwise similarity constraints. The composite kernel is constructed by combining a limited number of kernels through either averaging or augmenting the associated kernel matrices. A set of orthogonal matrices are then generated by eigen-decomposition of the resulting Gram matrix. The final kernel matrix is created by weighted averaging of the orthogonal matrices, while the weights are determined via a learning process. In fact, through the learning process, the axes of the new feature space (which is the result of the eigen-decomposition process) are rescaled so that the pairwise similarity constraints are satisfied.

In this paper, we present a new metric learning algorithm using composite kernels to generalize the method proposed in [26]. We reformulate the optimization problem so that the effect of the supervisory information, which is expressed in the form of both the pairwise similarity and dissimilarity constraints, is taken into account. During optimization, a limited number of variables are learned such that the resulting distance between similar pairs from the pairwise similarity set becomes as low as possible while the distance between dissimilar pairs from the pairwise dissimilarity set becomes as large as possible. An important characteristic of the proposed method is that the optimization process does not require any iterative algorithm to find the solution.

The proposed approach is inspired by the kernel-β method introduced in [21], and the optimization algorithm has been proposed in [26]. However, in contrast to [21] and [26], in this work, we considered pairwise dissimilarity as well as similarity constraints in the optimization problem. Moreover, compared to [21], instead of a pre-determined kernel, we made use of composite kernels to improve the flexibility of the method and to avoid the problem of choosing an inappropriate kernel function. Furthermore, throughout the eigen-decomposition operation, the number of optimization variables is reduced by keeping those that preserve a pre-specified level of total variation of the data. Also noting that the matrix augmentation process generates a high dimensional kernel matrix when a large set of candidate kernel matrices is available, we avoided the computational complexity problem by grouping the base kernels using a kernel alignment measure. A representative kernel was then used for each group. In fact, in our previous work [26], we were not able to increase the number of base kernels within the framework of the matrix augmentation method. This problem was here removed by the proposed grouping process. In the next section, the proposed method is detailed.

3. Proposed metric learning method

In this section, our formulation of the underlying optimization problem is presented. The proposed method falls within the framework of kernel-based distance metric learning using pairwise similarity and dissimilarity constraints. Since composite kernels are used as the kernel function, the adopted approaches for producing composite kernels are subsequently reviewed. We used the following notations in this section: $\mathbf{A}$ represents a matrix, a denotes a vector, a^j denotes the j-th column of matrix $\mathbf{A}$, and a^{ij} is its i-th element (i.e. $a^{ij} = \mathbf{A}(i,j)$.).

3.1. Problem formulation

Denote by $X = \{\mathbf{x}_i\}_{i=1}^N$ a set of data points, where $\mathbf{x}_i \in R^{r_x}$, $i = 1,...,N$, and N is the total number of samples. Also suppose that ϕ is a feature space induced by a non-linear transformation $\phi: R^{r_x} \rightarrow H$. For a positive semi-definite kernel function k, a Mercer kernel is computed as the inner product of samples in H, and $k(\mathbf{x},\mathbf{y}) = \langle \phi(\mathbf{x}), \phi(\mathbf{y}) \rangle$. Also suppose that from the data points in X, we can construct two sets of training data S and D satisfying $S = \{(\mathbf{x}_i,\mathbf{x}_j) \mid \mathbf{x}_i \text{ and } \mathbf{x}_j \text{ belong to the same class}\}$ and $D = \{(\mathbf{x}_i,\mathbf{x}_j) \mid \mathbf{x}_i \text{ and } \mathbf{x}_j \text{ belong to different classes}\}$ As we focus on the semi-supervised setting of the distance metric learning problem, we assume that the size of the S and D datasets is very limited and a large number of unlabelled data points are available in X. Our goal is that by virtue of learning, distances between similar pairs are reduced, while distances between dissimilar pairs are increased. Accordingly, the objective function can be defined as:

$$J = \sum_{(\mathbf{x}_i,\mathbf{x}_j) \in S} \left\| \phi(\mathbf{x}_i) - \phi(\mathbf{x}_j) \right\|_2^2 \tag{1}$$
$$- \beta \sum_{(\mathbf{x}_i,\mathbf{x}_j) \in D} \left\| \phi(\mathbf{x}_i) - \phi(\mathbf{x}_j) \right\|_2^2$$

The above criterion function is, in fact, a weighted sum of squares of the Euclidean distances between the similar and dissimilar pairs of points measured in the feature space. This function should be minimized using the learned distance metric so that the pairs of the samples that belong to the same class will be as close as possible, and vice versa, for the dissimilar pairs. The role of parameter β is to balance the contributions of the similarity and dissimilarity pairs. In practice, β can be estimated using the cross-validation procedure or it can simply be set to $\dfrac{|D|}{|S|}$, where $|.|$ denotes the cardinality of a set. Using the kernel representation for the Euclidean distances in (1), we can express J as:

$$J = \sum_{(\mathbf{x}_i,\mathbf{x}_j) \in S} \left[k^{ii} + k^{jj} - 2k^{ij} \right] \tag{2}$$
$$- \beta \sum_{(\mathbf{x}_i,\mathbf{x}_{j'}) \in D} \left[k^{i'i'} + k^{j'j'} - 2k^{i'j'} \right]$$

where, k^{ab}'s are elements of the kernel or Gram matrix, i.e. $k^{ab} = \mathbf{K}(a,b)$. Elements of $\mathbf{K}$ are actually the values of the kernel function corresponding to the respective pairs of data samples. This objective function is used in order to find the optimum kernel function, i.e. the optimum feature space ϕ. Since the corresponding kernel matrix contains N^2 elements, the number of variables that should be optimized is very large. To avoid this computational burden, we suppose that an initial Gram matrix is available a priori. This matrix is not necessarily the optimal one but it highly likely contains the relevant information. Then, new variables facilitating adaptation are introduced in the objective function to achieve a better performance. In particular, we assume that by decomposing the Gram matrix into orthogonal components, it is written as:

$$\mathbf{K} = \sum_{n=1}^N \alpha_n \mathbf{u}_n \mathbf{u}_n^T = \sum_{n=1}^N \alpha_n \mathbf{U}_n \tag{3}$$

where, α_n are positive eigen-values of $\mathbf{K}$ and $\mathbf{u}_1, \mathbf{u}_2,...,\mathbf{u}_N$ are the corresponding normalized eigen-vectors. Now by remixing the bases with different weighting coefficients, λ_n^2, we have:

$$\tilde{\mathbf{K}} = \sum_{n=1}^N \lambda_n^2 \mathbf{U}_n \tag{4}$$

The remixing idea is based upon the well-known fact that while coefficients α_n are ideal for good reconstruction of matrix $\mathbf{K}$, they are not necessarily optimal for good discrimination. By replacing the eigen-values by a set of positive coefficients λ_1^2, λ_2^2,..., and λ_N^2, we reformulate the distance metric learning problem as one determining the optimum value of λ_n^2's. Thus instead of matrix $\mathbf{K}$, which is commonly used in kernel-based metric learning approaches, the matrix $\tilde{\mathbf{K}}$ is used, and the learning process optimizes these mixing parameters (λ_n^2).

The exponent of λ_n^2 emphasises that the coefficients are positive. It will also simplify the subsequent equations.

An important issue in problem formulation is selecting the initial kernel matrix, $\mathbf{K}$, so that (5) provides a scope for finding a good solution to our problem. The objective function described in (1) or (2) can then be used for learning the variables λ_n^2. Using this technique, the number of variables reduces from the order of N^2 to N. The number of variables can be reduced even more by preserving a specific level (for example, 99%) of the total variance of the data during the eigen-decomposition operation. Hence, (4) can be re-written as:

$$\tilde{\mathbf{K}} = \sum_{n=1}^{P} \lambda_n^2 \mathbf{U}_n \qquad (5)$$

where, $P < N$ is the number of the eigen-values α_n, $n = 1, 2, ..., P$ capturing the specified amount of variance of the data in the original kernel space. By substituting the kernel function of (5) in (2), we have:

$$J = \sum_{n=1}^{P} \lambda_n^2 \sum_{(\mathbf{x}_i, \mathbf{x}_j) \in S} \left[u_n^{ii} + u_n^{ij} - 2u_n^{ij} \right]$$
$$- \beta \sum_{n=1}^{P} \lambda_n^2 \sum_{(\mathbf{x}_{i'}, \mathbf{x}_{j'}) \in D} \left[u_n^{i'i'} + u_n^{j'j'} - 2u_n^{i'j'} \right] \qquad (6)$$

Let $\mathbf{e}^i (i = 1, ..., N)$ be the i-th column of an $N \times N$ identity matrix. We can rewrite the objective function in (6) as:

$$J = \sum_{n=1}^{P} \lambda_n^2 \sum_{(\mathbf{x}_i, \mathbf{x}_j) \in S} (\mathbf{e}^i - \mathbf{e}^j)^T \mathbf{U}_n (\mathbf{e}^i - \mathbf{e}^j)$$
$$- \beta \sum_{n=1}^{P} \lambda_n^2 \sum_{(\mathbf{x}_{i'}, \mathbf{x}_{j'}) \in D} (\mathbf{e}^{i'} - \mathbf{e}^{j'})^T \mathbf{U}_n (\mathbf{e}^{i'} - \mathbf{e}^{j'})$$
$$= \sum_{n=1}^{P} \lambda_n^2 a_n - \beta \sum_{n=1}^{P} \lambda_n^2 b_n \qquad (7)$$

where, $a_n = \sum_{(\mathbf{x}_i, \mathbf{x}_j) \in S} (\mathbf{e}^i - \mathbf{e}^j)^T \mathbf{U}_n (\mathbf{e}^i - \mathbf{e}^j)$ and $b_n = \sum_{(\mathbf{x}_{i'}, \mathbf{x}_{j'}) \in D} (\mathbf{e}^{i'} - \mathbf{e}^{j'})^T \mathbf{U}_n (\mathbf{e}^{i'} - \mathbf{e}^{j'})$. Now, if $\mathbf{A}_S$ and $\mathbf{B}_D$ matrices are defined as $\mathbf{A}_S = diag(a_1, a_2, ..., a_P)$ and $\mathbf{B}_D = diag(b_1, b_2, ..., b_P)$, then (7) can be re-written as:

$$J = \lambda^T \mathbf{A}_S \lambda - \beta \lambda^T \mathbf{B}_D \lambda = \lambda^T (\mathbf{A}_s - \beta \mathbf{B}_D) \lambda \qquad (8)$$

where $\lambda = [\lambda_1, \lambda_2, ..., \lambda_P]$. To prevent λ from being a vector of zero values, we consider an extra constraint on λ such that $\mathbf{1}^T \lambda = c$ for some constant value of $c > 0$. In order to preserve the total variance of the data, we set this value as: $c = \sum_{n=1}^{P} \sqrt{\alpha_n}$. The constraint optimization problem in (8) with this equality constraint can be solved using the method of Lagrange multipliers, leading to the following constraint objective function:

$$L = \lambda^T (\mathbf{A}_s - \beta \mathbf{B}_D) \lambda + \mu (c - \mathbf{1}^T \lambda) \qquad (9)$$

where, μ is a Lagrange multiplier. The partial derivatives of the above expression are as:

$$\frac{\partial L}{\partial \lambda} = 2(\mathbf{A}_s - \beta \mathbf{B}_D) \lambda - \mu \mathbf{1} \qquad (10)$$

$$\frac{\partial L}{\partial \mu} = c - \mathbf{1}^T \lambda$$

The optimal vector of λ is obtained by setting the partial derivatives to zero as:

$$\lambda = \frac{c(\mathbf{A}_s - \beta \mathbf{B}_D)^{-1} \mathbf{1}}{\mathbf{1}^T (\mathbf{A}_s - \beta \mathbf{B}_D)^{-1} \mathbf{1}} \qquad (11)$$

As mentioned earlier, we assume that the initial kernel matrix, $\mathbf{K}$, is available at the beginning. The optimization process modifies the associated mapping process by replacing the eigen-values of the kernel with the values obtained via the learning process. It should be noted that the structure of the initial kernel matrix, $\mathbf{K}$, is important, as it should contain the "optimal" kernel. It means that we cannot expect to achieve the best possible results if a totally inappropriate kernel function is adopted. Thus the most important issue now is how to choose the initial kernel function. The usual approaches such as the cross-validation procedure that try to find the best kernel are not useful for this purpose. Therefore, we focus on the composite kernels instead of choosing a specific kernel function.

The general optimization goal in the proposed optimization process is somehow similar to that of the optimization method in [28], where the authors have proposed a semi-supervised metric learning technique for learning a projection matrix that is used for the dimensionality reduction purpose. Both optimization processes try to minimize the average distance between similarity pairs and maximize the average distance between dissimilarity pairs. However, their final objective and the adopted methodologies are different. In our proposed method, within the clustering framework, the optimization process is performed in the kernel space considering a weighted sum of a set of kernel functions and the main purpose is to find the optimal weights, while in [28], the optimization process is done in the feature space, and the main purpose is to learn a projection matrix for the dimensionality reduction purpose. Moreover, in their learning process, all the data points including the unlabeled ones are used. However, we utilize only the similarity and/or dissimilarity pairs in order to learn the weights of the adopted kernels.

3.2. Composite kernels

Let $\{\mathbf{K}_1, \mathbf{K}_2, ..., \mathbf{K}_M\}$ be M different kernel matrices that map the data points to M Hilbert spaces as:

$$\mathbf{K}_m = \left[k_m(\mathbf{x}_i, \mathbf{x}_j) \right]_{N \times N} \tag{12}$$
$$= \left[\left\langle \phi_m(\mathbf{x}_i), \phi_m(\mathbf{x}_j) \right\rangle \right]_{N \times N}$$

where, $\phi_m \in \mathbb{R}^{r_{\phi_m}}$ is the feature space corresponding to the m-th Hilbert space, and r_{ϕ_m} is the number of dimensions of ϕ_m. These different kernels correspond to different feature spaces and they contain different sources of information. This suggests that complimentary information which leads to a better performance can be extracted by a suitable combination of the kernel functions. In what follows, we briefly review two popular combining methods, namely the unweighted sum [19] and matrix augmentation methods [25].

3.2.1 Unweighted sum method

The unweighted sum of a set of base kernels is denoted by:

$$\mathbf{K}_{un} = \sum_{m=1}^{M} \mathbf{K}_m \tag{13}$$

Since the kernel matrices are positive semi-definite, the summation of them is also a positive semi-definite matrix. Thus the new kernel satisfies the mercer's condition, and it is a valid kernel. It can be shown that the new kernel corresponds to a new feature space that is obtained by unweighted concatenation of the base feature vectors, i.e.:

$$\mathbf{\Phi}_{un} = \left[\phi_1^T, \phi_2^T, ..., \phi_M^T \right]^T \tag{14}$$

One of the advantages of this composite kernel is that there is no limit on the number of base kernels, and a large number of base kernels can be combined without increasing the computational complexity. Moreover, the reported results confirm the effectiveness of the method [19].

3.2.2 Augmenting kernel matrices

In [25], Yan *et al.* have proposed a novel method of creating composite kernels that involves augmenting kernel matrices. An augmented kernel matrix (AKM) is defined as:

$$\mathbf{K}_{aug} = \begin{bmatrix} \mathbf{K}_1 & 0 & 0 \\ 0 & \ddots & 0 \\ 0 & 0 & \mathbf{K}_M \end{bmatrix}_{(M \times N)(M \times N)} \tag{15}$$

It can be shown that this kernel is also a valid Mercer's kernel [25]. This formulation indicates that the discriminative importance of the data points in different feature spaces is preserved by augmenting the kernel matrices. One of the limitations of AKM is that by increasing the number of base kernels, a large amount of memory space is needed, resulting in a high computational complexity. This makes AKM inapplicable to large datasets, especially when the number of base kernels, M, is large.

We deal with this problem by initial grouping of the base kernels according to their similarity. We use the Kernel Alignment (KA) method proposed in [27] as a measure of similarity between kernels in order to group them in an unsupervised manner. Considering two kernel matrices as $\mathbf{K}_k$ and $\mathbf{K}_l$, the Frobenius inner product between the matrices is defined as: $\left\langle \mathbf{K}_k, \mathbf{K}_l \right\rangle_F = \sum_{i,j=1}^{N} \mathbf{K}_k(\mathbf{x}_i, \mathbf{x}_j) \mathbf{K}_l(\mathbf{x}_i, \mathbf{x}_j)$. The empirical alignment between these two kernel matrices can be measured by:

$$\text{KA}(\mathbf{K}_k, \mathbf{K}_l) = \frac{\left\langle \mathbf{K}_k, \mathbf{K}_l \right\rangle_F}{\sqrt{\left\langle \mathbf{K}_k, \mathbf{K}_k \right\rangle_F \left\langle \mathbf{K}_l, \mathbf{K}_l \right\rangle_F}} \tag{16}$$

We group the kernels in an agglomerative manner using the kernel alignment measure. For this purpose, first, we initialize all kernels as separate clusters and merge two most similar clusters at a time. Similarity between two clusters is defined as the largest distance between all possible pairs of cluster members. The merging process is then continued until G groups are obtained. After determining the members of each group, we find a representative kernel for each of them. In this study, the representative kernels are determined by unweighted summation of the kernels of each group. In fact, we use the beneficial effects of unweighted sum within each group and the discriminative effect of the augmenting method over the representative kernels. The proposed algorithm is summarized in figure 1.

Algorithm 1. *The proposed algorithm*

Input: *Input data,* $X = \{x_i\}_{i=1}^{N}$ *a set of similarity pairs S and a set of dissimilarity pairs D.*
Output: *Clustering the input data.*

Step 1: *Compute the basis kernels* $\{\mathbf{K}_m\}_{m=1}^{M}$.

Step 2: *Compute composite kernel using unweighted or augmenting method,* $\{\mathbf{K}_{Com}\} = \mathbf{K}_{un}$ *or* $\{\mathbf{K}_{Com}\} = \mathbf{K}_{aug}$.

Step 3: *Eigen-decomposition of composite kernels in previous the step,* $\mathbf{K}_{Com} = \sum_{n=1}^{N} \alpha_n \mathbf{u}_n \mathbf{u}_n^T = \sum_{n=1}^{N} \alpha_n \mathbf{U}_n$.

Step 4: *Specify the eigen-values that preserve a specific level (for example, 99%) of the total variance of the data.*

Step 5: *Replace the eigen-values in the previous step with new variables and remove the rest,* $\tilde{\mathbf{K}}_{Com} = \sum_{n=1}^{P} \lambda_n^2 \mathbf{U}_n$.

Step 6: *Compute the optimal coefficient vector as* $\lambda = \dfrac{c(\mathbf{A}_S - \beta \mathbf{B}_D)^{-1} \mathbf{1}}{\mathbf{1}^T (\mathbf{A}_S - \beta \mathbf{B}_D)^{-1} \mathbf{1}}$.

Step 7: *Compute new kernel matrix using the coefficients in the previous step,* $\tilde{\mathbf{K}}_{Com} = \sum_{n=1}^{P} \lambda_n^2 \mathbf{U}_n$.

Step 8: *Use* $\tilde{\mathbf{K}}_{Com}$ *in kernelized k-means algorithm to cluster data, and repeat the k-means algorithm until a stopping criterion is met.*

Figure 1. Proposed algorithm.

To study the computational complexity of the above solution, we exploit the complexity of different parts of it. Without considering any structure for the kernel matrix $\mathbf{K}$, the eigen-decomposition of $\mathbf{K}$ to express it in the form of (3) takes $O(N^3)$ time. The diagonal matrices $\mathbf{A}_S$ and $\mathbf{B}_D$ take $O(P|S|)$ and $O(P|D|)$ times, respectively. The optimal value for λ can be computed according to (11) in $O(P)$ time. Note that $P < N$ and typically $|S|, |D| \ll N$, so the overall complexity of the proposed algorithm is $O(N^3)$, which is dominated by the complexity of the eigen-decomposition step. The kernel alignment can also be computed in $O(N^2)$. The computational complexity of kernel-based algorithms is summarized in table 1. It can be seen that the computational complexity of all kernel-based algorithms is approximately $O(N^3)$.

Table 1. Computational complexity of the proposed algorithm.

Kernel-β	Unweighted sum	Augmenting
$O(N^3)$	$O(N^3 + N^2)$	$O(GN^3 + N^2)$

4. Experimental results

In this section, our experimental results on both the synthetic and real-world data are reported, and the performance of the proposed method for semi-supervised metric clustering is evaluated.

4.1. Experimental setup

We compare our kernel-based metric learning method with some other benchmark approaches. The Euclidean distance without metric learning is used as the baseline in our comparative study. The RCA method proposed in [14] is one of the benchmark methods. The RCA algorithm assigns lower weights to the irrelevant directions in the input space by applying whitening transformation on the dataset. The Xing *et al.*'s method in [13] is the other adopted method. This method considers both the pairwise similarity and dissimilarity constraints in contrast to the RCA method that makes use of only the similarity constraint. As one of the recently proposed kernel-based methods, we also report the results using the Kernel-β method [21]. This method uses the pairwise similarity constraint as well. Thus overall, we compare the performance of our kernel-based metric learning algorithm with the following algorithms (the short names inside the brackets will be used subsequently):

1) k-means without metric learning (Euclidean);
2) k-means with the RCA metric learning method (RCA) [14];
3) k-means with Xing *et al.*'s metric learning method (Xing's) [13];
4) Kernelized k-means with the kernel obtained by the Kernel-β method (Kernel-β) [21];
5) Kernelized k-means with the unweighted composite kernel obtained by the proposed method using only the similarity constraints (unweighted-*S*) [26];
6) Kernelized k-means with the unweighted composite kernel obtained by the proposed method using both the similarity and dissimilarity constraints (unweighted-*SD*);
7) Kernelized k-means with the augmented composite kernel obtained by the proposed method using only the similarity constraints (augmented-*S*) [26];
8) Kernelized k-means with the augmented composite kernel obtained by the proposed method using both the similarity and dissimilarity constraints (augmented-*SD*);

We utilize the RBF kernels as the primary non-linearity inducing function for all the kernel-based metric learning methods. The RBF kernel is given as:

$$k(\mathbf{x}_i, \mathbf{x}_j) = \exp\left(\frac{\|\mathbf{x}_i - \mathbf{x}_j\|^2}{2\sigma^2}\right) \tag{17}$$

This kernel is widely used in kernel-based methods. An appropriate selection of the kernel parameter, σ, is an important issue. The value for σ should be selected to reflect the distribution of data points. The distribution is usually unknown, especially in the case of high dimensional data. Instead of choosing a specific value for σ, we combine Gaussian kernels with different widths. The composite kernel encloses information for all the kernels. It is expected to automatically extract the most useful information via the learning process.

In this study, the performance of the metric learning clustering algorithms is measured using the Rand Index (RI) value. RI is a measure of agreement between the clustering result and the ground truth. Let n_s be the number of pairs assigned to the same partitions by both the clustering and the ground truth annotation, and n_d be the number of pairs assigned to different partitions by them. The RI is defined as $RI = 2(n_s + n_d)/(N(N-1))$, i.e. it is the ratio of correctly assigned pairs to the total number of pairs. When there are more than two clusters, the standard Rand index, as defined above, will tend to assign data pairs to different clusters. We use the modified Rand index as in [13, 18, 21, 23]. In the modified Rand index, the equal chance of occurrence (0.5) is considered for both the similarity and dissimilarity pairs, and RI is defined as:

$$RI(C, \hat{C}) = \frac{0.5 \times \sum_{i>j} \delta(c_i = c_j \wedge \hat{c}_i = \hat{c}_j)}{\sum_{i>j} \delta(\hat{c}_i = \hat{c}_j)} \\ + \frac{0.5 \times \sum_{i>j} \delta(c_i \neq c_j \wedge \hat{c}_i \neq \hat{c}_j)}{\sum_{i>j} \delta(\hat{c}_i \neq \hat{c}_j)} \tag{18}$$

where, $\delta(.)$ is an indicator function (i.e. $\delta(True) = 1$ and $\delta(False) = 0$), $\hat{c}_i$ is the cluster to which $\mathbf{x}_i$ is assigned by the clustering algorithm, and c_i is the correct cluster assignment. The indicator $\wedge$ is used as "*and*" operator.

Each dataset is normalized to zero mean and unit standard deviation before applying the clustering algorithm. As described in Section 3, the proposed

metric learning approach uses the similarity and dissimilarity pairwise constraints in the learning process. This data plays an important role. Therefore, for each dataset, we randomly generate 20 different similarity (S) and dissimilarity (D) sets. We also perform 20 runs of k-means with random initialization for each pairwise constraint (SD) set. Thus each clustering experiment is repeated for 400 times and the statistical characteristics of the results are reported.

As mentioned in Section 3.2, the main aim in creating the augmented structure is to retain the discriminative importance of the data points in different feature spaces. After clustering the base kernels into G groups using kernel alignment as the similarity measure, we will have G representations of a data point at the same time. Thus we define the distance between two data points in the augmented feature space as the mean of the distances between these two points in the different feature spaces induced by the base kernels.

In the kernel-β method, the kernel parameter, σ, is set using the following equation [21]:

$$\sigma^2 = (\theta / N(N-1)) \sum_{i,j=1}^{N} \|\phi(\mathbf{x}_i) - \phi(\mathbf{x}_j)\|^2 \tag{19}$$

where, similar to the associated reference, $\theta = 5$ is used.

4.2. Experiments on Synthetic Dataset

We first perform some experiments on a synthetic XOR dataset. Figure 2(a) shows a scatter plot of the dataset. Two different signs with different colours are used to show the data points with their labels. The solid green and pink lines are used to show, respectively, the adopted similarity (S) and dissimilarity (D) pairs. We randomly pick 10 similarity pairs (i.e. $|S| = 10$) and 5 dissimilarity pairs (i.e. $|D| = 5$). Based on the experiments performed on the UCI datasets, which will be reported later, we set $G = 2$. The parameter σ_i varies from 1 to 8, which is in steps of 0.7 to obtain 11 base kernels.

The scatter plots of the data points projected into the new feature spaces induced by the different distance metric-based clustering approaches are shown in figure 2 (b-h). The RCA and Xing's method learn global Mahalanobis metric in the original input space. For the kernel-based methods, in order to represent the transformed data in the learned kernel space, we apply the kernelized PCA to the data points using the learned kernel matrix. The resulting two-dimensional (2-D) feature space is then displayed.

Figure 2 (b) and (c) show the transformed data points using the RCA and Xing's methods, respectively. Note that the linear transformation using the RCA and Xing's methods cannot yield significant clustering results for non-linearly distributed data points such as the XOR data. As shown in figure 2(d), the non-linear kernel-β method yields a good clustering result for this type of dataset but the main problem with this method is that it is very sensitive to the choice of the RBF kernel parameter, σ. Slight changes can highly degrade the performance of the method. Moreover, although the data points of different classes are separated, the scattering of the data points in each class is quite high. Figures 2 (e) and (g) show the mapped data points using the proposed method with the unweighted averaging and augmenting strategies, respectively, in a scenario when just similarity constraints are available. Compared to the kernel-β method, combining the base kernels, i.e. combining the information for different feature spaces induced by different kernels, reduces the scattering of the data points in each class. As shown in figures 2 (f) and (h), using additional information in the form of dissimilarity pairwise constraints, the performance of the proposed kernel-based method is meaningfully improved. It can be seen that by adding this information, more compacted and separated clusters are created. It has to be noted that in the eigen-decomposition step of the experiments, 99% of the variance of the overall kernel matrix, $\mathbf{K}$, is preserved. As a result, the number of variables that have to be learned is significantly reduced (for instance, from $N = 200$ to $P = 7$).

Figure 3 contains schematic plots of the initial and learned kernel matrices computed over the XOR dataset using the kernel-β and unweighted-SD methods. We arrange the data points according to their class label. The kernel matrix for these arranged data points is then computed. The top row of the figure shows the initial kernel that has been obtained from a single Gaussian kernel for the kernel-β method and a combination of the base kernels for the unweighted-SD method. It can be seen that the initial kernel matrix of both methods consists of four parts, meaning that the samples are cast into four clusters, which is due to the geometrical distribution of the data. Although the data points in both initial kernels are

incorrectly partitioned, the kernel values for each part of the data in the composite methods are much higher than those of the single kernel. The kernel matrices after the learning process are shown in the next row of the figure. The learning process leads to a better association of kernel values and data point labels (i.e. the matrix can be divided into two parts). Using the composite kernels, the kernel matrix is perfectly divided into two distinct parts that correspond to the ideal kernel for this dataset.

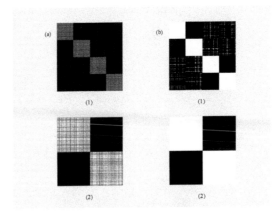

Figure 3. Kernel matrices for XOR dataset before and after kernel-based metric learning algorithms. (1) initial kernel matrix used in metric learning, (2) learned kernel matrix in metric learning process. (a) kernel-β, (b) unweighted-SD.

The semi-supervised clustering results for the XOR dataset are displayed as the box-plots in figure 4. All the kernel-based methods achieve remarkably good semi-supervised clustering. The kernel-based methods always lead to perfect results ($RI = 1$), and the variance of the results is zero.

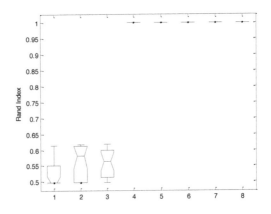

Figure 4. Clustering results of different algorithms for XOR dataset. Eight algorithms (numbered in Section 4.1) are as follow: (1) Euclidean, (2) RCA, (3) Xing's, (4) kernel-β, (5) unweighted-S, (6) unweighted-SD, (7) augmented-S, and (8) augmented-SD.

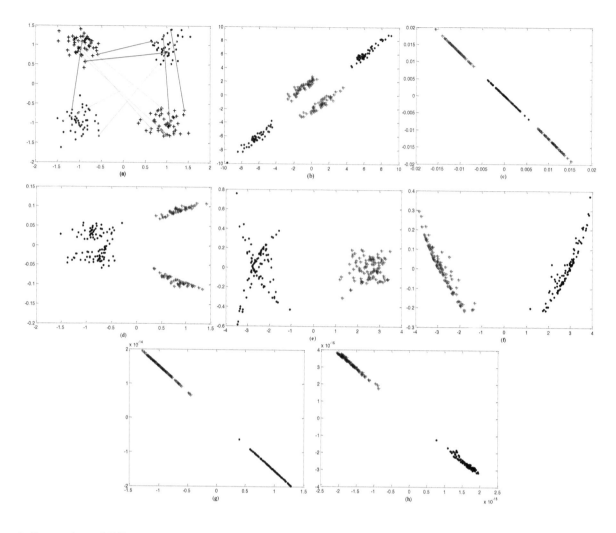

Figure 2. Comparison of different metric learning methods on XOR dataset. (a) Original dataset with two classes, and dataset after applying (b) RCA, (c) Xing's, (d) kernel-β, (e) unweighted-S, (f) unweighted-SD, (g) augmented-S, and (h) augmented-SD.

We also repeat the experiments for the XOR with overlapping clusters. Parameters are set similar to the previous experiment. Figure 5 shows new XOR data and the corresponding clustering results of different algorithms. It can be seen that the proposed methods outperform the others. Figure 6 (b-h) shows the new XOR data points projected into the feature spaces induced by the different distance metric-based clustering approaches.

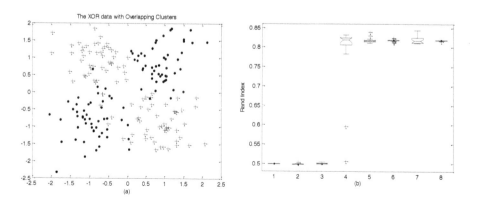

Figure 5. Clustering results of different algorithms for XOR data with overlapping clusters. (a) original data, (b) eight algorithms (numbered in Section 4.1) are as follow: (1) Euclidean, (2) RCA, (3) Xing's, (4) kernel-β, (5) unweighted-S, (6) unweighted-SD, (7) augmented-S, and (8) augmented-SD.

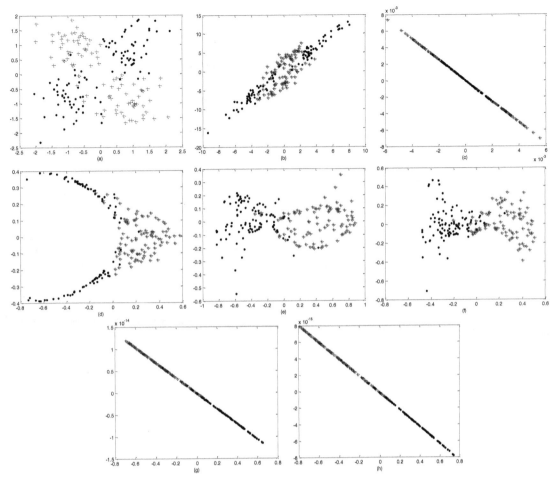

Figure 6. Comparison of different metric learning methods on XOR dataset with overlapping clusters. (a) original dataset with two classes, and dataset after applying (b) RCA, (c) Xing's, (d) kernel-β, (e) unweighted-S, (f) unweighted-SD, (g) augmented-S, and (h) augmented-SD.

4.3. Experiments on UCI Data

We repeated our experiments on six real-world datasets from the University of California at Irvine (UCI) Machine Learning Repository. Some details about the main characteristics of these datasets and our experimental settings are shown in table 2. These details include the size of dataset (N), number of features (r_x), number of clusters (C), and number of randomly selected similarity and dissimilarity pairs ($|S|$ and $|D|$). $|S|$ was selected to be the same as that in [21] and [23].

In the case of multiple kernel learning, Gaussian kernels with different parameter values, σ, were utilized. The number of Gaussian kernels (M) and the adopted range of this parameter (σ_i) have also been reported in the table. For each dataset, the lower bound of variance value, σ, has been chosen by computing the variance of the associated data points in the original feature space. For each dataset, M Gaussian kernels are computed by extracting M parameter σ_i from the

interval $\left[\dfrac{1}{2}\sigma, 2\sigma\right]$. In the experiments, the number of Gaussian kernels has been chosen as $M = 11$ for all datasets. M is randomly selected. The datasets are normalized before applying the clustering algorithms.

The performance of the proposed method may be affected by the value of a few parameters. The main parameters are the number of kernel groups, G, and number of the similarity/dissimilarity pairs. Some discussions about the parameter settings are in the following order:

(i) G: As mentioned, the number of base kernels is reduced to G groups using a kernel alignment procedure. The grouping process reduces the computational complexity of the method, especially in the case of the kernel augmentation method. A number of experiments were performed using different values of G. Figure 7 contains samples of the results, where the average Rand Index is plotted versus the number of groups, G, for different datasets using the unweighted-SD method. These plots demonstrate that the performance of the proposed method is not highly affected by the number of the groups. Therefore, we set $G = 2$ in the experiments.

(ii) $|S|$ and $|D|$: The plots in figure 8 show the relationship between the average Rand Index and the number of constraints. These are the results obtained using the unweighted-SD method on different datasets. As expected, the performance of the proposed method normally improves when the number of the constraints is increased. Since this study focuses on semi-supervised learning, a limited amount of supervisory information has to be provided. Hence, in the rest of the paper, we report the results obtained using the number of superiority constraints, as specified in table 2.

Figure 9 contains the clustering results on the UCI datasets using different algorithms (numbered as discussed in Section 4.1). From these results, the findings of the paper can be summarized as follow:

1)   As expected, the kernel-based methods (4 to 8 in Section 4.1) outperform the simple Euclidean distance measure or the linear metric learning approaches. This is thanks to the benefits obtained by the non-linear mapping induced by the kernel functions.

2)   It can be seen that the proposed kernel learning methods (5 to 8 in Section 4.1) generally lead to better results compared to the kernel-β and the other approaches. The main exception is the Wine dataset. As mentioned earlier, in this study, a set of RBF kernels is considered as the primary kernels. Perhaps, there still is a need for including a greater variety of kernels as the base kernels in order to capture the inherent clustering characteristics of different datasets with better efficiency. This is a matter of interest in the future studies. Also in some cases, although the average Rand Index of the proposed methods is higher, a low confidence interval (i.e. high variance) has been observed. As mentioned earlier, for any sets of pairwise similarity/dissimilarity constraints, the k-means clustering process is repeated for 20 times. The high variance problem could be due to the problem of local optima in some runs of the algorithm. This problem can be reduced by automatically selecting the best clustering results using the relevant solutions such as using the silhouette measure [29].

3)   Among the advocated approaches (5 to 8 in Section 4.1), the kernel augmentation process usually leads to slightly better results. Also adding the dissimilarity pairs as a part of the supervisory information usually improves the clustering quality.

Table 2. Main characteristics of UCI datasets and associated experimental settings.

Dataset	N	r_x	C	$|S|$	$|D|$	σ_i
Soybean	47	35	4	10	5	[5-20]
Heart	270	13	2	30	10	[5-20]
Ionosphere	351	34	2	30	10	[5-20]
Wine	178	13	3	20	10	[5-20]
Sonar	208	60	2	30	10	[10-40]
Iris	150	4	3	20	10	[3-12]

4.4. Experiments on MNIST digits dataset

To evaluate the performance of the proposed methods on real datasets, we also performed some experiments on the hand-written digits from the MNIST database[1]. This database contained 60000 hand-written numerical characters as the training set and another 10000 as the test set. All the relevant images were centred and normalized to 28×28 gray level images. In our experiments, the clustering process was performed on three subsets of the numerical characters.

These subsets contained {0,1}, {1,5}, and {1,9} digits, respectively. We randomly picked 200

[1] http://yann.lecun.com/exdb/mnist/

samples for each digit. Also 10 different constraint sets were randomly generated, where each set contained 20 similarity pairs ($|S| = 20$) and 5 dissimilarity pairs ($|D| = 5$). For each pairwise constraint set (S and D), 20 runs of the k-means clustering algorithm were performed by different random initializations.

The number of groups was set to $G = 2$, and the kernel parameter σ_i varied from 10 to 60 in steps

of 5. Thus overall, each clustering experiment was repeated for 200 times, and the mean and standard deviation of the Rand Index were calculated. Table 3 contains the results obtained using different approaches. It can be seen that the proposed optimization process leads to better results.

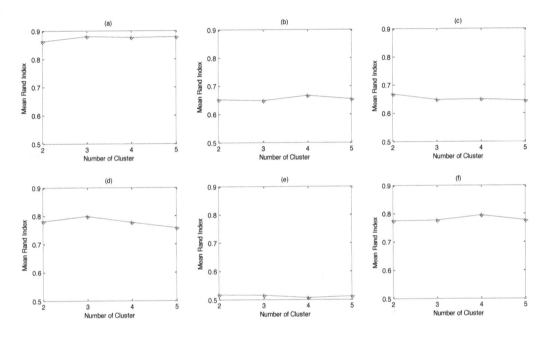

Figure 7. Clustering results of unweighted-*SD* method versus number of groups, *G*, for UCI datasets: (a) Soybean, (b) Heart, (c) Ionosphere, (d) Wine, (e) Sonar, and (f) Iris.

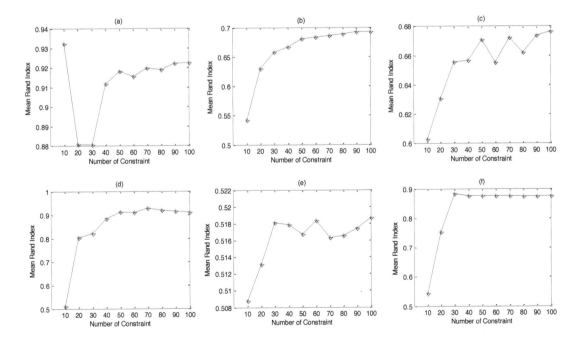

Figure 8. Clustering results of unweighted-*SD* method versus number of constraints for UCI datasets: (a) Soybean, (b) Heart, (c) Ionosphere, (d) Wine, (e) Sonar, and (f) Iris.

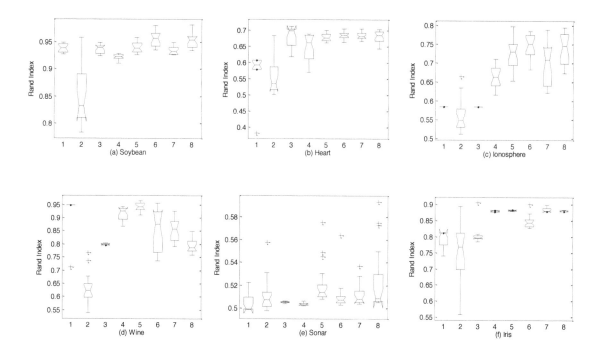

Figure 9. Clustering results of different algorithms for UCI datasets. Algorithms (numbered in Section 4.1) are as follow: (1) Euclidean, (2) RCA, (3) Xing's, (4) kernel-β, (5) unweighted-*S*, (6) unweighted-*SD*, (7) augmented-*S*, and (8) augmented-*SD*.

5. Conclusion

In this paper, we proposed a new metric learning method that makes use of the concept of composite kernels. We formulated a semi-supervised metric learning approach, which utilizes both the similarity and dissimilarity pairwise constraints. Within the framework of the proposed method, the merits of two groups of composite kernels, namely unweighted-average and augmented kernels, were investigated. The learning process concentrates on determining the weights of the eigen-matrices obtained by the eigen-decomposition of the associated composite kernel matrix. In the learning process, a set of similarity and/or dissimilarity constraints have to be jointly satisfied. Our experimental results on the synthetic and real world datasets confirm that overall, the proposed methods are superior to the existing approaches. The proposed methods are suitable for the case that all data points are available in advance. However, extending the proposed methods for dealing with stream data (on-line clustering) could be a matter of interest in the future studies.

Table 3. Clustering results on three subsets of the MNIST dataset.

Subset	Euclidean	RCA	Xing's	kernel-β	unweighted-*S*	unweighted-*SD*	augmented-*S*	augmented-*SD*
{0,1}	0.9781 ±0.0000	0.9812 ±0.0125	0.9850 ±0.0031	0.9851 ±0.0000	0.9900 ±0.0000	0.9950 ±0.0000	0.9888 ±0.0146	0.9851 ±0.0120
{1,5}	0.8249 ±0.0012	0.8314 ±0.0311	0.8401 ±0.0170	0.8528 ±0.0336	0.9003 ±0.0015	0.9184 ±0.0023	0.8731 ±0.0037	0.8839 ±0.0031
{1,9}	0.9524 ±0.0035	0.9531 ±0.0412	0.9549 ±0.0359	0.9366 ±0.0059	0.9611 ±0.0034	0.9760 ±0.0031	0.9550 ±0.0261	0.9588 ±0.0192

6. Acknowledgment

The partial supports of the Ministry of Science, Research, and Technology of Iran, EPSRC/dstl project EP/K014307/1, and the EPSRC project EP/N007743/1 are gratefully acknowledged.

References

[1] Yang, L., Jin, R. (2006). Distance metric learning: a comprehensive survey. Technical Report, Michigan State University.

[2] Yang, L. (2007). An Overview of Distance Metric Learning. Technical Report, Michigan State University.

[3] Domeniconi, C., Peng, J., Gunopulos, D. (2002). Locally adaptive metric nearest neighbor classification. IEEE Transactions on Pattern Analysis and Machine Intelligence, vol. 24, no. 9, pp. 1281-1285.

[4] Domeniconi, C., Gunopulos, D. (2005). Large margin nearest neighbor classifiers. IEEE Transactions on Neural Networks, vol. 16, no.4, pp. 899-909.

[5] Wang, D., Lim, J. S., Han, M. M. & Lee, B. W. (2005) Learning similarity for semantic images classification. Neurocomputing, vol. 6, pp. 363-368.

[6] Goldberger, J., Roweis, S., Hinton, G. & Salakhutdinov, R. (2005) Neighbourhood components analysis. In Advances in Neural Information Processing Systems (NIPS).

[7] Weinberger, K., Blitzer, J. & Saul, L. (2006). Distance metric learning for large margin nearest neighbor classification. In Advances in Neural Information Processing Systems (NIPS).

[8] Saul, L. K. & Roweis, S. T. (2003). Think globally, fit locally: Unsupervised learning of low dimensional manifolds. Journal of Machine Learning Research, vol. 4, pp. 119–155.

[9] Xiang, S., Nie, F. & Zhang, C. (2008). Learning a Mahalanobis distance metric for data clustering and classification. Pattern Recognition, vol. 41, no. 12, pp. 3600-3612.

[10] Kumar, N. & Kummamuru, K. (2007). Semi-supervised clustering with metric learning using relative comparisons. IEEE Transactions on Knowledge and Data Engineering, vol. 20, no. 4, pp. 496-503.

[11] Chang, H. & Yeung, D. Y. (2006). Locally linear metric adaptation with application to semi-supervised clustering and image retrieval. Pattern Recognition, vol. 39, no. 7, pp. 1253-1264.

[12] Schultz, M. & Joachims, T. (2004). Learning a distance metric from relative comparisons. In Advances in Neural Information Processing Systems (NIPS).

[13] Xing, EP., Ng, A. Y., Jordan M. I & Russell, S. (2003). Distance metric learning, with application to clustering with side-information. In Advances in Neural Information Processing Systems (NIPS).

[14] Bar-Hillel, A., Hertz, T., Shental, N. & Weinshall. D. (2003). Learning distance functions using equivalence relations. In Proceedings of 20th International Conference on Machine Learning, Washington, DC.

[15] Chang, H. & Yeung, D. Y. (2006). Extending the relevant component analysis algorithm for metric learning using both positive and negative equivalence

constraints. Pattern Recognition, vol. 39, no. 5, pp. 1007-1010.

[16] Nguyen, N. & Guo, Y. (2008). Metric Learning: A Support Vector Approach. In Proceedings of European Conference on Machine Learning /PKDD.

[17] Kwok, J. T. & Tsang, I. W. (2003). Learning with idealized kernels. In Proceedings of International Conference on Machine Learning.

[18] Yeung, D. Y. and Chang, H. & Dai, G. (2008). A scalable kernel-based semi-supervised metric learning algorithm with out-of-sample generation ability. Neural computation, vol. 20, no.11, pp. 2839-2861.

[19] Cristianini, N. & Shawe-Taylor, J. (2000). An introduction to support vector machines and other kernel-based learning methods. Cambridge University Press.

[20] Yan, F., Mikolajczyk, K., Kittler, J. & Tahir, MA. (2010). Combining Multiple Kernels by Augmenting the Kernel Matrix. In Proceedings of Multiple Classifier Systems.

[21] Yeung, D. Y. & Chang, H. (2007). A kernel approach for semisupervised metric learning. IEEE Transactions on Neural Networks, vol. 18, no. 1, pp. 141-149.

[22] Hoi, S. CH, Jin, R. & Lyu, M. R. (2007). Learning nonparametric kernel matrices from pairwise constraints. In Proceedings of 20th International Conference on Machine Learning, New York, USA.

[23] Soleymani Baghshah, M. & Bagheri Shouraki, S. (2010). Kernel-based metric learning for semi-supervised clustering. Neurocomputing, vol. 73, no. 1, pp. 1352-1361.

[24] Wang, J., Do, H., Woznica, A. & Kalousis, A. (2011). Metric learning with multiple kernels. In Advances in Neural Information Processing Systems (NIPS).

[25] Yan, F., Mikolajczyk, K. & Kittler, J. (2011). Multiple Kernel Learning via Distance Metric Learning for Interactive Image Retrieval. In Proceedings of Multiple Classifier Systems.

[26] Zare, T., Sadeghi, M. T. & Abutalebi, H. R. (2012). Semi-supervised Metric Learning Using Composite Kernels. In Proceedings of 6th International Telecommunication symposium (IST).

[27] Cristianini, N., Shawe-Taylor, J., Elisseeff, A. & Kandola, J. (2001). On Kernel-Target Alignment. In Advances in Neural Information Processing Systems (NIPS).

[28] Zhang, D., .Zhou, ZH., & Chen, S. (2007). Semi-supervised dimensionality. In Proceedings of the 7th SIAM International Conference on Data Mining (SDM'07), Minneapolis, MN.

[29] Rousseeuw, P. J. (1987). Silhouettes: a Graphical Aid to the Interpretation and Validation of Cluster Analysis. Computational and Applied Mathematics.

18

A Hybrid MOEA/D-TS for Solving Multi-Objective Problems

Sh. Lotfi and F. Karimi[*]

Department of Computer Science, University of Tabriz, Tabriz, Iran.

*Corresponding author: f.karimi@tabrizu.ac.ir (F. Karimi).

Abstract

In many real-world applications, various optimization problems with conflicting objectives are very common. In this work, we employ Multi-Objective Evolutionary Algorithm based on Decomposition (MOEA/D), a newly developed method beside Tabu Search (TS) accompaniment to achieve a new manner for solving multi-objective optimization problems (MOPs) with two or three conflicting objectives. This improved hybrid algorithm, namely MOEA/D-TS, uses the parallel computing capacity of MOEA/D along with the neighborhood search authority of TS for discovering Pareto optimal solutions. Our goal is to exploit the advantages of evolutionary algorithms and TS to achieve an integrated method to cover the totality of the Pareto front by uniformly distributed solutions. In order to evaluate the capabilities of the proposed method, its performance based on various metrics is compared with SPEA, COMOEATS, and SPEA2TS on the well-known Zitzler-Deb-Thiele's ZDT test suite and DTLZ test functions with separable objective functions. According to the experimental results obtained, the proposed method could significantly outperform the previous algorithms and produce fully satisfactory results.

Keywords: *Multi-objective Problems, Evolutionary Algorithms, Hybrid Method, MOEA/D, Tabu Search.*

1. Introduction

Multi-objective optimization problems (MOPs) with the aim of optimizing a collection of various objectives, systematically and simultaneously, are among important challenges in the today's world. Unlike single-objective optimization, finding an optimal trade-off among conflicting objectives in a multi-objective problem is often more complex and challenging [1]. Also it is necessary to determine a community of points, which are compatible with a pre-determined definition for an optimum. For trading off between solutions, a vast piece of information about the desired problem is required to opt the best solutions and omit the unwanted ones based on the problem constraints. Typically, a number of potentially Pareto optimal solutions are good candidates as optimal trade-off for these kinds of problems [2].

Many researchers believe that Evolutionary Algorithms (EAs), which make use of the strategy of population evolutionary to optimize the problems, are able to perform better than other blind search strategies confronting MOPs [3-5]. Within the last decade, various techniques have been proposed, which demonstrate the power of Multi-Objective Evolutionary Algorithms (MOEAs) for solving MOPs [7-16]. These kinds of methods can produce a set of Pareto-optimal solutions in a single run using a population of candidate solutions [17]. As an important population-based EA, Genetic Algorithm (GA) is well-suited to solve multi-objective optimization problems. Multi-Objective Genetic Algorithm (MOGA) [18], Niched Pareto Genetic Algorithm (NPGA) [19], and Non-dominated Sorting Genetic Algorithm (NSGA) [5] are among the first efforts to take advantage of GA having specialized fitness functions and various methods to promote solution diversity [8].

One fundamental shortcoming of these methods is the neglect of elitism strategy, which was recognized and supported experimentally in the multi-objective searches a few years later [20, 21]. Strength Pareto Evolutionary Algorithm (SPEA) [21] was one of the first techniques that outperformed the (non-elitist) alternative approaches [21,22]. An improved version of

SPEA, namely SPEA2 [23], is a powerful algorithm with the ability to overcome its predecessor shortcomings and achieve acceptable results. This updated method was the basis of our previous hybrid algorithm, namely Strength Pareto Evolutionary Algorithm2 Tabu Search (SPEA2TS) [24], which uses the exploration capacity of SPEA2 along with the power of TS in neighborhood research to find Pareto optimal solutions in different multi-objective problems.

A majority of the current MOEAs do not employ the decomposition concept. The manner these algorithms adopt is considering the whole MOP, and do not affiliate each separate solution with any particular scalar optimization problem [25]. This idea is adopted by a limited number of MOEAs to a certain amount [26-28], and Multi-Objective Evolutionary Algorithm based on Decomposition (MOEA/D) is the more recent one [25]. MOEA/D transforms the task of approximating the Pareto front (PF) into a number of single-objective optimization sub-problems using the traditional aggregation methods, and then optimizes these sub-problems simultaneously [6]. Considering the best solution found so far (i.e. from the start of algorithm's run) at each generation, the population is composed of each sub-problem. According to the distances between their aggregation coefficient vectors, these sub-problems find the neighborhood relations among them. The only information used for optimization of each sub-problem by MOEA/D comes from its neighbors.

In this work, we improved our earlier work (SPEA2TS) [24] by taking the advantage of MOEA/D as the optimization tool beside the capabilities of Tabu Search for dealing with various multi-objective optimization problems. Our goal was to exploit the advantages of EA and TS to achieve an integrated method to cover the totality of the Pareto front by uniformly distributed solutions.

The structure of this paper is as what follows. Section 2 introduces the main concepts of the multi-objective optimization. Section 3 provides a comprehensive literature review on the different methods used for solving MOPs. The Multi-Objective Evolutionary Algorithm based on Decomposition is described with more details in Section 4, while as a general overview of our proposed method, MOEA/D-TS is available in Section 5. Section 6 provides the experimental settings that are used in Section 7 to elaborate the experimental results for selected benchmark problems. Finally, a brief summary and conclusion are provided in Section 8.

2. Multi-objective optimization

We could define a multi-objective optimization problem as follows [6]:

$$\text{Max } F(x) = \left(f_1(x), f_2(x), ..., f_m(x) \right)$$

Subject to
$$g_i(x) \leq 0, \qquad i = 1, 2, ..., q \qquad (1)$$
$$h_i(x) = 0, \qquad i = 1, 2, ..., p$$

where, $x = (x_1, ..., x_n) \in X \subset R^n$ is called the decision variable, and X is the n-dimensional decision space. $f_i(x)(i = 1, ..., m)$ is the i-th objective to be minimized, $g_j(x)(j = 1, 2, ..., q)$ defines the j-th inequality constraint, and $h_j(j = 1, 2, ..., p)$ defines the j-th equality constraint. Furthermore, all the constraints determine the set of feasible solutions, which is denoted by Ω. To be specific, we tried to find a feasible solution $x \in \Omega$ minimizing each objective function $f_i(x)(i = 1, ..., m)$ in F.

Suppose $x, v \in \Omega$. We say x *dominates* $v (x \succ v)$ if and only if $f_i(x) \geq f_i(v)$ for every $i \in \{1, 2, ..., m\}$, and $f_j(x) > f_j(v)$ for at least one index $j \in \{1, 2, ..., m\}$. A solution vector x is said to be Pareto optimal with respect to Ω if $\nexists z \in \Omega : z \succ x$. The set of Pareto optimal solutions (PS) is defined as $PS = \{x \in \Omega \mid \nexists z \in \Omega : z \succ x\}$. Finally, the Pareto optimal front (PF) is defined as all $f(x)$, where $x \in PS$. It should be mentioned that usually multi-objective optimization problems (MOPs) refer to those with two or three objectives, while those with more than three objectives are known as many-objective optimization problems (MaOPs) [29].

3. Related work

Recently, the development of EAs to solve multi-objective optimization problems has had considerable progresses [12-16, 30-31]. One significant goal in the field of MOEAs is to find a set of representative Pareto optimal solutions in a single run. Try to produce a set of Pareto optimal solutions to represent the whole PF as diverse as possible. For a desired MOP, a Pareto optimal solution is defined as a set of optimal solution for all scalar optimization problems with the aim of optimizing their aggregation function [30]. Hence, the PF approximation can be divided into a number of scalar objective optimization sub-problems and is the basis of many previous mathematical programming methods [32].

The first multi-objective GA that uses Pareto-based ranking and niching techniques explicitly together is MOGA [18]. This algorithm encourages the search toward the true Pareto front, while maintaining diversity in the population. Hence, it could be a considerable evidence to demonstrate how Pareto-based ranking and fitness sharing can be integrated in a multi-objective GA. The concept of elitism has not yet been considered in this method. In another non-elitist strategy, NSGA, the population is classified into non-dominated fronts, and then a dummy fitness value is assigned to each front (F_1, F_2,..) using a fitness sharing function so that the worst fitness value assigned to F_i is better than the best fitness value assigned to F_{i+1}.

In the MOEA literatures, many algorithms use population categorization based on the non-dominance strategy to assign a fitness value based on the non-dominance rank of the members [6]. For example, Non-dominated Sorting Genetic Algorithm II (NSGAII) [10], proposed by Deb et al. in 2002, uses the crowding distance method and the elitism strategy to obtain a uniform spread of solutions along the best-known Pareto front without using a fitness sharing parameter [8].

Zitzler et al. [33] have proposed the strength Pareto evolutionary algorithm (SPEA) [22], which assigns better fitness values to non-dominated solutions using a ranking procedure at the under-represented regions of the objective space [8]. SPEA is among the first techniques that clearly outperformed the (non-elitist) alternative approaches. It employs a fixed size external list E to store non-dominated solutions that have been investigated during the search hitherward, and a strength value is defined for each solution $y \in E$. Finally, according to these strength values, the ranking of the solution is calculated. SPEA2 [23], which is also based on the elitism strategy, differentiates between solutions with the same rank using a density estimation measure, where the density of a solution is a simple inverse of the distance of its k-th nearest neighbor in objective function space [8].

In contrast to the mentioned algorithms, which mainly rely on Pareto dominance to guide their search, MOEA/D [25] makes use of the traditional aggregation methods to transform the task of approximating the Pareto front (PF) into a number of single-objective optimization sub-problems. During the years, many metaheuristic algorithms applied the idea of decomposition for MOPs [34] [35]. In the two-phase local search (TPLS), for instance, at first, an initial solution is generated by optimizing only one single-objective, and then a search is started from this solution exploiting for non-dominated solutions based on aggregations of the objectives. The multi-objective genetic local search (MOGLS) tries to optimize all aggregations produced by the weighted sum approach or Tchebycheff approach simultaneously [36]. Various multi-objective problems with different characteristics like many objectives, discrete decision variables, and complicated Pareto set could achieve admissible results using MOEA/D [37, 38].

Moreover, some hybrid algorithms have employed the MOEA/D strategy as their basic element. For example, MOEA/D with differential evolution and particle swarm optimization has been proposed by Mashwani [39]. Ke et al. [17] have proposed a MOEAD-ACO, in which each ant (i.e. agent) is responsible for solving one sub-problem and records the best solution found so far for its sub-problem during the search. An ant combines information from its group's pheromone matrix, its own heuristic information matrix, and its current solution to construct a new solution. Li and Landa-Silva [40] have combined MOEA/D and Simulated Annealing (SA) to solve MOPs. In their proposed method, EMOSA, the weight vector of each sub-problem is adaptively modified at the lowest temperature in order to diversify the search towards the unexplored parts of the Pareto optimal front. Moreover, MOEA/D has been used to solve various kinds of problems (e.g. [37, 38]).

This paper proposes a combination of MOEA/D and Tabu Search (TS) [4] to achieve a new manner for solving multi-objective optimization problems.

This improved hybrid algorithm, namely MOEA/D-TS, uses the parallel computing capacity of MOEA/D for a comprehensive exploration of the search space along with the exploitation power of TS for discovering Pareto optimal solutions. The following sections provide more details about the proposed method.

4. Multi-objective evolutionary algorithm based on decomposition

Decomposition of MOP into N scalar optimization sub-problems and solving them altogether is a general manner of MOEA/D. By exchanging information at each generation, these sub-problems collaborate with each other [25]. There are some primary features of MOEA/D: (1) In the current population, there is the best solution found so far per each scalar optimization problem. (2) There are many sub-problems in the neighboring of each scalar optimization problem so that each two neighbor sub-problems have analogous optimal solutions. (3) In MOEA/D, information from neighboring of each sub-problem is used for its optimization. (4) Since each solution is associated with a scalar optimization problem, using scalar optimization methods in MOEA/D is very common [1].

Although decomposition of a high-dimensional MOP into a set of simpler and low-dimensional sub-problems is interesting, without a prior knowledge about the objective function, it is not clear how to decompose it [33]. Moreover, it is difficult to use such a decomposition method to solve all the multi-objective optimization problems (MOPs) because their objective functions are commonly conflicting with one another. That is to say, changing decision variables will generate incomparable solutions. Basically, a separability function means that the decision variables involved in the problem can be optimized independent from any other variable, while a non-separability function means that there exist interactions between at least two decision variables. Formal definition of separable and non-separable functions can be found in [33].

There are several approaches available to convert the problem of Pareto front approximation to some scalar optimization problems [25]. The weight sum and Tchebycheff approach are the most popular ones [41,42]. In this research work, we employed the Tchebycheff approach as the basic method, although the results of applying weight sum approach was also evaluated.

4.1. Tchebycheff and weighted sum approaches

Suppose that $\lambda = (\lambda_1,...,\lambda_m)^T$ shows a collection of weight vectors and Z^*, $Z^* = (z_1^*,...,z_m^*)^T$ is the ideal vector, where $Z_i^* = \max\{f_i(x) | x \in \Omega\}$ for $i = 1, . . . , m$. Using the Tchebycheff approach, decomposition of the main problem into N scalar sub-problems could be done in a way that the objective function of the j-th sub-problem is:

Minimize

$$g^{te}(X | \lambda^j, z^*) = \max_{1 \le i \le m} [\lambda_i^j |f_i(X) - Z_i^*|] \quad (2)$$

Subject to $x \in \Omega$

where, $\lambda^j = (\lambda_1^j,...,\lambda_m^j)^T$ [25].

In the weighted sum approach, if $\sum_{i=1}^{m} \lambda_i = 1$ for weight vector λ, then the optimal solution to the following scalar optimization problem is a Pareto optimal point to (1):

$$Maximize \ g^{ws}(X | \lambda^j) = \sum_{i=1}^{m} \lambda_i^j f_i(X) \quad (3)$$

Subject to $x \in \Omega$

If PF is concave (convex in the case of minimization), this approach could work well. However, not every Pareto optimal vector can be obtained by this approach in the case of non-concave PFs. Also it should be noted that minimization of z by MOEA/D is not essential when the weight sum approach is used [25].

MOEA/D, which uses the Tchebycheff approach, keeps some information at each generation t including:

(1) N individual $X^1,...,X^N \in \Omega$ (population), where the current solution to the i-th subproblem is X^i;
(2) $FV^1, ..., FV^N$, where $FV^i = F(X^i)$;
(3) $z = (z_1,...,z_m)^T$ is the vector of the best value found so far for objective f_i; and
(4) An External Population (EP), which is used to store non-dominated solutions found during the search.

The desired algorithm receives MOP as input and output EP. In this process, other inputs include the number of considered sub-problems, N, the number of weight vectors in the neighborhood of each weight vector, T, a uniform distribution of N weight vectors $\lambda^1, ..., \lambda^N$, and the maximum number of generations, gen_{max}. In accordance with [24,43], the proposed method utilizes a binary tournament strategy as the selection operator. Two important procedures in evolutionary algorithms, recombination, and mutation operators apply on different individuals in order to replace the old population by the resulting off-spring. Also it is necessary to keep the non-dominated solutions found during the search; for this purpose, MOEA/D employs an archive namely the external population (EP). The overall pseudo-code of MOEA/D is shown in Algorithm 1 [25].

During the initialization step, for each index I, $B(i) = \{i_1,...,i_T\}$ is computed. The Euclidean distance is used in order to compute the proximity of any two weight vectors, and also always $i \in B(i)$. As $j \in B(i)$, the j-th sub-problem is considered as a neighbor of the i-th sub-problem [1]. The T neighbors around the i-th sub-problem are considered in the i-th pass of the loop in Step 2 [40]. The available solutions to the neighbors of the i-th sub-problem are represented by x_k and x_j in part 1 of Step 2; hence, the resulting off-spring probably is a good candidates to be considered as an appropriate solution for the i-th sub-problem. When y violates any constraint, and/or optimizes the i-th $\mathbf{g^{te}}$, a heuristic is employed to repair y in Step 2.3. Thus the obtained solution y' is feasible with a lower function value for the neighbors of the i-th sub-problem. Step 2.4 considers the whole neighbors of the i-th sub-problem, and if y' accomplishes better than x_j due to the j-th sub-problem, it replaces x_j with y'. Since finding the actual ideal

vector z^* is often very time-consuming, z is used, and Step 1 initializes and Step 2.5 updates it. At the end off Step 2.6, the external population EP utilizes the newly-generated solution y' for its update.

In order to compare the effects of the decomposition methods on the results obtained, we also considered the weight sum approach in MOEA/D. In the whole document, T-MOEA/D stands for MOEA/D using the Tchebycheff approach as a decomposition method (i.e. using $\mathbf{g^{te}}$ function (2)) [25], whereas W-MOEA/D represents MOEA/D that decomposes MOP using the weight sum approach (i.e. using $\mathbf{g^{ws}}$ function (3)).

Algorithm 1. The MOEA/D general framework

Step 1 Initialization

- Set $EP = \varnothing$ and gen $= 0$.

- Generate an initial population $P_0\{X^1,...,X^N\}$ and initialize $z = (z_1,...,z_m)^T$ using the lowest value for f_i found in the initial population as z_i. Set $FV^i = F(X^i)$.

- Consider any two weight vectors, then calculate between them, and then work out the T closest weight vectors to each weight vector. For each I = 1,..., N, set $B(i) = \{i_1,...,i_T\}$, where $\lambda_1^i,...,\lambda_T^i$ are the T closet weight vectors to λ^i.

Step 2 Update: For I = 1, ..., N do

1. **Reproduction:** In a random manner, pick out two indices **k** and **l** from B(i), and then utilizing appropriate genetic operators generate a new solution y from X^k and X^l.

2. **Mutation:** Apply Mutation operator on y to produce Y'.

3. **Update of z:** For each $j = 1$, ..., m, if $f_j(Y') < z_j$, then set $z_j = f_j(Y')$.

4. **Update of Neighboring Solutions:** For each index $j \in B(i)$, if $g^{te}(Y'|\lambda^j,z) \leq g^{te}(X^j|\lambda^j,z)$, then set $X^j = Y'$ and $FV^j = F(Y')$.

5. **EP Update:**
   - Remove the whole vectors dominated by $F(Y')$ from EP.
   - If no vectors in EP dominates $F(Y')$, add $F(Y')$ to EP.

6. **Replacement:** Use binary tournament replacement strategy

Step 3 Stopping Criteria: If gen = gen$_{max}$, stop and output EP. Otherwise, gen = gen + 1, go to **Step 2**.

---

5. Hybrid multi-objective evolutionary algorithm/D-Tabu search

The main idea behind this work was to introduce a combination of recently developed multi-objective optimization algorithms, MOEA/D and Tabu Search, for an extensive and precise probe on different multi-objective problems. The result of this hybrid method is Pareto optimal solutions with uniform distribution that cover the Pareto front as much as possible [24]. Tabu search (TS), proposed by Glover [4], is a kind of metaheuristic algorithm that aims at finding good quality solutions in an admissible time using a local

search method. During the process of solution improvement, at first, the problem space was searched by TS for a potential solution x, and then other similar solutions in its neighboring N(x) were checked.

Trapping in the local optima were avoided in TS using a tabu list that remembers the history of the previous searches. Then the candidate solution with a better fitness value in the N(x) was selected as a destination for algorithm movement. The only forbidden moves are those leading to the solutions on the tabu list. The pseudo-code of Tabu Search is shown in Algorithm 2 [42].

Algorithm 2. TS general framework

Step 1: In a search space S, consider an initial solution

Set $i^* = i$ and $k = 0$

Step 2: $k = k + 1$

Make a subset of solutions in N(i,k) in a way that:
- The tabu movements are not chosen
- The aspiration criterion a(i,m) is applied
- At iteration k, N(i,k) is the neighborhood of the current solution i.

Step 3: Among N(i,k), find the best solution i', then apply $i = better\ i'$

Step 4: If $f(i) \leq f(i^*)$, then apply $i^* = i$

Step 5: Update the list T and aspiration criterion.

Step 6: If a stop condition is reached, then stop. Otherwise, return to Step 2.

For each individual, MOEA/D directly defines a single-objective optimization sub-problem, and then the computational effort is distributed among these sub-problems. This process is among the major reasons why MOEA/D outperforms NSGA-II-DE on a set of continuous test instances with complicated PS shapes [30]. The proposed method in this manuscript is based on Zhang and Hui [25], and our previous work [24] was based on cooperation between SPEA2 and TS. This method, namely MOEA/D-TS, employs a comprehensive search in two levels, one global and one local, among problem spaces. The areas with high potential solutions are found during the first level search, and at the second level, a local search tries to explore the best solutions with good distribution. In what follows, the main steps of the proposed method are described:

- Applying a global search to discover multiple optimal solutions at the first step is the MOEA/D's responsibility. A Pareto front of non-dominated solutions is produced within each iteration by MOEA/D, and then it generates and sets them as the starting points for the next steps.

- In the next step, a local search should be done among the solutions obtained from MOEA/D. The Improved Diversificator Tabu Search (IDTS) [24] is a good candidate to perform a local search in order to detect new solutions [24, 43]. The covering of the Pareto front with well-distributed solutions is a significant aim in this step.

The local search using IDTS for multi-objective problems includes two steps:

1. The first step detects a less explored zone of the search space, and performs a local search in order to discover new solutions. It finds two most distant and consecutive points (SL1 or SL2) on the Pareto Front. Then it calculates the middle point Cm (the middle vector cost of SL1 and SL2) to mark the best solution belonging to the hatched dominant zone Cm.

2. During the second step, this procedure continues IDTS between SL1 and Cm (finding a new point Cm1) and between Cm and SL2 (finding a new point Cm2) to explore the best solutions in the specified dominant regions [24].

Figure 1 shows the process of IDTS for a local search in a bi-objective problem space. This method, in comparison with the simple DTS [43], reduces unexplored areas within the problem space and distributes the resulting solution on the Pareto front uniformly [24].

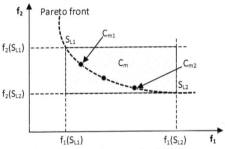

Figure 1. Search space for IDTS.

As mentioned earlier, in order to update the old population with promising solutions discovered by IDTS, the algorithm employs the binary tournament strategy. This population is used as an initial solution in the next generation. Figure 2 shows the pseudo-code of the proposed algorithm.

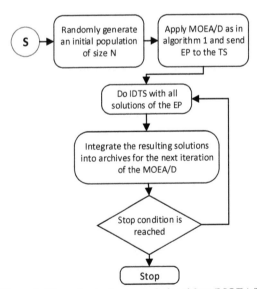

Figure 2. Flow chart of proposed algorithm (MOEA/D-TS).

6. Experimental study

In order to evaluate the capability of the proposed method and compare it with the other works in this field, namely SPEA, COMOEATS [43], and our previous algorithm SPEA2TS [24], the similar parameters as in [43] were considered and all three methods were implemented separately. The population size N was set to 100 and T in

MOEA/D-TS was considered 10% of N for all of the test instances. Table 1 illustrates the desired values for all parameters [43].

Table 1. Experimental parameters.

Parameter	Value
Initial Pop-Size (N)	100
Generation#	400
Crossover Probability (Pc)	0.9
Mutation Probability (Pm)	0.01
Tabu list size	50
Number of TS iterations	200
Tabu Life	50

The performance of the algorithm was studied on widely used bi-objective Zitzler-Deb-Thiele's test suite, namely (ZDT1 to ZDT4 and ZDT6) [44]. The test problems in the ZDT package introduce five basic functions including a distribution function f_1, a distance function g, and a shape function f_2, in which f_1 tests the ability of an MOEA to maintain diversity along the PF, function g is used for testing the ability of an MOEA to converge to PF, and function f_2 is used

to define the shape of PF. These various test problems have different characteristics. Specifically, ZDT3 has a disconnected PF, which is partly convex and partly concave; ZDT4 contains a large number of local PFs and ZDT6 has a non-uniform fitness landscape. All these test instances are minimization of the objectives, and except ZDT5, which is binary-coded, the others are real-coded.

Unlike test problems in the ZDT suite, which are all bi-objective, in the DTLZ package, the test problems are scalable to have any number of objectives [33]. Each one of the nine problems in the DTLZ test suite has many unique characteristics. For instance, DTLZ1 and DTLZ3 contain a large number of local PFs in their fitness landscape, and the Pareto optimal solutions of DTLZ4 have highly non-uniform distributions. According to the similar research works [6, 25], here, we evaluated the performance of the proposed method on DTLZ1 and DTLZ2 with three objective functions. Table 2 shows the properties of these test problems.

Table 2. Experimental parameters.

Test function	Search space	Objectives	Pareto front type
ZDT1	$[0,1]^n$	$f_1(x) = x_1$ $f_2(x) = g(x)[1 - \sqrt{f_1(x)/g(x)}]$ $g(x) = 1 + 9(\sum_{i=2}^{n}(x_i - 0.2)^2)/(n-1)$	convex
ZDT2	$[0, 1]^n$	$f_1(x) = x_1$ $f_2(x) = g(x)[1 - (f_1(x)/g(x))^2]$ $g(x) = 1 + 9(\sum_{i=2}^{n}(x_i - 0.2)^2)/(n-1)$	Non-convex
ZDT3	$[0, 1]^n$	$f_1(x) = x_1$ $f_2(x) = g(x)[1 - \sqrt{f_1(x)/g(x)} - \frac{x_1}{g(x)}\sin(10\pi x_1)]$ $g(x) = 1 + 9(\sum_{i=2}^{n}(x_i - 0.2)^2)/(n-1)$	disconnected
DTLZ1	$[0, 1]n$	$f_1(x) = (1+g(x))x_1 x_2$ $f_2(x) = (1+g(x))x_1(1-x_2)$ $f_3(x) = (1+g(x))(1-x_1)$ $g(x) = 100(n-2) + 100(\sum_{i=3}^{n}\{(x_i - 0.5)^2 - \cos[20\pi(x_i - 0.5)]\}$	Non-convex
DTLZ2	$[0, 1]^n \times [-1, 1]^{n-2}$	$f_1(x) = (1+g(x))\cos(\frac{x_1\pi}{2})\cos(\frac{x_2\pi}{2})$ $f_2(x) = (1+g(x))\cos(\frac{x_1\pi}{2})\sin(\frac{x_2\pi}{2})$ $f_3(x) = (1+g(x))\sin(\frac{x_1\pi}{2})$ $g(x) = \sum_{i=3}^{n}x_i^2$	Non-convex

There are some well-known metrics that are used to have comparison among the developed approaches [45]. These four metrics include:
Spacing: In an objective space, this metric expresses the uniformity of the solution

distribution. The spacing metric calculates the distance between solutions and gives an interesting indication on the convergence of the considered method [46].

Contribution: This metric evaluates the proportion of Pareto solution brought by each one of the two (or three) foreheads F1 and F2 (and F3) [47].

Entropy: Solution entropy should be calculated to evaluate the distribution of solutions on the Pareto front. The closer the values to 1, the better the solution distribution.

Metric S: This metric (that is also known as hyper-volume) measures the quality for solution sets in Pareto optimization. The Pareto front and a desired reference point are considered, and this metric calculates the hyper-volume of the multi-dimensional region between them [46].

7. Results and discussion

In this section, some simulation results and comparisons that prove the potential of MOEA/D-TS are presented. Table 3 represents a comparison between the results obtained using different algorithms (SPEA, COMOEATS, and SPEA2TS) at the level of four mentioned metrics on ZDT1 benchmark. The attained results of applying MOEA/D-TS on this convex POF show significant improvements in all the four metric values. The different values related to the spacing metric prove the capability of MOEA/D-TS to generate more uniform Pareto optimal solutions than the three other methods. In this way, more discovered zones can be covered with a good uniform distribution. Moreover, the outcomes of table 3 depict that using the Tchebycheff approach as a decomposition method in MOEA/D-TS (i.e. T-MOEA/D) in most cases (except metric S) leads to better results in comparison with exploiting the weighted sum approach for decomposition (i.e. W-MOEA/D).

The statistics of the values obtained by each algorithm in ZDT2 are represented in table 4. Here, we are faced with a non-convex POF. It is obvious from the results that MOEA/D-TS outperforms other methods due to the three metrics except entropy. Although the new method did not have enough power to overcome SPEA2TS, it achieved better results in comparison with the other algorithms.

Tables 5-7 depict the various results obtained by each algorithm in ZDT3 (with a discontinuous PF), ZDT4, and ZDT6 test functions, respectively. For these problems, our proposed algorithm

shows its ability to achieve interesting results at the level of all four metrics.

Tables 8 and 9 compare the results obtained by different algorithms in the three-objective problems DTLZ1 and DTLZ2. It is quite clear from these results that MOEA/D-TS performs much better than the other algorithms at the level of four criteria, and using the Tchebycheff decomposition approach compared with the weighted sum approach mainly achieves more satisfactory outcomes in these three-objective instances.

According to the attained results presented in table 3-9, the MOEA/D-TS is able to handle various multi-objective problems having two and three objective and convex, non-convex, and discontinuous POFs. In addition, it is obvious that T-MOEA/D achieves better results than W-MOEA/D at most of the metrics except *metric S* at ZDT1, ZDT2, and DTLZ1, and also metric *Spacing* at ZDT3. These results may be due to the one weakness of the Tchebycheff approach, in which the aggregation function is not smooth for continuous MOPs (i.e. ZDT1, ZDT2, and DTLZ1) [25]. In this case, calculation of the hyper-volume of the multi-dimensional region between Pareto front and desired reference point (i.e. metric S) is complicated.

In order to visually compare the performance of the four algorithms, the solutions obtained by them in these test problems are shown in figures 4 and 5. These figures show the distributions of the solutions on Pareto fronts in 30 independent runs. The comparisons mainly focus on two aspects: 1) the coverage of the solutions obtained to the true PF; and 2) the diversity of the solutions obtained. Obviously, both SPEA and COMOEATS cannot locate the global PF in any instance, and the results attained by SPEA2TS are not completely satisfactory. In contrast, MOEA/D-TS can approximate the PFs of these instances quite well. These solutions obtained by MOEA/D-TS have covered most of less discovered zones, with a uniform distribution that confirm our claim about the effect of IDTS to cover most of the unexplored zones of the Pareto front. These results indicate that the diversity and coverage of solutions obtained by the algorithm MOEA/D-TS are better than those obtained by SPEA, COMOEATS, and even SPEA2TS on these test problems.

Table 3. Metrics values for ZDT1.

Algorithm Metric	SPEA	COMOEATS	SPEA2TS	MOEA/D-TS	
				W-MOEA/D	T-MOEA/D
Spacing	0.0203861	0.0256606	0.0234362	0.0206327	0.018847
Contribution	0.492958	0.507042	0.556231	0.56035	0.591044
Entropy	0.360803	0.367399	0.505162	0.58183	0.61354
Metric S	0.5524335	0.55787	0.56085	0.55572	0.55924

Table 4. Metrics values for ZDT2.

Algorithm Metric	SPEA	COMOEATS	SPEA2TS	MOEA/D-TS	
				W-MOEA/D	T-MOEA/D
Spacing	0.0203861	0.0276606	0.018173	0.014208	0.011386
Contribution	0.492958	0.507092	0.566471	0.58363	0.62043
Entropy	0.360803	0.371775	0.517232	0.42522	0.48803
Metric S	0.5524335	0.55689	0.542853	0.40917	0.47261

Table 5. Metrics values for ZDT3.

Algorithm Metric	SPEA	COMOEATS	SPEA2TS	MOEA/D-TS	
				W-MOEA/D	T-MOEA/D
Spacing	0.0206785	0.0116797	0.0074512	0.002258	0.009341
Contribution	0.496454	0.507042	0.627452	0.84512	0.95386
Entropy	0.365199	0.373243	0.387123	0.402102	0.449638
Metric S	0.750998	0.741164	0.725361	0.677366	0.651146

Table 6. Metrics values for ZDT4.

Algorithm Metric	SPEA	COMOEATS	SPEA2TS	MOEA/D-TS	
				W-MOEA/D	T-MOEA/D
Spacing	0.0224316	0.0263217	0.023267	0.018803	0.012651
Contribution	0.462758	0.507092	0.523716	0.58363	0.60342
Entropy	0.362131	0.40721	0.503571	0.52058	0.54507
Metric S	0.529386	0.52309	0.5201453	0.50152	0.48713

Table 7. Metrics values for ZDT6.

Algorithm Metric	SPEA	COMOEATS	SPEA2TS	MOEA/D-TS	
				W-MOEA/D	T-MOEA/D
Spacing	0.0220126	0.0270117	0.023267	0.018803	0.012651
Contribution	0.483217	0.490278	0.523716	0.58363	0.60342
Entropy	0.362891	0.41834	0.503571	0.52058	0.54507
Metric S	0.741834	0.725037	0.720341	0.693617	0.67571

Table 8. Metrics values for DTLZ1.

Algorithm Metric	SPEA	COMOEATS	SPEA2TS	MOEA/D-TS	
				W-MOEA/D	T-MOEA/D
Spacing	0.27318	0.24533	0.13867	0.10391	0.08651
Contribution	0.52174	0.57723	0.60265	0.63241	0.65829
Entropy	0.394321	0.43145	0.577141	0.70148	0.72328
Metric S	0.83307	0.82198	0.80721	0.71057	0.75251

Table 9. Metrics values for DTLZ2.

Algorithm Metric	SPEA	COMOEATS	SPEA2TS	MOEA/D-TS	
				W-MOEA/D	T-MOEA/D
Spacing	0.15257	0.12324	0.10015	0.08391	0.05651
Contribution	0.54812	0.57034	0.59107	0.67763	0.69135
Entropy	0.362031	0.39557	0.421972	0.53261	0.58204
Metric S	0.78307	0.731078	0.70681	0.67152	0.63142

8. Summary and conclusion

In this paper, we proposed a hybrid method derived from Multi-Objective Evolutionary Algorithm based on Decomposition (MOEA/D) and Tabu Search (TS) for solving various multi-objective optimization problems. This algorithm, namely MOEA/D-TS, at its first level uses the capabilities of MOEA/D for exploration of the problem space by decomposing MOP into single-objective optimization sub-problems. An Improved Diversificator Tabu Search (IDTS) is utilized to perform local search among the problem space at the second level. The main goal of IDTS is achievement to a Pareto front with minimum unknown parts and well-distributed solutions. The experimental results considering seven benchmarks with different numbers of objective functions and various POF demonstrate that MOEA/D-TS has more functionality than SPEA, COMOEATS, and SPEA2TS to discover solution sets with a better quality. Also the results obtained indicate that using the Tchebycheff approach as a decomposition method in these kinds of problems will lead to better values than using the weighted sum decomposition approach. The main reason is that the weighted sum approach is compatible with concave (convex in the case of minimization) PFs, and not every Pareto optimal vector can be obtained by this approach in the case of non-concave PFs.

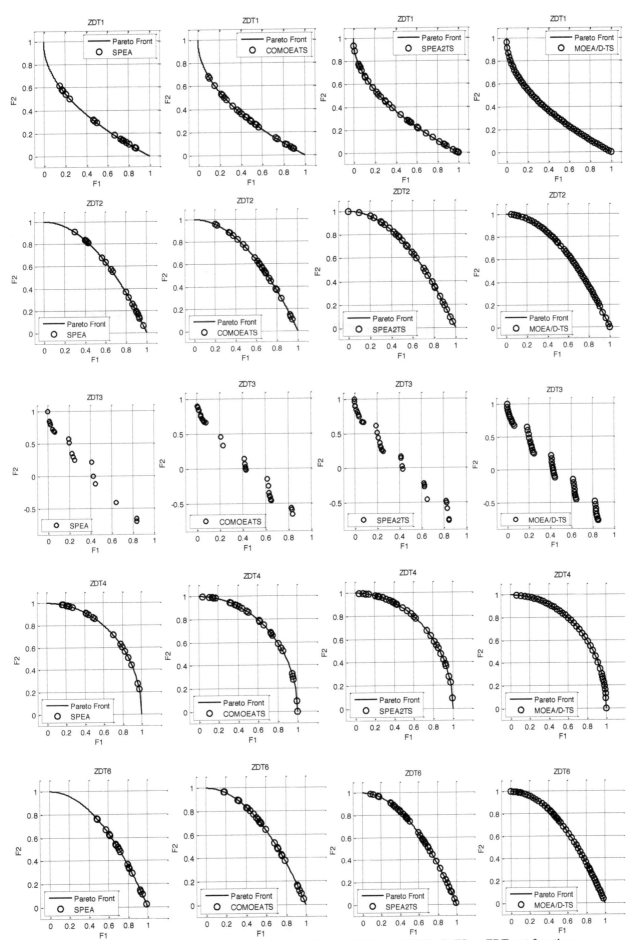

Figure 3. Solutions obtained by SPEA, COMOEATS, SPEA2TS, and MOEA/D-TS on ZDT test functions.

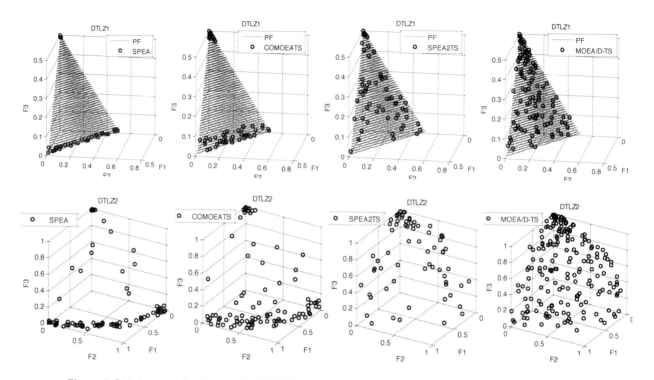

Figure 4. Solutions obtained by SPEA, COMOEATS, SPEA2TS, and MOEA/D-TS on DTLZ test function.

References

[1] Marler, R. T. & Arora, J. S. (2004). Survay of multi-objective optimization methods for engineering. Structural and Multidisciplinary Optimization, vol. 26, no. 6, pp. 369-395.

[2] Suman, B. (2004). Study of simulated annealing based algorithms for multiobjective optimization of a constrained problem. Computers and Chemical Engineering, vol. 28, pp. 1849-1871.

[3] Fonseca, C. M. & Fleming, P. J. (1995). An overview of evolutionary algorithms in multiobjective optimization, Evolutionary Computation., vol. 3, no. 1, pp. 1-16.

[4] Valenzuela-Rend'on, M. & Uresti-Charre, E. (1997). A nongenerational genetic algorithm for multiobjective optimization, 7th Int. Conf. GeneticAlgorithms, T. B"ack, Ed. San Francisco, CA: Morgan Kaufmann, pp. 658-665.

[5] Srinivas N. & Deb K., (1994). Multiobjective optimization using nondominated sorting in genetic algorithms, Evolutionary Computation vol. 2, no. 3, pp. 221-248.

[6] Dai, C. & Wang, Y. (2014). A New Multiobjective Evolutionary Algorithm Based on Decomposition of the Objective Space for Multiobjective Optimization, Journal of Applied Mathematics, vol. 2014, Article ID 906147, 9 pages, 2014. doi:10.1155/2014/906147.

[7] Gong, M., et al. (2008). Multiobjective immune algorithm with nondominated neighbor-based selection, Evolutionary Computation, vol. 16, no. 2, pp. 225-255.

[8] Konak, A., Coit, D. W. & Smith, A. E. (2006) Multi-objective optimization using genetic algorithms: a tutorial, Reliability Engineering and System Safety, vol. 91, no. 9, pp. 992-1007.

[9] Chang, P.-C. & Chen, S.-H. (2009). The development of a sub-population genetic algorithm II (SPGA II) for multi-objective combinatorial problems, Appl. Soft Comput., vol. 9, no. 1, pp. 173-181.

[10] Deb, K., et al. (2002). A fast and elitist multiobjective genetic algorithm: NSGA-II, IEEE Transactionson Evolutionary Computation, vol. 6, no. 2, pp. 182-197.

[11] Liu, R., et al. (2013). A preference multi-objective optimization based on adaptive rank clone and differential evolution, Natural Computing, vol. 12, no. 1, pp. 109-132.

[12] Matjaz, D., Roman, T. & Bogdan, F. (2013). Asynchronous masterslave parallelization of differential evolution for multi-objective optimization, Evolutionary Computation, vol. 21, no. 2, pp. 261-291.

[13] Goh, C. K., et al. (2010). A competitive and cooperative co-evolutionary approach to multi-objective particle swarm optimization algorithm design, European Journal of Operational Research, vol. 202, no. 1, pp. 42-54.

[14] Gómez, R., Coello Coello, C. A. & Alba Torres E. (2016). A Multi-Objective Evolutionary Algorithm based on Parallel Coordinates, In Proceedings of the Genetic and Evolutionary Computation Conference 2016 (GECCO '16), Tobias Friedrich (Ed.). ACM, New York, NY, USA, pp. 565-572.

[15] Guo, W., et al. (2016). Hyper multi-objective evolutionary algorithm for multi-objective optimization problems, soft computing, pp. 1-9, doi:10.1007/s00500-016-2163-5.

[16] Guo, W., et al. (2016). A multiobjective evolutionary algorithm based on decision variable analyses for multiobjective optimization problems with large-scale variables, IEEE Transactions on Evolutionary Computation, vol. 20, no. 2, pp. 275-298.

[17] Paquete, L. & Stutzle, T. (2013). MOEA/D-ACO: A Multiobjective Evolutionary Algorithm Using Decomposition and Ant Colony, IEEE Transactions On Cybernetics, vol. 43, no. 6, pp. 1845-1859.

[18] Fonseca, C. M. & Fleming, P. J. (1993). Genetic algorithms for multiobjective optimization: Formulation, discussion and generalization, In S. Forrest (Ed.), Proceedings of the Fifth International Conference on Genetic Algorithms, San Mateo, California, pp. 416-423.

[19] Horn, J., Nafpliotis, N. & Goldberg, D. E. (1994). A niched pareto genetic algorithm for multiobjective optimization, First IEEE Conferenceon Evolutionary Computation, IEEE World Congress on Computational Computation, vol. 1, Piscataway, NJ, pp. 82-87.

[20] Naujoks, B., Beume, N. & Emmerich, M. (2005). Multi-objective Optimisation using S-metric Selection: Application to three-dimensional Solution Spaces, 2005 IEEE Congress on Evolutionary Computation, pp. 1282-1289.

[21] Zitzler, E., Deb, K. & Thiele, L. (2000). Comparison of multiobjective evolutionary algorithms: Empirical results, Evolutionary Computation, vol. 8, no. 173, pp. 173-195.

[22] Zitzler E. & Thiele, L. (1998). Multiobjective optimization using evolutionary algorithms: A comparative case study, In A. E. Eiben, T. Back, M. Schoenauer, H. P. Schwefel (Eds.), Parallel problem solving from Nature, vol. V, p. 292-301, Berlin, Germany: Springer.

[23] Zitzler E., Laumanns, M. & Thiele, L. (2002). SPEA2: Improving the Strength Pareto Evolutionary Algorithm, from Evolutionary Methods for Design, Optimisation and Control, CIMNE, Barcelona, Spain.

[24] Karimi, F. & Lotfi, Sh. (2014). Solving multi-objective problems using SPEA2 and Tabu search, Intelligent Systems (ICIS), Iranian Conference on, IEEE.

[25] Zhang, Q. & Hui, L. (2007). A Multi-objective Evolutionary Algorithm Based on Decomposition, Evolutionary Computation, IEEE Transactions on, vol. 11, no. 6, pp. 712-731.

[26] Ishibuchi, H. & Murata, T. (1998). Multi-objective genetic local search algorithm and its application to flowshop scheduling, IEEE Transactions on Systems, Man and Cybernetics, vol. 28, no. 3, pp. 392-403.

[27] Leung, Y. W. & Wang, Y. (2000). Multiobjective programming using uniform design and genetic algorithm. IEEE Transactions on Systems, Man, and Cybernetics, Part C, vol. 30, no. 3, pp. 293-304.

[28] Jin, Y., Okabe, T. & Sendhoff, B. (2001). Adapting weighted aggregation for multiobjective evolutionary strategies, in EMO '01: Evolutionary Multicriterion OPtimization, Springer LNCS, pp. 96-110.

[29] Cheng, R., et al. (2016). Test Prblems for Large-Scale Multiobjective and Many-Objective Optimization, IEEE Transactions on Cybernetics, Epub, vol. PP, Issue 99, pp. 1-14.

[30] Zhang, Q. & Li, H. (2009). Comparison Between NSGA-II and MOEA/D on a Set of Multiobjective Optimization Problems with Complicated Pareto Sets, Evolutionary Computation, IEEE Transactions on, vol. 13, no. 2, pp. 284-302.

[31] Motameni, H. (2016). PSO for multi-objective problems: Criteria for leader selection and uniformity distribution, Journal of AI and Data Mining, Vol. 4, No. 1, pp. 67-76.

[32] Miettinen, K. (1999). Nonlinear Multiobjective Optimization. Kluwer Academic Publishers.

[33] Ma, X., et al. (2016). Multiobjective Evolutionary Algorithm Based on Decision Variable Analyses for MultiobjectiveOptimization Problems With Large-Scale Variables, IEEE Transactions On Evolutionary computation, vol. 20, no. 2, pp. 275-298.

[34] Ulungu, E., et al. (1999). Mosa method: A tool for solving multiobjective combinatorial optimization problem, Journal of Multi-Criteria Decision Analysis, vol. 8, no. 4, pp. 221-236.

[35] Paquete, L. & Stutzle, T. (2003). A two-phase local search for the biobjective traveling salesman problem. in EMO, pp. 479-493.

[36] Jaszkiewicz, A. (2002). On the performance of multiple-objective genetic local search on the 0:1 knapsack problem-a comparative experiment, IEEE Trans. Evolutionary Computation, vol. 6, no. 4, pp. 402-412.

[37] Shim, V. A., Tan, K. C. & Tan, K. K. (2012). A hybrid estimation of distribution algorithm for solving the multi-objective multiple traveling salesman problem, in Proceedings of the IEEE Congress on Evolutionary Computation (CEC'12), pp. 1-8.

[38] Chan, Y.-H., Chiang, T.-C. & Fu, L.-C. (2010). A two-phase evolutionary algorithm for multiobjective mining of classification rules, in Proceedings of the IEEE Congress on Evolutionary Computation (CEC'10).

[39] Mashwani, W. K. (2011). MOEA/D with DE and PSO: MOEA/DDE+PSO, in Proceedings of the 31st SGAI International Conference on Innovative Techniques and Applications of Artificial Intelligence, pp. 217-221.

[40] Özdemir, S., Attea, B. A. & Khalil, Ö. A. (2012). Multi-Objective Evolutionary Algorithm Based on Decomposition for Energy Efficient Coverage in Wireless Sensor Networks, springer, pp. 1-6.

[41] Miettinen, K. (1999). Nonlinear Multiobjective Optimization. Kluwer Academic Publishers.

[42] Jaszkiewicz, A. (2002). On the performance of multiple-objective genetic local search on the 0/1 knapsack problem - a comparative experiment, IEEE Trans. Evolutionary Computation, vol. 6, no. 4, pp. 402-412.

[43] Hajlaoui, R., Gzara, M. & Abdelaziz, D. (2011). Hybrid Model for Solving Multi-Objective Problems Using Evolutionary Algorithm and Tabu Search, World of Computer Science and Information Technology Journal, vol. 1, no. 1, pp. 5-9.

[44] Okabe, T., et al. (2004). On test functions for evolutionary multi-objective optimization, in Parallel Problem Solving from Nature. Springer, pp. 792-80.

[45] ZeinEldin, R. A. (2014). A Hybrid SS-SA Approach for Solving Multi-Objective Optimization Problems, European Journal of Scientific Research, vol. 121, no. 3, pp. 310-320.

[46] Naujoks, B., Beume, N. & Emmerich, M. (2005). Multi-objective Optimisation using S-metric Selection: Application to three-dimensional Solution Spaces, IEEE.

[47] Haussler, D. & Opper, M. (1997). Mutual information, metric entropy and cumulative relative entropy risk, Ann. Statist., vol. 25, no. 6, pp. 2451-2492.

19

Winner Determination in Combinatorial Auctions using Hybrid Ant Colony Optimization and Multi-Neighborhood Local Search

M. B. Dowlatshahi and V. Derhami[*]

Computer Engineering Department, Yazd University, Yazd, Iran.

*Corresponding author: vderhami@yazduni.ac.ir (V. Derhami).

Abstract

A combinatorial auction is an auction where the bidders have the choice to bid on bundles of items. The Winner Determination Problem (WDP) in combinatorial auctions is the problem of finding winning bids that maximize the auctioneer's revenue under constraint, where each item can be allocated to at most one bidder. WDP is known as an NP-hard problem with practical applications like electronic commerce, production management, games theory, and resource allocation in multi-agent systems. This has motivated the quest for efficient approximate algorithms in terms of both the solution quality and computational time. This paper proposes a hybrid Ant Colony Optimization with a novel Multi-Neighborhood Local Search (ACO-MNLS) algorithm for solving WDP in combinatorial auctions. Our proposed MNLS algorithm uses the fact that using various neighborhoods in local search can generate different local optima for WDP and that the global optima of WDP is a local optima for a given neighborhood. Therefore, the proposed MNLS algorithm simultaneously explores a set of three different neighborhoods to get different local optima and to escape from the local optima. The comparisons between ACO-MNLS, Genetic Algorithm (GA), Memetic Algorithm (MA), Stochastic Local Search (SLS), and Tabu Search (TS) on various benchmark problems confirm the efficiency of the ACO-MNLS algorithm in terms of both the solution quality and computational time.

Keywords: *Winner Determination Problem, Combinatorial Auctions, Ant Colony Optimization, Multi-Neighborhood Local Search, Combinatorial Optimization.*

1. Introduction

Auctions play a significant role in multi-agent systems, where the auction mechanisms are used for task distribution and resource allocation. The items that are auctioned range from network bandwidth to radio frequencies, and pollution rights. Combinatorial Auction (CA) is a sort of auctions in which bidders (agents) can place bids on combinations of items (goods) rather than only the individual ones. Buyers offer their bids to auctioneer, each bid being defined by a subset of items with a price (bidder's valuation). Two bids are conflicting if they share at least one item. The main advantage of combinatorial auction is that it produces a high economic efficiency [1].

The Winner Determination Problem (WDP) in combinatorial auctions is defined as finding a conflict-free allocation of items that maximize the

auctioneer's revenue. WDP is equivalent to the weighted set packing problem, a well-known NP-hard problem [2-4]. From a practical viewpoint, WDP has many applications in electronic commerce, production management, game theory, and resource allocation in multi-agents systems [5-8].

The computational challenge of WDP and its wide practical applications have motivated a variety of algorithms. These algorithms can be classified as either "exact" or "approximate". Exact algorithms can obtain optimal solutions and guarantee their optimality for every instance of WDP. However, it has been shown that for optimization problems that are NP-hard, no polynomial time algorithm exists unless $P = NP$ [3,9]. Therefore, exact algorithms for WDP require exponential time, and this makes them impractical for most real-world applications. In contrast to exact algorithms, approximate algorithms do not guarantee the optimality of the solutions obtained. In these algorithms, the optimal solution is sacrificed for the sake of obtaining good solutions in a reasonable time [10-12].

Approximate algorithms may be classified into three classes: approximation algorithms, problem-specific heuristics, and metaheuristics. Unlike problem-specific heuristics and metaheuristics, approximation algorithms provide a provable solution quality and run-time bounds. Problem-specific heuristics are problem-dependent and are designed for a particular problem, whereas metaheuristics represent more general approximate algorithms and are applicable to a large variety of optimization problems. Metaheuristics solve complex optimization problems by "exploring" the large solution space and achieve this goal by effectively reducing the size of this space and "exploiting" the reduced space efficiently [10,11,13]. This class of algorithms includes Evolutionary Computation (EC) [14], Ant Colony Optimization (ACO) [15], Greedy Randomized Adaptive Search Procedure (GRASP) [16], Tabu Search (TS) [17], Variable Neighborhood Search (VNS) [18], Iterated Local Search (ILS) [19], Particle Swarm Optimization (PSO) [20], Gravitational Search Algorithm (GSA) [21], etc.

In this paper, we propose a hybrid Ant Colony Optimization with Multi-Neighborhood Search (ACO-MNLS) algorithm for solving WDP. The experimental results obtained by the proposed algorithm are compared with the results of Genetic Algorithm (GA), Memetic Algorithm (MA), Stochastic Local Search (SLS), and Tabu Search (TS). The comparisons confirm the efficiency of ACO-MNLS in terms of solution quality and computational time.

The rest of the paper is organized as what follows. In Section 2, we present the formal definition of WDP and provide an overview of the existing algorithms for WDP. Section 3 provides a review of ACO. In Section 4, the proposed ACO-MNLS algorithm for WDP is presented. Section 5 contains the experimental part of the paper, in which the performance of the proposed approach is evaluated. Finally, in Section 6, conclusion is given.

2. Winner Determination Problem and existing algorithms
2.1. Winner Determination Problem

In this section, we discuss WDP and winner determination algorithms for combinatorial auctions. Let us say that the auctioneer has a set of items, $M = \{1, 2, ..., m\}$, to sell, and the buyers propose a set of bids, $B = \{b_1, b_2, ..., b_n\}$. A bid is a tuple $b_j = (S_j, p_j)$, where $S_j \subseteq M$ is a set of items and $p_j \geq 0$ is price of b_j, which is a positive real number that shows the value the buyer is willing to pay for bundle S_j. Further, consider a matrix $a_{m \times n}$ having m rows and n columns, where $a_{ij} = 1$ if item i belongs to S_j, $a_{ij} = 0$, otherwise. Finally, the decision variables are defined as follow: $x_j = 1$ if bid b_j is accepted (a winning bid), and $x_j = 0$ otherwise (a losing bid). WDP is the problem of finding the winning bids that maximize the auctioneer's revenue under the constraint that each item can be allocated to the most bidder. WDP can be modeled as the following integer optimization problem [22]:

$$Maximize \quad \sum_{j=1}^{n} p_j x_j, \tag{1}$$

$$Subject\ to \quad \sum_{j=1}^{n} a_{ij} x_j \leq 1, \quad i \in \{1,...,m\}, \tag{2}$$

$$x_j \in \{0,1\}, \tag{3}$$

where, the objective function given in (1) maximizes the auctioneer's revenue that is computed as the sum of prices of the winning bids. The constraints given in (2) mean that the item can be allocated to at most one bidder. The inequality $(a_{ij} x_j \leq 1)$ allows that some items could be left uncovered. This is due to the free disposal assumption.

Example 1: Consider a combinatorial auction with a set of five items $M = \{1, 2, 3, 4, 5\}$ to be auctioned and a set of five bids $B = \{b_1, b_2, b_3, b_4, b_5\}$ that are the following:

$$b_1 = (\{1, 3\}, 5.5)$$
$$b_2 = (\{1, 3, 4\}, 15)$$
$$b_3 = (\{2\}, 1)$$
$$b_4 = (\{2, 4\}, 12)$$
$$b_5 = (\{4\}, 8)$$
$$b_6 = (\{4, 5\}, 10).$$

Note that the combined value of the two bids for the individual items 2 and 4 is lower than the value of the bundle bid for both (b_4), which reflects the complementarity of these items. Let us consider the allocations $A_1 = \{b_2, b_4\}$ and $A_2 = \{b_1,$

b_4}. While A_2 is feasible, A_1 is infeasible because b_2 and b_4 both require item 4. The value for A_2 is 17.5, which is the maximum value over all possible feasible allocations for this problem instance. Under the optimal allocation A_2, bids b_1 and b_4 win, with items 1 and 3 assigned to b_1 and items 2 and 4 assigned to b_4. Note that item 5 remains unassigned under this allocation; there is a feasible allocation that assigns all items to bids ($A_3 = \{b_1, b_3, b_6\}$) but its value is lower than 17.5.

2.2. Existing algorithms

Attempts to exactly solve WDP (under the name of set packing) can be found as early as in the beginning of 1970s [23]. Many studies have appeared ever since. Most exact algorithms are based on the general branch-and-bound (B&B) technique. Some examples include the combinatorial auction structural search (CASS) [2], Combinatorial Auction Multi-Unit Search (CAMUS) [24], BOB algorithm [25], CABOB algorithm [26], and linear programming-based B&B algorithm [27]. Other interesting exact methods for WDP are a branch-and-price algorithm based on a set packing formulation [28], a branch-and-cut algorithm [29], and a dynamic programming algorithm [30]. The general integer programming approach based on CPLEX has been intensively studied in [31,32], showing an excellent performance in many cases. In [33], a clique-based branch-and-bound approach has been introduced for WDP, which relies on a transformation of WDP into the maximum weight clique problem. To ensure the efficiency of the proposed search algorithm, specific bounding and branching strategies using a dedicated vertex coloring procedure and a specific vertex sorting technique has been proposed. In [34], Complete Set Partitioning problem captures the special case of WDP in combinatorial auctions, where bidders place bids on every possible bundle of goods, and the goal is to find an allocation of goods to bidders that maximizes the profit of the auctioneer.

On the other hand, given the intrinsic intractability of WDP, various heuristic algorithms have been devised to handle problems whose optimal solutions cannot be reached by exact approaches. For instance, Casanova [35] is a well-known stochastic local search algorithm that explores the space of feasible allocations (non-overlapping subsets of bids) by adding at each step an unallocated bid and removing from the allocation the bids that are conflicting with the added bid. The selection rule employed by Casanova takes into consideration both the quality and history information of the bid. Casanova has been shown to be able to find high quality solutions much faster than the CASS algorithm [2]. WDP is also modeled as a set packing problem and is solved by a simulated annealing algorithm (SAGII) with three different local move operators: an embedded branch-and-bound move, greedy local search move, and exchange move [32]. SAGII outperforms dramatically Casanova and the CPLEX 8.0 solver for realistic test instances. A memetic algorithm has been proposed by [36], which combines a local search component with a specific crossover operator. The local search component adds at each iteration either a random bid with a probability p or a best bid with the largest profit with probability 1-p, and then removes the conflicting bids from the allocation. This hybrid algorithm reaches excellent results on the tested realistic instances. Other interesting heuristics include greedy algorithm [37], a tabu search algorithm [38], an equilibrium-based local search method [39], and a recombination-based tabu search algorithm [40]. In [41], a new mathematical formulation for WDP (under the name of set packing) and an efficient method for generating near-optimal solution have been proposed. In [42], a mathematical model that aims to maximize the expected economization of procurement has been established and a solution algorithm based on genetic algorithm (GA), where an order encoding scheme is designed and a special repair method is employed to accomplish the translation from the individual encoding to the corresponding solution of WDP, has been proposed. In [43], a stochastic hyper-heuristic (SHH) for combining heuristics for solving WDP has been proposed, in which a new idea is developed for hyper-heuristics by combining choice function and randomness strategies. In [44], an agent learning approach has been proposed for solving WDP, in which a Lagrangian relaxation approach is used to develop an efficient multi-agent learning algorithm. In [45], the authors have presented a metaheuristic approach for the bi-objective WDP, which integrates the greedy randomized adaptive search procedure with a two-stage candidate component selection procedure, large neighborhood search, and self-adaptive parameter setting in order to find a competitive set of non-dominated solutions.

From the above-mentioned review, we observe that the existing (exact and heuristic) methods follow two solution strategies. The first one is to consider directly WDP and design dedicated algorithms. This is the case for most of the reviewed methods. The second one is to recast WDP as another related problem P and then solved with a solution method designed for P. Examples have been given in [23,32], where WDP is modeled as the set packing problem and in [26, 31], where WDP is reformulated as an integer programming problem and solved by the general CPLEX solver.

2.3. Disadvantages of existing algorithms

The existing exact algorithms to solve WDP [23-34] have an exponential time complexity, and this makes them impractical for most real-world instances of WDP. On the other hand, although heuristic algorithms used to solve WDP [35-45] have a polynomial time complexity, they have a low efficiency and a low effectiveness. To the best of our knowledge, the best results of direct heuristic methods come from a Memetic Algorithm (MA) proposed by [34]. In Section 5, we will see that the proposed ACO-MNLS algorithm outperforms the GA, MA, SLS, and TS algorithms in terms of the computational time, and overcomes the GA, TS, MA, and SLS algorithms in terms of the solution quality in most problems, whereas in the case of other problems, both ACO-MNLS and other algorithms get the same results.

3. Ant Colony Optimization

Ant Colony Optimization (ACO) algorithms are constructive stochastic metaheuristics that make use of a pheromone model and heuristic information on the problem being tackled in order to probabilistically construct solutions. A pheromone model is a set of pheromone trail parameters whose numerical values can be obtained by a reinforcement type of learning mechanism and show the search experience of the algorithm. Therefore, the pheromone model can be used to bias the solution construction over time towards the regions of the solution space containing high quality solutions. Note that the stochastic procedure in ACO permits the ants to explore a much larger number of solutions; meanwhile, the use of heuristic information guides the ants towards the most promising solutions.

Several ACO algorithms for NP-hard problems have been proposed in the literature. Ant System (AS) was proposed as the first ACO algorithm for the well-known Traveling Salesman Problem (TSP) [49]. The Ant Colony System (ACS) [50] and the MAX–MIN Ant System (MMAS) algorithm [51] are among the most successful ACO variants in practice. In order to provide a unifying view to identify the most important

aspects of these algorithms, [52], put them in a general framework by defining the ACO metaheuristic. The template of this ACO metaheuristic has been shown in Algorithm (1). After initializing parameters and pheromone trails, the metaheuristic iterates over three phases. At each iteration, a number of solutions are constructed by the ants; these solutions are then improved through a local search (this step is optional), and finally, the pheromone trails are updated.

Algorithm (1): Template of Ant Colony Optimization.
Set parameters;
Initialize the pheromone trails;
Repeat
For *each ant* ***Do***
Solution construction using the pheromone trail;
Solution improvement using local search;
Update the pheromone trails:
Evaporation ;
Reinforcement ;
Endfor
Until *stopping criteria are satisfied.*
Output: *Best solution found.*

The *solution construction* is done by a probabilistic rule. Each artificial ant can be considered as a stochastic greedy algorithm that constructs a solution probabilistically by adding solution components to partial ones until a complete solution is derived. This stochastic greedy algorithm takes into account the followings:

Pheromone trails that memorize the patterns of "good" constructed solutions, and will guide the construction of new solutions. The pheromone trails change dynamically during the search to store the obtained knowledge of problem.

Heuristic information that gives more hints about most promising solutions to ants in their decisions to construct solutions.

The *solution improvement* is a local search method that starts with an initial solution and follows moves from the current solution to a neighbor. Many strategies can be used in the selection of a neighbor such as: (1) Best improvement selection strategy, in which the best neighbor (i.e. the neighbor that improves the objective function the most) is selected, (2) First improvement selection strategy, which consists of choosing the first improving neighbor that is better than the current solution, and (3) Random selection strategy, in which a random selection is applied to the neighbors of the current solution. The process of exchanging the current solution with a neighbor is continued until the stopping criteria are satisfied [53]. Note that solution improvement is an optional component of ACO, although it has been shown that it can improve the performance of ACO when static combinatorial optimization problems are considered. An explanation of the good performance of a combination of ACO with local search can be found in the fact that these two search methods are complementary. An ACO algorithm usually performs a rather coarse-grained search. Therefore, it is a good idea to try and improve its solutions locally.

The *pheromone update* is done using the constructed solutions. A good pheromone updating rule is used in two phases:

An **evaporation phase** that decreases the pheromone trail value. The goal of the evaporation is to escape from premature convergence toward "good" solutions and then to encourage the exploration in the solution space.

A **reinforcement phase** that updates the pheromone trail using constructed solutions. Three different strategies can be used [54]: *off-line pheromone update* [55], *online step-by-step pheromone update* [50], and *online delayed pheromone update* [56]. Among these strategies, the off-line pheromone update is the most popular approach, in which different strategies can be applied: quality-based pheromone update [49], rank-based pheromone update [57], worst pheromone update [58], and elitist pheromone update [51].

4. Proposed algorithm for winner determination

In this section, we present a hybrid ant colony optimization and multi-neighborhood search (ACO-MNLS) algorithm for solving WDP. In addition to common search components in all metaheuristics (e.g. representation of solutions and definition of the objective function), the main components of the proposed ACO-MNLS are pheromone information, solution construction, local search, and pheromone update.

4.1. Solution representation

To design a metaheuristic, representation is necessary to encode each solution of the problem. The representation used in the proposed ACO-MNLS is the binary representation [11]. For a WDP of n bids, a vector $X=\{x_1, x_2, ..., x_n\}$ of binary variables x_j may be used to represent a solution:

$$\forall j \in \{1,2,...,n\}, \quad x_j = \begin{cases} 1 & if\ b_j\ is\ in\ solution \\ 0 & otherwise \end{cases} \quad . (4)$$

In other words, a solution will be encoded by a vector X of n binary variables, where the jth decision variable of X denotes the presence or absence of the jth bid in the solution. For example, consider a set of five bids $B = \{b_1, b_2, b_3, b_4, b_5\}$ and the feasible allocation $A_1 = \{b_2, b_4\}$ in which bids b_1 and b_4 are won. Figure 1 illustrates a binary representation used by ACO-MNLS for a solution.

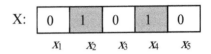

Figure 1. A candidate solution in proposed ACO-MNLS for a WDP with five bids.

4.2. Fitness evaluation

Each metaheuristics must use a fitness evaluation function that associates with each solution of the search space a numeric value that describes its quality. An effective fitness evaluation function must yield better evaluations to solutions that are closer to the optimal solution than those that are farther away. The fitness evaluation function for a given problem is chosen by the problem solver, and it is not given with the problem but is directly related to the specifications for that problem. Fortunately, the definition of fitness evaluation function for WDP is straightforward. It specifies the originally formulated objective function. The objective function defined in (1) is used to measure the quality of a candidate solution X. Thus for a candidate solution X, its quality is just equal to the sum of the valuations of the winning bids [48]:

$$Fitness(X) = \sum_{j=1}^{n} p_j x_j, \qquad (5)$$

where, $X=\{x_1, x_2, ..., x_n\}$ is a $1\times n$ matrix, and $P=\{p_1, p_2, ..., p_n\}$ is a $1\times n$ matrix in which p_j is the price of b_j.

4.3. Pheromone information

Pheromone information consists of defining a vector of model parameters τ called *pheromone trail parameters*, where pheromone values $\tau_i \in \tau$ should give the relevant information for solution construction. Here, a pheromone τ_j is associated with each bid j (i.e. b_j). Therefore, the pheromone information is represented by a $1\times n$ matrix τ, where each element τ_j of the matrix says the desirability to have the b_j in the solution. The pheromone matrix is initialized by the same values. During the search, the pheromone is updated to estimate the utility of any bid.

4.4. Solution construction

In addition to the pheromone trails, the main question in the solution construction is concerned with the definition of the problem-specific heuristic to be used in guiding the search. As stated in Section 3, artificial ants can be considered as stochastic greedy algorithms that construct a solution in a probabilistic manner by considering two important parameters: *pheromone trails* and *problem-dependent heuristic information*.

Given an initial arbitrary solution A, we define set C composed of each bid $b_j = (S_j, p_j)$ such that $S_j \bigcap (\bigcup_{i \in A} S_i) = \phi$. In this case, an ant selects the next bid $b_j \in C$ with the probability:

$$p_j = \frac{(\tau_j)^\alpha \times (\eta_j)^\beta}{\sum_{k \in C} (\tau_k)^\alpha \times (\eta_k)^\beta}, \qquad (6)$$

where:

- $\eta_j \in \eta$ is the value of problem-specific heuristic for b_j. The problem-specific heuristic information is represented by a $1 \times n$ matrix η, where the value for each element η_j of the matrix is equal to the normalized price of b_j, i.e. $\eta_j = p_j / \sum_{k=1}^{n} p_k$.

- α and β are the parameters representing the relative influence of the pheromone values and the problem-specific heuristic values. The ACO algorithm will be similar to a stochastic greedy algorithm if we have $\alpha = 0$. In this case, the bids with a large price are more likely to be selected. If $\beta = 0$, only the pheromone trails will guide the search direction. In this case, *stagnation* may occur, in which all ants will construct similar solutions. Hence, a suitable balance must be done in using this kind of information [11].

Note that the process of adding a new bid to the current solution A is repeated until set C is not empty.

4.5. Local search: Multi-Neighborhood Local Search (MNLS)

Definition of the *neighborhood space* is the common search concept for all local search algorithms. The neighborhood space is defined by an undirected graph $H=(N, E)$ associated with the solution space of the problem, where the nodes in

N correspond to candidate solutions and the edges in E correspond to moves in the neighborhood space, i.e. $(i, j) \in E$ if and only if $i \in N, j \in N, j \in N(i)$, and $i \in N(j)$, where $N(y)$ denotes the neighbors of a solution $y \in N$. The structure of the neighborhood depends on the target optimization problem. A neighbor solution y' for a given solution y is constructed by applying a move m to the solution y using a move operator $\oplus$, denoted by $y' = y \oplus m$. The neighborhood space is called single-neighborhood if for constructing it we use only a one-move operator, and is called multi-neighborhood if for constructing it we use several-move operators [11].

A local search may be seen as a walk in the neighborhood space. A walk is performed by move operators that move from the current solution to another one in the neighborhood space. Here, we define three basic move operators for WDP, denoted by *ADD*, *EXCHANGE*, and *REMOVE*. Suppose an initial arbitrary allocation A composed of some non-conflicting bids.

The $ADD(b_j)$ move operator consists of adding to A a bid $b_j = (S_j, p_j)$ from the set of bids that are excluded from the A and have no conflict with bids in A. In example 1, let us consider the feasible allocation $A = \{b_1, b_3\}$. There are only two bids b_5 and b_6 that are excluded from the A and have no conflict with bids in the A. Note that after the $ADD(b_j)$ move, the change in the fitness of solution is $+p_j$. Since the value for p_j is always positive, the move gain is always positive for an *ADD* move, and therefore, such a move always leads to an improved neighboring solution.

$EXCHANGE(b_i, b_j)$ move operator consists of exchanging a bid $b_i = (S_i, p_i)$ (from the set of bids that are excluded from the A and have no conflict with bids in set $A-b_j$) with only bid b_j of A that have conflict with b_i. In example 1, let us consider the feasible allocation $A = \{b_1, b_3\}$. Bid b_2 is a candidate bid to exchange with bid b_1, and bid b_4 is a candidate bid to exchange with bid b_3. The move gain of the $EXCHANGE(b_i, b_j)$ move operator is $p_i - p_j$. Note that the move gain can be either positive or negative for an *EXCHANGE* move. Hence, we can see that an *EXCHANGE* move can increase or decrease the fitness of A.

The $REMOVE(b_j)$ move operator removes a bid $b_j = (S_j, p_j)$ from the A. The move gain of the removed bid b_j is $-p_j$. Note that the move gain is always negative for a *REMOVE* move because p_j is always positive. Hence, we can see that a

REMOVE move always leads to a decrease in the fitness of *A*.

For the three move operators *ADD*, *ECXHANGE*, and *REMOVE*, there is no absolute dominance of one operator over the other ones. Therefore, the best move operator to be applied depends on the current situation. These facts lead us to generate a combined neighborhood space *H*, which corresponds to the union of the three neighborhoods H_1, H_2, and H_3, denoted by $H = H_1 \cup H_2 \cup H_3$. Using this multi-neighborhood, our local search algorithm, i.e. Multi-Neighborhood Local Search (MNLS), at each iteration selects the move with the largest gain among all the *ADD*, *ECXHANGE*, and *REMOVE* moves if the move gain is positive, and selects a random move among all possible moves if the move gain is negative. Note that the MNLS algorithm simultaneously explores a set of three neighborhoods H_1, H_2, and H_3 to get different local optima and to escape from local optima. MNLS uses the fact that using various neighborhoods in local search can generate different local optima and that the global optima is a local optima for a given neighborhood. The template of the MNLS algorithm is shown in Algorithm (2).

Algorithm (2): Template of Multi-Neighborhood Local Search algorithm for WDP.

Input: X as the initial solution, and maxiter as the maximum iteration of MNLS algorithm.
*For i = 1 to maxiter **Do***
   Generate candidate neighbors to X by three move operators ADD, ECXHANGE, and REMOVE;
   X' = the best neighbor of X;
   *If Fitness(X')-Fitness(X) > 0 **Then***
      X = X';
   Else
      X = a random neighbor of X;
   Endif
Endfor
***Output:** Best solution found.*

4.6. Pheromone update

As stated in Section 3, a general pheromone updating strategy is used in two phases: **evaporation phase** and **reinforcement phase**. Here, we use the classical evaporation method for the pheromone trails so that each pheromone value is reduced by a fixed proportion. For each b_j, its pheromone τ_j will evaporate as follows:

$$\tau_j = (1-\rho)\tau_j, \quad \forall j \in \{1,...,n\}, \tag{7}$$

where, $\rho \in [0, 1]$ shows the reduction rate of the pheromone.

Now the pheromone update method has to be specified. Here, we use elitist pheromone update

[35], in which the best solution found so far will increment the pheromone matrix to reinforce exploitation ability of the search. This operation is done by (8):

$$\tau_j = \tau_j + \Delta, \quad if\ b_j\ is\ a\ winner\ bid, \tag{8}$$

where, $\Delta = Fitness(X) \Big/ \sum_{k=1}^{n} p_k$, and $P=\{p_1, p_2, ..., p_n\}$ is a $1 \times n$ matrix, in which p_k is the price of b_k.

4.7. General framework of ACO-MNLS

The pseudo-code of ACO-MNLS is described in Algorithm (3). At first, the initial values for the parameters are determined. After initialization, the main search loop is entered. It is repeated until a maximum number of iterations is satisfied. In the main loop itself, four important phases exist: Solution construction, Solution improvement, pheromone evaporation, and pheromone reinforcement.

Algorithm (3): Template of ACO-MNLS.

Set the value of below parameters:
   the number of ants;
   the initial value of pheromone matrix ;
   the relative influence of the pheromone values, i.e. α;
   the problem-dependent parameter β;
   the reduction rate of the pheromone, i.e. ρ ;
   the maximum number of iterations;
   the maximum iteration of MNLS algorithm;
Repeat
   *For each ant **Do***
      Solution construction using the pheromone trail;
      Solution improvement using MNLS algorithm;
      Pheromone evaporation using Eq. (7);
      Pheromone reinforcement using Eq. (8);
   Endfor
***Until** maximum number of iterations are satisfied.*
***Output:** Best solution found.*

---

5. Experimental results

In this Section, the performance of the proposed algorithm is measured on several benchmark instances. In order to show the effectiveness of our approach, we compared the ACO-MNLS algorithm with four different approaches for solving the WDP reported in [48], i.e. Stochastic Local Search (SLS), Tabu Search (TS), Genetic Algorithm (GA), and Memetic Algorithm (MA). The structure of this section is as what follows. First we describe the characteristics of the selected benchmarks. Then we present the results obtained from ACO-MNLS for benchmark instances. Finally, we present a comparison of ACO-MNLS with the other four metaheuristics.

5.1. Benchmarks

To evaluate the performance of algorithms on the WDP problem, [59] has created the program

Combinatorial Auction Test Suite (CATS) to generate benchmarks. Recently, [37] has provided new benchmarks of various sizes consisting of up to 1500 items and 1500 bids. The CATS instances are easily solved by CPLEX and CABoB [60]. In this paper, we use the realistic benchmarks by [37] for which CPLEX cannot find the optimal solution in a reasonable period of time. These benchmarks include 500 instances, and are available at the Zhuyi's home page (http://logistics.ust.hk/~zhuyi/instance.zip). These benchmarks are divided into five groups of problems, where each group contains 100 instances given in table 1. In this table, m is the number of items and n is the number of bids.

5.2. Results and comparisons
In this section, the performance of the proposed ACO-MNLS is measured by applying the proposed algorithm to solve different benchmarks. The proposed ACO-MNLS was implemented in C language and run on a PC with an Intel 2.2 GHz CPU. The ACO-MNLS parameters are fixed on the following values: the number of ants is set to 100, the initial value of pheromone matrix is set to 10, the relative influence of the pheromone values, i.e. α parameter, is set to 0.5, the relative influence of the problem-dependent heuristic values, i.e. β parameter, is set to 5, the reduction rate of the pheromone, i.e. ρ parameter, is set to 0.1, the stopping criterion of ACO-MNLS is satisfied after 200 iterations, and the maximum iteration of MNLS algorithm is set to 50. All of these values for the parameters are obtained experimentally.

Tables 2–6 present the computational results of the ACO-MNLS algorithm in comparison with different metaheuristics reported in [48]. Each table is designed to one of the 5 groups of the REL benchmarks.
In these tables, the first column shows the name of the instance, columns with *sol* caption correspond to the maximum revenue obtained by each algorithm, and columns with *time* caption

correspond to CPU time in seconds for each algorithm.

From tables 2-6, it can be observed that the ACO-MNLS algorithm outperforms the GA, MA, SLS, and TS algorithms in terms of computational time in all the REL instances. Also ACO-MNLS outperforms GA in terms of the solution quality in all REL instances and overcomes the TS, MA, and SLS algorithms in most instances, whereas in the case of other instances, both the ACO-MNLS and other algorithms get the same results. The proposed ACO-MNLS is ranked in the first place among five metaheuristics in terms of both the solution quality and computational time. In order to determine the statistical significance of the advantage of ACO-MNLS, *t*-test (all compared with ACO-MNLS) is applied. In the first row of each table, the symbols + and $\approx$ represent that other methods are statistically inferior to or equal to the proposed algorithm, respectively. The last three rows of each table summarize how many cases ACO-MNLS perform better, similar or worse than the other algorithms. From these results, we can conclude that the ACO-MNLS algorithm dominates the GA [48], MA [48], SLS [48], and TS [48] algorithms in terms of both the solution quality and computational time.

Note that from an optimization viewpoint, ACO-MNLS combine global and local search using ACO to perform exploration, while the MNLS algorithm performs exploitation. ACO ensures that ACO-MNLS can explore new bids that may have not been seen in the search process yet. In fact, ACO makes the entire search space reachable, despite the finite population size. Furthermore, the MNLS algorithm was able to enhance the convergence rate of ACO-MNLS by finely tuning the search on the immediate area of the landscape being considered.

Table 1. Main characteristics of benchmarks used.

Benchmarks	m	n	Description
REL-1000-500	500	1000	100 instances from in 101 to in 200
REL-1000-1000	1000	1000	100 instances from in 201 to in 300
REL-500- 1000	1000	500	100 instances from in 401 to in 500
REL-1500-1000	1000	1500	100 instances from in 501 to in 600
REL-1500-1500	1500	1500	100 instances from in 601 to in 700

Table 2. Experimental results of proposed ACO-MNLS, GA, MA, SLS, and TS on some instances of REL-1000-500.

Instances	ACO-MNLS		GA		MA		SLS		TS	
	sol	time	sol	time	sol	time	sol	time	sol	time
in101	**69840.07**	**16.84**	42100.71$^+$	336.90	67101.93$^{\approx}$	129.62	66170.61$^+$	23.51	66170.61$^+$	57.86
in102	**70897.46**	**16.02**	39641.22$^+$	432.76	67797.61$^+$	132.18	65466.95$^+$	23.89	64716.31$^+$	63.43
in103	**69791.25**	**15.36**	43376.54$^+$	338.89	66350.99$^+$	133.34	66350.99$^+$	24.79	66350.99$^+$	128.68
in104	**67268.71**	**15.64**	42790.65$^+$	376.37	64618.41$^+$	135.14	67268.71$^{\approx}$	22.92	62524.23$^+$	120.56
in105	**69834.28**	**17.14**	40841.21$^+$	331.31	66376.83$^+$	153.96	67268.71$^{\approx}$	22.92	62524.23$^+$	120.56
in106	**66436.08**	**13.48**	41770.07$^+$	385.43	65481.64$^{\approx}$	140.96	63479.26$^+$	22.37	64591.70$^{\approx}$	129.42
in107	**69182.25**	**14.28**	38781.82$^+$	379.15	66245.70$^+$	146.40	66245.70$^+$	23.18	63972.62$^+$	128.51
in108	**74588.51**	**16.14**	43881.51$^+$	337.35	**74588.51**$^{\approx}$	161.03	71505.66$^+$	24.01	68776.34$^+$	119.84
in109	**66239.28**	**13.56**	42001.62$^+$	336.89	62492.66$^+$	144.71	61751.22$^+$	22.20	64343.07$^{\approx}$	80.98
in110	**67395.07**	**14.28**	38632.49$^+$	320.84	65171.19$^{\approx}$	149.01	64083.64$^+$	23.25	60275.66$^+$	115.31
Average	69147.30	15.28	41381.78	357.59	66622.55	142.64	65959.15	23.30	64424.58	106.52
Rank	1	1	5	5	2	4	3	2	4	3
Better	-	-	10	-	6	-	8	-	8	-
Similar	-	-	0	-	4	-	2	-	2	-
Worse	-	-	0	-	0	-	0	-	0	-

Table 3. Experimental results of proposed ACO-MNLS, GA, MA, SLS, and TS on some instances of REL-1000-1000.

Instances	ACO-MNLS		GA		MA		SLS		TS	
	sol	time	Sol	time	Sol	time	sol	time	sol	time
in201	**81557.74**	**6.10**	56640.60$^+$	697.65	77499.82$^+$	98.26	56640.60$^+$	697.65	77499.82$^+$	98.26
in202	**90464.19**	**7.32**	59029.76$^+$	693.14	**90464.19**$^{\approx}$	106.68	59029.76$^+$	693.14	**90464.19**$^{\approx}$	106.68
in203	**86239.21**	**7.00**	59476.80$^+$	562.29	**86239.21**$^{\approx}$	102.28	59476.80$^+$	562.29	**86239.21**$^{\approx}$	102.28
in204	**87075.42**	**6.98**	57671.10$^+$	732.71	81969.05$^+$	97.40	57671.10$^+$	732.71	81969.05$^+$	97.40
in205	**82469.19**	**6.16**	59915.07$^+$	573.98	**82469.19**$^{\approx}$	91.26	59915.07$^+$	573.98	**82469.19**$^{\approx}$	91.26
in206	**86881.42**	**6.32**	58674.13$^+$	627.01	**86881.42**$^{\approx}$	93.99	58674.13$^+$	627.01	**86881.42**$^{\approx}$	93.99
in207	**91033.51**	**6.38**	60383.29$^+$	667.75	**91033.51**$^{\approx}$	100.90	60383.29$^+$	667.75	**91033.51**$^{\approx}$	100.90
in208	**91782.20**	**7.22**	63052.38$^+$	646.34	83667.76$^+$	101.29	63052.38$^+$	646.34	83667.76$^+$	101.29
in209	**81966.65**	**6.82**	59333.98$^+$	655.09	**81966.65**$^{\approx}$	96.42	59333.98$^+$	655.09	**81966.65**$^{\approx}$	96.42
in210	**87569.19**	**6.52**	64762.35$^+$	547.09	85079.98$^{\approx}$	97.78	64762.35$^+$	547.09	85079.98$^{\approx}$	97.78
Average	86703.87	6.68	59893.95	640.31	84727.08	98.63	59893.95	640.31	84727.08	98.63
Rank	1	1	4	4	2	2	4	4	2	2
Better	-	-	10	-	3	-	10	-	3	-
Similar	-	-	0	-	7	-	0	-	7	-
Worse	-	-	0	-	0	-	0	-	0	-

Table 4. Experimental results of proposed ACO-MNLS, GA, MA, SLS, and TS on some instances of REL-500-1000.

Instances	ACO-MNLS		GA		MA		SLS		TS	
	sol	time	sol	time	sol	time	sol	time	sol	time
in401	**77417.48**	**3.52**	56437.68$^+$	1193.89	72948.07$^+$	37.07	72948.07$^+$	5.67	68485.81$^+$	44.14
in402	**74469.07**	**3.94**	56637.00$^+$	1272.06	71454.78$^+$	37.20	71454.78$^+$	5.79	72820.03$^{\approx}$	23.57
in403	**74843.96**	**3.80**	57024.78$^+$	1299.01	**74843.96**$^{\approx}$	38.81	**74843.96**$^{\approx}$	6.01	**74843.96**$^{\approx}$	34.15
in404	**78761.68**	**3.84**	61123.14$^+$	1088.39	**78761.68**$^{\approx}$	38.78	**78761.68**$^{\approx}$	6.12	73385.62$^+$	16.85
in405	**74899.12**	**4.02**	58852.75$^+$	1030.96	72674.25$^{\approx}$	39.29	72674.25$^{\approx}$	6.04	72674.25$^{\approx}$	15.90
in406	**71791.03**	**3.56**	58714.53$^+$	1318.40	**71791.03**$^{\approx}$	38.09	**71791.03**$^{\approx}$	5.87	**71791.03**$^{\approx}$	37.12
in407	**73935.28**	**4.16**	58239.19$^+$	1021.79	**73935.28**$^{\approx}$	40.95	73278.66$^{\approx}$	6.35	71578.48$^+$	15.57
in408	**77018.73**	**3.98**	59185.08$^+$	1348.82	72580.04$^+$	39.07	72580.04$^+$	5.95	70144.19$^+$	27.37
in409	**73188.62**	**3.36**	54950.59$^+$	1342.28	68724.53$^+$	36.28	67177.35$^+$	5.48	67177.35$^+$	25.48
in410	**73791.66**	**4.24**	59764.76$^+$	1005.54	71791.57$^+$	41.90	71791.57$^+$	6.37	72791.68$^{\approx}$	14.01
Average	75011.66	3.84	58092.95	1192.11	72950.52	38.74	72730.14	5.97	71569.24	25.42
Rank	1	1	5	5	2	4	3	2	4	3
Better	-	-	10	-	5	-	5	-	5	-
Similar	-	-	0	-	5	-	5	-	5	-
Worse	-	-	0	-	0	-	0	-	0	-

Table 5. Experimental results of proposed ACO-MNLS, GA, MA, SLS, and TS on some instances of REL-1500-1000.

Instances	ACO-MNLS		GA		MA		SLS		TS	
	sol	Time	sol	time	sol	time	sol	time	sol	time
in501	**84165.23**	**6.28**	64961.36$^+$	1624.84	79132.03$^+$	107.82	77140.72$^+$	15.62	82216.35$^\approx$	98.71
in502	**83163.66**	**6.16**	56954.75$^+$	1707.18	80340.76$^+$	108.71	78574.26$^+$	15.98	74127.61$^+$	120.82
in503	**83277.71**	**5.98**	59161.13$^+$	1450.79	**83277.71**$^\approx$	114.15	79554.65$^+$	15.99	77005.81$^+$	114.11
in504	**83947.13**	**5.66**	59691.51$^+$	1662.53	81903.02$^\approx$	116.11	81903.02$^\approx$	16.48	81903.02$^\approx$	155.54
Average	83638.43	6.02	60192.19	1611.34	81163.38	111.70	79293.16	16.02	78813.20	122.30
Rank	1	1	5	5	2	3	3	2	4	4
Better	-	-	4	-	2	-	3	-	2	-
Similar	-	-	0	-	2	-	1	-	2	-
Worse	-	-	0	-	0	-	0	-	0	-

Table 6. Experimental results of proposed ACO-MNLS, GA, MA, SLS, and TS on some instances of REL-1500-1500.

Instances	ACO-MNLS		GA		MA		SLS		TS	
	sol	time	sol	time	sol	time	sol	time	sol	time
in601	**105286.68**	**5.88**	73665.13$^+$	1489.40	99044.32$^+$	110.62	96255.53$^+$	15.54	97473.85$^+$	100.76
in602	**101150.89**	**5.22**	76006.38$^+$	1810.56	98164.23$^+$	114.18	95328.21$^+$	15.71	93873.31$^+$	155.34
in603	**96628.98**	**5.22**	71585.28$^+$	1685.07	94126.96$^\approx$	110.71	94126.96$^\approx$	15.48	92568.61$^+$	137.95
in604	**106127.19**	**5.50**	71958.50$^+$	1627.37	103568.86$^+$	110.60	103568.86$^+$	15.59	92869.78$^+$	96.70
in605	**106273.50**	**6.02**	71348.06$^+$	1634.68	102404.76$^+$	122.40	98799.71$^+$	17.36	95787.59$^+$	175.14
in606	**105218.21**	**5.42**	72505.09$^+$	1656.29	104346.07$^\approx$	107.79	104346.07$^\approx$	15.60	104346.07$^\approx$	334.12
in607	**105869.44**	**5.52**	72162.60$^+$	1625.37	**105869.44**$^\approx$	113.26	100417.40$^\approx$	15.89	98674.39$^+$	267.79
in608	**99541.75**	**5.38**	76189.79$^+$	1625.46	95671.77$^+$	109.15	95671.77$^+$	15.26	91554.61$^+$	95.62
in609	**104602.39**	**5.26**	71664.87$^+$	1581.18	98566.94$^+$	111.12	98566.94$^+$	16.76	96652.44$^+$	103.10
in610	**109008.35**	**6.12**	72393.14$^+$	1572.06	102468.60$^+$	120.17	99975.09$^+$	17.57	99975.09$^+$	146.03
Average	103970.70	5.54	72947.88	1630.74	100423.20	113.00	98705.65	16.08	96377.57	161.26
Rank	1	1	5	5	2	3	3	2	4	4
Better	-	-	10	-	7	-	7	-	9	-
Similar	-	-	0	-	3	-	3	-	1	-
Worse	-	-	0	-	0	-	0	-	0	-

6. Conclusions

A hybrid Ant Colony Optimization with a novel Multi-Neighborhood Local Search (ACO-MNLS) algorithm was proposed for solving Winner Determination Problem (WDP) in combinatorial auctions. Our proposed MNLS algorithm used the fact that using various neighborhoods in local search could generate different local optima for WDP and that the global optima of WDP was a local optima for a given neighborhood. Therefore, in the proposed MNLS algorithm, a set of three different neighborhoods was simultaneously explored to get different local optima and to escape from local optima. To the best of our knowledge and the research in the literature, no study has been done to solve WDP with combining general-purpose Ant Colony Optimization (ACO) metaheuristic and problem-specific Multi-Neighborhood Local Search (MNLS) algorithm.

The performance of the proposed algorithm was evaluated in terms of solution quality and computational time by several well-known benchmarks. Its performance was compared with four different metaheuristics for solving WDP, i.e. Stochastic Local Search (SLS), Tabu Search (TS),

Genetic Algorithm (GA), and Memetic Algorithm (MA). The experimental results confirmed that the proposed ACO-MNLS outperformed the current best performing WDP metaheuristics in terms of both the solution quality and computational efficiency.

A first step toward extending this paper would be to hybrid the proposed MNLS algorithm in other swarm and evolutionary algorithms. Secondly, the MNLS algorithm could be changed to simultaneously explore a set of other different neighborhoods. Finally, the proposed approach could be adopted for solving Multi-objective WDP (MOWDP) [45].

References

[1] Parsons, S., Rodriguez-Aguilar, J. A. & Klein, M. (2011). Auctions and bidding: A guide for computer scientists. ACM Computing Surveys, vol. 43, no. 2, pp. 1-10.

[2] Fujishima, Y., Leyton-Brown, K. & Shoham, Y. (1999). Taming the computational complexity of combinatorial auctions: optimal and approximate approaches. Sixteenth international joint conference on artificial intelligence, Stockholm, Sweden, 1999.

[3] Garey, M. & Johnson, D. (1979). Computers and Intractability: A Guide to the Theory on NP-Completeness. W.H. Freeman and Co. Publishers, New York.

[4] Sandholm, T. (2006). Optimal Winner Determination Algorithms, In: Cramton, P. (Eds.), Combinatorial Auctions. MIT Press, pp. 337-368.

[5] Abrache, J., Crainic, T. G., Gendreau, M. & Rekik, M. (2007). Combinatorial auctions. Annals of Operations Research, vol. 153, no. 1, pp. 131–164.

[6] Fontanini, W. & Ferreira, P. A. V. (2014). A game-theoretic approach for the web services scheduling problem. Expert Systems with Applications, vol. 41, no. 10, pp. 4743–4751.

[7] Ray, A. K., Jenamani, M. & Mohapatra, P. K. J. (2011). Supplier behavior modeling and winner determination using parallel MDP. Expert Systems with Applications, vol. 38, no. 5, pp. 4689–4697.

[8] Vries, S. & Vohra, R. (2003). Combinatorial auctions: a survey. INFORMS Journal on Computing, vol. 15, pp. 284-309.

[9] Lipton, R. J. (2010). The P=NP Question and Godel's Lost Letter, Springer.

[10] Safaee, B. & Kamaleddin Mousavi Mashhadi, S. K. (2017). Optimization of fuzzy membership functions via PSO and GA with application to quad rotor. Journal of AI and Data Mining, vol. 5, no. 1, pp. 1-10.

[11] Talbi, E. G. (2009). Metaheuristics: From Design to Implementation. John Wiley & Sons.

[12] Dowlatshahi, M. B., Nezamabadi-pour, H. & Mashinchi, M. (2014). A discrete gravitational search algorithm for solving combinatorial optimization problems. Information Sciences, vol. 258, pp. 94–107.

[13] AllamehAmiri, M., Derhami, V. & Ghasemzadeh, M. (2013). QoS-Based web service composition based on genetic algorithm. Journal of AI and Data Mining, vol. 1, no. 2, pp. 63-73.

[14] Holland, J. H. (1975). Adaptation in Natural and Artificial Systems. University of Michigan Press, Ann Arbor, MI.

[15] Dorigo, M. (1992). Optimization, learning and natural algorithms. Dissertation, Politecnico di Milano, Italy.

[16] Kirkpatrick, S., Gelatt, C. D. & Vecchi, M. P. (1983). Optimization by simulated annealing. Science, vol. 220, pp. 671–680.

[17] Feo, T. A. & Resende, M. G. C. (1989). A probabilistic heuristic for a computationally difficult set covering problem. Operations Research Letters, vol. 8, pp. 67–71.

[18] Glover, F. & Laguna, M. (1997). Tabu Search. Kluwer Academic Publishers.

[19] Mladenovic, M. & Hansen, P. (1997). Variable neighborhood search. Computers and Operations Research, vol. 24, pp. 1097–1100.

[20] Stützle, T. (1999). Local search algorithms for combinatorial problems: Analysis, algorithms and new applications. Dissertation, Germany.

[21] Kennedy, J. & Eberhart, R. (1999). Particle swarm optimization. In: Proceedings of the IEEE International Conference on Neural Networks, Piscataway, N.J., pp. 1942–1948.

[22] Rashedi, E., Nezamabadi-pour, H. & Saryazdi, S. (2009). GSA: A Gravitational Search Algorithm. Information Sciences, vol. 179, pp. 2232–2248.

[23] Sandholm, T. (1999). Algorithms for optimal winner determination in combinatorial auctions. Artificial Intelligence, vol. 135, pp. 1–54.

[24] Padberg, M. W. (1973). On the facial structure of set packing polyhedra. Mathematical Programming, vol. 5, no. 1, pp. 199–215.

[25] Leyton-Brown, K., Shoham, Y. & Tennenholz, M. (2000). An algorithm for multi-unit combinatorial auctions. In: Proceedings of the 7th international conference on artificial intelligence pp. 56–61.

[26] Sandholm, T. & Suri, S. (2003). BOB: Improved winner determination in combinatorial auctions and generalizations. Artificial Intelligence, vol. 145, pp. 33–58.

[27] Sandholm, T., Suri, S., Gilpin, A. & Levine, D. (2005). CABOB: A fast optimal algorithm for winner determination in combinatorial auctions. Management Science, vol. 51, no. 3, pp. 374–390.

[28] Nisan, N. (2000). Bidding and allocation in combinatorial auctions. In: Proceedings of the 2nd ACM conference on electronic commerce, pp. 1–12.

[29] Gunluk, O., Laszlo, L. & de Vries, S. (2005). A branch-and-price algorithm and new test problems for spectrum auctions. Management Science, vol. 51, no. 3, pp. 391–406.

[30] Escudero, L. F., Landete, M. & Marin, A. (2009). A branch-and-cut algorithm for the winner determination problem. Decision Support Systems, vol. 46, no. 3, pp. 649–659.

[31] Rothkopf, M. H., Pekec, A. & Harstad, R. M. (1998). Computationally manageable combinatorial auctions. Management Science, vol. 44, no. 8, pp. 1131–1147.

[32] Andersson, A., Tenhunen, M. & Ygge, F. (2000). Integer programming for combinatorial auction winner determination. In: Proceedings of the 4th international conference on multi-agent systems, New York: IEEE Computer Society Press, pp. 39–46.

[33] Guo, Y., Lim, A., Rodrigues, B. & Zhu, Y. (2006). Heuristics for a bidding problem. Computers & Operations Research, vol. 33, no. 8, pp. 2179-2188.

[34] Wu, Q. & Hao, J.K. (2016). A clique-based exact method for optimal winner determination in combinatorial auctions. Information Sciences, vol. 334, pp. 103-121.

[35] Michalak, T., Rahwan, T., Elkind, E., Wooldridge, M. & Jennings, N.R. (2016). A hybrid exact algorithm for complete set partitioning. Artificial Intelligence, vol. 230, pp. 14-50.

[36] Hoos, H. H. & Boutilier, C. (2000). Solving combinatorial auctions using stochastic local search. In: Proceedings of the Seventeenth National Conference on Artificial Intelligence and Twelfth Conference on Innovative Applications of Artificial Intelligence, pp. 22-29.

[37] Boughaci, D., Benhamou, B. & Drias, H. (2009). A memetic algorithm for the optimal winner determination problem. Soft Computing - A Fusion of Foundations, Methodologies and Applications, vol. 13, pp. 905-917.

[38] Lau, H. C. & Goh, Y. G. (2002). An intelligent brokering system to support multi-agent web-based 4th-party logistics. In: Proceedings of the 14th international conference on tools with artificial intelligence, pp. 54–61.

[39] Boughaci, D., Benhamou, B. & Drias, H. (2010). Local search methods for the optimal winner determination problem in combinatorial auctions. Journal of Mathematical Modelling and Algorithms, vol. 9, no. 2, pp. 165–180.

[40] Tsung, C., Ho, H. & Lee, S. (2011). An equilibrium-based approach for determining winners in combinatorial auctions. In: Proceedings of the 9th IEEE international symposium on parallel and distributed processing with applications, pp.47–51.

[41] Sghir, I., Hao, J. K., Ben Jaafar, I. & Ghedira, K. (2014). A recombination-based tabu search algorithm for the winner determination problem. In: Legrand, P., et al. (Eds.), AE 2013. Lecture notes in computer science, vol. 8752, pp. 157–169.

[42] Nguyen, T. D. (2014). A fast approximation algorithm for solving the complete set packing problem. European Journal of Operational Research, vol. 237, no. 1, pp. 62-70.

[43] Wang, N. & Wang, D. (2014). Model and algorithm of winner determination problem in multi-item E-procurement with variable quantities. In: The 26th Chinese Control and Decision Conference, pp. 5364-5367.

[44] Boughaci, D. & Lassouaoui, M. (2014). Stochastic Hyper-Heuristic for the Winner Determination Problem in combinatorial auctions. In: Proceedings of the 6th International Conference on Management of Emergent Digital EcoSystems, pp. 62-66.

[45] Hsieh, F. S. & Liao, C. S. (2014). Multi-agent Learning for Winner Determination in Combinatorial Auctions. In: International Conference on Industrial, Engineering and Other Applications of Applied Intelligent Systems, pp. 1-10.

[46] Buer, T. & Kopfer, H. (2014). A Pareto-metaheuristic for a bi-objective winner determination problem in a combinatorial reverse auction. Computers & Operations Research, vol. 41, pp. 208-220.

[47] Holte, R. (2001). Combinatorial Auctions, Knapsack Problems, and Hill-Climbing Search. In: Stroulia, E. & Matwin, S. (Eds.), Advances in Artificial Intelligence, vol. 2056 of Lecture Notes in Computer Science, pp. 57-66.

[48] Schwind, M., Stockheim, T. & Rothlauf, F. (2003). Optimization heuristics for the combinatorial auction problem. In: Evolutionary Computation, 2003. CEC '03. The 2003 Congress on, vol. 3, pp. 1588-1595.

[49] Boughaci, D. (2013). Metaheuristic approaches for the winner determination problem in combinatorial auction. In: Yang, X.S. (Eds.), Artificial Intelligence, Evolutionary Computing and Metaheuristics, vol. 427 of Studies in Computational Intelligence, pp. 775-791.

[50] Dorigo, M., Maniezzo, V. & Colorni, A. (1996). Ant System: Optimization by a colony of cooperating agents. IEEE Transactions on Systems, Man, and Cybernetics – Part B, vol. 26, no. 1, pp. 29–41.

[51] Dorigo, M. & Gambardella, L. M. (1997). Ant Colony System: A cooperative learning approach to the traveling salesman problem. IEEE Transactions on Evolutionary Computation, vol. 1, no. 1, pp. 53–66.

[52] Stützle, T. & Hoos, H. H. (2000). MAX–MIN Ant System. Future Generation Computer Systems, vol. 16, no. 8, pp. 889–914.

[53] Dorigo, M., Caro, G. D. & Gambardella, L. M. (1999). Ant algorithms for discrete optimization. Artificial Life, vol. 5, no. 2, pp. 137–172.

[54] Aarts, E. H. L. & Lenstra, J. K. (1997). Local Search in Combinatorial Optimization. J. Wiley & Sons, Chichester, UK.

[55] Corne, D., Dorigo, M. & Glover, F. (1999). New Ideas in Optimization. McGraw-Hill.

[56] Merkle, D. & Middendorf, M. (2005). Swarm intelligence. In Search Methodologies. Springer, pp. 401–435.

[57] Maniezzo, V. (1999). Exact and approximate nondeterministic tree-search procedures for the quadratic assignment problem. INFORMS Journal on Computing, vol. 11, no. 4, pp. 358–369.

[58] Bullnheimer, B., Hartl, R. F. & Strauss, C. A. (1999). New rank based version of the ant system: A computational study. Central European Journal for Operations Research and Economics, vol. 7, no. 1, pp. 25–38.

[59] Cordon, O., Fernandez, I., Herrera, F. & Moreno, L. (2000). A new ACO model integrating evolutionary algorithms concepts: The best-worst ant system. In: 2nd International Workshop on Ant Algorithms, Brussels, Belgium, pp. 22–29.

[60] Leyton-Brown, K., Pearson, M. & Shoham, Y. (2000). Towards a universal test suite for combinatorial auction algorithms. In: ACM conference on electronic commerce, pp. 66–76.

[61] Sandholm, T., Suri, S., Gilpin, A. & Levine, D. (2001). CABoB: a fast optimal algorithm for combinatorial auctions. In: Proceedings of the international joint conferences on artificial intelligence, pp. 1102–1108.

20

Drought Monitoring and Prediction using K-Nearest Neighbor Algorithm

E. Fadaei-Kermani[*], G. A. Barani and M. Ghaeini-Hessaroeyeh

Department of Civil Engineering, Faculty of Engineering, Shahid Bahonar University of Kerman, Kerman, Iran.

*Corresponding author: E-mail: ehsanhard@gmail.com (E. Fadaei-Kermani).

Abstract

Drought is a climate phenomenon that might occur in any climate condition and all regions on the earth. An effective drought management depends on the application of appropriate drought indices. Drought indices are variables that are used to detect and characterize drought conditions. In this work, it is tried to predict drought occurrence based on the standard precipitation index (SPI) using k-nearest neighbor modeling. The model is tested using the precipitation data of Kerman, Iran. The results obtained show that the model gives reasonable predictions of the drought situation in the region. Finally, the efficiency and precision of the model is quantified by some statistical coefficients. Appropriate values for the correlation coefficient (r = 0.874), mean absolute error (MAE = 0.106), root mean square error (RMSE = 0.119) and coefficient of residual mass (CRM = 0.0011) indicate that the presented model is suitable and efficient.

Keywords: *Drought Monitoring, Standard Precipitation Index, Nearest Neighbor Model, Model Evaluation.*

1. Introduction

Drought is a natural and repeatable phenomenon caused by a decline in the rainfall level during a specified time period. This phenomenon is a climatic event because its characteristics depend on its intensity and continuation as well as the extent of the affected area. Its occurrence can be short-term and harmless or harmful and long-term. It starts slowly, and its effects appear gradually and in a relatively long period of time in different sectors such as water resources, agriculture, environment and economy. Therefore, determining the exact starting and ending points of this phenomenon is rather difficult. That is why drought has been often described as a creeping phenomenon [1].

Drought monitoring and forecasting play a crucial role in the management of water resource systems, and can considerably reduce the losses caused by this phenomenon. Generally, drought indices are used to monitor and predict this phenomenon. The overall objective of these indices is to express this phenomenon quantitatively and to incorporate the combined effects of various factors on the occurrence of droughts in the form of more quantitative and convenient relationships [2].

A number of different indices have been developed to monitor and quantify a drought, each with its own characteristics. They include the Palmer drought severity index (PDSI; Palmer [3]), rainfall anomaly index (RAI; Van Rooy [4]), deciles (Gibbs and Maher [5]), crop moisture index (CMI; Palmer [3]), Bhalme and Mooly drought index (BMDI; Bhalme and Mooley [6]), surface water supply index (SWSI; Shafer and Dezman [7]), national rainfall index (NRI; Gommes and Petrassi [8]), standardized precipitation index (SPI; McKee et al. [9]), reclamation drought index (RDI; Weghorst [10]).

Examples of the drought damage to agricultural systems and other sectors around the world are well-documented, and various efforts have been made to investigate and characterize the mechanism of this phenomenon. Cancelliere et al. [11] have provided two methodologies for the seasonal forecasting of SPI, under the hypothesis of uncorrelated and normally distributed monthly precipitation aggregated at various time scales. Han et al. [12] have proposed a method for drought forecasting based on the remote sensing data using the ARIMA models. The method was used for drought forecasting in the Guanzhong Plain. Farokhnia et al. [13] have utilized the adaptive neurofuzzy inference system (ANFIS) model to forecast possible drought conditions in Tehran plain. Du et al. [14] have defined the synthesized drought index (SDI) as a principal component of vegetation condition index (VCI), temperature condition index (TCI) and precipitation condition index (PCI) for drought monitoring in Shandong province, China. Farahmand and AghaKouchak [15] have introduced the Standardized Drought Analysis Toolbox (SDAT), which can be applied to different climatic variables including precipitation, soil moisture, and relative humidity without having to assume representative parametric distributions. Hao et al. [16] have proposed the optimized meteorological drought index (OMDI) and the optimized vegetation drought index (OVDI) using the multi-source satellite data to monitor drought in three bio-climate regions of SW China.

Non-parametric methods can be used as appropriate approaches to estimate the status of droughts. In the cases where the relationship between input and output is not already fully-determined, utilizing non-parametric algorithm can be instrumental. Therefore, in this study, using the nearest neighbor model, a method was applied to monitor and predict droughts based on the standard precipitation index.

2. Standard precipitation index (SPI)

The understanding that a deficit of precipitation can have different impacts on the ground water, reservoir storage, soil moisture, and streamflow led McKee et al. [9] to develop the Standardized Precipitation Index (SPI) to enhance the detection of onset and monitoring of drought for multiple time scales. These time scales reflect the impact of drought on the availability of the different water resources. Soil moisture conditions respond to precipitation anomalies on a relatively short scale, while ground water, streamflow, and reservoir storage reflect the longer term precipitation anomalies. The standardized precipitation index (SPI) was calculated, based on the long-term precipitation record for a desired period (at least 30 years). The long-term record was fitted to a probability distribution, most probably gamma distribution. Then the cumulative probability was transformed to a Z-standard normal distribution with mean zero and

variance of one using the following equations [9,17]:

$$Z = SPI = -[t - \frac{C_0 + C_1 t + C_2 t^2}{1 + d_1 t + d_2 t^2 + d_3 t^3}] \quad (1)$$

$$t = \sqrt{\ln[\frac{1}{H(x)^2}]} \qquad 0 < H(x) \leq 0.5$$

$$Z = SPI = +[t - \frac{C_0 + C_1 t + C_2 t^2}{1 + d_1 t + d_2 t^2 + d_3 t^3}] \quad (2)$$

$$t = \sqrt{\ln[\frac{1}{1 - H(x)^2}]} \qquad 0.5 < H(x) \leq 1$$

where, $H_{(x)}$ is the cumulative probability function, and the constants C_1 to C_3 and d_1 to d_3 can be calculated as follows:

$C_1 = 2.51557$	$d_1 = 1.432788$
$C_2 = 0.802853$	$d_2 = 0.189269$
$C_3 = 0.010328$	$d_3 = 0.001308$

Using the time series obtained by precipitation data, sorting data in increasing order, the empirical probability distribution can be calculated (Eq. 3).

$$ECP = \frac{m}{n+1} \quad (3)$$

where, m is the row number of sorted precipitation data and n is the total number of precipitation data. Using the standard normal cumulative distribution curve, the standard precipitation index (SPI) can be calculated related to the precipitation data for every corresponding time scale.

Table 1 shows the classification system defining drought intensities resulting from SPI. According to this table, drought occurs any time SPI is continuously negative and reaches intensity where SPI is -1.0 or less. The drought event ends when SPI becomes positive. Each drought event, therefore, has a duration defined by its beginning and end, and the intensity for each month that the event continues.

SPI has several advantages over other indices including its simplicity and temporal flexibility, which allow its application for water resources on all timescales. Moreover, as SPI is adaptable for the analysis of drought at variable time scales, it can be used for monitoring agricultural and hydrological aspects [18]. Despite all these advantages, this index has some limitations as well. SPI uses only the precipitation data, and it is loosely connected to ground conditions [19].

3. K-Nearest neighbor modeling

The k-nearest neighbor modeling (k-NN) is a nonparametric machine learning algorithm that has found wide usage in pattern recognition and data mining. It tries to classify an unknown sample based on the known classification of its neighbors. In this method, the model is fed with a training set, and it uses this training set to classify objects. Each one of the samples in the training set is labeled. The input objects are classified based on the K parameter, meaning that they are assigned to the class that is most pervasive among its closest K neighbors [20,21].

Table 1. Drought classification of SPI [9].		
Class	SPI Values	Drought Status
1	+2 and more	extremely wet
2	1.5 to 1.99	very wet
3	1 to 1.49	moderately wet
4	0.99 to -0.99	near normal
5	-1.49 to -1	moderately dry
6	-1.99 to -1.5	very dry
7	-2 and less	extremely dry

Despite its simplicity, the k-NN algorithm has been widely studied from various perspectives, pursuing the improvement of its classification accuracy. The K-NN modeling has been used for traffic flow forecasting [22], streamflow simulation [23, 24], prediction of intake vortex risk [25], and prediction of cavitation damage on dam spillways [26]. The advantages of the K-NN model are (1) it is highly effective, especially where use is made of large datasets; (2) algorithm efficiency allows various combinations of the factors to be tested, and insignificant combinations are detected and eliminated, minimizing the risk of overfitting; and (3) the K-NN algorithm is robust even where noisy data is used [20, 25].

The first step in the K-NN model is to find the distance between the training and test data. The choice of the distance measure is an important consideration. Commonly, the Euclidean distance measure is used (Eq. 4).

$$d(X,Y) = \sqrt{\sum_{i=1}^{n}(x_i - y_i)^2} \qquad (4)$$

where X refers to the training data with specific parameters (x_1 to x_n), and Y refers to the test data with specific parameters (y_1 to y_n).

$$X = (x_1, x_2, ..., x_n)$$

$$Y = (y_1, y_2, ..., y_n)$$

The next step involves sorting the distances for all the objects in the training set and determining the nearest neighbor based on the minimum distance (maximum similarity). The most important step in this model is to identify the K parameter, which is the number of the closest neighbors in the space of interest. If K is too large, classes with a great number of classified samples can overwhelm small ones and the results will be biased or the neighborhood may include too many points from other classes. On the other hand, if K is too small, the advantage of using many samples in the training set is not exploited, and the result can be sensitive to noise points [27,28].

The best value for K can be obtained by the n-fold cross-validation method. In this method, the data set is divided into K roughly equal-sized parts. For the Kth part, the model is fitted to the other $K-1$ parts of the data, and calculating the prediction error of the fitted model when predicting the kth part of the data. This is done for all values of K (k= 1, 2, ..., K), combining the K estimates of prediction error [27,29].

4. Model preprocessing and methodology

In this work, the precipitation data of the city of Kerman during 1995 to 2005 was used. This city is the capital city of the Kerman Province, which is located in the SE of Iran, situated on a sandy plain with 1749 meters above the sea level, and has an area of 181,714 km².

Based on the precipitation data, determining the moving time series and standard normal distribution function for different time scales, the standard precipitation index was calculated. Figs. 1- 3 show the precipitation cumulative probability distribution function and standard normal probability distribution function for 3-, 6-, and 12-month time scales. Finally, the SPI values were calculated for different periods of 3-month, 6-month, and 12-month during 1995 to 2005. Figs. 4 and 5 show the SPI values for the first 3- and 6-month time scales.

Before working with the K-NN model, to avoid bias toward one attribute or the other, the data is required to be normalized. Therefore all the input attributes are transformed to obtain temporary variables with a distribution having zero means and a standard deviation of 1 using the following equation:

$$X' = \frac{x - \bar{x}}{\sigma(x)} \qquad (5)$$

standard deviations of the observed value of the attribute in the reference data set, respectively.

where, X' represents the value for the normalized attribute, and $\bar{x}$ and $\sigma(x)$ represent the mean and

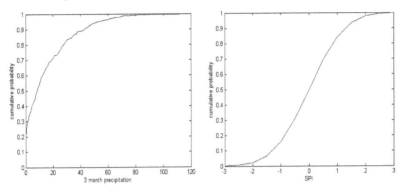

Figure 1. 3-month SPI values.

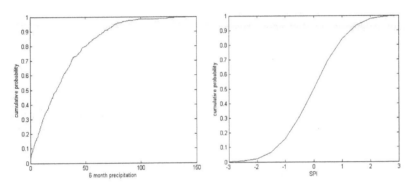

Figure 2. 6-month SPI values.

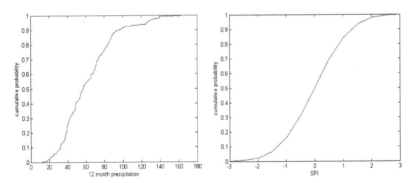

Figure 3. 12-month SPI values.

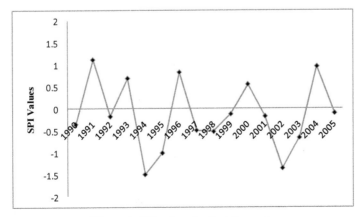

Figure 4. SPI values for first 3-month.

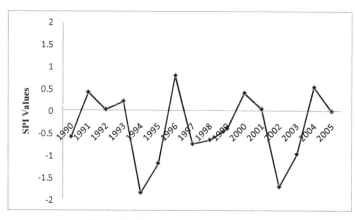

Figure 5. SPI values for first 6-month.

Finally, the efficiency and precision of the model could be evaluated by some statistical coefficients. The Pearson correlation coefficient (r) is a measure indicating the strength and direction of a linear relationship between two variables (model output and observed values). The Pearson correlation coefficient can be obtained by (6).

$$r = \frac{n[\sum_{i=1}^{n} y_i x_i] - [\sum_{i=1}^{n} y_i][\sum_{i=1}^{n} x_i]}{\sqrt{[n\sum_{i=1}^{n} y_i^2 - (\sum_{i=1}^{n} y_i)^2][n\sum_{i=1}^{n} x_i^2 - (\sum_{i=1}^{n} x_i)^2]}} \qquad (6)$$

where, y_i is the value for the ith predicted attribute, x_i is the value for the ith measured attribute, and n represents the number of attributes.

The values for the correlation coefficients range from −1 (a perfect decreasing linear relationship) to +1 (a perfect increasing linear relationship). The absolute value for the coefficient indicates the strength of the relationship, with larger absolute values indicating stronger relationships [30].

In addition to the correlation coefficient, Mean Absolute Error (MAE), Root Mean Square Error (RMSE) and Coefficient of Residual Mass (CMR) were used to evaluate the model.

$$MAE = \frac{\sum_{i=1}^{n} |x_i - y_i|}{n} \qquad (7)$$

$$RMSE = [\frac{\sum_{i=1}^{n} (x_i - y_i)^2}{n}]^{0.5} \qquad (8)$$

$$CRM = \frac{(\sum_{i=1}^{n} x_i) - (\sum_{i=1}^{n} y_i)}{\sum_{i=1}^{n} x_i} \qquad (9)$$

The RMSE value indicates how much the model under- or over-estimates the measurements, and the CRM value is a measure of the tendency of the model to overestimate or underestimate the measurements. Positive values for CRM indicate that the model underestimates the measurements,

and negative values for CRM indicate a tendency to overestimate. For a perfect fit between the observed and predicted data, the values for MAE, RMSE, and CRM should equal 0.0 [31].

5. Results and discussion

According to the calculated SPI values for different time scales, the k-nearest neighbor model was utilized to predict the most likely drought occurrence for the studied region during different years. In the beginning of computations, the optimum value for the K was obtained by the two-fold cross-validation method. Fig. 6 shows the precision of the method based on the Sum of Squares Error (SSE) coefficient. According to Fig. 6, three K values (15, 16, and 19) produced the same lowest error. The SSE value equal to 19 was selected because larger K values often smooth the K-NN model, thereby minimizing the risk of over-fitting. Then the most likely drought status for the region was predicted by the K-NN model. Fig. 7 shows the region drought status based on the standard precipitation index during the desired time period.

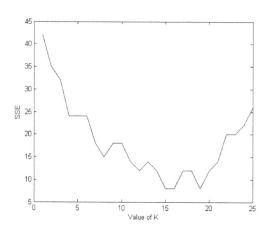

Figure 6. Two-fold cross-validation error rate for K-NN model.

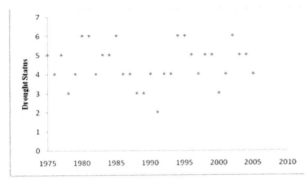

Figure 7. Region drought status based on SPI.

According to the results of the *K*-NN model, it can be found that the studied region has faced droughts over the years. Moreover, according to the presented moving time series, the standard precipitation index can be estimated for future years, and the most likely drought status can be determined.

In order to quantify the prediction accuracy and precision of the model, the Pearson correlation coefficient (r), mean absolute error (MAE), root mean square error (RMSE), and coefficient of residual mass (CRM) were calculated (Table 2). A high value for the Pearson correlation coefficient indicates strong relationships between the variables, and the low MAE, RMSE and CRM values show a reasonable precision and a low error of the *k*-NN model.

Comparing the results obtained for the K-NN modeling with the other SPI-based studies including Cancelliere et al. [11] (r = 0.715, MAD = 0.551 and RMSE = 0.731) indicates that the presented model gives appropriate predictions of the drought situation. Moreover, different time scales were considered in the model so that the drought predictions can be more reliable and efficient.

Table 2. Evaluation of K-NN model by some statistical coefficients.

r	MAE	RMSE	CRM
0.874	0.106	0.119	0.0011

6. Conclusion

Given the importance of drought monitoring in managing this phenomenon as well as the design and management of natural resources, water resource system planning, and various sectors of agriculture, in this study, using the standard precipitation index and *K*-NN model, a method was developed to predict drought occurrence. The model was evaluated using the precipitation and meteorological data of the city of Kerman, Iran. The results obtained indicate that this region has faced moderate-to-severe droughts for many years, which is consistent with the local

observations. Finally, the efficiency and accuracy of the proposed model was evaluated by some statistical coefficients. The reasonable values for the Pearson correlation coefficient (r = 0.874), mean absolute error (MAE = 0.106), root mean square error (RMSE = 0.119), and coefficient of residual mass (CRM = 0.0011) indicate that the developed model is suitable and efficient.

References

[1] Mishra, A. K. & Singh, V. P. (2010). A review of drought concepts. Journal of Hydrology, vol. 391, pp. 202–216.

[2] Moreira, E. E., Coelho, C. A. & Paulo, A. A. (2008). A SPI-based drought category prediction using log linear models. Journal of Hydrology, vol. 354, pp. 116–130.

[3] Palmer, W. C. (1968). Keeping track of crop moisture conditions, nationwide: the new crop moisture index. Weatherwise, vol. 21, pp. 156–161.

[4] Van Rooy, M. P. (1965). A rainfall anomaly index independent of time and space. Notos, 14, 43.

[5] Gibbs, W. J. & Maher, J. V. (1967). Rainfall Deciles as Drought Indicators. Bureau of Meteorology Bull. 48. Commonwealth of Australia, Melbourne, Australia.

[6] Bhalme, H. N. & Mooley, D. A. (1980). Large-scale droughts/floods and monsoon circulation. Mon. Weather Rev, vol. 108, pp. 1197–1211.

[7] Shafer, B. A. & Dezman, L. E. (1982). Development of a Surface Water Supply Index (SWSI) to Assess the Severity of Drought Conditions in Snowpack Runoff Areas. In: Preprints, Western SnowConf., Reno, NV, Colorado State University, pp. 164–175.

[8] Gommes, R. & Petrassi, F. (1994). Rainfall Variability and Drought in Sub-Saharan Africa Since 1960. Agro-meteorology Series Working Paper 9, Food and Agriculture Organization, Rome, Italy.

[9] McKee, T. B., Doesken, N. J. & Kleis, J. 1993. The Relationship of Drought Frequency and Duration to Time Scales, Eighth Conference on Applied Climatology. 17-22 January, Anaheim, California.

[10] Weghorst, K. M. (1996). The Reclamation Drought Index: Guidelines and Practical Applications. Bureau of Reclamation, Denver, CO, p. 6 (Available from Bureau of Reclamation, D-8530, Box 25007, Lakewood, CO 80226).

[11] Cancelliere, A., Di Mauro, G., Bonaccorso, B. & Rossi, G. (2007). Drought forecasting using the standardized precipitation index. Water resources management, vol. 21, no. 5, pp. 801-819.

[12] Han, P., Wang, P. X., Zhang, S. Y. & Zhu, D. H. (2010). Drought forecasting based on the remote

sensing data using ARIMA models. Mathematical and Computer Modelling, vol. 51, no. 11, pp.1398-1403.

[13] Farokhnia, A., Morid, S. & Byun, H. R. (2011). Application of global SST and SLP data for drought forecasting on Tehran plain using data mining and ANFIS techniques. Theoretical and applied climatology, vol. 104, no. (1-2), pp.71-81.

[14] Du, L., Tian, Q., Yu, T., Meng, Q., Jancso, T., Udvardy, P. & Huang, Y. (2013). A comprehensive drought monitoring method integrating MODIS and TRMM data. International Journal of Applied Earth Observation and Geoinformation, vol. 23, pp.245-253.

[15] Farahmand, A. & AghaKouchak, A. (2015). A generalized framework for deriving nonparametric standardized drought indicators. Advances in Water Resources, vol. 76, pp.140-145.

[16] Hao, C., Zhang, J. & Yao, F. (2015). Combination of multi-sensor remote sensing data for drought monitoring over Southwest China. International Journal of Applied Earth Observation and Geoinformation, vol. 35, pp.270-283.

[17] Narasimhan, B. & Srinivasan, R. (2005). Development and evaluation of Soil Moisture Deficit Index (SMDI) and Evapotranspiration Deficit Index (ETDI) for agricultural drought monitoring. Agricultural and Forest Meteorology, vol. 113, pp. 69–88.

[18] Türkeş, M. & Tatlı, H. (2009). Use of the standardized precipitation index (SPI) and a modified SPI for shaping the drought probabilities over Turkey. International Journal of Climatology, vol. 29, no. 15, pp. 2270-2282.

[19] Vasiliades, L., Loukas, A. & Liberis, N. (2011). A water balance derived drought index for Pinios River Basin, Greece. Water Resources Management, vol. 25, no. 4, pp.1087-1101.

[20] Dhaliwal, D. S., Sandhu, P. S. & Panda, S. N. (2011). Enhanced K-Nearest Neighbor Algorithm, World Academy of Science Engineering and Technology Journal, vol. 49, pp. 681-685.

[21] Mucherino, A., Papajorgji, P. & Pardalos, P. M. (2009). Data Mining in Agriculture, Springer.

[22] Smith, B. L., Williams, B. M., & Oswald, R. K. (2002). Comparison of parametric and nonparametric models for traffic flow forecasting, Transportation Research, vol. 10, no. 4, pp. 303–321.

[23] Prairie, J. R., Rajagopalan, B., Fulp, T. J., & Zagona, E. A. (2006). Modified K-NN model for stochastic streamflow simulation, Journal of Hydrologic Engineering, vol. 11, no. 4, pp. 371–378.

[24] Salas, J. D. & Lee, T. (2010). Nonparametric Simulation of Single-Site Seasonal Streamflows, Journal of Hydrologic Engineering, vol. 15, no. 4, pp. 284–296.

[25] Travis, Q. B., & Mays, L. W. (2011). Prediction of Intake Vortex Risk by Nearest Neighbors Modeling, Journal of Hydraulic Engineering, vol. 126, no. 5, pp. 701–705.

[26] Fadaei-Kermani., E, Barani, G. A., & Ghaeini-Hessaroeyeh., M. (2015). Prediction of cavitation damage on spillway using K-nearest neighbor modeling. Water science and technology. vol. 71, no. 3, pp. 347–352.

[27] Hastie, T., Tibshirani, R., & Friedman, J. (2008). The Elements of Statistical Learning, Second edition, Springer series, California.

[28] Xindung, W. & Kumar, V. (2009). Top Ten Algorithm in Data Mining, First edition, Taylor & Francis Group, USA.

[29] Bokharaeian, B. & Diaz, A. (2016). Extraction of Drug-Drug Interaction from Literature through Detecting Linguistic-based Negation and Clause Dependency. Journal of AI and Data Mining, vol. 4, no. 2, pp. 203-212.

[30] Izakian, Z. & Mesgari, M. (2015). Fuzzy clustering of time series data: A particle swarm optimization approach. Journal of AI and Data Mining, vol. 3, no. 1, pp. 39-46.

[31] Dashtaki., S. G, Homaee, M., & Mahdian., M. H. (2009). Site-Dependence Performance of Infiltration Models, Water Resour Manage, vol. 23, pp. 2777–2790.

21

An improved algorithm for network reliability evaluation

M. Ghasemzadeh[*]

Electrical and Computer Engineering Department, Yazd University

*Corresponding author: m.ghasemzadeh@yazd.ac.ir (M. Ghasemzadeh)

Abstract

Binary Decision Diagram (BDD) is a data structure proved to be compact in representation and efficient in manipulation of Boolean formulas. Using Binary decision diagram in network reliability analysis has already been investigated by some researchers. In this paper, we show how an exact algorithm for network reliability can be improved and implemented efficiently by using a Colorado University Decision Diagram (CUDD).

Keywords: *Network Reliability, Efficienty, CUDD, Binary Decision Diagram.*

1. Introduction

In many systems, such as a computer or electricity networks the connectivity of the network components is of a great concern. Sometimes we are only interested in the connectivity of some components or connectivity of just two special components. In this paper, we review the properties of a Binary Decision Diagram [12,3] which is a modern data structure in representation and manipulation of Boolean formulas, then we see how a network reliability can be measured efficiently by using this data structure. We also consider the CUDD [16], which is a standard open source package for construction and the manipulation of BDD and its variants, such as ZDD, Zero-suppressed Binary Decision Diagram.

The network model is an undirected graph where vertices of the graph stand for the sites and the edges of the graph stand for the links between the sites. In practice each site or link can fail accidentally, but we suppose that sites (vertices) are perfect, but links may independently fail with some known probabilities. The problem of checking the connectivity is known to be NP-hard [1, 2].

There are two classes for computation of network reliability. The first class is for approximate computation while the second class is concerned with exact computation of network reliability computation. The existing algorithms in an exact computation are in two different categories: The first category deals with the enumeration of all the minimum paths or cuts. A path is defined as a set of network components in such a way that if these components are all failure-free, the system remains up. A path is minimal if it has no proper sub-paths. Conversely, a cut is a set of network components such that if any of the components fail, the system goes down. Using the enumeration method, one may only compute the reliability of networks consisting of a small number of components. In the second category, the algorithms are based on reducing the graph representing the network by removing some of its components.

These reductions allow us to compute the reliability in a simpler way[15], that is, decompose the problem into two sub-problems: The first one is assumed the component has failed, and the second one is assumed it functions. These reductions are recursively applied until it reaches very primitive instances. It is shown that the idea of eduction lets solve this problem more efficiently [17].

Binary Decision diagram is the state-of-the-art

data structure in Boolean formula representation and manipulation. It has been successfully used in VLSI CAD and widely integrated in commercial tools[11,4]. As a data structure for representation of Boolean functions it was first introduced by Lee and further popularized by Akers[13]. Bryant[4] introduced its restricted form OBDD (Reduced Ordered BDD), which is a canonical representation. He also proved that OBDDs allow efficient manipulations of Boolean formulas. This data structure and its variants can be implemented efficiently in modern computers using a programming language, such as C. CUDD (Colorado University Decision Diagram) Package, provided at the university of Colorado by Fabio Somenzi [16], is an open source package written in C. This package is known to be the most useful package for construction and manipulation of BDD and its variants.

Using BDD in the reliability analysis framework was first introduced by Madre and Coudert [5], and developed by Odeh and Rauzy [14]. In the network reliability framework, Sekine and Imai [10], and Trivedi [18] have shown how to functionally construct the corresponding BDD. Gary Hardy, Corinne Lucet and Nikolaos Limnios [9] improved existing techniques by using the concept of partitions of network nodes. They presented an exact algorithm for computing the K-terminal reliability of a network graph with perfect vertices.

The rest of this paper is organized as follows. First, we introduce BDD with an emphasis on its brilliant properties. In Section 3, we discuss about the network reliability problem and employ BDD in solving them. We give our CUDD based implementation for constructing the desired BDD in Section 4. Finally, we give conclusions in Section 5.

2. Binary decisions diagram and its variants

Binary Decision diagram (BDD) is the state-of-the-art data structure in Boolean formula representation and manipulation. They have been successfully used in VLSI CAD and widely integrated in commercial tools. In this section we review the basic definitions of BDD and learn about their theoretical and practical aspects. There are several extensions of BDD, of which we are interested in ZDD, shown to be more efficient in solving some related problems [6].

2.1. Definition and examples of BDD

Mostly BDD is meant to be an ordered BDD or OBDD. An OBDD is a graphic description of an algorithm for the computation of a Boolean function. The following definition describes the syntax of OBDD, i.e., the properties of the underlying graph. The semantics of OBDD, i.e., the functions represented by OBDD, are specified by the following definitions.

Definition 1: An OBDD G representing the Boolean functions $f^1,...,f^m$ over the variables $x_1,...,x_n$ is a directed acyclic graph with the following properties:

1. For each function f^i there is a pointer to a node in G.
2. The nodes without outgoing edges, which are called *sinks* or *terminal nodes*, are labeled by 0 or 1.
3. All non-sink nodes of G, which are also called *internal* nodes, are labeled by a variable and have two outgoing edges, a *0-edge* and a *1-edge*.
4. On each directed path in the OBDD, each variable occurs at most once as the *label of a node*.
5. There is a variable ordering π, which is a permutation of $x_1,...,x_n$, and on each directed path the variables occur according to this ordering. This means, if x_i is arranged before x_j in the variable ordering, then it must not happen that on some path there is a node labelled by x_j before a node labeled by x_i.

In Figure 1, we draw sink nodes as squares and internal nodes as circles. We always assume that edges are directed downwards. 0-edges are drawn as dashed lines while 1-edges are drawn as solid lines. Figure 1 shows an OBDD G_f with the variable ordering x_1, x_3, x_2 and an OBDD G_g with the variable ordering x_1, y_1, x_0, y_0.

Definition 2: Let G be an OBDD for the functions $f^1,...,f^m$ over the variables $x_1,...,x_n$, and let $a = (a_1,...,a_n)$ be an input. The *computation path* for the node v of G and the input a is the path starting at v obtained by choosing at each internal node labelled by x_i the outgoing a_i-edge.

Each node v represents a function f_v,

where $f_v(a)$ is defined as the value of the sink at the end of the computation path starting at v for the input a. Finally, f^j is defined as the function represented at the head of the pointer for f^j. Definition 2 can be seen as the description of an algorithm to obtain the computation path and therefore the value of $f^j(a)$ for each function f^j and each input a.

In the OBDD G_f in Figure 1, the computation path for the input $(x_1, x_2, x_3) = (1, 1, 0)$ passes from x_1 in the root, then from the right x_3, then from the right x_2 and finally goes to the 0-Sink. Furthermore, for each node v of G_f the function f_v represented at v is given. Definition 2 is easy to verify that the OBDD G_f in Figure 1, represents the function $f(x_1, x_2, x_3) = x_1 \oplus x_2 \oplus x_3$ and the OBDD G_g represents function $g(x_1, y_1, x_0, y_0) = (s_2, s_1, s_0)$, where (s_2, s_1, s_0) is the sum of the two 2-bit numbers (y_1, y_0) and (x_1, x_0).

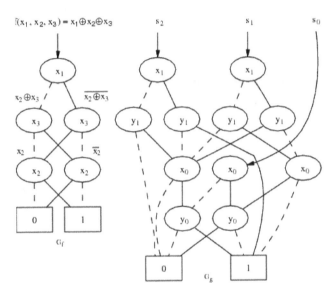

Figure 1. Examples of OBDDs.

The function represented at the sink labelled by $c \in \{0, 1\}$ is the constant function c. Now let v be an internal node which is labelled by x_i. Let v_0 be the 0-successor of v, i.e., the node reached via the 0-edge leaving v, and let v_1 be the 1-successor of v. We consider the computation of f_v for some input. If in the input the value of x_i is 0, then by definition 2 we may obtain f_v by evaluating f_{v_0} and, if the value of x_i is 1, by evaluating f_{v_1}. This can be expressed by the equation:

$$f_v = \overline{x}_i . f_{v_0} \vee x_i . f_{v_1} \qquad (1)$$

Using equation 1 we may compute the functions represented at the nodes of an OBDD in a bottom-up fashion. However, the opposite is also true. If a node v labelled by x_i represents the function f_v,

then the 0-successor of v represents the subfunction (sometimes called cofactor) $f_{v|x_i=0}$ and the 1-successor the subfunction $f_{v|x_i=1}$. In other words, at v the function f_v is decomposed using *Shannons decomposition rule*:

$$f_v = \overline{x}_i . f_{v|x_i=0} \vee x_i . f_{v|x_i=1} \qquad (2)$$

We point out that there are variants of OBDDs where Shannons decomposition rule is replaced by a different decomposition rule. Equation 2 shows that we can decompose the function f_v in different ways by choosing different variables x_i for decomposition. Hence, we may get different OBDDs for the same function if we use different variable orderings. Later on, we will see that the size of an OBDD usually depends strongly on the chosen variable ordering.

2.2. Synthesis

Synthesis is probably the most important operation, because it is needed in almost all applications. The usual way of generating a new BDD is to combine existing BDDs with connectives like AND, OR, EX-OR. If we want to make an OBDD for a given Boolean function. First, we make OBDDs for each variable of the Boolean function, and then we parse the Boolean function and combine the existing OBDDs to make OBDDs for the needed sub functions. Finally the OBDD representing the whole given Boolean function would be obtained. As suggested by Brace, Rudell, and Bryant [3], in OBDD packages, the synthesis algorithm is usually called an *ITE* ("if-then-else") where:

$$ite(f,g,h) = f.g \lor \bar{f}.h$$

The *ITE()* procedure receives OBDDs for two Boolean functions f and g, builds the OBDD for $f < op > g$. In fact, it receives three arguments: *I,T,E* which are OBDDs and returns the OBDD representing: $(I \land T) \lor (I \land E)$. All binary Boolean operations can be simulated by the ite-operator, e.g.: $f \lor g = ite(f,1,g)$, $f \land g = ite(f,g,0)$ or $f \oplus g = ite(f,g,g)$. *ITE()* is a combination of depth-first traversal and dynamic programming. (A recursive, Bottom-up procedure with tabulation). The basic idea of *ITE()* comes from the expansion theorem:

$$F < op > G = v(F_v < op > G_v) + v'(F_{v'} < op > G_{v'})$$

ITE() maintains a table called *Computed Table* to avoid computing the same combination repeatedly. It also maintains another table called *Unique Table* to avoid producing subgraphs representing the same sub-function. The benefit of this technique is the important result that *ITE()* becomes polynomial rather than exponential. Figure 2 displays the pseudocode for the *ITE* operator.

If f and g are given by OBDDs with different variable orderings, the *ITE()* procedure would not work, because for the simultaneous traversal, the variables have to be encountered in the same ordering in both OBDDs. In this situation the synthesis method would be much harder.

2.3. The variable ordering problem for OBDDs

OBDDs share a fatal property with all kinds of representations of switching functions: The representation of almost all functions need exponential space. Bryant [4] discovered that

OBDD size strongly depends on the chosen variable ordering. Figure 3, shows the effect of variable ordering for a switching function. Notice that both OBDDs represent the same Boolean function: $F = (a_1 \land b_1) \lor (a_2 \land b_2) \lor (a_3 \land b_3)$.

```
ITE(f, g, h)
   {
      If (f == 1) return g;
      If (f == 0) return h;
      If (g == h) return g;
      if(
   p=IN_COMPUTED_TABLE(f,g,h))
   return p;
      v = TOP_VARIABLE(f, g, h );
      fn = ITE(f_v0,g_v0,h_v0);
      gn = ITE(f_v1,g_v1,h_v1);
      if(f_n == g_n) return g_n;

   if(!p=IN_UNIQUE_TABLE(v,f_n,g_n))
         p = CREATE_NODE(v,f_n,g_n);

   NSERT_COMPUTED_TBL(p,HASH(
   f,g,h));
      return p;
   }
```

Figure 2. The ITE algorithm for ROBDDs.

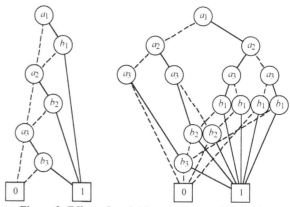

Figure 3. Effect of variable ordering on OBDD size (Bryant, 1986).

Different functions have different ordering sensitivities. Some functions have a high and others have a low variable order sensitivity. The practicability of OBDDs strongly depends on the existence of suitable algorithms and tools for minimizing the graphs in the relevant applications. There are many improvements, optimization algorithms, and additions to the basic OBDD model. It is known by experience that:

- Many tasks have reasonable OBDD

representations.

  • Algorithms remain practical for up to 100,000 OBDD nodes.

  • Most proposed heuristic ordering methods are generally satisfactory.

However, because of the practical applicability of this data structure, investigation and development of new optimization techniques for OBDDs is still a rewarding research topic.

3. Reliability measurment

As mentioned above, the exact method in evaluating the reliability can be achieved in two different methods. In this section we introduce these methods and discuss a how BDD can be used to gain considerable improvements.

3.1. Enumeration method

We consider the model used in most publications and used by Lucet and Limnios [9]. In this regard, a network model is an undirected stochastic graph $G=(V,E)$, where V stands for vertices representing sites, and E stands for edge set representing the links between the sites. Each edge e_i of the graph G is subject to failure with known probability $q_i(q_i \in [0,1])$. The probability that edge e_i functions can be obtained from $p_i = 1 - q_i$. In the following, we consider the vertices as perfect. In classical enumerative methods, all the states of the graph are generated, evaluated as a failing state or as a functioning state, then probabilistic methods are used to compute the resulting reliability. Since there are two states for each edge, there are 2^m possible states for the graph G. Let X_i be the binary random variable state of the link e_i in G'', defined by $X_i = 1$ when link e_i is operational, and when $X_i = 0$ link e_i is down. $X = (X_1, X_2, \ldots X_m)$ is the *random network state vector*. A state x of G is denoted by $x = (x_1, x_2, \ldots x_m)$ where x_i stands for the state of edge e_i, $x_i = 0$ if e_i is down and $x_i = 1$ if it works. Probability of x is can be computed by:

$$Pr(X = x) = \prod_{i=1}^{m}(x_i.p_i + (1-x_i)q_i)$$

K-terminal network reliability is defined by:

$$R_k(p;G) = \sum_{x \, is \, a \, functioning \, state} Pr(X = x)$$

Because of exponential number of states, if classical methods are applied, the complexity would be $O(m.2^m)$. So, these methods are not applicable in large networks.

3.2. Graph reduction

In order to avoid drawbacks of the enumeration method, Lucet and Limnios [9] define two graph operations: The *edge deletion*, and the *edge contraction*. $G = (V, E)$ is a given graph such that there is an edge $e_i \in E$. G_i is to be the subgraph obtained from G by deleting $e_i, (G\_i = G \backslash e_i)$.

If $e_i = (x, y)$ such that $x, y in V$, then edge contraction consists of merging vertices x and y in one single vertex. We denote G_*i to represent the subgraph obtained from G by contracting e_i. When edge e_i fails, the network behavior is equivalent to G_i; and when functions, the network behavior is equivalent to $G_8 i$. According to this decomposition the following result is emerged and could be applied recursively:

$$R_k(p;G) = p_i.R_k(p;G_{*i}) + q_i.R_k(p;G_{-i})$$

if we consider e_i and e_j as two edges of E then G_{*i-j} means subgraph obtained by contracting e_i and deleting e_j. Figure 4 shows how this idea works.

4. Employing BDD in encoding and evaluation

We can learn from the ITE() operation on BDDs that although in its primitive form it is exponential, by embedding the idea of tabulation, its complexity has been reduced to quadratic. When we look at the algorithm of evaluating network reliability based on reducing the graph representing the network by removing some of its components (decompose the problem into two sub-problems) we can realize that the same technique and also be employed for this problem to gain similar benefits. In this section, we compute network reliability by taking advantage of the BDD data structure.

The mystery of BDD is merging equivalent subfunctions of a Boolean formula to get compact representation of the entire formula. All main operations on BDD, such as the ITE() function, perform this kind of merging in a recursive manner and in a systematic way to get the most benefits of it, while preserving the canonicity of representation. In has been shown that the recursive network reliability relation in BDD can be formulated as:

$$\forall i \in [1\ldots m]: \quad R_k(p;G) = Pr(f=1)$$

$$R_k(p;G) = p_i.Pr(f_{X_{i=1}} = 1) + q_i.Pr(f_{X_{i=0}} = 1)$$

We obtain values of $f_{X_{i=0}}$ and $f_{X_{i=1}}$ recursively untill it reaches the sink nodes. The probability is stored in each internal node. We may use the CUDD package to implement the corresponding algorithm and operations.

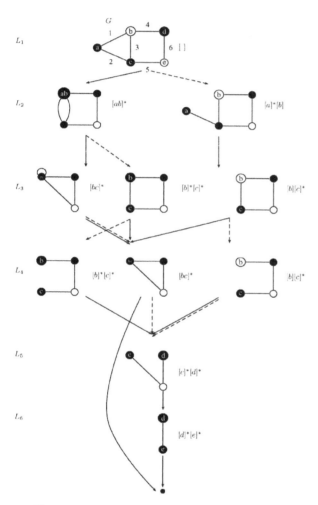

Figure 4: Network decomposition based on edge deletion/contraction (Lucet and Limnios).

4.1. Implementation in the CUDD Package

In this section, we introduce the CUDD package, which is known to be the best open source package for manipulating the BDD and its variants. Content of this subsection is prepared very briefly from its help manual [16].

The CUDD package provides functions to manipulate Binary Decision Diagram (BDD), Algebraic Decision Diagram (ADD), and Zero-suppressed Binary Decision Diagram (ZDD). BDDs are used to represent switching functions;

ADDs are used to represent function from $\{0,1\}^n$ to an arbitrary set. ZDDs represent switching functions like BDDs; however, they are more efficient than BDDs when the functions to be represented are characteristic functions of cube sets, or in general, when the ON-Set of the function to be represented is sparse. They are inferior to BDDs in other cases.

The CUDD package can be used in three ways:

- As a black box. The application program that needs to manipulate decision diagrams only uses the exported functions of the package. The rich set of functions included in the CUDD package allows many applications to be written in this way. An application written in terms of the exported functions of the package needs not concern itself with the details of variable reordering, which may take place behind the scenes.

- As a clear box. When writing a sophisticated application based on decision diagrams, efficiency often dictates that some functions be implemented as direct recursive manipulation of the diagrams, instead of being written in terms of existing primitive functions.

- Through an interface. Object oriented languages like C++ can free the programmer from the burden of memory management. A C++ interface is included in the distribution of CUDD. It automatically frees decision diagrams that are no longer used by the application. Almost all the functionality provided by the CUDD exported functions is available through the C++ interface, which is especially recommended for fast prototyping.

Figure 5 shows the main procedure in CUDD for the algorithm of evaluating the probability of network reliability.

The decomposition shown in Figure 3 can be mapped into BDD construction. Its root corresponds to the original network graph and in each level, one edge is deleted or contracted. Children of a node in each level represent sub-graphs obtained by successive edge deletion or edge contractions.

```
float ComputeNetRel( DdNode *DecBDD )
    {
        float Rk;

        if ( DecBDD==CuddOne) return 1;
        if ( DecBDD==CuddZero) return 0;
        if ( Rk = Computed(DecBDD) )
         return(Rk);
        Pr1          =           CaculReliability(
        Cudd_T(DecBDD));
        Pr0          =           CaculReliability(
        Cudd_E(DecBDD));
        Rk = (1-q[i]) * Pr1 + q[i] * Pr0;
        InsertComputed( DecBDD , Rk);
         return(Rk);
    }
```

Figure 5. Network reliability evaluation / part of cudd code.

5. Conclusion

Two exact methods for evaluation of network reliability were discussed. We saw how by inspiration from the ITE() operator in BDD construction, an algorithm with lower complexity for evaluation of network reliability can be obtained. In fact employing a variant of BDD called ZDD can lead to even more advantages.

References

[1] Ball, M. O. (1980). Complexity of network reliability computations. Networks, 10,153-165.

[2] Ball, M. O. (1986). Computational complexity of network reliability analysis:An overview. IEEE Trans. Reliability. R-35:230-239.

[3] Karl, S. (1990). Brace and Richard L. Rudell and Randal E. Bryant. Efficient Implementation of a BDD Package. DAC: Design Automation Conf. 40-45.

[4] Randal, E. (1986). Bryant. Graph-Based Algorithms for Boolean Function Manipulation. IEEE Transactions on Computers. 35(8),677-691.

[5] Coudert, O. and Madre, J. C. (1992). Implicit and incremental computation of primes and essential primes of Boolean functions. Proceedings of the 29th ACM/IEEE Design Automation Conference. 36-39.

[6] Drechsler, R. and Sieling, D. (2001). Binary decision diagrams in theory and practice. International Journal on Software Tools for Technology Transfer (STTT). 3(2),112-136.

[7] GhasemZadeh, M., Klotz, V. and Meinel, C. (2004). Embedding Memoization to the Semantic Tree Search for Deciding QBFs. Australian Conference on Artificial Intelligence. 681-693.

[8] GhasemZadeh, M. and Meinel, C. (2005). Splitting Versus Unfolding. 7th International Symposium on Representations and Methodology of Future Computing Technology, Tokyo, Japan, 2005.

[9] Hardy, G., and Lucet, C. and Limnios, N. (2007). K-Terminal Network Reliability Measures With Binary Decision Diagrams. IEEE Transactions on Reliability. 56(3), 506-515.

[10] Imai, H., Sekine, K. and Imai, K. (1999). Computational investigations of allterminal network reliability via BDDs. IEICE Transactions on Fundamentals. E82-A(5),714--721.

[11] Christoph Meinel and Jochen Bern and Anna Slobodová. Efficient OBDD-Based Boolean Manipulation in CAD beyond Current Limits. Design Automation Conf.(DAC), pp 408-413, San Francisco, CA, 1995.

[12] Meinel, C. and Theobald, T. (1998). Algorithms and data structures in VLSI design: OBDD - foundations and applications. Berlin, Heidelberg. New York: Springer-Verlag.

[13] Moret, B. (1982). Decision trees and diagrams. Computer Survey. (14), 593-623.

[14] Rauzy, A. (2003). A new methodology to handle Boolean models with loops. IEEE Trans. Reliability. R-52(1),96-105.

[15] Satyanarayana, A. and Chang, M. K. (1983). Network reliability and the factoring theorem. Networks, 13,107-120.

[16] Somenzi, F. CUDD Package. ftp://vlsi.colorado.edu/pub/.

[17] Theologou, O. and Carlier, J. (1991). Factoring and reductions for networks with imperfect vertices. IEEE Trans. R-40, 210-217.

[18] Zang, X., Sun, H. and Trivedi, K. (1999). A BDD-based algorithm for reliability evaluation of phased mission systems. IEEE Trans. Reliability. R-48(1),50-60.

22

Image retrieval using the combination of text-based and content-based algorithms

H. Mohamadi[1], A. Shahbahrami[2*] and J. Akbari[1]

1. Islamic Azad University of Arak
2. Department of Computer Engineering, University of Guilan

*Corresponding author: shahbahrami@guilan.ac.ir (A. Shahbahrami)

Abstract

Image retrieval is an important research field, which has received great attention in the last decades. The main purpose of research in this field is to improve the process of finding the desired image in the large and variable database. In this paper, we present an approach for the image retrieval based on the combination of text-based and content-based features. For text-based features, keywords and for content-based features, color and texture features have been used. A query in this system contains some keywords and an input image. At first, the images are retrieved based on the input keywords. Then, visual features are extracted to retrieve ideal output images. For extraction of color features, we have used color moments and for texture, we have calculated color co-occurrence matrix for each Red, Blue and gray component. The COREL image databas have been used for our experimental results. The experimental results show that the performance of the combination of both text-based and content-based features is much higher than each of them, which is applied separately.

Keywords: *Text-Based Image Retrieval, Content-Based Image Retrieval, Color Moments, Color Co-occurrence Matrix.*

1. Introduction

Image retrieval techniques are divided into two text-based and content-based categories. In text-based algorithms, some special words like keywords are used. Keywords and annotations should be assigned to each image, when each image is stored in a database. The annotation operation is time consuming and tedious. In addition, it is subjective. Furthermore, the annotations are sometimes incomplete and it is possible that some image features may not be mentioned in annotations [1]. To overcome on mentioned limitation, Content-Based Image Retrieval (CBIR) techniques have been proposed. In a CBIR system, images are automatically indexed by their visual contents through extracted low-level features, such as shape, texture, color, size and so on [1, 2, 3].

However, extracting all visual features of an image is a difficult task and there is a problem namely semantic gap in the semantic gap, presenting high-level visual concepts using low-level visual concept is very hard. In order to alleviate these limitations, some researchers use both techniques together using different features. This combination improves the performance compared to each technique separately [4-11].

In this paper, there are two steps for answering a query to retrieve an image. First, some keywords are used to retrieve similar images and after that some special visual features such as color and texture are extracted. In other words, in the second step, CBIR is applied. Color moments for color feature and co-occurrence matrix for extraction of texture features have been computed. We have designed this system, and we have tested it using a COREL standard image dataset. The rate of the accuracy of the proposed system has been improved in comparison to text-based and content-based methods.

This paper is organized as follows. the next session focuses on the related works in the field. In section 3, content-based image retrieval systems have been explained. In section 4, the combination technique has been explained. Section 5 presents the implementation and experimental results and finally, in section 6, the conclusions have been presented.

2. Related works

In the some systems, a content-based approach is combined with a text-based approach. As an example Blobworld system, automatically segments each image into regions, which correspond to objects or parts of objects in an image. In this system, users can view the results of the segmentation of both the query image and the returned results highlighting how the segmented features have influenced the retrieval results [6].

QBIC system supports queries based on example images. The visual features used in the system include color, texture, and shape. In this system, color was represented using a k-bin color histogram and the texture was described by an improved tamura texture the visual features [7].

In the VisualSEEK, a system uses two content-based and text-based queries. The system uses color and texture visual features. The color feature is represented by color set, texture based on wavelet transform, and spatial relationship between image regions. A binary tree was used to index the feature vectors [8].

Chabot uses a relational database management system called postgres, which supports search through a combination of text and color [9] and Photobook, computes features vectors for the image characteristics, which are then compared to compute a distance measure utilizing one of the systems matching algorithms, including euclidean, mahalanobis, divergence, vector space angle, histogram, Fourier peak, wavelet tree distances and user-defined matching algorithms via dynamic code loading [10].

In [11], a system has presented a combination of text-based and content-based algorithms. For text retrieval, the Apache Lucene engine has been used and for content-based retrieval, images have been segmented to different areas and regions and histogram has calculated for each section.

3. Features extraction

In a CBIR system, feature extraction is an important stage and different features can be extracted in this stage. Some of these features are explained in the following sections.

3.1. Color feature

Color is an important low-level feature for image retrieval. Due to the fact that color features are very stable and robust and are not sensitive to rotation, translation and scale changes. Color describers containing color distribution, color histogram, color sets and color moments [1, 2, 14, 19].

3.1.1. Color moments

Color moments are one of the best color describers. Most of the color distribution information is captured by the three low-order Moments. Suppose an image has N and M pixels. The first-order moment (μ) calculates the mean color, the second-order Moment (σ) calculates the standard deviation, and the third-order moment calculates the skewness (θ) of color. These three moments are extracted using the following mathematical formulation [14, 22].

$$\mu = \frac{1}{N} \sum_{i=1}^{N} \sum_{j=1}^{M} f_{ij} \tag{1}$$

$$\sigma = \left(\frac{1}{N} \sum_{i=1}^{N} \sum_{j=1}^{M} (f_{ij} - \mu_i)^2 \right)^{\frac{1}{2}} \tag{2}$$

$$\theta = \left(\frac{1}{N} \sum_{i=1}^{N} \sum_{j=1}^{M} (f_{ij} - \mu_i)^3 \right)^{\frac{1}{3}} \tag{3}$$

Where f_{ij} is the value of pixel in the ith row and jth column of the image.

3.2. Texture feature

Texture is an important property in image retrieval and is a regional descriptor in the retrieval process. The texture descriptor provides measures, such as smoothness, coarseness and regularity [13, 17, 18]. Texture description algorithms are divided into some categories, such as structural and statistical. Statistical methods, including Fourier power spectra, co-occurrence matrices, tamura features, word decomposition, Markov random field, fractal model, and filter-based techniques, such as Gabor and wavelet transform, characterize texture by the statistical distribution of the image intensity [16, 20, 21, 22].

3.2.1. Gray-level co-occurrence matrix (GLCM)

Gray-level co-occurrence approach is one of the most commonly used statistical methods whose calculated Gray-Level Co-occurrence Matrix (GLCM). The elements in this matrix are the relative frequencies of occurrence of grey level combinations among pairs of image pixels. This matrix considers the relationship of image pixels in different directions, such as horizontal, vertical, diagonal and ant diagonal [5, 8].

The GLCM, first introduced by Haralick is a powerful technique for measuring texture features. Suppose the input image has N and M pixels in the horizontal and vertical directions respectively. Suppose that the grey level appearing at each pixel is quantised to Z levels. Assume $N = \{1, 2, ..., N\}$ is a horizontal space domain, $N_y = \{1, 2, ..., M\}$ is a vertical space domain and $G = 0,1,2,...,Z$ be the set of Z quantized grey levels. When the direction θ and distance d are given, the matrix element C (i, j/d, θ) can be expressed by calculating the pixel logarithm of co-occurrence grey level i and j. The (i, j) of C (i,j) is the number of co-occurrences of the pair of gray-level i and j which are a distance d apart. Suppose the distance is 1 and θ equals 0°, the formulae is following[13, 23]:

$$C(i,j/1,0) =$$
$$Card \begin{cases} ((x_1, y_1), (x_2, y_2)) \in (N \times N_y) \\ \\ |x_1 - x_2| = 0, \\ |y_1, y_2| = 1, \\ f(x_1, y_1) = i, \\ f(x_2, y_2) = j \end{cases} \quad (4)$$

3.2.2. Haralick textural features

The following statistical properties are calculated from the co-occurrence matrix [12, 13, 17, 22]:

1- Energy
The Energy is the image homogeneity, and $c(i,j)$ is the (i,j)th element of the normalized GLCM.

$$F1 = \sum_{i=0}^{G-1} \sum_{j=0}^{G-1} c(i,j)^2 \quad (5)$$

2- Entropy
Entropy shows the amount of information of the image that is needed for image compression.

$$F2 = -\sum_{i=0}^{G-1} \sum_{j=0}^{G-1} c(i,j) \times \log(c(i,j)) \quad (6)$$

3- Contrast
Contrast is a measure of intensity or gray-level variations between the reference pixel and its neighbor.

$$F3 = \sum_{i=0}^{G-1} \sum_{j=0}^{G-1} C(i,j)(i-j)^2 \quad (7)$$

4- Homogeneity
Homogeneity, measures the local homogeneity of a digital image.

$$F4 = \sum_{i=0}^{G-1} \sum_{j=0}^{G-1} \frac{C(i,j)}{1-|i-j|^2} \quad (8)$$

5- Correlation
Correlation calculates the linear dependency of the gray level values in the co-occurrence matrix or the correlation presenting along a scan line of an image [22].

$$F5 = \sum_{i=0}^{G-1} \sum_{j=0}^{G-1} \frac{(i-\mu_x)(j-\mu_y)C(i,j)}{\sigma_x \times \sigma_y} \quad (9)$$

Where, $\mu_x, \mu_y, \sigma_x, \sigma_y$ are the means and the variances of the row and column sums respectively and define as follows:

$$\mu = \sum_{i=0}^{G-1} \sum_{j=0}^{G-1} i \times C(i,j) \quad (10)$$

$$\mu_y = \sum_{i=0}^{G-1} \sum_{j=0}^{G-1} j \times C(i,j) \quad (11)$$

$$\sigma^2 = \sum_{i=0}^{G-1} \sum_{j=0}^{G1}(i-\mu)^2 \times C(i,j) \quad (12)$$

$$\sigma_y^2 = \sum_{i=0}^{G-1} \sum_{j=0}^{G-1}(j-\mu_y)^2 \times C(i,j) \quad (13)$$

6 - Sum of squares
Sum of squares is a measure of gray tone variance.

$$Variance = \sqrt{\sum_{i=0}^{G-1} \sum_{j=0}^{G-1}(i-\mu)^2 C(i,j)} \quad (14)$$

Where:

$$\mu = \frac{\sum_{i=0}^{G-1} \sum_{j=0}^{G-1} C(i,j)}{G*G} \quad (15)$$

7- Mean

$$F7 = \sum_{k=0}^{2G-2} k \times P_{x+y}(k) \quad (16)$$

Where:

$$P_{x+y}(K) = \sum_{i=0}^{G-1} \sum_{j=0}^{G-1} C(i,j)_{|i+j|=k} \quad (17)$$

that $k = 0..(2G-2)$

8- Sum entropy

$$F8 = -\sum_{k=0}^{2G-2} p_{x+y}(K) \times Log\left(p_{x+y}(K)\right) \quad (18)$$

Due to the log (0) is not defined, it is recommended to use log (p+e) that e is an arbitrarily small positive constant, instead of log (p).

9- Sum variance

$$F9 = \sum_{k=0}^{2G-2}(k - F8)^2 \times P_{x+y}(K) \qquad (19)$$

10- Difference variance

$$F10^2 = \sigma_{p_{x-y}}^2 = \sum_{I=0}^{G-1}\left(p_{x-y}(K) - \mu_{p_{x-y}}\right)^2 \qquad (20)$$

Where:

$$P_{x-y}(K) = \sum_{I=0}^{G-1}\sum_{j=0}^{G-1} C(i,j)_{|i-j|=k} \qquad \text{that k =}$$
$$0 \dots \dots G - 1 \qquad (21)$$

$$\mu_{p_{x-y}} = \frac{\sum_{K=0}^{G-1} P_{x-y}(K)}{G} \qquad (22)$$

11-Difference entropy

$$F11 = -\sum_{k=1}^{G-1} p_{x-y}(K) \times \log(p_{x-y}(K)) \qquad (23)$$

12-Information measures of correlation 1

$$F12 = \frac{HXY - HXY1}{MAX\{HX,HY\}} \qquad (24)$$

Where Hxy is entropy and:

$$Hxy1 = -\sum_{i=0}^{G-1}\sum_{j=0}^{G-1} C(i,j) \times Log\left(p_x(i) \times P_y(j)\right) \qquad (25)$$

$$P_y(K) = \sum_{i=0}^{G-1} i \times C(i,k) \qquad (26)$$

$$P_x(K) = \sum_{j=0}^{G-1} j \times C(k,j) \qquad (27)$$

$$Hxy2 = -\sum_{i=0}^{G-1}\sum_{j=0}^{G-1} p_x(i) \times P_y(j) \times Log\left(p_x(i) \times P_y(j)\right) \qquad (28)$$

$$Hx = -\sum_{i=0}^{G-1} p_x(i) \times Log(p_x(i)) \qquad (29)$$

$$Hy = -\sum_{i=0}^{G-1} p_y(i) \times Log\left(p_y(i)\right) \qquad (30)$$

13- Information measures of correlation 2

$$F13 = (1 - e^{-2(HXY2-HXY)})^{\frac{1}{2}} \qquad (31)$$

14- Maximal correlation coefficient

$$F14 = \sqrt{\text{second largest eigen value of Q}} \qquad (32)$$

Where: $Q(i,j) = \sum_K \frac{C(i,k) \times C(j,k)}{p_x(i) \times p_y(k)}$ that $k = 0 \dots (G - 1)$ (33)

These features are the commonly used texture descriptors and can effectively reflect the texture features [15].

3.3. Shape
Shape is a low-level visual feature for image content description. Shape based image retrieval needs to edge reorganization algorithms. These algorithms have lower precision. Therefore, shape feature has a lower precision rather than color and texture features [21, 24, 26, 29].

4. Combined algorithm
In this paper, a two-step system, which is a combination of text-based and content-based methods has been presented and tries to improve the accuracy of image retrieval results. In the first step query, an image is searched based on text, then output enters to the second step, which is retrieval based on content. In the second step, we have used color moments for extraction of color feature, and we have used color co-occurrence matrix for extraction of texture feature. For each color image, we have extracted the co-occurrence matrix of the following color components:

1- Red and Blue Components of RGB color space. There is a linear correlation between the components; therefore, we have not applied the Green component.

2- Gray component I, is defined as follow:

I =0.2 R +0.7G +0.07B (34)

Then the total of statistical features from each matrix should be extracted. Image retrieval steps showed in Figure1.

5. Experimental results
5.1. Image Database
The simulation has been performed on a PC with a processor 2.2 GHz and visual C# 2010 software. The Corel image database has been used as the input data. It consists of 1000 color images with size of 128×96 [6, 14, 18, 27, 28, 30]. Table 1 depicts the different category of this image database.

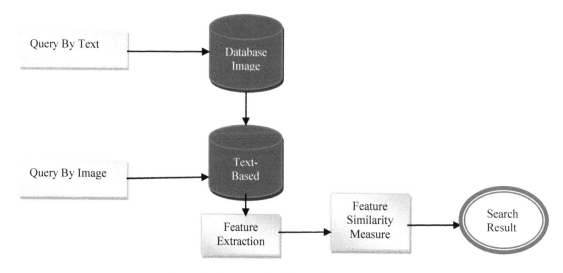

Figure 1. Image retrieval steps in the combined system.

Table 1. Different categories of image database [14].

Category number	1	2	3	4	5	6	7	8	9	10
Category name	Flowers	Buses	Textures	People	Food	Beach	Elephant	Dinosaur	Mountain	Horses

5.2. Similarity Measure Function

For each color image, we have calculated color moments and the total of statistical features from each color co-occurrence matrix (F1-F14 features) for each of Red, Blue and I component. Therefore, feature vectors for two color images A and B can be defined as the following equations.

$F_A = [F_{RedA}, F_{BlueA}, F_{IA}, F_{Color\ A}] = \{F_{A1}, F_{A2}....,$
$F_{A45}\}$
$F_B = [F_{RedB}, F_{BlueB}, F_{IB}, F_{Color\ B}] = \{F_{B1}, F_{B2},...,$
$F_{B45}\}$

The similarity function is defined as follow:

$S(A,B) = W_1 D_E (F_{RedA}, F_{RedB}) + W_2 D_E (F_{BlueA}, F_{BlueB}) + W_3 D_E (F_{IA}, F_{IB}) + W_4 D_E (F_{Color\ A}, F_{Color\ B})$ (34)

Where D_E is the Euclidean distance of the feature vector [14] and wi ($1 \leq i \leq 4$) are weights for each component and they are subject to $0 < W_i < 1$, $\sum_{i=1}^{4} W_i = 1$, and we suppose $W_1 = W_2 = W_3 = W_4 = 0.25$

$S(A, B)$ is the similarity of texture feature of two color images. If $S(A, B) = 0$, the two images are completely similar, and if $S(A, B) = 1$, the two images are completely dissimilar.

The effectiveness of the extracted features has been measured by precision and recall parameters. Precision is the ratio of relevant retrieved images

to the total number of retrieved images. Recall is the ratio of relevant retrieved images to the total number of relevant images in the database, which is defined as follow [14]:

$$p = \frac{Number\ of\ relevant\ retrieved\ images}{Total\ number\ of\ retrieved\ images}$$ (35)

$$R = \frac{Number\ of\ relevant\ retrieved\ images}{Total\ number\ of\ relevant\ images\ in\ database}$$ (36)

Table 2 presents precision and recall comparisons between the proposed method, text-based and content-based algorithms for each category. Average precision and recall for proposed techniques are 0.82 and 0.87, respectively. These are shown in Table 3. As this table shows, the precision and recall of the proposed algorithm is higher than the Chabot system.

6. conclusion

Image retrieval performs through using the text-based and content-based algorithms. In order to use the advantages of both techniques, some research along with this study combines these techniques together. The proposed algorithm has two steps: First, the text-based algorithm using some keywords has been applied and after that content-based algorithms have been used. In content-based algorithms, we focused on color and texture features. Specifically, we have extracted color moments for color features and texture features, which have been extracted by using color co-occurrence matrix. The proposed algorithms have been implemented and tested by using a COREL standard image database and compared with text-based, content-based, and a combined system Chabot system. The experimental results show that the precision and recall of the proposed techniques are higher than other techniques.

Table 2. Precision and Recall Comparisons between proposed Algorithm, Text-Based and content-based algorithms.

Category name	Method name	R	P
Flowers	Proposed method	0.9	0.9
	Text-based method	0.35	0.2
	Content-based method	0.9	0.71
Buses	Proposed method	1	0.88
	Text-based method	0.3	0.2
	Content-based method	1	0.78
Textures	Proposed method	0.65	0.65
	Text-based method	0.3	0.2
	Content-based method	0.6	0.6
People	Proposed method	0.8	0.65
	Text-based method	0.25	0.2
	Content-based method	0.5	0.6
Food	Proposed method	0.9	0.7
	Text-based method	0.35	0.25
	Content-based method	0.7	0.6
Beach	Proposed method	1	0.92
	Text-based method	0.3	0.2
	Content-based method	0.98	0.7
Elephant	Proposed method	0.9	0.8
	Text-based method	0.35	0.2
	Content-based method	0.8	0.72
Dinosaur	Proposed method	1	0.85
	Text-based method	0.3	0.25
	Content-based method	1	0.59
Mountain	Proposed method	0.9	0.92
	Text-based method	0.3	0.2
	Content-based method	0.8	0.7
Horses	Proposed method	0.75	0.65
	Text-based method	0.25	0.2
	Content-based method	0.6	0.6

Table 3. Precision and Recall Comparisons between Proposed Method and Chabot system [9].

	Proposed method	chabot system[9]
Average Precision	0.82	0.78
Average Recall	0.87	0.69

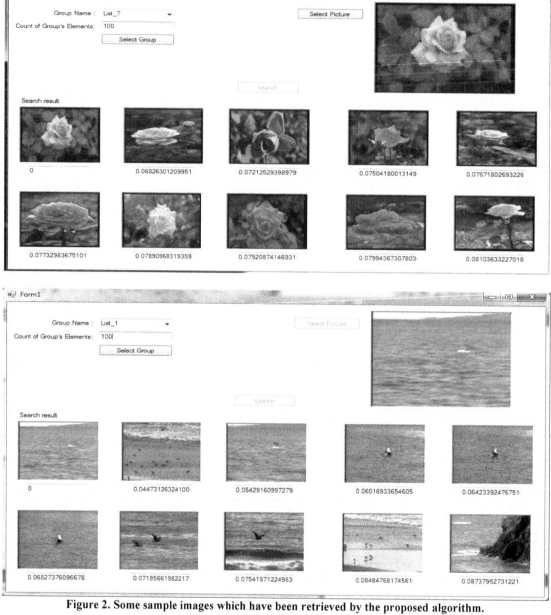

Figure 2. Some sample images which have been retrieved by the proposed algorithm.

References

[1] Li, X., Chen, S., Shyu, M. and Furht, B. (2002). Image Retrieval By Color, Texture and Spatial Information. Processing International Conference on Distributed Multimedia Systems. 152-159.

[2] Pabboju , S. and gopal, R. (2009). A Novel Approach For Content- Based Image Global and Region Indexing and Retrieval System Using Features. International Journal of Computer Science And Network Security. 9(2), 15-21.

[3] Leung, C. H. C., Hibler, D. and Mwara, N. (1992). Image retrieval by Content Description, Journal of Information science. 18, 111-119.

[4] Li, X., Shou, L., Chen, G., Hu, T. and Dong, J. (2008). Modeling Image Data For Effective Indexing and Retrieval In Large General Image Database. IEEE Transaction on Knowledge And Data Engineering. 20(11), 1566-1580.

[5] Chang, Y. and Chen, H. (2006). Approaches of Using a Word-Image Ontology and an Annotated Image Corpus as Intermedia for Cross-Language Image Retrieval, Image CLEF Working Notes.

[6] Belongie, S., Carson, C., Greenspan, H. and Malik, J. (1998). Color And Texture-Based Image Segmentation Using Em and Its Application To Content-Based Image Retrieval, In Processing of 6th International Conference on Computer Vision.

[7] Flickner, M., Sawhney, H., Niblack, W. and Yanker, p. (1995). Query By Image And Video Content: The Qbic System. Computer. 23–32.

[8] Smith, J. R. and Chang, S. (1996). Visual seek: A Fully Automated Contentbased Image Query System. In Processing of 4th Acm International Conference on Multimedia. 211–218.

[9] Virginia, E. and Stonebraker, M. (2005). Chabot: Retrieval from a relational database of images. IEEE Computer. 28(9), 40-48.

[10] Pentland, A., Picard, R. W. and Sclaroff, S. (1994). Photobook: Contentbased Manipulation of Image Databases, In Spie Storage And Retrieval Image and Video Databases. 2185, 34-47.

[11] Demerdash, O., Kosseim, L. and Bergler, S. (2008). CLaC at ImageCLEFphoto 2008, ImageCLEF Working Notes.

[12] Yue, J. Li, Z., Liu, L. and Fu, Z. (2010). Content-Based Image Retrieval Using Color And Texture Fused Features. Mathematical And Computer Modelling. 1121-1127.

[13] Yuan, W., Feng, C. and Jia, Y. (2011). An Effective Method For Color Image Retrieval Based on Texture. Computer Standards and Interfaces. 1121-1127.

[14] Shahbahrami, A., Borodin, D. and Juurlink, B. (2008). Comparison Between Color And Texture Features For Image Retrieval, Processing 19th Annual Workshop on Circuits. Systems And Signal Processing. 361-371.

[15] Manjunath, B. S. and Ma, W. Y. (1996).Texture Feature For Browsing And Retrieval of Image Data. IEEE Trans. on Pattern Analysis And Machin Intelligence. 18(8), 331-339.

[16] Kokare, M. P., Biswas, K. and Chatterji, B. N. (2005). Texture Image Retrieval Using New Rotated Complex Wavelet filters. IEEE Transactions on Systems. Man and Cybernetics. 35(6), 1168-1178.

[17] Haralick, R. M., Shanmugan, K. and Dinstein, I. (1973). Textural Features For Image Classification. IEEE Transactions on Systems. Man, And Cybernetics. Smc-3, 610-621.

[18] Wang, J., li, j. and Wiederhold, G. (2001). Simplicity: Semantics-Sensitive Integrated Matching For Picture Libraries. IEEE Transactions on Pattern Analysis And Machine Intelligence. 23(9), 963-947.

[19] Sakhare, S. V. and Nasre, V. (2011). Design of Feature Extraction In Content Based Image Retrieval Using Color And Texture. International Journal of Computer Science and Informatics. 1, 445-449.

[20] Andrysiak, T. and Chora′S, M. (2005). Image Retrieval Based on Heirarchical Gabor Filter. International Journal on Applied Mathematics and Computer Science. 15, 471–480.

[21] Choras, R. (2007). Image Feature Extraction Techniques And Their Application For Cbir and Biometrics System, International Journal of Biology And Biomedical Engineering, 1, 6-16.

[22] Akoushideh, A. and Shahbahrami, A. (2010). Accelerating Texture Features Extraction Algorithms using FPGA Architecture. International Conference on ReConFigurable Computing and FPGAs. 232-237.

[23] Davis, L., Clearman, S. M. and Aggarwal, J. K. (1981). Anempirical evaluation of generalized Co-Occurrencematrices. IEEE Transactions on Pattern Analysis And Machine Intelligence. 3(2), 214-221.

[24] Vailaya, A., Zhong, Y. and Jain, K. (1996). A hierarchical system for efficient image retrieval. In 13th International Conference on Pattern Recognition. 25-30.

[25] Boland, M. V. (1999). Quantitative Description and Automated Classification of Cellular Protein Localization Patterns in Fluorescence Microscope Images of Mammalian Cells. Ph.D. dissertation. University of Pittsburgh.

[26] Antani, S., Kasturi, R. and Jain, R. (2002). A survey on the use of pattern recognition methods for abstraction, indexing and retrieval of images and video. Pattern Recognition. 35, 945–965.

[27] Carson, C., Thomas, M. and Malik, J. (1999). Blobworld: A System for Region-Based Image Indexing and Retrieval. 509-517.

[28] Laaksonen, J., Koskela, M. and Oja, E. (2000). Content-based image retrieval using self-organizing maps.Elsevier, Journal Pattern Recognition. 21(13-14), 1199-1207.

[29] Mahmoudi, F., Shanbehzadeh, J., Eftekhari Moghada, Soltanianzadeh, A. H. (2003). Image retrieval Based on shape similarity by edge orientation autocorrelogram. Elsevier, Journal Pattern Recognition. 36, 1725-1736.

[30] Subrahmanyam, M. and Maheshwari, R. P. (2011). A correlogram algorithm for image indexing and retrieval using wavelet and Rotated Wavele t Filters. International Journal Signal and Imaging Systems Engineering. 4(1), 27-34.

23

QoS-Based web service composition based on genetic algorithm

M. AllamehAmiri, V. Derhami, M. Ghasemzadeh[*]

Department of Electrical and Computer Engineering, Yazd University, Yazd, Iran.

Corresponding author: m.ghasemzadeh@yazd.ac.ir (M. Ghasemzadeh)

Abstract

Quality of service (QoS) is an important issue in the design and management of web service composition. QoS in web services consists of various non-functional factors, such as execution cost, execution time, availability, successful execution rate, and security. In recent years, the number of available web services has proliferated, and then offered the same services increasingly. The same web services are distinguished based on their quality parameters. Also, clients usually demand more value added services rather than those offered by single, isolated web services. Therefore, selecting a composition plan of web services among numerous plans satisfies client requirements and has become a challenging and time-consuming problem. This paper has proposed a new composition plan optimizer with constraints based on genetic algorithm. The proposed method can find the composition plan that satisfies user constraints efficiently. The performance of the method is evaluated in a simulated environment.

Keywords: *Web Service, Web Service Composition, Quality of Service, QoS, Genetic Algorithm.*

1. Introduction

According to W3C definition "a web service is a software system designed to support interoperable machine-to-machine interaction over a network". It is an XML based, self-described software entity which can be published, located, and used across the internet using a set of standards, such as Simple Object Access Protocol (SOAP), Web Service Description Language (WSDL), and Universal Description, Discover and Integration (UDDI) [1]. Since web services can enable computer-computer communication in a heterogeneous environment, hence they are very suitable for an environment such as the internet. People can use the standardized web service model for rapid design, implement and extended applications. Many enterprises and corporations provide different web services to be more responsive and cost-effective. Google's SOAP Search API for information inquiry [2] and Amazon web services for doing enormous e-commerce activities [3] are good examples of such systems. A number of standards and protocols have been designed to use and publish web services over the internet. Some of the most commonly used standards are UDDI, SOAP and WSDL. Universal Description Discovery and Integration (UDDI) is an XML-based registry that provides a standard set of specifications for service description and discovery. It defines the information model, the service providers API for registering and publishing services and the API for service requesters to inquire for services. Web service provider registers their web services into UDDI registries. Simple Object Access Protocol (SOAP) is an XML based protocol specification for exchanging information between peers in the decentralized, distributed environment. SOAP provides a simple and lightweight mechanism to communicate with web services. SOAP can form the foundation layer of a web services protocol stack. Web Service Description Language (WSDL) is used to describe the interfaces of all web services regardless of the underlying technology. The WSDL is defined: Services as collections of network endpoints, or ports. When service provider wants to register a web service to UDDI server (web service directory), it describes web service by WSDL and puts it in UDDI registry. As service requester looks for a web service in UDDI server, s/he receives the WSDL file of web services Figure 1 shows the IBM standard architecture of web services. This architecture provides a three level procedure to find an appropriate web service. First, service provider describes its web services in WSDL Format and puts them in a web service directory (registering web service). Then, service requester searches into web service directory to find a suitable web service. Finally, after selecting the web service, service requester can interact with the web service using SOAP protocol. There are some sophisticated applications that cannot be performed using a single, isolated web service. Consequently we need to use a composition of web services to perform complex tasks. An Example of synthesizing web services is a travel planning web service. When the client uses web

service based system to plan a trip, the following steps will be taken into consideration in the service process.

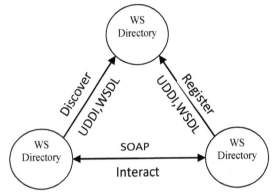

Figure 1. Standard architecture of web services.

At first, the client contacts a travel agency web service to reserve a hotel room and an airplane seat. Then the client selects the best reservation plan among the plans suggested to him/her by considering factors like schedule, financial condition, weather conditions and some other factors. In addition, the client may request services, such as a car rental agency or insurance. After all web services are selected, the client pays the reservation fee to the travel agency. Figure 2 provides an example of travel agency candidate web services and Figure 3 represents all composition plans of the candidate web services.

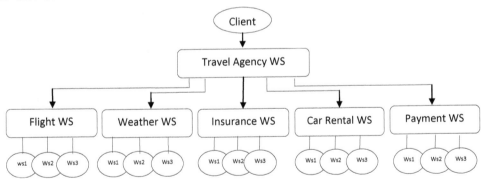

Figure 2. An example of travel Agency web service and candidate web services for each task.

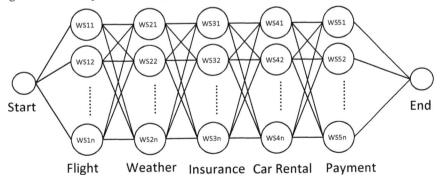

Figure 3. All composition plans for travel agency example.

Web service composition creates new functionalities by aggregating different services based on a specific workflow [4]. When there are more than one candidate web services for a task or process, there will be various combinations of web services having the same functionality with different qualities. For instance, if there are m tasks and n candidate web services, the number of all possible plans is n^m. In general, finding a composition plan that fulfils a client's QoS requirement is a time-consuming optimization problem. Combining web services of high QoS values in a reasonable computation time has been recognized as an important problem of web service composition [6]. We need to find a composition plan satisfying client's constraints without checking all combinations. This will be impractical even if there are a few services and tasks in the workflow. Typical QoS factors associated with a web service are executive cost and time, availability, successful execution rate, reputation, and usage frequency [5]. Also, there are other properties other than the above-mentioned factors, such as reliability, security and so on. To obtain a composition plan, we should first create a QoS model to describe the QoS aspects of web services. To create an appropriate model, service requester and service provider should agree on same definitions to the extent possible. After creating a QoS model, the second step is QoS based on web service discovery and selection. Unfortunately, WSDL only addresses functional aspects of a web service and does not contain any useful description for non-functional requirements [14]. Using the QoS model, service requester can filter inappropriate web services. A number of studies on web service selection have been carried out [7, 8]. One of the most well known techniques is "matchmaking" that is employed in situations where services with semantic descriptions for their functional attributes are available on the Internet search system [7]. It should be noted that the process of filtering web services consists of functional matchmaking and non-functional matchmaking. In functional matchmaking, web services that have different functionalities from the client are filtered out and on the other hand, in non-functional matchmaking, web services that don't have the appropriate quality are eliminated. At this stage, the candidate web services for each task are selected. In [8], a new QoS-based service registration and discovery model to explore the feasibility of QoS involving into UDDI registry

information is suggested. In this model, service providers have to send QoS claims to service QoS certifiers, responding to the third party or forum web services, for certification. The service customer is responsible for verifying QoS claims. Finally, if QoS claims pass QoS certifier verification, the QoS information will be registered in the UDDI registry associated with function description. In the last stage, we should obtain the optimized web service composition plan from all available plans. As mentioned above, trying all combinations of web services is time consuming. A problem of web service composition is usually an NP-hard [9]. Several solutions have been suggested so far to solve this problem that one of them such as [10] is based on Leaner programming and some are based on AI (e.g. [6]). Genetic algorithm is effective approach to solve some kind of hard problem [22, 23, 24, 25, 26]. Our approach uses the genetic algorithm [20, 21] to solve this problem. To escape from local optimums, we present some modifications in crossover, mutation and selection approach. The remaining sections of this paper are organized in order. Next section presents related work. The third section describes the QoS model of web service composition. The fourth section proposes our GA based on composition algorithm. The computational results of the algorithm are given in the fifth section and the sixth section includes conclusion and future work.

2. Related work

Web service discovery and QoS based on the web service composition offer interesting applications of constraint satisfaction methods. In [10] a multiple criteria decision making with weighted sum model (to select a service) and integer programming (IP) approaches with branch and bound (to select an optimal solution) have been proposed. In [6] constraint satisfaction based on solution which combine simulated annealing [17, 18, 19] approach with Tabu search [16] has been proposed. The Tabu search is used for generating neighbour plans and simulated annealing heuristic is applied for accepting or rejecting the neighbour plan. In [11] a QoS-based web service composition algorithm that combines local strategy and global strategy has the following features. Initially, the services that have low QoS value are eliminated by local strategy and then the problem has reduced to a multi-dimension multi-choice 0-1 knapsack problem solved by the heuristic method. In [12] a model that expands traditional UDDI to describe the QoS attributes of web services is presented. Also, a service proxy is added to this model by which all service compositions requested by service requester are found, bound and invoked. In [13] an automated web service composition is performed by hierarchical task network and SHOP2 HTN system is developed. This system takes OWL-S service model as input (client requirement) and executes the plan as a system result. High probability of Getting stuck in local optimum is the main problem of these methods. This is because it is unable to work more than one composition plan at the same time. At the same time, the probability in methods such as genetic algorithms and fish swarm algorithms working on several composition plans are less than above-mentioned method.

3. QoS based web service model
3.1. QoS properties description
The most important QoS properties used in this paper are response time, execution cost, availability, reputation and successful execution rate. The response time can be defined in several ways. For example, it can be defined as the time between sending request and receiving respond. This period involves receiving request massage time, queuing time, execution time and receiving response time by requester. Measuring these time sections is very difficult because they depend on network conditions. Alternatively, it can be measured as the time between receiving request by service provider and sending response to service requester. This time includes queuing time and execution time only affected by the web service workload. This value must be continuously updated for each web service because the work load of web service may change during the work time. Execution cost is a fee received by service provider from service requester for each execution. This fee is determined by service provider and may change according to web service provider's financial policy. Availability is the degree that a web service is accessible and ready for immediate use. This value can be defined as [uptime/ (uptime + downtime)]. Downtime includes the time that web service is inaccessible and time taken to repair it. This value should be updated by service provider. Reputation is the average reputation score of a web service evaluated by the clients. The individual reputation scores are likely to be subjective, but the average score becomes trustable as the total number of the usages increases [6]. The successful Execution Rate is the

percentage of requests that a web service perform successfully when web service is available. It is computed by dividing the number of successful performed requests by the total number of requests. The QoS properties used in this paper is summarized in Table 1.

Table 1. Description of QoS peoperties used in this paper

QoS property	Description
Response Time	Time between receiving request and sending response
Execution cost	Execution cost per request
Availability	$\dfrac{UpTime}{UpTime+DownTime}$
Reputation	$\dfrac{\sum Rep_i}{TotalNumber\ Of\ Usage}$
Successful Execution Rate	$\dfrac{Numer\ of\ Successful\ Request}{TotalNumber\ of\ Request}$

Notations
Descriptions of notations used in this paper are as follow:
m: number of tasks.
n: number of candidate web services for each task.
p_i: i-th atomic process of a composition schema ($1 \leq i \leq m$).
ws_{ij}: j-th candidate web service for the ith atomic process, ($1 \leq i \leq m$, $1 \leq j \leq n$).
d: index of QoS property.
w_d: weight of the d-th QoS constraint defined by a client.
Con_d: permissible value of the d-th QoS property (constraints).
Agg_d: aggregated value of the d-th QoS property of a composition plan.
b_{ij}: binary decision variable (0 or 1). If $b_{ij}=1$ then j-th candidate web service is selected for i-th process.

3.2. QoS-based evaluation of web services
Since each QoS property may be measured in various metrics, they should be normalized for appropriate evaluation. The QoS properties are divided into two categories: First, negative values, such as response time and execution cost, and second, positive values, such as availability and reputation. The higher value in negative properties indicates the lower quality and the higher one in positive properties represent higher quality and vice versa. The following equations are used to normalize positive and negative properties, respectively:

$$q_{nrm} = \begin{cases} \dfrac{q - q_{min}}{q_{max} - q_{min}} & q_{max} - q_{min} \neq 0 \\ 1 & q_{max} - q_{min} = 0 \end{cases} \quad (1)$$

$$q_{nrm} = \begin{cases} \dfrac{q_{max} - q}{q_{max} - q_{min}} & q_{max} - q_{min} \neq 0 \\ 1 & q_{max} - q_{min} = 0 \end{cases} \quad (2)$$

After normalization, the local value of each web service that is candidate for a task will be computed from the following formula. Where Q is the number of QoS properties.

$$Local\, Value\, of\, ws_{ij} = \sum_{i=0}^{q} w_i q_i \quad (3)$$

3.3. Aggregation value of QoS property

Generally, composition plans are constituted from serial, cycle, XOR-parallel, and AND-parallel execution patterns. According to the definition of QoS properties in section 3.1, the aggregative value of web service composition is calculated regarding to its workflow pattern. The description and aggregation values of workflow patterns are discussed below.

Serial pattern is an execution pattern in which services are executed one after another and there is no overlap between execution periods of web services. Figure 4 illustrates this pattern and Table 2 represents the aggregation value of this pattern. According to Table 3 to calculate aggregation value of response time and execution cost, each web service value should be added to each other. Besides, in order to calculate aggregation value of availability and successful execution rate, web services values should be multiplied by each other because web services are independent from each other. The aggregative value of reputation is obtained by taking average of reputation values of web services.

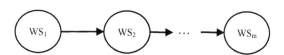

Figure 4. Serial Pattern.

Cycle pattern is a kind of sequential pattern in which the web service executes for limited cycles. According to Table 3, the aggregation values of this pattern are similar to sequential pattern. Figure 5 describes this pattern.

Table 2. Aggregative QoS value for serial pattern

Response Time	$\displaystyle\sum_{i=0}^{m} WS.RT$
Execution Cost	$\displaystyle\sum_{i=0}^{m} WS.EC$
Availability	$\displaystyle\prod_{i=0}^{m} WS.Ava$
Successful Execution rate	$\displaystyle\prod_{i=0}^{m} WS.Suc$
Reputation	$\dfrac{\displaystyle\sum_{i=0}^{m} WS.\mathrm{Re}\,p}{m}$

Figure 5. A cycle pattern.

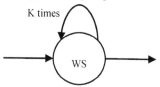

K times

WS

Table 3. Aggrigative QoS value for a cycle pattern

Response Time	$m*(WS.RT)$
Execution Cost	$m*(WS.RT)$
Availability	$WS.Ava$
Successful Execution rate	$WS.Suc$
Reputation	$WS.\mathrm{Re}\,p$

XOR-parallel pattern is an execution pattern in which after the completion of the prior web service, one of the following web services just executes. In this pattern execution of each component is non-deterministic; therefore, to calculate the aggregation QoS effect of this pattern, the worst case should be calculated. We can obtain aggregative QoS values of this pattern as described in Table 4. Figure 6 depicts this pattern.

AND-parallel pattern is an execution pattern in which after the completion of the prior web service, the entire subsequent web services are executed simultaneously. The aggregative QoS values of this pattern are described in Table 5. Notice that to obtain aggregative response time, we use the Max function, because all subsequent components are executed simultaneously. Figure 7 describes this pattern.

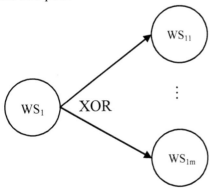

Figure 6. XOR-parallel pattern.

Table 4. Aggregative QoS value for XOR-parallel pattern

Response Time	$Max(WS.RT)$
Execution Cost	$Max(WS.EC)$
Availability	$Min(WS.Ava)$
Successful Execution rate	$Min(WS.Suc)$
Reputation	$Min(WS.Re\, p)$

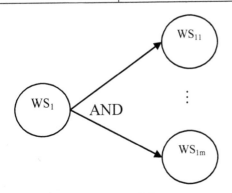

Figure. 7. AND-parallel pattern.

Table 5. Aggrigative QoS value for XOR-parallel pattern

Response Time	$Max(WS.RT)$
Execution Cost	$\sum_{i=0}^{m} WS.EC$
Availability	$\prod_{i=0}^{m} WS.Ava$
Successful Execution rate	$\prod_{i=0}^{m} WS.Suc$
Reputation	$\dfrac{\sum_{i=0}^{m} WS.Re\, p}{m}$

4. The GA based algorithm

In this section, we present our approach to find an optimal web service composition plan Since the number of all composition plans of this problem is very large (n^m), some ideas to improve GA are presented so that it quickly converges the appropriate composition plan. We introduce some idea for initialization, crossover and mutation of chromosomes. Also the method to escape from local optimum is represented. If the algorithm cannot find the optimal plan in a specific time, without losing best plans of previous step, the algorithm will escape from local optimum.

Constraints

There are two constraints. The first constraint is that only one web service among candidate web services should be chosen for a task. In other words, the equation (4) has to be satisfied. The second constraint is that the service composition must satisfy user constraints. For negative QoS properties, such as execution cost and time the aggregation values must be smaller than user constraints. For positive QoS properties, aggregation values must be greater than user constraints. Equation (5) describes this constraint.

$$\sum_{i=0}^{n} b_{ij} = 1 \quad 1 \le i \le m \tag{4}$$

$$\begin{cases} Agg_d \le Con_d & \text{For negetive constraints} \\ Agg_d \ge Con_d & \text{For posotive constraints} \end{cases} \tag{5}$$

Algorithm construction

To obtain relation between local optimum and global optimum chromosomes, several experiments have been carried out. We design a small example of composition plan with m=10 and n=6 in which the number of plans is 10^6. Initially, all web services should be sorted according to their local values. Then, the best composition plan is found by using enumeration methods. In this method, all composition plans are obtained and evaluated. Table 6 shows the percentage of web services that are selected for global optimum plan. The closer this amount is to 9, the higher its local value will be. About 36.6% of web services in the composition plans have best local values too. It can be inferred that about 70% of web services that are selected for the best composition plan belong to 30% of the best web services that have high local values. Figureure. 8 depicts the values of fitness function of all plans.

In this diagram, each two adjacent points that demonstrate two adjacent plans, differ only in one web service. As depicted in this figure, for this small example, several local optimums exist so the algorithm should be changed so that it can escape from them; to escape from these local optimums, the various forms of randomness is required.

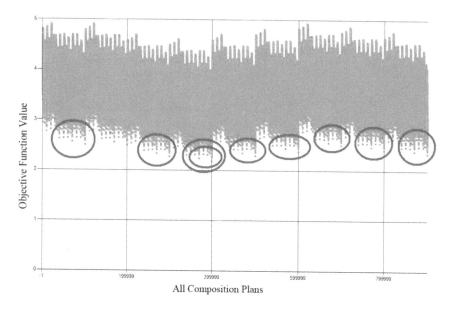

Figure. 8. Value of all plans in example with 6 tasks and 10 web services.

Table 6. Relation between Local and global optimum

WS number	Percentage of repeat in best plan
1	2.2%
2	1.6%
3	4.4%
4	5.5%
5	6.2%
6	9.0%
7	12.2%
8	22.3%
9	36.6%

Construction of chromosome is described in Figure 9. Each chromosome consists of m genes and each gene has a value between 1 to n.

1...n	1...n	...	1...n	1...n
Gene$_1$	Gene$_2$		Gene$_{m-1}$	Gene$_m$

Figure 9. Chromosome structure.

The main body of the algorithm is summarized in Table 7 and specifications of its functions are described in Tables 8, 9, 10, 11 and 12. At first, we should calculate local value of each web service. This is done prior to execution of composition plan optimization. Local value is a criterion of goodness among the candidate web services of a specific task. To obtain the local value, the QoS properties are normalized according to equations (1) and (2), and then the local value is calculated using equation (3). To obtain an optimized composition plan at first, web services candidate for a task are sorted according to their local values. In the next step, chromosomes are generated. 20% of all chromosomes are selected from 20% of best web services that have high local value and the remaining 80% is selected randomly. For each chromosome fitness function is calculated by using equation (9). It is derived from objective functions of [6, 10, 15]. D_1 is used for negative values and D_2 is used for positive values. If the fitness function value is equal or smaller than 0, it will mean that the appropriate composition plan satisfying user constraints is found.

$$D_1 = \sum w_d \cdot (\frac{Agg_d}{Con_d} - 1) \quad if \ Agg_d \geq Con_d$$

(For negetive values)

$$D_2 = \sum w_d \cdot (\frac{Agg_d}{Con_d} - 1) \quad if \ Agg_d \leq Con_d$$

(For posotive values)

Fitness Function $= D_1 - D_2$ \hfill (9)

Crossover is a function to combine two or more parent chromosomes and obtain one or more child chromosomes. We define two kinds of crossover. In crossover type 1 shown in Figure 10, genes of a child are inherited from parents alternatively. In crossover type 2 shown in Figure 11, a certain percentage of genes are inherited from one parent and the other genes are inherited from the other parent. For crossover operation, 20% of best chromosomes having high fitness are combined with each other by crossover type 1 and for the remaining 80%, each chromosome is combined with a randomly selected chromosome belonging to 20% of chromosomes with high fitness function by crossover type 2.

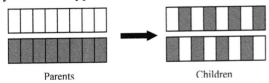

Figure 10. Crossover type 1.

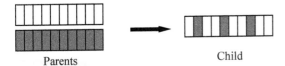

Figure 11. Crossover type 2.

To select chromosomes for the next step (selection function), constant number of best chromosomes from the previous step are selected and replaced with worst chromosomes in current step. This results in preservation of best chromosomes but accelerates the convergence of the algorithm to the local optimum. To escape from local optimum we design mutation and partial initialization chromosomes functions. In mutation, some genes of some chromosomes that are selected randomly will change with probability of P_m.

To fix the selection function accelerating the convergence of the algorithm to the local optimum, the Partial initialization chromosomes function is presented. In this function, a constant number of best chromosomes are kept and other chromosomes are generated randomly again.

5. Experiments

We have accomplished several experiments to evaluate our algorithm. The programming language used to do the evaluation is Java and the algorithm is executed on desktop PC with Pentium 2.2 GHz dual core CPU and 3 GB of RAM. We compare the execution time of our algorithm with enumeration method. The first experiment was performed with 30, 50 and 100 tasks. For each task we have 30, 40 and 50 web services. As shown in Figureure. 12, the maximum execution time of the algorithm is 377 milliseconds. In a separate run, another experiment is performed with 100 web services in which the number of tasks is 20, 40 and 50. In this experiment the maximum time is equal to 240 milliseconds. The results are shown in Figureure.

13. Figure 14 shows the result of enumeration method. In enumeration method, the plans are generated until the suitable plan is founded. From this diagram, it can be inferred that the time of execution increases exponentially when number of tasks increase linearly. Furthermore, we compare our work with the work represented in [6]. They provide a solution for composition plan optimization using a combination of Tabu search and simulated annealing approach. The result of this comparison is shown in Figure 15.

Table 7. Main body of algorithm

Function Composition_Plan_Optimizer
Sort all web services according to their local value;
Initialize chromosomes ();
Sort all chromosomes according to their local score;
Counter=0;
While not find appropriate plan do
Crossover ();
Sorts all web services according to their local score;
Selection ();
Sorts all web services according to their local score;
Mutation ();
Sorts all web services according to their local score;
Counter=counter+1;
If (counter % T=0) Do
Partial_initialization_Chromosome();
End if
End While
End Function

Table 8. Initialization chromosomes function

Function Initialization Chromosome
For 20% of population do
Select chromosome genes are selected randomly from 20% of best web services
End For
For 80% of population do
Select chromosome genes are selected randomly.
End For
End Function

Table 9. Crossover function

Function Crossover
20% of best chromosomes are combined with each other by   crossover type 1.
80% of remaining chromosomes are combined with 20% of best chromosomes with crossover type 2.
End Function

Table 10. Selection function

Function Selection
Replace N number of best chromosomes from previous step with N worst chromosomes of current step
End Function

Table 11. Mutation function

Function Mutation
With probability of P_m, some genes of some chromosomes are changed randomly
End Function

Table 12. partial_initialization_chromosomes function

Function Partial_initialization_chromosomes
Keep N number of the best chromosomes and other chromosomes are initialized again.
End Function

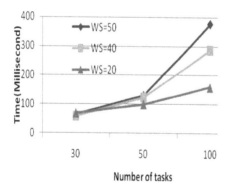

Figure 12. Performance of GA based algorithm

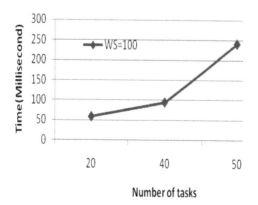

Figure 13. Performance of GA based algorithm with 100 tasks.

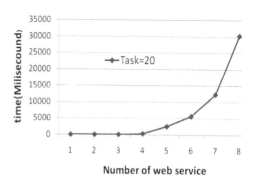

Figureure. 14. Performance of enumeration method

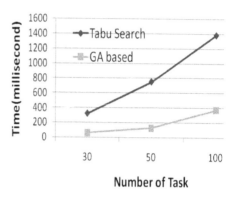

Figureure. 15. Compare with Tabu search approach

Furthermore, one of the important factors having the significant impact on the execution time is the population size. Figureure. 16 shows the impact of the population size on the execution time. In this experiment, the number of web services is 100 and the numbers of tasks are 20, 40 and 50 respectively. As it can be inferred from the diagram, the best population size is in range of 300 to 500.

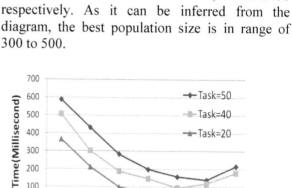

Figure 16. Impact of population number on the performance of algorithm (web service=100).

6. Conclusion

In this paper, we showed how can find the suitable web service composition using genetic algorithms. Some new ideas for generating chromosomes, selection and crossover functions were proposed. The experimental results demonstrated the advantages of the proposed ideas are to overcome local optimums. Experimental results show that since GA is a K beam search, it can find suitable composition plan much faster than other random search approaches. Therefore, it can be concluded that applying genetic algorithms in such problems has a great effect on improving computation time. As a future work, we suggest examining effects of using different formulas for fitness function.

Acknowledgements

This work was partially supported by Iranian Telecommunication Research Center (ITRC).

References

[1] CURBERA, F., M. DUFTLER, R. KHALAF, W. NAGY, N. MUKHI, S. WEERAWARANA, Unraveling the Web Services web, An Introduction to SOAP, WSDL and UDDI, IEEE Internet Computing, Vol. 6, (2002), pp. 86–93.

[2] KOSHMAN, S., Visualization-based Information Retrieval on the Web, Library and Information Science Research Vol. 28, (2006), pp. 192–207.

[3] CHEN, L.S., F.H. HSU, M.C. CHEN, Y.C. HSU, Developing Recommender Systems With the Consideration of Product Profitability for Sellers, Information Sciences, Vol 178, (2008), pp. 1032–1048.

[4] CHEN, Y., L. ZHOU, D. ZHANG, Ontology-Supported Web Service Composition: An Approach to Service-Oriented Knowledge Management in Corporate Services, Database Management Vol 17, (2006), pp. 67–84.

[5] O'SULLIVAN, J., D. EDMOND, A.T. HOFSTEDE, What's in a service? Distributed and Parallel Databases Vol 12, (2002), pp. 117–133.

[6] KO, J.M, C.O. KIM, I. KWON, Quality-of-Service Oriented Web Service Composition Algorithm and Planning Architecture, Systems and Software, Vol. 81, (2008), pp. 2079–2090.

[7] WANG, P., K.M. CHAO, C.C. LO, On Optimal Decision for Qos-Aware Composite Service Selection, Expert Systems with Applications, Vol 37, (2010), pp. 440–449

[8] RAN, S., A Model for Web Services Discovery with QoS, ACM SIGecom Exchanges, Vol 4, 2003, pp. 1 – 10.

[9] CANFORA, G., M.D. PENTA, R. ESPOSITO, M.L. VILLANI. An Approach for Qos-Aware Service Composition Based on Genetic Algorithms. Proc. Int. Conf. on Genetic and evolutionary computation, Washington DC, USA, (2005), pp. 1069–1075.

[10] HUANG, A.F.M., C.W. LAN, S.J.H. YANG, An Optimal Qos-Based Web Service Selection Scheme, Systems and Software, Vol 81, (2008), pp. 2079–2090.

[11] AI, W.H, Y.X. HUANG, H. ZHANG, N. ZHOU, Web Services Composition and Optimizing Algorithm Based on QoS, Proc. Int. Conf. on Wireless Communications, Networking and Mobile Computing, Dalian, (2008), pp. 1-4.

[12] LIU, Z., J. LI, J, LI, A. AN, J. XU, A Model for Web Services Composition Based on Qos and Providers' Benefit, Proc. Int. Conf. on Wireless communications, networking and mobile computing, Beijing, China, (2009), pp. 4562-4565.

[13] SIRIN, E., B. PARSIA, D. WU, J. HENDLER, D. NAU, HTN Planning for Web Service Composition Using SHOP2, Web Semantics Vol 1, (2004), pp. 377–396.

[14] D'AMBROGIO, A, A Model-driven WSDL Extension for Describing the QoS of Web Services, Proc. IEEE Int. Conf. on Web Services, (2006), pp. 789 – 796.

[15] LIANG, W.Y., C.C. HUANG, H.F. CHUANG, The Design With Object (DWO) Approach to Web Services Composition, Computer Standards & Interfaces, Vol 29, (2007), pp. 54-68.

[16] FERCHICHI, S.E., K. LAABIDI, S. ZIDI Genetic Algorithm and Tabu Search for Feature Selection, Studies in Informatics and Control, Vol. 18, No. 2, (2009).

[17] AARTS, E.H.L., P.J.M. VAN LAARHOVEN, Simulated Annealing: Theory and Applications, D. Reidel Publishing Company, (1987).

[18] CHAISEMARTIN, P., G. DREYFUS, M. FONTET, E. KOUKA, P. LOUBIÈRES, SIARRY P., Placement and Channel Routing by Simulated Annealing: Some Recent Developments, Computer Systems Science and engineering, Vol. 41, (1989).

[19] METROPOLIS, N., A.W. ROSENBLUTH, M.N. ROSENBLUTH, A.H. TELLER, E. TELLER, Simulated Annealing, J. Chem. Phys. 21, (1953).

[20] PATNAIK, S., Genetic Algorithms: A Survey, IEEE computer society, Vol. 27, No. 6, pp.17-26, (1994).

[21] ZOMAYA, P.F., Parallel Genetic Algorithms, Parallel & Distributed Computing, Handbook, McGraw Hul, (1996).

[22] RAJKUMAR, R. , P. SHAHABUDEEN, P. NAGARAJ, S. ARUNACHALAM, T. PAGE, A Bi-Criteria Approach to the M-machine Flowshop Scheduling Problem, Studies in Informatics and Control, Vol. 18, No. 2, (2009).

[23] DRIDI, H., R. KAMMARTI, M. KSOURI, PIERRE BORNE, A Genetic Algorithm for the Multi-Pickup and Delivery Problem with Time Windows, Studies in Informatics and Control, Vol. 18, No. 2, (2009).

[24] KAMMARTI, R., I. AYACHI , M. KSOURI, P. BORNE, Evolutionary Approach for the Containers Bin-Packing Problem, Studies in Informatics and Control, Vol. 18, No. 4, (2009).

[25] BOUKEF, H., M. BENREJEB, P. BORNE, A Proposed Genetic Algorithm Coding for Flow-ShopScheduling Problems, International Journal of Computers, Communications & Control, Vol. 2 , No. 3, (2007), pp. 229-240.

[26] CUBILLOS, C., E. URRA, N. RODRÍGUEZ, Application of Genetic Algorithms for the DARPTW Problem, International Journal of Computers, Communications & Control, Vol. 4, No. 2, (2009), pp. 127-136.

24

Estimation of LPC coefficients using Evolutionary Algorithms

H. Marvi[1], Z. Esmaileyan[2], A. Harimi[3*]

1.Electrical engineering department, Shahrood university of technology, Shahrood, Iran
2.Electrical engineering department science and research branch, Islamic Azad Univercity, Shahrood, Iran
3.Electrical engineering department, Shahrood branch, Islamic Azad Univercity, Shahrood, Iran

*Corresponding author: a.harimi@gmail.com (A. Harimi)

Abstract

The vast use of Linear Prediction Coefficients (LPC) in speech processing systems has intensified the importance of their accurate computation. This paper is concerned with computing LPC coefficients using evolutionary algorithms: Genetic Algorithm (GA), Particle Swarm Optimization (PSO), Differential Evolution (DE) and Particle Swarm Optimization with Differentially perturbed Velocity (PSO-DV). In this method, evolutionary algorithms try to find the LPC coefficients which can predict the original signal with minimum prediction error. To this end, the fitness function is defined as the maximum prediction error in all evolutionary algorithms. The coefficients computed by these algorithms are compared to coefficients obtained by traditional autocorrelation method in terms of the prediction accuracy. Our results showed that coefficients obtained by evolutionary algorithms predict the original signal with less prediction error than autocorrelation methods. The maximum prediction error is achieved by autocorrelation method: GA, PSO, DE and PSO-DV are 0.35, 0.06, 0.02, 0.07 and 0.001, respectively. This finding shows that the hybrid algorithm, PSO-DV, is superior to other algorithms in computing linear prediction coefficients.

Keywords: *Linear prediction coefficients, evolutionary, algorithms, PSO, DE, PSO-DV*

1. Introduction

Linear predictive coding (LPC) is a very powerful method for speech analysis [1, 2]. This method is widely used because it is fast and simple and yet an effective way of estimating the main parameters of speech signals. Linear predictive coding gets its name from the fact that it predicts the current sample of speech signal, x[n], as a linear combination of its past p samples, as follow:

$$x[n] = \sum_{k=1}^{p} a_k x[n-k] + e[n] \quad (1)$$

where a_k and en[n] represent the LPC coefficients and the estimation error, respectively. The linear prediction model described by equation (1) can be schematically shown as Figure 1 wherein z^{-1} indicates the transfer function of a delay system.

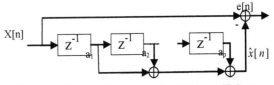

Figure 1. Signal estimation using LPC coefficients.

The prediction error can be written as follow:

$$e[n] = x[n] - \tilde{x}[n] = x[n] - \sum_{k=1}^{p} a_k x[n-k] \quad (2)$$

where $\hat{x}[n]$ is the estimated signal. The basic approach is to find a set of a_k coefficients that minimize the mean square prediction error over a short time of speech signal. There are several traditional methods, such as the covariance method, the autocorrelation method, and the lattice method to determine the LPC coefficients [1-3]. The vast use of Linear Prediction Coefficients (LPC) in speech processing systems has intensified the importance of their accurate computation.

Our contribution in this work is to determine LPC coefficients using four evolutionary algorithms: Genetic Algorithm (GA), Particle Swarm Optimization (PSO), DE (Differential Evolution) and PSO-DV. These algorithms try to find the best LPC coefficients which predict the speech signal with less prediction error. The LPC coefficients obtained from traditional autocorrelation method are used here as a benchmark to verify whether the proposed evolutionary methods can find better coefficients.

The paper is organized as follows: Next section focuses on the evolutionary algorithms include GA, PSO, DE and PSO-DV are detailed by the proposed method in section 3. The experimental results for applying evolutionary algorithms to determine optimal LPC coefficients are presented and discussed in section 4, and finally the paper is concluded in section 5.

2.Evolutionary algorithms

The use of *evolutionary* strategies (ESs) is to solve non-linear optimization problems has attracted much attention recently. The common underlying idea behind all the evolutionary algorithms is the same: A population of individuals tries to survive under the environmental pressure. The fittest individuals have the more chance to survive and this yields a rise in the fitness of the population. Given a fitness function to be maximized (or minimized), a set of candidate solutions can randomly be created. Based on the fitness function, some of the better candidates are chosen to generate the next population using various generation operators, such as recombination and mutation. Recombination is an operator applied to two or more selected candidates (the so-called parents) and generate one or more new candidates (the children). Mutation is applied to one candidate and generates one new candidate. Various evolutionary algorithms take different strategies to upgrade a population in consecutive generations. In this section, four evolutionary algorithms, GA, PSO, DE and PSO-DV are described.

2.1.Genetic Algorithm (GA)

A basic element of the biological genetics is the chromosomes. Chromosomes cross over each other, and mutate themselves, and a new set of chromosomes is generated. Based on the requirement, some of the chromosomes survive. This is the cycle of one generation in biological

genetics. The above process is repeated for many generations and finally the best set of chromosomes based on the requirement are available. The Mathematical algorithm equivalent to the above behavior used as the optimization technique is called as an Artificial Genetic Algorithm [4, 5]. GA flowchart is shown in Figure 2.

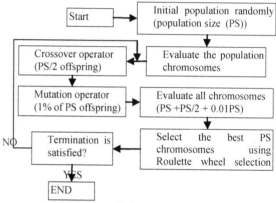

Figure 2. GA flowchart.

As can be seen from figure 2, at the step 1 the chromosomes are initialized randomly, and then GA iteratively examines various sets of coefficients generated during the genetic operators crossover and mutation [6]. In each iteration, GA chooses the qualified chromosomes, which result in the minimum estimation error using Roulette wheel selection method. This algorithm is detailed in [7-9]. The classic crossover and mutation operators are schematically shown in Figure 3.

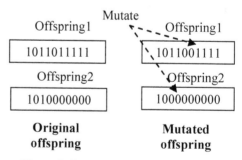

Figure 3. Genetic operators: crossover and mutation.

Table 1 shows the parameter setup for the GA employed here.

Table 1. Genetic Algorithm (GA) parameters setup.

Modeling description	setting
Population size	100
Selection technique	Roulette wheel
Crossover type	One point crossover
Crossover rate	0.9
Mutation rate	0.001
Iteration number	100

2.2. Particle Swarm Optimization (PSO)

In PSO, there is a society, wherein each of the members named as a particle is considered as a possible solution for the available problem. The number of particles which is usually chosen below 100 is named as swarm size. In step 1 the particles are initialized randomly at the position $x_i(0)$. Then, particles are evaluated using a fitness function. The best position each particle has been so far, and The position of the best particle in the society are named pbest (personal best) and gbest (global best). Each particle has its own velocity, which is updated in each iteration. The velocity and position of i-th particle at current iteration could be written as [10, 11]:

$$v_i(t+1) = \zeta[\,\omega.v_i(t) \tag{3}$$
$$+c_1.\Phi_1.(pbest_i(t) - x_i(t))]$$
$$+c_2.\Phi_2.(gbest(t) - x_i(t))$$

and

$$x_i(t+1) = x_i(t) + v_i(t+1) \tag{4}$$

where $v_i(t)$ and $x_i(t)$ are vectors which denote the previous velocity and position of the i-th particle in sequence. ζ is called the constriction factor. Venter and Sobeiski termed c_1 as 'self confidence' and c_2 as 'swarm confidence' [4,12]. Since in this problem each particle represents an one possible solution for linear prediction coefficients, dimensionality of problem (each vector dimension) depends on the number of LPC coefficients or estimation degree. Φ_1 and Φ_2 stand for a uniformly distributed random number in the interval (0, 1). There are many suggestions from researchers about ζ, c_1 and c_2. In this study, these parameters are determined as [4, 13]:

$$\zeta = 2/|4 - \phi - \sqrt{\phi^2 - 4\phi}| \tag{5}$$

where

$$c_1 = (c_{1f} - c_{1i})(t/t_{Max}) + c_{1i} \tag{6}$$

and

$$c_2 = (c_{2f} - c_{2i})(t/t_{Max}) + c_{2i} \tag{7}$$

where $c_{1i} = c_{2f} = 2.5$, $c_{2i} = c_{1f} = 0.5$ and t_{Max} is the number of maximum allowable iterations. In this study the swarm size is set to 100.

2.3. Differential Evolution (DE)

In 1995, Price and Storn proposed a new floating point encoded evolutionary algorithm for global optimization and named it DE owing to a special kind of differential operator invoked to create new offspring from parent chromosomes instead of classical crossover or mutation [4, 14]. Easy methods of implementation and negligible parameter tuning made the algorithm quite popular very soon.

Like any other evolutionary algorithm, DE also starts with a population of PS D-dimensional search variable vectors. We will represent subsequent generations in DE by discrete time steps like t=0, 1, 2 ...t, t+1 etc. Since the vectors are likely to be changed over different generations we may adopt the following notation for representing the i-th vector of the population at the current generation (i.e. at time t=t) as:

$$\vec{X}_i(t) = [x_{i,1}(t), x_{i,2}(t),..., x_{i,D}(t)] \tag{8}$$

These vectors are referred in literature as 'genomes' or 'chromosomes'. DE is a very simple evolutionary algorithm and works through a simple cycle, presented in Figure 3.

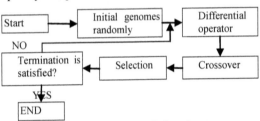

Figure 4. DE flowchart.

In step 1 the chromosomes are initialized randomly at position $x_i(0)$. Now in each generation (or one iteration of the algorithm) to change each population member $\vec{x}_i(t)$, a donor vector $\vec{v}_i(t)$ is created. To create $\vec{v}_i(t)$ for i-th member, three other parameter vectors (e.g., the r1, r2, and r3-th vectors) are chosen in a random fashion from the current population. Next, a scalar number F scales the difference of any two of the three vectors and the scaled difference is added to the third one whence we obtain the donor vector $\vec{v}_i(t)$. The process for the, j-th component of each vector can be expressed as [15,16]:

$$V_{i,j}(t) = X_{r1,j}(t) + F(X_{r2,j}(t) - X_{r3,j}(t)) \tag{9}$$

Next, to increase the potential diversity of the population, a crossover scheme comes into play. The crossover is performed on each of the D variables whenever a randomly picked number between 0 and 1 is lower the Crossover Rate (CR). Then the trial vector forms as:

$$\vec{U}_i(t) = [U_{i,1}(t), U_{i,2}(t)..U_{i,D}(t)] \tag{10}$$

wherein:

$$U_{i,j}(t) = \begin{cases} V_{i,j}(t), rand(0,1) < CR \\ X_{i,j}(t), otherwise \end{cases} \qquad (11)$$

CR and F are two control parameters for DE. For each trial vector, $\vec{x}_i(t)$, an offspring vector, $\vec{U}_i(t)$, is created. To keep the population size constant over subsequent generations, the next step of the algorithm calls for 'selection' to determine which one of the target vectors and trial vectors will survive in the next generation (i.e. at time t = t+1). DE actually involves the Darwinian principle of 'Survival of the fittest' in its selection process which may be outlined as:

$$\vec{X}_i(t+1) = \begin{cases} \vec{U}_i(t), f(\vec{U}_i(t)) \leq f(\vec{X}_i(t)) \\ \vec{X}_i(t), f(\vec{X}_i(t)) < f(\vec{U}_i(t)) \end{cases} \qquad (12)$$

where f( ) is the function to be minimized. So, if the new trial vector yields a better value of the fitness function, it replaces its target in the next generation; otherwise, the target vector is retained in the population. Hence the population either gets better (the fitness function) or remains constant but the population never deteriorates. Table 2 shows the parameter setup for the DE employed here.

Table 2. Differential Evolution (DE) parameters setup.

Modeling description	setting
Number of genomes	100
Crossover rate (CR)	0.9
Scaling factor (F)	0.01
Iteration number	100

2.4. PSO-DV

PSO-DV is a hybrid evolutionary algorithm introduces a differential operator (borrowed from DE) in the velocity-update scheme of PSO [4, 11]. The operator is invoked on the position vectors of two randomly chosen particles, not on their individual best positions. Further, unlike the PSO scheme, a particle is actually shifted to a new location only if the new location yields a better fitness value, that is,, a selection strategy has been incorporated into the swarm dynamics. In the proposed algorithm, for each particle i in the swarm two other distinct particles, say j and k ($i \neq j \neq k$) are selected randomly. The difference between their positional coordinates is taken as a difference vector:

$$\vec{\delta} = \vec{X}_k - \vec{X}_j, k \neq j \neq i \qquad (13)$$

Then the d-th velocity component (1 < d < n) of the target particle i is updated as:

$$V_{id}(t+1) = \begin{cases} \omega V_{id}(t) + \beta\delta_d + c_2\varphi_2.(p_{gd} \\ - X_{id}(t)), rand(0,1) \leq CR \\ V_{id}(t), otherwise \end{cases} \qquad (14)$$

where CR is the crossover rate, d is the d-th component of the difference vector defined earlier, and β is a scale factor in [0, 1]. Now, a new trial location Tr_i is created for the particle by adding the updated velocity to the previous position X_i :

$$\vec{Tr}_i = \vec{X}_i(t) + \vec{V}_i(t+1) \qquad (15)$$

The particle is placed at this new location only if the coordinates of the location yield a better fitness value. Thus, if we are seeking the minimum of an n-dimensional function $\vec{f}(x)$, then the target particle is relocated as follows:

$$\vec{X}_i(t+1) = \begin{cases} \vec{Tr}_i, f(\vec{Tr}_i) \leq f(\vec{X}_i(t)) \\ \vec{X}_i(t), otherwise \end{cases} \qquad (16)$$

Therefore, every time its velocity changes, the particle either moves to a better position in the search space or sticks to its previous location. The current location of the particle is thus the best location it has ever found [4]. Table 3 shows the parameter setup for the DE employed here.

Table 3. Differential Evolution (DE) parameters setup.

Modeling description	setting
Swarm size	100
Crossover rate (CR)	0.5
Scaling factor (β)	0. 1
Iteration number	100

3. Proposed method

Designing the individuals and the fitness function are two common parts of coding a non-linear optimization problem to be solved by ESs. Each individual is known as chromosome in GA and a particle in PSO should be able to represent a possible solution for the available problem. The fitness function must be capable to evaluate individuals as possible solutions for the optimization problem.

In this study, the problem is to find LPC coefficients which can estimate the speech signal with less prediction error. Therefore, each set of LPC coefficients can be an individual in the ES and all individual construct the population. Since the main problem is to minimize the prediction error, the fitness functions is defined as the maximum prediction error as:

$$f(i) = \max(|\hat{s}[n] - s[n]|), 1 \leq i \leq N \qquad (17)$$

Where $\hat{s}[n]$ and $s[n]$ indicate the predicted signal and original signal, respectively. N is the number of individuals presented in the population. Minimizing the fitness function during the algorithm improves the prediction accuracy. Figure 5 represents the diagram of the proposed evolutionary algorithm to find the optimal LPC coefficients.

In Figure 5, Ci , $1 \leq i \leq 8$ represents the ith LPC coefficient. In this study, we use 8 LPC coefficients to predict the speech signal (order 8 LPC).

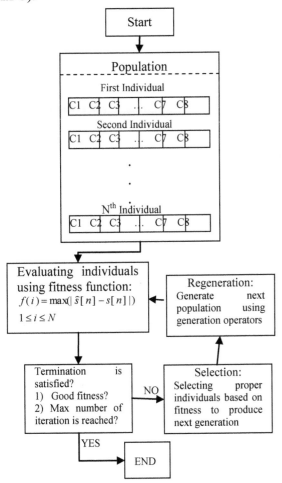

Figure 5. Diagram of the proposed method.

As can be seen from Figure 5, each individual include 8 LPC coefficients, which can be a possible solution for the problem. In step 1, individuals are initialized randomly. After that, the population is upgraded in an evaluation-selection-regeneration loop. In this loop individuals are evaluated using fitness function described by equation (17). The best individuals are chosen in the selection stage to reconstruct the next generation. Finally, next population is produced using generation operators. Various evolutionary algorithms are usually different in the employed selection and generation strategies.

In this study, we employ four different evolutionary algorithms (GA, PSO, DE and PSO-DV) to find optimal LPC coefficients which can estimate the speech signal with less prediction error. The results of our experiments are presented and discussed in the next section.

4. Experimental results

In this section, we compare the proposed evolutionary algorithms and traditional autocorrelation method by means of the prediction error. The first 8 LPC coefficients estimated from autocorrelation, GA, PSO, DE and PSO-DV algorithms are used to estimate two 20ms frames of speech.

Figures 6 to 15 show the original signals, estimated signals and the prediction error curves obtained for the two frames using autocorrelation method, GA, PSO, DE and PSO-DV algorithms.

As can be seen from these figures, all of the evolutionary algorithms employed to estimate signal using LPC coefficients outpoint the traditional autocorrelation method in term of prediction error. The error reduction rate of these algorithms is shown in Figure 16 and 17, respectively for the two speech frames.

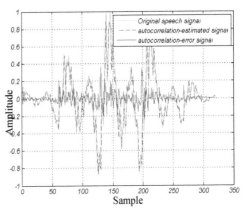

Figure 6. Autocorrelation method (frame 1).

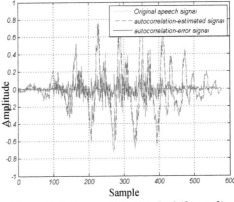

Figure 7. Autocorrelation method (frame 2).

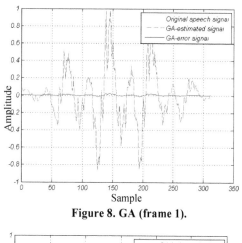

Figure 8. GA (frame 1).

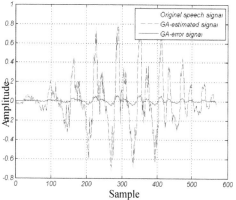

Figure 9. GA (frame 2).

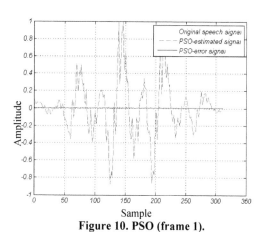

Figure 10. PSO (frame 1).

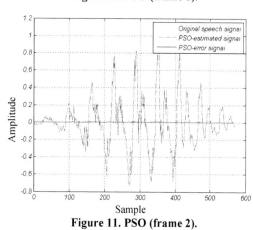

Figure 11. PSO (frame 2).

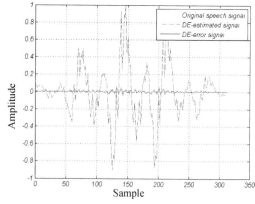

Figure 12. DE (frame 1).

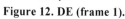

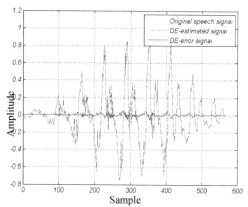

Figure 13. DE (frame 2).

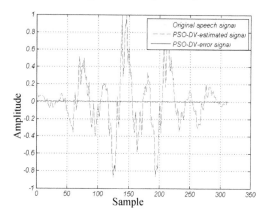

Figure.14. PSO-DV (frame 1).

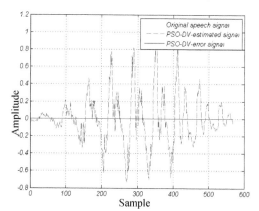

Figure 15. PSO-DV (frame 2).

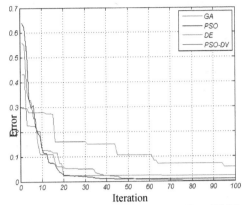

Figure 16. Error rate for GA, PSO, DE and PSO-DV (frame 1).

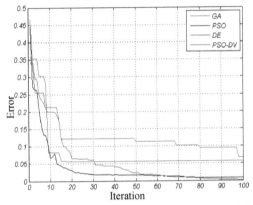

Figure.17. Error rate for GA, PSO, DE and PSO-DV (frame 2).

From Figures16 and 17, it can be seen that after 50 iterations the error rates of the GA, PSO and PSO-DV are converged, while DE is not converged yet. Also, it could be seen that PSO-DV outperforms other techniques in term of convergence speed and predicted error. It is interesting to see that all the evolutionary algorithms reached to the error rate lower that autocorrelation scheme after just 10 iterations. According to Figures 16 and 17, PSO seems to be the most efficient method for iteration number below 50, while PSO-DV is superior since then.

Figure 18 shows the minimum prediction error obtained using each method.

As can be seen from Figure 18, the proposed PSO-DV is superior to autocorrelation and also other evolutionary algorithms. Also, the success of evolutionary algorithms in computing efficient LPC coefficients which result in minimum prediction error encourages the idea of employing these algorithms for this problem.

The LPC coefficients obtained by each method are presented in Tables 4 and 5 for first and second speech frames, respectively. As can be seen from these tables, the computed coefficients are by no means similar, but all of them estimate the original speech signal properly.

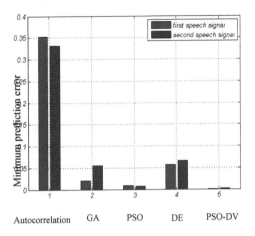

Figure 18. minimum prediction error achieved each various methods (frame 1 and 2).

5.Conclusion

The purpose of the current study was to determine the LPC coefficients for speech signal using evolutionary algorithms: GA, PSO, DE and PSO-DV. The findings in this study suggest that the evolutionary algorithms are superior to traditional methods, such as Autocorrelation method in terms of prediction accuracy. The following conclusions can be drawn from the present study.

First, evolutionary algorithms, such as GA, PSO, DE and PSO-DV can predict speech signal more accurate than traditional autocorrelation method.

Second, our experiments show that the hybrid algorithm, PSO-DV, which resulted from the contribution of PSO and DE, is the fastest algorithm and DE is the slowest one. According to our experiments, GA, PSO and PSO-DV converged after 50 iterations while DE did not converge after 100 iterations.

Moreover, PSO-DV achieved the best results after 100 iterations. After the PSO-DV, PSO and GA were the most powerful methods to estimate the speech signal with less prediction error.

Another flexibility of evolutionary algorithms is to find solutions with any desirable criterion. In other words, we can limit our results with more constrictions, such as stability of the constructed LPC filter. This could be realized by designing a proper fitness function for the problem. Algorithms try to find the fittest solution to the function. In this work the fitness function is defined as maximum prediction error, therefore, algorithms tried to find LPC coefficients with less prediction error.

It is clear that for the hardware implementation of a signal processing system, the LPC coefficients should be quantized and its effect on the efficiency of the system would not remain optimal after the quantization procedure the coefficients.

Evolutionary algorithms can be employed to find the optimal quantized coefficients. Moreover, applying LPC coefficients obtained by evolutionary algorithms for speech processing applications may improve their efficiency.

Table 4. LPC coefficients obtained by each method for frame 1.

Method	C1	C2	C3	C4	C5	C6	C7	C8
Autocorrelation	1.4849	-0.8596	0.0345	0.7340	-0.7169	0.3087	0.3699	-0.4936
GA	0.0389	-0.1377	0.0643	-0.0688	0.1961	-0.1710	0.1506	0.8969
PSO	-0.0212	0.0475	-0.0489	0.0162	0.0369	-0.0602	0.0489	0.9794
DE	-0.0336	0.0425	-0.1215	0.1630	-0.1065	0.0468	0.0562	0.9379
PSO-DV	-0.0008	0.0008	0.0007	-0.0015	0.0015	-0.0011	0.0003	1

Table 5. LPC coefficients obtained by each method for frame 2.

Method	C1	C2	C3	C4	C5	C6	C7	C8
Autocorrelation	1.6647	-1.1798	0.5273	0.3132	-0.9179	1.1388	-0.8051	0.1637
GA	-0.1694	0.3606	-0.3501	0.0077	0.3515	-0.5047	0.5034	0.7723
PSO	0.0020	-0.0066	0.0210	-0.0349	0.0116	0.0176	-0.0253	1.0136
DE	-0.0520	0.0916	-0.1205	0.1200	-0.1426	0.0844	-0.0608	1.0789
PSO-DV	-0.0019	0.0042	-0.0039	-0.0006	0.0042	-0.0049	0.0051	0.9978

References

[1] Huang, X., Acero, A. and Hon, H. W. (2001). Spoken Language Processing. Upper saddle River. NJn And Prentice Hall.

[2] Rabiner, L. R. and Schafer, R. W. (1978). Digital processing of speech signals. Englewood cliffs. NJ, Prentice Hall.

[3] Gopal, E. S. (2007). Algorithm collections for digital signal processing applications using matlab. Natural institute of Technology, Tiruchi, India.

[4] Das, S., Abraham, A. and Konar, A. (2007). Particle Swarm Optimization and differential Evolution Algorithms: Technical analysis, Applications and Hybridization perspectives. Dept of Electronics and Telecomunications Engineering, Jadavpur University, Kolkata, 700032.

[5] Manoj, V. J. and Elias, E. (2009). Design of multiplier-less non uniform filter bank trans multiplexer using genetic algorithm. Signal Processing. Volume 89, Issue 11.

[6] Lim, Y. H., Tana, J. and Abramsonb, D. (2012). Solving Optimization Problems in Nimrod/OK using a Genetic Algorithm. Procedia Computer Science. 9, 1647 – 1656.

[7] Xiang , L., Gang, D. and BSTBGA. (2013). A hybrid genetic algorithm for constrained multi-objective optimization problems. Computers & Operations Research. 40, 282–302.

[8] Gen, M., Cheng, R. (2000). Genetic Algorithms and Engineering Optimization. vol. 68, Wiley Interscience Publication.

[9] Goldberg, D.E. (1989). Genetic Algorithm in search, optimization and machine learning. Addison-Wesley, Reading, MA.

[10] Wong, T. C. and Ngan, S. C. (2012). A comparison of hybrid genetic algorithm and hybrid particle swarm optimization to minimize makespan for assembly job shop. Applied Soft Computing.

[11] Epitropakis, M. G., Plagianakos, V. P. and Vrahatis, M. N. (2012). Evolving cognitive and social experience in Particle Swarm Optimization through Differential Evolution: A hybrid approach. Information Sciences. 216, 50–92.

[12] Upendar, J., Gupta, C. P. and Singh, G.K. (2010). Design of two-channel quadrature mirror filter bank using particle swarm optimization. Digital Signal Processing. Volume 20, Issue 2.

[13] Khare, A. and Rangnekar, S. (2012). Particle swarm optimization: A review, Applied Soft Computing .

[14] Chang, W. D. (2009). Two-dimensional fractional-order digital differentiator design by using differential evolution algorithm. Digital Signal Processing. Volume 19, Issue 4.

[15] Mohamed, A. W. and Sabry, H. Z. (2012). Constrained optimization based on modified differential evolution algorithm. Information Sciences. 194, 171–208.

[16] Mohamed, A. W., Sabry, H. Z. and Khorshid, M. (2012). An alternative differential evolution algorithm for global optimization. Journal of Advanced Research. 3, 149–165.

Permissions

All chapters in this book were first published in JAIDM, by Shahrood University of Technology; hereby published with permission under the Creative Commons Attribution License or equivalent. Every chapter published in this book has been scrutinized by our experts. Their significance has been extensively debated. The topics covered herein carry significant findings which will fuel the growth of the discipline. They may even be implemented as practical applications or may be referred to as a beginning point for another development.

The contributors of this book come from diverse backgrounds, making this book a truly international effort. This book will bring forth new frontiers with its revolutionizing research information and detailed analysis of the nascent developments around the world.

We would like to thank all the contributing authors for lending their expertise to make the book truly unique. They have played a crucial role in the development of this book. Without their invaluable contributions this book wouldn't have been possible. They have made vital efforts to compile up to date information on the varied aspects of this subject to make this book a valuable addition to the collection of many professionals and students.

This book was conceptualized with the vision of imparting up-to-date information and advanced data in this field. To ensure the same, a matchless editorial board was set up. Every individual on the board went through rigorous rounds of assessment to prove their worth. After which they invested a large part of their time researching and compiling the most relevant data for our readers.

The editorial board has been involved in producing this book since its inception. They have spent rigorous hours researching and exploring the diverse topics which have resulted in the successful publishing of this book. They have passed on their knowledge of decades through this book. To expedite this challenging task, the publisher supported the team at every step. A small team of assistant editors was also appointed to further simplify the editing procedure and attain best results for the readers.

Apart from the editorial board, the designing team has also invested a significant amount of their time in understanding the subject and creating the most relevant covers. They scrutinized every image to scout for the most suitable representation of the subject and create an appropriate cover for the book.

The publishing team has been an ardent support to the editorial, designing and production team. Their endless efforts to recruit the best for this project, has resulted in the accomplishment of this book. They are a veteran in the field of academics and their pool of knowledge is as vast as their experience in printing. Their expertise and guidance has proved useful at every step. Their uncompromising quality standards have made this book an exceptional effort. Their encouragement from time to time has been an inspiration for everyone.

The publisher and the editorial board hope that this book will prove to be a valuable piece of knowledge for researchers, students, practitioners and scholars across the globe.

List of Contributors

M. Dashti and E. Ekhtiyari
Textile Engineering Department, Yazd University

V. Derhami
Electrical and Computer Engineering Department, Yazd University

Z. Dorrani
Department of Electrical Engineering, Payame Noor University (PNU), Tehran, Iran

M. S. Mahmoodi
Department of Computer Engineering, Payame Noor University (PNU), Tehran, Iran

M. Shafiee
Department of Computer Engineering, Kerman Branch, Islamic Azad University, Kerman, Iran

A. Latif
Department of Electrical and Computer Engineering, Yazd University, Yazd, Iran

A. Ghaffari and S. Nobahary
Department of Computer Engineering, Tabriz branch, Islamic Azad University, Tabriz, Iran

M. Asghari Esfandani and H. Nematzadeh
Department of Computer Engineering, Sari Branch, Islamic Azad University, Sari, Iran

S. M. Hosseinirad and S. K. Basu
Department of Computer Science, Banaras Hindu University, India

M. Niazi, J. Pourdeilami and A. A. Pouyan
Department of Computer Engineering, Shahrood University of Technology, Shahrood, Iran

B. Safaee and S. Kamaleddin Mousavi Mashhadi
School of Electrical Engineering, Iran University of Science and Technology, Tehran, Iran

Z. Amiri, A. A. Pouyan and H. Mashayekhi
Department of Computer & IT Engineering, University of Shahrood, Shahrood, Iran

H. Kiani Rad and Z. Moravej
Faculty of Electrical & Computer Engineering, Semnan University, Semnan, Iran

M. Zare-Baghbidi and K. Jamshidi
Computer Architecture Engineering Department, Faculty of Computer Engineering, University of Isfahan, Isfahan, Iran

S. Homayouni
Department of Geography, University of Ottawa, Ottawa, Canada

A. R. Naghsh-Nilchi
Artificial Intelligent Department, Faculty of Computer Engineering, University of Isfahan, Isfahan, Iran

S. M. Hosseinirad and S. K. Basu
Department of Computer Science, Banaras Hindu University, India

H. Khodadadi
Department of Computer Engineering, Minab Branch, Islamic Azad University, Minab, Iran

O. Mirzaei
Computer Security Lab, Department of Computer Science and Engineering, Universidad Carlos III de Madrid, Madrid, Spain

H. Shahamat and A. A. Pouyan
Computer Engineering and Information Technology Department, University of Shahrood, Shahrood, Iran

F. Soleiman Nouri, M. Haddad Zarif and M. M. Fateh
Department of Electrical Engineering and Robotics, University of Shahrood, Iran

H. Motameni
Department of Computer Engineering, Sari Branch, Islamic Azad University, Sari, Iran

Kh. Valipour and A. Ghasemi
Technical Engineering Department, University of Mohaghegh Ardabili, Ardabil, Iran

T. Zare, M. T. Sadeghi and H. R. Abutalebi
Signal Processing Research Group, Electrical Engineering Department, Yazd University, Yazd, Iran

J. Kittler
Centre for Vision, Speech and Signal Processing (CVSSP), Faculty of Engineering and Physical Sciences, University of Surrey, Guildford, Surrey

Sh. Lotfi and F. Karimi
Department of Computer Science, University of Tabriz, Tabriz, Iran

M. B. Dowlatshahi and V. Derhami
Computer Engineering Department, Yazd University, Yazd, Iran

E. Fadaei-Kermani, G. A. Barani and M. Ghaeini-Hessaroeyeh
Department of Civil Engineering, Faculty of Engineering, Shahid Bahonar University of Kerman, Kerman, Iran

M. Ghasemzadeh
Electrical and Computer Engineering Department, Yazd University

H. Mohamadi and J. Akbari
Islamic Azad University of Arak

A. Shahbahrami
Department of Computer Engineering, University of Guilan

M. AllamehAmiri, V. Derhami and M. Ghasemzadeh
Department of Electrical and Computer Engineering, Yazd University, Yazd, Iran

H. Marvi
Electrical engineering department, Shahrood university of technology, Shahrood, Iran

Z. Esmaileyan
Electrical engineering department science and research branch, Islamic Azad Univercity, Shahrood, Iran

A. Harimi
Electrical engineering department, Shahrood branch, Islamic Azad Univercity, Shahrood, Iran

Index

Printed in the USA
CPSIA information can be obtained
at www.ICGtesting.com
JSHW051431221024
72173JS00006B/1440